Fiesta Owners Workshop Manual

IM Coomber

Models covered
Ford Fiesta Popular, Popular Plus & L, 957 cc
Ford Fiesta Popular Plus, L & Ghia, 1117 cc
Ford Fiesta L & Ghia, 1296 cc
Ford Fiesta XR2, 1597 cc

Covers four- & five-speed manual transmissions
Does not cover Diesel engine models

ISBN 1 85010 030 6

Haynes Publishing Group
Sparkford Nr Yeovil
Somerset BA22 7JJ England

Haynes Publications, Inc
861 Lawrence Drive
Newbury Park
California 91320 USA

British Library Cataloguing in Publication Data

Coomber, Ian
  Ford Fiesta '83 to '85 owners workshop manual.–
  (Owners Workshop Manual)
  1. Fiesta automobile
  I. Title   II. Series
  629.28'722   TL215.F7
  ISBN 1–85010–030–6

Acknowledgements

Thanks are due to the Champion Sparking Plug Company Limited who supplied the illustrations showing the spark plug conditions. Certain other illustrations are the copyright of the Ford Motor Company, and are used with their permission. Thanks are also due to Sykes-Pickavant, who supplied some of the workshop tools, and also to the staff at Sparkford who assisted in the production of this manual.

About this manual

Its aim

The aim of this manual is to help you get the best value from your vehicle. It can do so in several ways. It can help you decide what work must be done (even should you choose to get it done by a garage), provide information on routine maintenance and servicing, and give a logical course of action and diagnosis when random faults occur. However, it is hoped that you will use the manual by tackling the work yourself. On simpler jobs it may even be quicker than booking the car into a garage and going there twice, to leave and collect it. Perhaps most important, a lot of money can be saved by avoiding the costs a garage must charge to cover its labour and overheads.

The manual has drawings and descriptions to show the function of the various components so that their layout can be understood. Then the tasks are described and photographed in a step-by-step sequence so that even a novice can do the work.

Its arrangement

The manual is divided into twelve Chapters, each covering a logical sub-division of the vehicle. The Chapters are each divided into Sections, numbered with single figures, eg 5; and the Sections into paragraphs (or sub-sections), with decimal numbers following on from the Section they are in, eg 5.1, 5.2, 5.3 etc.

It is freely illustrated, especially in those parts where there is a detailed sequence of operations to be carried out. There are two forms of illustration: figures and photographs. The figures are numbered in sequence with decimal numbers, according to their position in the Chapter – eg Fig. 6.4 is the fourth drawing/illustration in Chapter 6. Photographs carry the same number (either individually or in related groups) as the Section or sub-section to which they relate.

There is an alphabetical index at the back of the manual as well as a contents list at the front. Each Chapter is also preceded by its own individual contents list.

References to the 'left' or 'right' of the vehicle are in the sense of a person in the driver's seat facing forwards.

Unless otherwise stated, nuts and bolts are removed by turning anti-clockwise, and tightened by turning clockwise.

Vehicle manufacturers continually make changes to specifications and recommendations, and these, when notified, are incorporated into our manuals at the earliest opportunity.

Whilst every care is taken to ensure that the information in this manual is correct, no liability can be accepted by the authors or publishers for loss, damage or injury caused by any errors in, or omissions from, the information given.

Introduction to the Ford Fiesta

Although the Ford Fiesta range of models was first introduced in February 1977, this manual covers the 'New Fiesta' range produced from August 1983. As with the earlier models, the New Fiesta is a two-door hatchback with an upward lifting tailgate, but the external and internal features of the new models have been restyled and updated.

The mechanical layout remains similar; with a transverse-mounted engine, separate manual gearbox and integral final drive unit, and front-wheel-drive.

The engine types available are the previously used 957 cc and 1117 cc overhead valve units (which have had design modifications to improve the fuel consumption), and the 1298 cc and 1598 cc overhead camshaft CVH (Compound Valve Hemispherical head) units which provide good performance coupled with economy. A diesel-engined variant is also available, but this is not included in this manual.

The transmission types available are the four-speed or five-speed manual gearbox with full synchromesh and a central floor-mounted gearlever.

All models are fitted with disc front brakes and drum rear brakes.

The front suspension is fully independent MacPherson strut type with coil springs and double acting telescopic shock absorbers, whilst the rear suspension is of the five link type with Panhard rod and telescopic double-acting shock absorbers. Certain models have a rear anti-roll bar.

For the home mechanic, the Fiesta is an ideal car to maintain and repair since design features have been incorporated to reduce the actual cost of ownership to a minimum, with the result that components requiring relatively frequent attention (eg the exhaust system) are easily removed.

Contents

	Page
Acknowledgements	2
About this manual	2
Introduction to the Ford Fiesta	2
General dimensions, weights and capacities	6
Buying spare parts and vehicle identification numbers	7
Tools and working facilities	9
General repair procedures	11
Jacking and towing	12
Recommended lubricants and fluids	14
Safety first!	15
Routine maintenance	16
Fault diagnosis	23
Chapter 1 Engine	26
Chapter 2 Cooling, heating and ventilation systems	80
Chapter 3 Fuel, exhaust and emission control systems	93
Chapter 4 Ignition system	116
Chapter 5 Clutch	130
Chapter 6 Transmission	136
Chapter 7 Driveshafts	163
Chapter 8 Braking system	171
Chapter 9 Steering	186
Chapter 10 Suspension	196
Chapter 11 Electrical system	209
Chapter 12 Bodywork and fittings	259
Conversion factors	283
Index	284

Ford Fiesta XR2

Ford Fiesta Popular Plus

General dimensions, weights and capacities

Dimensions

	Saloons	XR2
Overall length:		
Without overriders	3648 mm (143.7 in)	–
With overriders	3695 mm (145.6 in) or 3712 mm (146.3 in)	3712 mm (146.3 in)
Overall width	1585 mm (62.4 in)	1620 mm (63.8 in)
Overall height:		
Maximum	1334 mm (52.6 in)	1334 mm (52.6 in)
Minimum	1316 mm (51.9 in)	1310 mm (51.6 in)
Wheelbase	2288 mm (90.1 in)	2288 mm (90.1 in)
Track:		
Front	1367 mm (53.9 in)	1385 mm (54.6 in)
Rear	1321 mm (52.0 in)	1339 mm (52.8 in)

Weights

Basic kerb weight:	
1.0 and 1.1 Base, L	765.0 kg (1687 lb)
1.1 Ghia	780.0 kg (1720 lb)
1.1 S (option)	797.5 kg (1758 lb)
1.3 Base, L, Ghia	800.0 kg (1764 lb)
1.3 S (option)	812.5 kg (1791 lb)
1.6 XR2	851.0 kg (1876 lb)
Gross vehicle weight:	
1.0 and 1.1 litre	1200 kg (2646 lb)
1.3 litre	1225 kg (2701 lb)
1.6 litre	1275 kg (2811 lb)

Capacities

Engine oil change:	
With filter:	
1.0 and 1.1 litre	3.25 litres (5.7 Imp pints)
1.3 and 1.6 litre	3.50 litres (6.2 Imp pints)
Without filter:	
1.0 and 1.1 litre	2.75 litres (4.8 Imp pints)
1.3 and 1.6 litre	3.25 litres (5.7 Imp pints
Cooling system:	
1.0 and 1.1 litre	5.5 litres (9.7 Imp pints)
1.3 litre	6.3 litres (11.1 Imp pints)
1.6 litre	8.0 litres (14.1 Imp pints)
Transmission:	
4-speed	2.8 litres (4.9 Imp pints)
5-speed	3.1 litres (5.5 Imp pints)

Buying spare parts and vehicle identification numbers

Buying spare parts

Spare parts are available from many sources, for example Ford garages, other garages and accessory shops, and motor factors. Our advice regarding spare part sources is as follows:

Official appointed Ford garages – This is the best source of parts which are peculiar to your vehicle and are otherwise not generally available (eg, complete cylinder heads, internal gearbox components, badges, interior trim etc). It is also the only place at which you should buy parts if your vehicle is still under warranty – non-Ford components may invalidate the warranty. To be sure of obtaining the correct parts it will always be necessary to give the storeman your vehicle's engine and chassis number, and if possible, to take the 'old' parts along for positive identification. Remember that some parts are available on a factory exchange scheme – any parts returned should always be clean! It obviously makes good sense to go straight to the specialists on your vehicle for this type of part for they are best equipped to supply you.

Other garages and accessory shops – These are often good places to buy materials and components needed for the maintenance of your vehicle (eg, spark plugs, bulbs, drivebelts, oils and greases, touch-up paint, filler paste, etc). They also sell general accessories, usually have convenient opening hours, charge lower prices and can often be found not far from home.

Motor factors –Good factors will stock all of the more important components which wear out relatively quickly (eg clutch components, pistons, valves, exhaust systems, brake cylinders/pipes/hoses/seals shoes and pads etc). Motor factors will often provide new or reconditioned components on a part exchange basis – this can save a considerable amount of money.

Vehicle identification numbers

The Vehicle Identification Number is located on the plate found in the engine compartment either on the bulkhead or on the front cross panel directly to the rear of the right-hand headlamp unit. The VIN plate also carries information concerning paint colour, final drive ratio, etc.

The engine number on ohv variants is located on the exhaust side at the flywheel end of the engine. On CVH engines the number is located at the timing case end on the exhaust side.

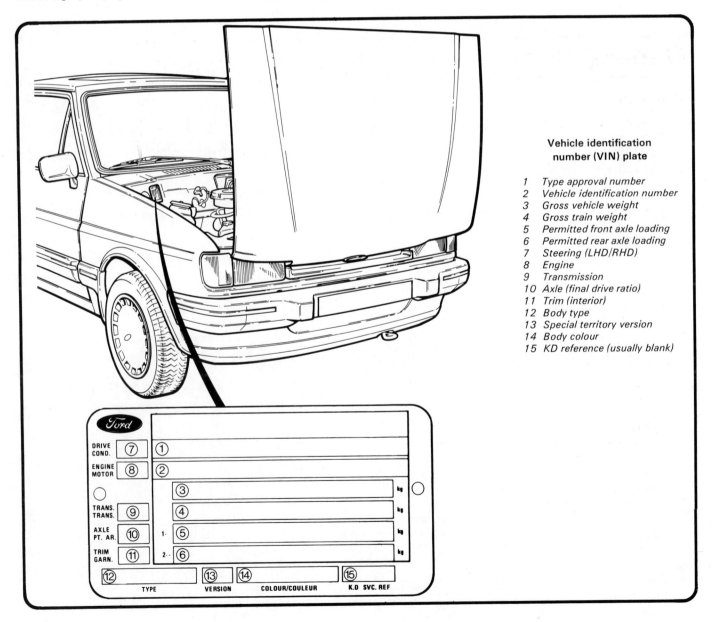

Vehicle identification number (VIN) plate

1   Type approval number
2   Vehicle identification number
3   Gross vehicle weight
4   Gross train weight
5   Permitted front axle loading
6   Permitted rear axle loading
7   Steering (LHD/RHD)
8   Engine
9   Transmission
10 Axle (final drive ratio)
11 Trim (interior)
12 Body type
13 Special territory version
14 Body colour
15 KD reference (usually blank)

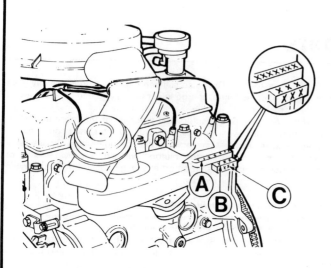

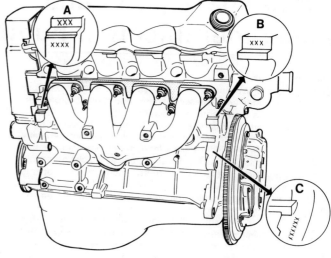

Engine number location – ohv engine

A Engine number
B Engine code

C Engine build date

Engine number location – CVH engine

A Engine number
B Engine code

C Engine number for repair reference

Tools and working facilities

Introduction

A selection of good tools is a fundamental requirement for anyone contemplating the maintenance and repair of a motor vehicle. For the owner who does not possess any, their purchase will prove a considerable expense, offsetting some of the savings made by doing-it-yourself. However, provided that the tools purchased are of good quality, they will last for many years and prove an extremely worthwhile investment.

To help the average owner to decide which tools are needed to carry out the various tasks detailed in this manual, we have compiled three lists of tools under the following headings: *Maintenance and minor repair, Repair and overhaul,* and *Special.* The newcomer to practical mechanics should start off with the *Maintenance and minor repair* tool kit and confine himself to the simpler jobs around the vehicle. Then, as his confidence and experience grow, he can undertake more difficult tasks, buying extra tools as, and when, they are needed. In this way, a *Maintenance and minor repair* tool kit can be built-up into a *Repair and overhaul* tool kit over a considerable period of time without any major cash outlays. The experienced do-it-yourselfer will have a tool kit good enough for most repair and overhaul procedures and will add tools from the *Special* category when he feels the expense is justified by the amount of use to which these tools will be put.

It is obviously not possible to cover the subject of tools fully here. For those who wish to learn more about tools and their use there is a book entitled *How to Choose and Use Car Tools* available from the publishers of this manual.

Maintenance and minor repair tool kit

The tools given in this list should be considered as a minimum requirement if routine maintenance, servicing and minor repair operations are to be undertaken. We recommend the purchase of combination spanners (ring one end, open-ended the other); although more expensive than open-ended ones, they do give the advantages of both types of spanner.

Combination spanners - 10, 11, 12, 13, 14 & 17 mm
Adjustable spanner - 9 inch
Spark plug spanner (with rubber insert)
Spark plug gap adjustment tool
Set of feeler gauges
Brake adjuster spanner
Brake bleed nipple spanner
Screwdriver - 4 in long x $\frac{1}{4}$ in dia (flat blade)
Screwdriver - 4 in long x $\frac{1}{4}$ in dia (cross blade)
Combination pliers - 6 inch
Hacksaw (junior)
Tyre pump
Tyre pressure gauge
Grease gun
Oil can
Fine emery cloth (1 sheet)
Wire brush (small)
Funnel (medium size)

Repair and overhaul tool kit

These tools are virtually essential for anyone undertaking any major repairs to a motor vehicle, and are additional to those given in the *Maintenance and minor repair* list. Included in this list is a comprehensive set of sockets. Although these are expensive they will be found invaluable as they are so versatile - particularly if various drives are included in the set. We recommend the $\frac{1}{2}$ in square-drive type, as this can be used with most proprietary torque wrenches. If you cannot afford a socket set, even bought piecemeal, then inexpensive tubular box spanners are a useful alternative.

The tools in this list will occasionally need to be supplemented by tools from the *Special* list.

Sockets (or box spanners) to cover range in previous list
Reversible ratchet drive (for use with sockets)
Extension piece, 10 inch (for use with sockets)
Universal joint (for use with sockets)
Torque wrench (for use with sockets)
'Mole' wrench - 8 inch
Ball pein hammer
Soft-faced hammer, plastic or rubber
Screwdriver - 6 in long x $\frac{5}{16}$ in dia (flat blade)
Screwdriver - 2 in long x $\frac{5}{16}$ in square (flat blade)
Screwdriver - 1$\frac{1}{2}$ in long x $\frac{1}{4}$ in dia (cross blade)
Screwdriver - 3 in long x $\frac{1}{8}$ in dia (electricians)
Pliers - electricians side cutters
Pliers - needle nosed
Pliers - circlip (internal and external)
Cold chisel - $\frac{1}{2}$ inch
Scriber
Scraper
Centre punch
Pin punch
Hacksaw
Valve grinding tool
Steel rule/straight-edge
Allen keys
Selection of files
Wire brush (large)
Axle-stands
Jack (strong scissor or hydraulic type)

Special tools

The tools in this list are those which are not used regularly, are expensive to buy, or which need to be used in accordance with their manufacturers' instructions. Unless relatively difficult mechanical jobs are undertaken frequently, it will not be economic to buy many of these tools. Where this is the case, you could consider clubbing together with friends (or joining a motorists' club) to make a joint purchase, or borrowing the tools against a deposit from a local garage or tool hire specialist.

The following list contains only those tools and instruments freely available to the public, and not those special tools produced by the vehicle manufacturer specifically for its dealer network. You will find occasional references to these manufacturers' special tools in the text of this manual. Generally, an alternative method of doing the job without the vehicle manufacturers' special tool is given. However, sometimes, there is no alternative to using them. Where this is the case and the relevant tool cannot be bought or borrowed, you will have to entrust the work to a franchised garage.

Valve spring compressor
Piston ring compressor
Balljoint separator
Universal hub/bearing puller
Impact screwdriver
Micrometer and/or vernier gauge
Dial gauge
Stroboscopic timing light
Dwell angle meter/tachometer
Universal electrical multi-meter
Cylinder compression gauge
Lifting tackle
Trolley jack
Light with extension lead

Buying tools

For practically all tools, a tool factor is the best source since he will have a very comprehensive range compared with the average garage or accessory shop. Having said that, accessory shops often offer excellent quality tools at discount prices, so it pays to shop around.

Remember, you don't have to buy the most expensive items on the shelf, but it is always advisable to steer clear of the very cheap tools. There are plenty of good tools around at reasonable prices, so ask the proprietor or manager of the shop for advice before making a purchase.

Care and maintenance of tools

Having purchased a reasonable tool kit, it is necessary to keep the tools in a clean serviceable condition. After use, always wipe off any dirt, grease and metal particles using a clean, dry cloth, before putting the tools away. Never leave them lying around after they have been used. A simple tool rack on the garage or workshop wall, for items such as screwdrivers and pliers is a good idea. Store all normal wrenches and sockets in a metal box. Any measuring instruments, gauges, meters, etc, must be carefully stored where they cannot be damaged or become rusty.

Take a little care when tools are used. Hammer heads inevitably become marked and screwdrivers lose the keen edge on their blades from time to time. A little timely attention with emery cloth or a file will soon restore items like this to a good serviceable finish.

Working facilities

Not to be forgotten when discussing tools, is the workshop itself. If anything more than routine maintenance is to be carried out, some form of suitable working area becomes essential.

It is appreciated that many an owner mechanic is forced by circumstances to remove an engine or similar item, without the benefit of a garage or workshop. Having done this, any repairs should always be done under the cover of a roof.

Wherever possible, any dismantling should be done on a clean, flat workbench or table at a suitable working height.

Any workbench needs a vice: one with a jaw opening of 4 in (100 mm) is suitable for most jobs. As mentioned previously, some clean dry storage space is also required for tools, as well as for lubricants, cleaning fluids, touch-up paints and so on, which become necessary.

Another item which may be required, and which has a much more general usage, is an electric drill with a chuck capacity of at least $\frac{5}{16}$ in (8 mm). This, together with a good range of twist drills, is virtually essential for fitting accessories such as mirrors and reversing lights.

Last, but not least, always keep a supply of old newspapers and clean, lint-free rags available, and try to keep any working area as clean as possible.

Spanner jaw gap comparison table

Jaw gap (in)	Spanner size
0.250	$\frac{1}{4}$ in AF
0.276	7 mm
0.313	$\frac{5}{16}$ in AF
0.315	8 mm
0.344	$\frac{11}{32}$ in AF; $\frac{1}{8}$ in Whitworth
0.354	9 mm
0.375	$\frac{3}{8}$ in AF
0.394	10 mm
0.433	11 mm
0.438	$\frac{7}{16}$ in AF
0.445	$\frac{3}{16}$ in Whitworth; $\frac{1}{4}$ in BSF
0.472	12 mm
0.500	$\frac{1}{2}$ in AF
0.512	13 mm
0.525	$\frac{1}{4}$ in Whitworth; $\frac{5}{16}$ in BSF
0.551	14 mm
0.563	$\frac{9}{16}$ in AF
0.591	15 mm
0.600	$\frac{5}{16}$ in Whitworth; $\frac{3}{8}$ in BSF
0.625	$\frac{5}{8}$ in AF
0.630	16 mm
0.669	17 mm
0.686	$\frac{11}{16}$ in AF
0.709	18 mm
0.710	$\frac{3}{8}$ in Whitworth; $\frac{7}{16}$ in BSF
0.748	19 mm
0.750	$\frac{3}{4}$ in AF
0.813	$\frac{13}{16}$ in AF
0.820	$\frac{7}{16}$ in Whitworth; $\frac{1}{2}$ in BSF
0.866	22 mm
0.875	$\frac{7}{8}$ in AF
0.920	$\frac{1}{2}$ in Whitworth; $\frac{9}{16}$ in BSF
0.938	$\frac{15}{16}$ in AF
0.945	24 mm
1.000	1 in AF
1.010	$\frac{9}{16}$ in Whitworth; $\frac{5}{8}$ in BSF
1.024	26 mm
1.063	$1\frac{1}{16}$ in AF; 27 mm
1.100	$\frac{5}{8}$ in Whitworth; $\frac{11}{16}$ in BSF
1.125	$1\frac{1}{8}$ in AF
1.181	30 mm
1.200	$\frac{11}{16}$ in Whitworth; $\frac{3}{4}$ in BSF
1.250	$1\frac{1}{4}$ in AF
1.260	32 mm
1.300	$\frac{3}{4}$ in Whitworth; $\frac{7}{8}$ in BSF
1.313	$1\frac{5}{16}$ in AF
1.390	$\frac{13}{16}$ in Whitworth; $\frac{15}{16}$ in BSF
1.417	36 mm
1.438	$1\frac{7}{16}$ in AF
1.480	$\frac{7}{8}$ in Whitworth; 1 in BSF
1.500	$1\frac{1}{2}$ in AF
1.575	40 mm; $\frac{15}{16}$ in Whitworth
1.614	41 mm
1.625	$1\frac{5}{8}$ in AF
1.670	1 in Whitworth; $1\frac{1}{8}$ in BSF
1.688	$1\frac{11}{16}$ in AF
1.811	46 mm
1.813	$1\frac{13}{16}$ in AF
1.860	$1\frac{1}{8}$ in Whitworth; $1\frac{1}{4}$ in BSF
1.875	$1\frac{7}{8}$ in AF
1.969	50 mm
2.000	2 in AF
2.050	$1\frac{1}{4}$ in Whitworth; $1\frac{3}{8}$ in BSF
2.165	55 mm
2.362	60 mm

General repair procedures

Whenever servicing, repair or overhaul work is carried out on the car or its components, it is necessary to observe the following procedures and instructions. This will assist in carrying out the operation efficiently and to a professional standard of workmanship.

Joint mating faces and gaskets

Where a gasket is used between the mating faces of two components, ensure that it is renewed on reassembly, and fit it dry unless otherwise stated in the repair procedure. Make sure that the mating faces are clean and dry with all traces of old gasket removed. When cleaning a joint face, use a tool which is not likely to score or damage the face, and remove any burrs or nicks with an oilstone or fine file.

Make sure that tapped holes are cleaned with a pipe cleaner, and keep them free of jointing compound if this is being used unless specifically instructed otherwise.

Ensure that all orifices, channels or pipes are clear and blow through them, preferably using compressed air.

Oil seals

Whenever an oil seal is removed from its working location, either individually or as part of an assembly, it should be renewed.

The very fine sealing lip of the seal is easily damaged and will not seal if the surface it contacts is not completely clean and free from scratches, nicks or grooves. If the original sealing surface of the component cannot be restored, the component should be renewed.

Protect the lips of the seal from any surface which may damage them in the course of fitting. Use tape or a conical sleeve where possible. Lubricate the seal lips with oil before fitting and, on dual lipped seals, fill the space between the lips with grease.

Unless otherwise stated, oil seals must be fitted with their sealing lips toward the lubricant to be sealed.

Use a tubular drift or block of wood of the appropriate size to install the seal and, if the seal housing is shouldered, drive the seal down to the shoulder. If the seal housing is unshouldered, the seal should be fitted with its face flush with the housing top face.

Screw threads and fastenings

Always ensure that a blind tapped hole is completely free from oil, grease, water or other fluid before installing the bolt or stud. Failure to do this could cause the housing to crack due to the hydraulic action of the bolt or stud as it is screwed in.

When tightening a castellated nut to accept a split pin, tighten the nut to the specified torque, where applicable, and then tighten further to the next split pin hole. Never slacken the nut to align a split pin hole unless stated in the repair procedure.

When checking or retightening a nut or bolt to a specified torque setting, slacken the nut or bolt by a quarter of a turn, and then retighten to the specified setting.

Locknuts, locktabs and washers

Any fastening which will rotate against a component or housing in the course of tightening should always have a washer between it and the relevant component or housing.

Spring or split washers should always be renewed when they are used to lock a critical component such as a big-end bearing retaining nut or bolt.

Locktabs which are folded over to retain a nut or bolt should always be renewed.

Self-locking nuts can be reused in non-critical areas, providing resistance can be felt when the locking portion passes over the bolt or stud thread.

Split pins must always be replaced with new ones of the correct size for the hole.

Special tools

Some repair procedures in this manual entail the use of special tools such as a press, two or three-legged pullers, spring compressors etc. Wherever possible, suitable readily available alternatives to the manufacturer's special tools are described, and are shown in use. In some instances, where no alternative is possible, it has been necessary to resort to the use of a manufacturer's tool and this has been done for reasons of safety as well as the efficient completion of the repair operation. Unless you are highly skilled and have a thorough understanding of the procedure described, never attempt to bypass the use of any special tool when the procedure described specifies its use. Not only is there a very great risk of personal injury, but expensive damage could be caused to the components involved.

Jacking and towing

Jacking

The jack supplied in the vehicle tool kit should only be used for emergency roadside wheel changing, unless it is supplemented with axle stands.

The jack supplied is of the side winding type. Check that the handbrake is fully applied before using the jack. Both the vehicle and the jack must be on firm ground when raising the car. Whenever possible, chock each side of the wheels on the opposite side to that being raised.

The jacking point on each side of the car is centrally positioned beneath the door sill. Check that the jack is fully engaged before raising the vehicle (photos).

When using a trolley or other type of workshop jack, it can be located beneath the longitudinal engine/transmission support member at the front or under the axle beam at the rear. In the latter case, care must be taken not to damage the Panhard rod and handbrake cable; to prevent this it is advisable to make up a suitable distance block to the dimensions shown in the accompanying illustration. The block is then fitted between the jack head and the axle beam.

If raising the vehicle completely, raise the rear end first. Axle stands must **only** be located under double-skinned side or chassis members.

Towing

Towing eyes are fitted to the front and the rear of the vehicle for attachment of a tow rope.

Always unlock the steering column if being towed by another vehicle. If servo-assisted brakes are fitted, remember that the servo is inoperative if the engine is not running.

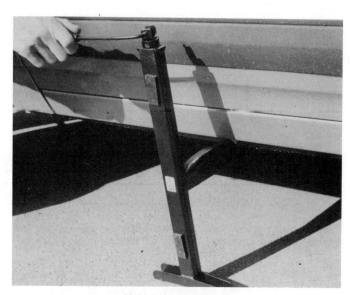

Vehicle jacking point

Prise free the wheel trim for access to the wheel nuts (if applicable)

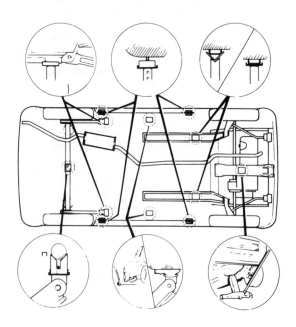

Jacking and support locations on underside of vehicle

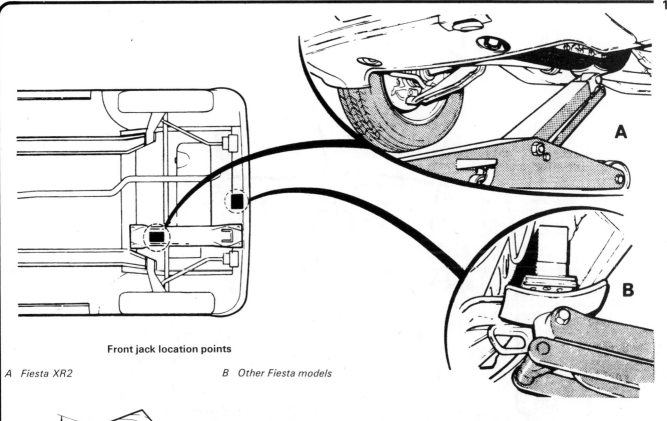

Front jack location points

A   Fiesta XR2   B   Other Fiesta models

Fabricate a distance block to dimensions shown for use when jacking at rear under the axle beam

A   133 mm (5.25 in)   D   13 mm (0.5 in)
B   108 mm (4.25 in)   E   38 mm (1.5 in)
C   51 mm (2.0 in)   F   127 mm (5.0 in)

Axle stand location points at front of vehicle

A   Body sill   B   Chassis runner

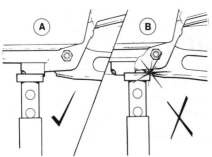

Axle stand location at rear must be forward of trailing arm (A), not under it (B)

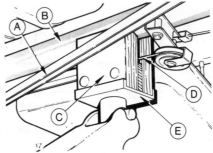

Distance block location when jacking/supporting under axle beam at rear

A   Panhard rod   D   Handbrake cable
B   Beam axle   E   Jack
C   Wooden block

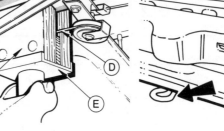

Vehicle towing eyes

H.12492

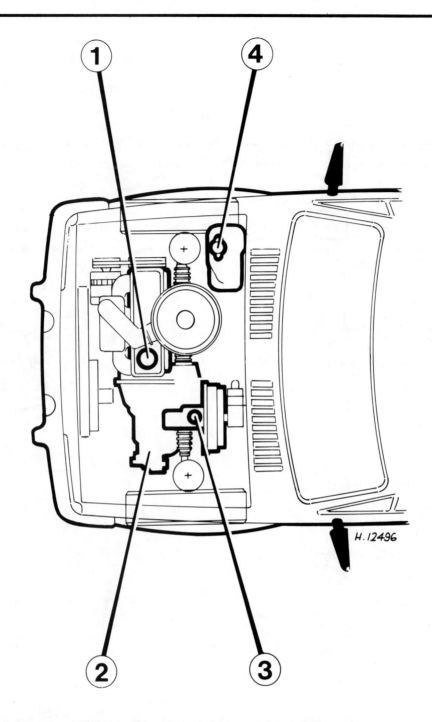

H.12496

Recommended lubricants and fluids

Component or system	Lubricant type or specification
Engine (1)	HD multigrade oil to SAE 10W/30, 10W/40 or 10W/50
Transmission (2)	SAE 80 EP gear oil to Ford specification SQM-2C9008-A
Braking system (3)	Brake fluid to Ford specification SAM-6C-9103A Amber
Cooling system (4)	Antifreeze to Ford specification SSM 97B 9103A

The above are general recommendations only: lubrication requirements vary from territory to territory. Consult your owners handbook or a Ford dealer.

Safety first!

Professional motor mechanics are trained in safe working procedures. However enthusiastic you may be about getting on with the job in hand, do take the time to ensure that your safety is not put at risk. A moment's lack of attention can result in an accident, as can failure to observe certain elementary precautions.

There will always be new ways of having accidents, and the following points do not pretend to be a comprehensive list of all dangers; they are intended rather to make you aware of the risks and to encourage a safety-conscious approach to all work you carry out on your vehicle.

Essential DOs and DON'Ts

DON'T rely on a single jack when working underneath the vehicle. Always use reliable additional means of support, such as axle stands, securely placed under a part of the vehicle that you know will not give way.

DON'T attempt to loosen or tighten high-torque nuts (e.g. wheel hub nuts) while the vehicle is on a jack; it may be pulled off.

DON'T start the engine without first ascertaining that the transmission is in neutral and the parking brake applied.

DON'T suddenly remove the filler cap from a hot cooling system — cover it with a cloth and release the pressure gradually first, or you may get scalded by escaping coolant.

DON'T attempt to drain oil until you are sure it has cooled sufficiently to avoid scalding you.

DON'T grasp any part of the engine or exhaust without first ascertaining that it is sufficiently cool to avoid burning you.

DON'T syphon toxic liquids such as fuel, brake fluid or antifreeze by mouth, or allow them to remain on your skin.

DON'T inhale brake lining dust — it is injurious to health.

DON'T allow any spilt oil or grease to remain on the floor — wipe it up straight away, before someone slips on it.

DON'T use ill-fitting spanners or other tools which may slip and cause injury.

DON'T attempt to lift a heavy component which may be beyond your capability — get assistance.

DON'T rush to finish a job, or take unverified short cuts.

DON'T allow children or animals in or around an unattended vehicle.

DO wear eye protection when using power tools such as drill, sander, bench grinder etc, and when working under the vehicle.

DO use a barrier cream on your hands prior to undertaking dirty jobs — it will protect your skin from infection as well as making the dirt easier to remove afterwards; but make sure your hands aren't left slippery.

DO keep loose clothing (cuffs, tie etc) and long hair well out of the way of moving mechanical parts.

DO remove rings, wristwatch etc, before working on the vehicle — especially the electrical system.

DO ensure that any lifting tackle used has a safe working load rating adequate for the job.

DO keep your work area tidy — it is only too easy to fall over articles left lying around.

DO get someone to check periodically that all is well, when working alone on the vehicle.

DO carry out work in a logical sequence and check that everything is correctly assembled and tightened afterwards.

DO remember that your vehicle's safety affects that of yourself and others. If in doubt on any point, get specialist advice.

IF, in spite of following these precautions, you are unfortunate enough to injure yourself, seek medical attention as soon as possible.

Fire

Remember at all times that petrol (gasoline) is highly flammable. Never smoke, or have any kind of naked flame around, when working on the vehicle. But the risk does not end there — a spark caused by an electrical short-circuit, by two metal surfaces contacting each other, or even by static electricity built up in your body under certain conditions, can ignite petrol vapour, which in a confined space is highly explosive.

Always disconnect the battery earth (ground) terminal before working on any part of the fuel system, and never risk spilling fuel on to a hot engine or exhaust.

It is recommended that a fire extinguisher of a type suitable for fuel and electrical fires is kept handy in the garage or workplace at all times. Never try to extinguish a fuel or electrical fire with water.

Fumes

Certain fumes are highly toxic and can quickly cause unconsciousness and even death if inhaled to any extent. Petrol (gasoline) vapour comes into this category, as do the vapours from certain solvents such as trichloroethylene. Any draining or pouring of such volatile fluids should be done in a well ventilated area.

When using cleaning fluids and solvents, read the instructions carefully. Never use materials from unmarked containers — they may give off poisonous vapours.

Never run the engine of a motor vehicle in an enclosed space such as a garage. Exhaust fumes contain carbon monoxide which is extremely poisonous; if you need to run the engine, always do so in the open air or at least have the rear of the vehicle outside the workplace.

If you are fortunate enough to have the use of an inspection pit, never drain or pour petrol, and never run the engine, while the vehicle is standing over it; the fumes, being heavier than air, will concentrate in the pit with possibly lethal results.

The battery

Never cause a spark, or allow a naked light, near the vehicle's battery. It will normally be giving off a certain amount of hydrogen gas, which is highly explosive.

Always disconnect the battery earth (ground) terminal before working on the fuel or electrical systems.

If possible, loosen the filler plugs or cover when charging the battery from an external source. Do not charge at an excessive rate or the battery may burst.

Take care when topping up and when carrying the battery. The acid electrolyte, even when diluted, is very corrosive and should not be allowed to contact the eyes or skin.

If you ever need to prepare electrolyte yourself, always add the acid slowly to the water, and never the other way round. Protect against splashes by wearing rubber gloves and goggles.

When jump starting a car using a booster battery, for negative earth (ground) vehicles, connect the jump leads in the following sequence: First connect one jump lead between the positive (+) terminals of the two batteries. Then connect the other jump lead first to the negative (−) terminal of the booster battery, and then to a good earthing (ground) point on the vehicle to be started, at least 18 in (45 cm) from the battery if possible. Ensure that hands and jump leads are clear of any moving parts, and that the two vehicles do not touch. Disconnect the leads in the reverse order.

Mains electricity

When using an electric power tool, inspection light etc, which works from the mains, always ensure that the appliance is correctly connected to its plug and that, where necessary, it is properly earthed (grounded). Do not use such appliances in damp conditions and, again, beware of creating a spark or applying excessive heat in the vicinity of fuel or fuel vapour.

Ignition HT voltage

A severe electric shock can result from touching certain parts of the ignition system, such as the HT leads, when the engine is running or being cranked, particularly if components are damp or the insulation is defective. Where an electronic ignition system is fitted, the HT voltage is much higher and could prove fatal.

Routine maintenance

Maintenance is essential for ensuring safety, and desirable for the purpose of getting the best in terms of performance and economy from the vehicle. Over the years the need for periodic lubrication – oiling, greasing and so on – has been drastically reduced, if not totally eliminated. This has unfortunately tended to lead some owners to think that because no such action is required the items either no longer exist or will last for ever. This is a serious delusion. It follows therefore that the largest initial element of maintenance is visual examination. This may lead to repairs or renewals.

Engine compartment – ohv

1	Coolant expansion tank	4	Ignition coil	7	Cooling fan	10	Alternator
2	Engine oil dipstick	5	Brake fluid reservoir	8	Oil filler cap	11	Washer reservoir
3	Oil filter	6	Battery	9	Carburettor (filter removed)		

Engine compartment – CVH

1 Coolant expansion tank
2 Engine oil dipstick
3 Carburettor (filter removed)

4 Fuel pump
5 Distributor
6 Ignition coil

7 Windscreen wiper motor
8 Ignition amplifier module
9 Battery

10 Brake fluid reservoir
11 Cooling fan

12 Oil filler cap
13 Washer reservoir

Underside view of car at front (CVH variant)

1	Suspension arm	5	Sump	9	Transmission
2	Driveshaft	6	Exhaust	10	Disc brake caliper
3	Tie-bar	7	Starter motor	11	Gearchange rod and
4	Alternator	8	Engine/transmission bearer		stabilizer rod

Underside view of car at rear

1 Rear silencer	4 Suspension coil spring	6 Panhard rod
2 Brake secondary cable	5 Shock absorber lower mounting	7 Anti-roll bar (certain models only)
3 Fuel tank		8 Towing eye
		9 Axle beam
		10 Exhaust system mounting

11 Handbrake adjustment check plunger
12 Suspension trailing arm
13 Brake pressure control valve

Engine oil dipstick

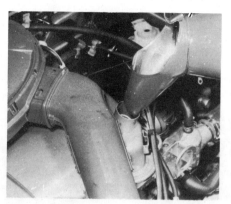

Topping-up the engine oil

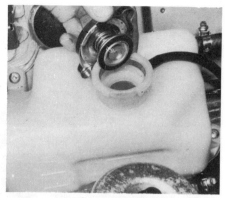

Coolant expansion tank

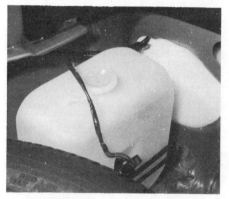

Washer reservoir (rear window)

Brake fluid reservoir

Check the tyre pressures

Weekly or every 250 miles (400 km)

Check the engine oil level and top up, if necessary (photos)
Check the coolant level in the expansion tank and top up, if necessary
Check the battery electrolyte level and top up, if necessary (where applicable – see Chapter 11)
Top up the fluid level in the washer reservoir (photos)
Check brake fluid level; investigate any sudden fall in level (photo)
Check the operation of all lights
Check the operation of the horn
Check the operation of washers and wipers
Check tyre pressures, including the spare (photo)
Check the tyres for wear or damage

At the first 1500 miles (2500 km) – new vehicles

Check the alternator/coolant pump drivebelt tension (see Chapter 2)
Check torque of intake and exhaust manifold bolts (cold)
Check brake hydraulic system connectors for leaks
Check idle speed, CO% (mixture) and choke for correct adjustment (see Chapter 3)
Check emission control system components and hoses for condition and security (as applicable) as given in Chapter 3

Every 6000 miles (10 000 km) or six months, whichever comes first

Drain and renew the engine oil. At the same time renew the oil filter (refer to Chapter 1) (photo)
Check for oil fuel and water leaks
Remove clean and adjust the spark plugs

Check the HT leads, distributor cap and ignition circuit connections for security and condition
On ohv engine models check and adjust, if necessary, the ignition timing and dwell angle
Check that the brake level warning indicator is operational
Check the disc pads for wear (front) and brake shoe linings for wear (rear), see Chapter 8

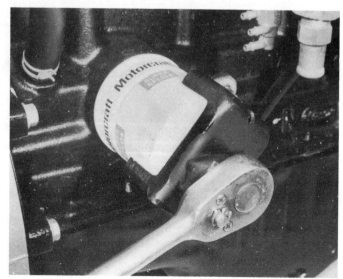

Renew the engine oil filter

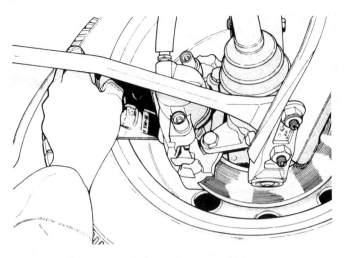

Use a mirror to check disc brake pads for wear

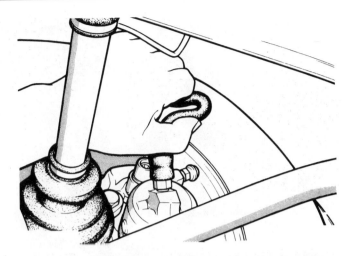

Bend flexible brake hoses to check for splitting and decay

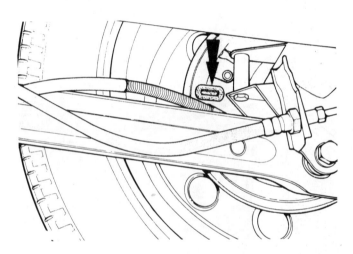

Remove inspection plug (arrowed) to check rear brake linings for wear

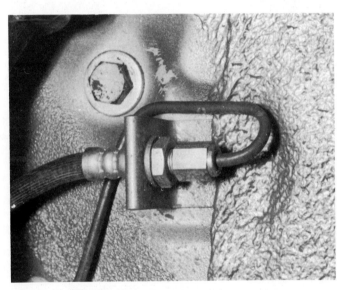

Check brake lines, connections and hoses

Every 12 000 miles (20 000 km) or 12 months, whichever comes first

Remove the rocker cover and check the valve clearances (on ohv engine variants)

Check the battery lead connections and terminals for security, clean any corrosion from them and smear the terminals posts with Vaseline for protection

Remove and renew the spark plugs. Check the electrode gap before fitting each plug

Check the HT leads and distributor cap connections for security and condition

Remove and renew the distributor contact breaker points and lubricate the distributor (ohv engines only)

Make a general check for engine oil, coolant or fuel line leaks

Check the transmission oil level and top up, if necessary

Lubricate the handbrake linkage

Check the brake lines and connections for security and signs of excessive corrosion (photo)

Check steering joints for wear and gaiters for deterioration (see Chapter 9) (photo)

Check tightness of roadwheel bolts

Check the tyres for signs of excessive wear or any signs of damage and renew, if necessary

Check the steering joints

Check the driveshaft gaiters

Inspect the driveshaft joint gaiters for deterioration, splits or insecurity (photo)

Check the exhaust system for signs of excessive corrosion, leaks or insecurity

Inspect the vehicle underside for signs of damage or excessive corrosion, particularly around the suspension mounting points

Check the windscreen wiper blades for signs of excessive wear or deterioration and renew, if necessary. At the same time also check the operation of the washers

Lubricate the controls, hinges, locks and cables

Check the seat belts for condition, operation and security at the mountings (see Chapter 12)

Every 24 000 miles (40 000 km) or 2 years, whichever comes first

Remove and renew the air cleaner element (see Chapter 3)
Check the air cleaner temperature control (see Chapter 3)
Remove and clean the emission control orifice in the oil filler cap (ohv)
Renew the emission control filter in the air cleaner unit (ohv)

Every 2 years

Drain and renew the engine coolant, together with the specified antifreeze/inhibitor (see Chapter 2)

Every 3 years

Make a thorough inspection of all brake components for signs of leaks, general deterioration and wear in mechanical parts
Drain and renew the hydraulic fluid (see Chapter 8)

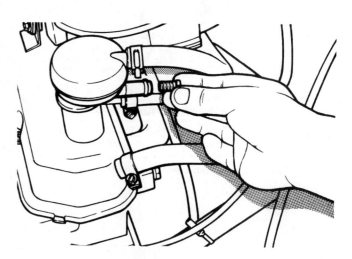

Clean emission control orifice in solvent (ohv engine)

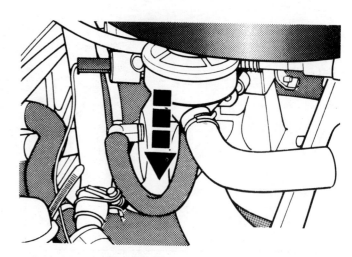

Detach hose downwards from filter for access to crankcase emission filter in air cleaner body

Fault diagnosis

Introduction

The vehicle owner who does his or her own maintenance according to the recommended schedules should not have to use this section of the manual very often. Modern component reliability is such that, provided those items subject to wear or deterioration are inspected or renewed at the specified intervals, sudden failure is comparatively rare. Faults do not usually just happen as a result of sudden failure, but develop over a period of time. Major mechanical failures in particular are usually preceded by characteristic symptoms over hundreds or even thousands of miles. Those components which do occasionally fail without warning are often small and easily carried in the vehicle.

With any fault finding, the first step is to decide where to begin investigations. Sometimes this is obvious, but on other occasions a little detective work will be necessary. The owner who makes half a dozen haphazard adjustments or replacements may be successful in curing a fault (or its symptoms), but he will be none the wiser if the fault recurs and he may well have spent more time and money than was necessary. A calm and logical approach will be found to be more satisfactory in the long run. Always take into account any warning signs or abnormalities that may have been noticed in the period preceding the fault – power loss, high or low gauge readings, unusual noises or smells, etc – and remember that failure of components such as fuses or spark plugs may only be pointers to some underlying fault.

The pages which follow here are intended to help in cases of failure to start or breakdown on the road. There is also a Fault Diagnosis Section at the end of each Chapter which should be consulted if the preliminary checks prove unfruitful. Whatever the fault, certain basic principles apply. These are as follows:

Verify the fault. This is simply a matter of being sure that you know what the symptoms are before starting work. This is particularly important if you are investigating a fault for someone else who may not have described it very accurately.

Don't overlook the obvious. For example, if the vehicle won't start, is there petrol in the tank? (Don't take anyone else's word on this particular point, and don't trust the fuel gauge either!) If an electrical fault is indicated, look for loose or broken wires before digging out the test gear.

Cure the disease, not the symptom. Substituting a flat battery with a fully charged one will get you off the hard shoulder, but if the underlying cause is not attended to, the new battery will go the same way. Similarly, changing oil-fouled spark plugs for a new set will get you moving again, but remember that the reason for the fouling (if it wasn't simply an incorrect grade of plug) will have to be established and corrected.

Don't take anything for granted. Particularly, don't forget that a 'new' component may itself be defective (especially if it's been rattling round in the boot for months), and don't leave components out of a fault diagnosis sequence just because they are new or recently fitted. When you do finally diagnose a difficult fault, you'll probably realise that all the evidence was there from the start.

Electrical faults

Electrical faults can be more puzzling than straightforward mechanical failures, but they are no less susceptible to logical analysis if the basic principles of operation are understood. Vehicle electrical wiring exists in extremely unfavourable conditions – heat, vibration and chemical attack – and the first things to look for are loose or corroded connections and broken or chafed wires, especially where the wires pass through holes in the bodywork or are subject to vibration.

All metal-bodied vehicles in current production have one pole of the battery 'earthed', ie connected to the vehicle bodywork, and in nearly all modern vehicles it is the negative (–) terminal. The various electrical components – motors, bulb holders etc – are also connected to earth, either by means of a lead or directly by their mountings. Electric current flows through the component and then back to the battery via the bodywork. If the component mounting is loose or corroded, or if a good path back to the battery is not available, the circuit will be incomplete and malfunction will result. The engine and/or gearbox are also earthed by means of flexible metal straps to the body or subframe; if these straps are loose or missing, starter motor, generator and ignition trouble may result.

Assuming the earth return to be satisfactory, electrical faults will be due either to component malfunction or to defects in the current supply. Individual components are dealt with in Chapter 11. If supply wires are broken or cracked internally this results in an open-circuit, and the easiest way to check for this is to bypass the suspect wire temporarily with a length of wire having a crocodile clip or suitable connector at each end. Alternatively, a 12V test lamp can be used to verify the presence of supply voltage at various points along the wire and the break can be thus isolated.

If a bare portion of a live wire touches the bodywork or other earthed metal part, the electricity will take the low-resistance path thus formed back to the battery: this is known as a short-circuit. Hopefully a short-circuit will blow a fuse, but otherwise it may cause burning of the insulation (and possibly further short-circuits) or even a fire. This is why it is inadvisable to bypass persistently blowing fuses with silver foil or wire.

Spares and tool kit

Most vehicles are supplied only with sufficient tools for wheel changing; the *Maintenance and minor repair* tool kit detailed in *Tools and working facilities*, with the addition of a hammer, is probably sufficient for those repairs that most motorists would consider attempting at the roadside. In addition a few items which can be fitted without too much trouble in the event of a breakdown should be carried. Experience and available space will modify the list below, but the following may save having to call on professional assistance:

Spark plugs, clean and correctly gapped
HT lead and plug cap – long enough to reach the plug furthest from the distributor
Distributor rotor, condenser and contact breaker points
Drivebelt(s) – emergency type may suffice
Spare fuses
Set of principal light bulbs
Tin of radiator sealer and hose bandage
Exhaust bandage
Roll of insulating tape
Length of soft iron wire
Length of electrical flex
Torch or inspection lamp (can double as test lamp)
Battery jump leads
Tow-rope
Ignition waterproofing aerosol
Litre of engine oil
Sealed can of hydraulic fluid
Emergency windscreen
Worm drive clips
Tube of filler paste

If spare fuel is carried, a can designed for the purpose should be used to minimise risks of leakage and collision damage. A first aid kit and a warning triangle, whilst not at present compulsory in the UK, are obviously sensible items to carry in addition to the above.

When touring abroad it may be advisable to carry additional spares which, even if you cannot fit them yourself, could save having to wait while parts are obtained. The items below may be worth considering:

Clutch and throttle cables
Cylinder head gasket
Alternator brushes
Tyre valve core

One of the motoring organisations will be able to advise on availability of fuel etc in foreign countries.

Engine will not start

Engine fails to turn when starter operated
Flat battery (recharge, use jump leads, or push start)
Battery terminals loose or corroded
Battery earth to body defective
Engine earth strap loose or broken
Starter motor (or solenoid) wiring loose or broken
Ignition/starter switch faulty
Major mechanical failure (seizure)
Starter or solenoid internal fault (see Chapter 11)

Starter motor turns engine slowly
Partially discharged battery (recharge, use jump leads, or push start)
Battery terminals loose or corroded
Battery earth to body defective
Engine earth strap loose
Starter motor (or solenoid) wiring loose
Starter motor internal fault (see Chapter 11)

Starter motor spins without turning engine
Flat battery
Starter motor pinion sticking on sleeve
Flywheel gear teeth damaged or worn
Starter motor mounting bolts loose

Engine turns normally but fails to start
Damp or dirty HT leads and distributor cap (crank engine and check for spark)
Dirty or incorrectly gapped distributor points (if applicable)
No fuel in tank (check for delivery at carburettor)
Excessive choke (hot engine) or insufficient choke (cold engine)
Fouled or incorrectly gapped spark plugs (remove, clean and regap)
Other ignition system fault (see Chapter 4)
Other fuel system fault (see Chapter 3)
Poor compression
Major mechanical failure (eg camshaft drive)

Engine fires but will not run
Insufficient choke (cold engine)
Air leaks at carburettor or inlet manifold
Fuel starvation (see Chapter 3)
Ballast resistor defective, or other ignition fault (see Chapter 4)

Engine cuts out and will not restart

Engine cuts out suddenly – ignition fault
Loose or disconnected LT wires
Wet HT leads or distributor cap (after traversing water splash)
Coil or condenser failure (check for spark)
Other ignition fault (see Chapter 4)

Engine misfires before cutting out – fuel fault
Fuel tank empty
Fuel pump defective or filter blocked (check for delivery)

Fuel tank filler vent blocked (suction will be evident on releasing cap)
Carburettor needle valve sticking
Carburettor jets blocked (fuel contaminated)
Other fuel system fault (see Chapter 3)

Engine cuts out – other causes
Serious overheating
Major mechanical failure (eg camshaft drive)

Engine overheats

Ignition (no-charge) warning light illuminated
Slack or broken drivebelt – retension or renew (see Chapter 2)

Ignition warning light not illuminated
Coolant loss due to internal or external leakage (see Chapter 2)
Thermostat defective
Low oil level
Brakes binding
Radiator clogged externally or internally

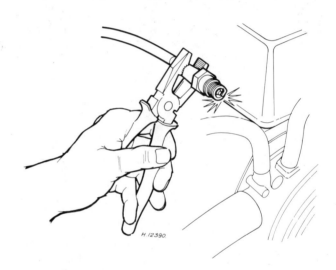

H.12390

Crank engine and check for a spark. Note use of insulated tool

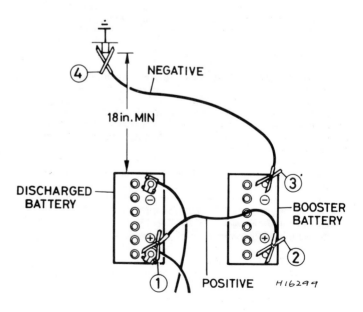

H16299

Jump start lead connections for negative earth vehicles – connect leads in order shown

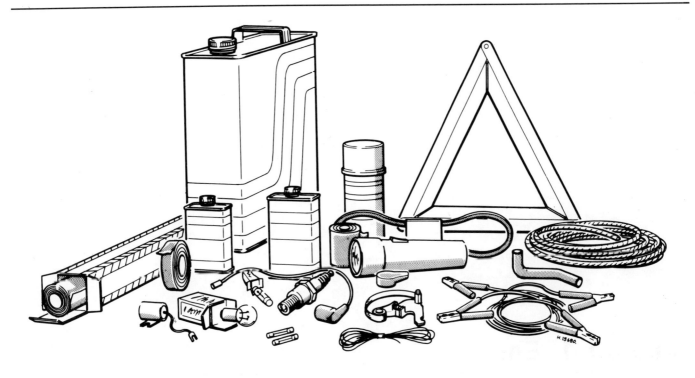

Carrying a few spares can save you a long walk!

Electric cooling fan not operating correctly
Engine waterways clogged
Ignition timing incorrect or automatic advance malfunctioning
Mixture too weak

Note: *Do not add cold water to an overheated engine or damage may result*

Low engine oil pressure

Gauge reads low or warning light illuminated with engine running
    Oil level low or incorrect grade
    Defective gauge or sender unit
    Wire to sender unit earthed
    Engine overheating
    Oil filter clogged or bypass valve defective
    Oil pressure relief valve defective
    Oil pick-up strainer clogged
    Oil pump worn or mountings loose
    Worn main or big-end bearings
Note: *Low oil pressure in a high-mileage engine at tickover is not necessarily a cause for concern. Sudden pressure loss at speed is far more significant. In any event, check the gauge or warning light sender before condemning the engine.*

Engine noises

Pre-ignition (pinking) on acceleration
    Incorrect grade of fuel
    Ignition timing incorrect
    Distributor faulty or worn
    Worn or maladjusted carburettor
    Excessive carbon build-up in engine

Whistling or wheezing noises
    Leaking vacuum hose
    Leaking carburettor or manifold gasket
    Blowing head gasket

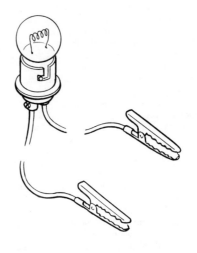

Simple test lamp is useful for tracing electrical faults

Tapping or rattling
    Incorrect valve clearances
    Worn valve gear
    Worn timing chain or belt
    Broken piston ring (ticking noise)

Knocking or thumping
    Unintentional mechanical contact (eg fan blades)
    Worn fanbelt
    Peripheral component fault (generator, water pump etc)
    Worn big-end bearings (regular heavy knocking, perhaps less under load)
    Worn main bearings (rumbling and knocking, perhaps worsening under load)
    Piston slap (most noticeable when cold)

Chapter 1 Engine

Contents

Part A: ohv engine

Crankcase ventilation system – description 13
Crankshaft front oil seal – renewal 9
Cylinder head – removal and refitting 5
Cylinder head and pistons – decarbonising 19
Engine – complete dismantling 17
Engine – examination and renovation 18
Engine – method of removal 15
Engine – reassembly 20
Engine and transmission – removal 16
Engine mountings – removal and refitting 14
Engine/transmission – reconnection and refitting 21
Fault diagnosis – ohv engine 22
General description 1
Lubrication system – description 12
Oil filter and pump – removal and refitting 11
Operations only possible with engine removed from vehicle 4
Operations possible without removing engine from vehicle 3
Piston/connecting rod – removal and refitting 10
Rocker gear – dismantling and reassembly 8
Routine maintenance – ohv engine 2
Sump – removal and refitting 7
Valve clearances – adjustment 6

Part B: CVH engine

Camshaft – removal and refitting 29
Camshaft oil seal – renewal 28
Crankcase ventilation system – description 37
Crankshaft front oil seal – renewal 31
Cylinder head – removal and refitting 30
Cylinder head and pistons – decarbonising 42
Engine – complete dismantling 40
Engine – examination and renovation 41
Engine – method of removal 38
Engine – reassembly 43
Engine/transmission – reconnection and refitting 44
Engine/transmission – removal and separation 39
Engine/transmission mountings – removal and refitting 34
Fault diagnosis – CVH engine 45
General description 23
Lubrication system – description 36
Oil filter – removal and refitting 35
Operations only possible with engine removed from vehicle 26
Operations possible without removing engine from vehicle 25
Piston/connecting rods – removal and reftting 33
Routine maintenance – CVH engine 24
Sump – removal and refitting 32
Timing belt – inspection, removal and refitting 27

Specifications

Part A: ohv engine
General

Engine type	Four-cylinder, overhead valve, mounted transversely, water-cooled	
Data:	**1.0 litre**	**1.1 litre**
Firing order (No. 1 at timing cover end)	1-2-4-3	1-2-4-3
Bore	73.96 mm (2.91 in)	73.96 mm (2.91 in)
Stroke	55.70 mm (2.19 in)	64.98 mm (2.56 in)
Cubic capacity	957 cc (58.4 cu in)	1117 cc (68.16 cu in)
Compression ratio	8.5:1	9.5:1
Compression pressure at starter speed	9.5 to 11.5 kgf/cm^2 (137 to 166 lbf/in^2)	13.3 to 15.3 kgf/cm^2 (189 to 217 lbf/in^2)
Idle speed (rpm)	750 to 850	750 to 850
Maximum continuous engine speed (rpm)	5950	5450
Engine output (DIN)	33 kW at 5750 rpm	37 kW at 5000 rpm
Engine torque (DIN)	6.9 kgf m at 3700 rpm	8.4 kgf m at 2700 rpm

Cylinder block

Number of main bearings	3
Cylinder bore diameter – mm (in)	
Standard (1)	73.940 to 73.950 (2.9110 to 2.9114)
Standard (2)	73.950 to 73.960 (2.9114 to 2.9118)
Standard (3)	73.960 to 73.970 (2.9118 to 2.9122)
Standard (4) and service	73.970 to 73.980 (2.9122 to 2.9126)
Oversizes – mm (in):	
0.5 (0.02)	74.500 to 74.510 (2.9330 to 2.9334)
1.0 (0.04)	75.000 to 75.010 (2.9527 to 2.9531)
Central main bearing width (less thrust washers) – mm (in) ...	22.04 to 22.10 (0.868 to 0.870)
Main bearing bore – mm (in):	
Standard	60.623 to 60.636 (2.3867 to 2.3872)
Oversize	61.003 to 61.016 (2.4017 to 2.4022)
Camshaft bearing bore – mm (in):	
Standard	42.888 to 42.918 (1.6885 to 1.6897)
Oversize	43.396 to 43.420 (1.7085 to 1.7094)

Crankshaft

Endfloat – mm (in)	0.072 to 0.285 (0.003 to 0.011)
Main journal diameter – mm (in):	
Standard	56.990 to 57.000 (2.2437 to 2.2441)
Yellow dot	56.980 to 56.990 (2.2433 to 2.2436)
0.254 (0.01) undersize	56.726 to 56.746 (2.2333 to 2.2340)
0.508 (0.02) undersize	56.472 to 56.492 (2.2233 to 2.2240)
0.762 (0.03) undersize	56.218 to 56.238 (2.2133 to 2.2140)
Main bearing shell width – mm (in)	21.2 to 21.6 (0.834 to 0.850)
Main bearing shell play – mm (in)	0.009 to 0.046 (0.0003 to 0.0018)
Crankpin (big-end) diameter – mm (in):	
Standard	42.99 to 43.01 (1.6925 to 1.6933)
0.254 (0.01) undersize	42.74 to 42.76 (1.6827 to 1.6835)
0.508 (0.02) undersize	42.49 to 42.51 (1.6728 to 1.6736)
0.762 (0.03) undersize	42.24 to 42.26 (1.6630 to 1.6638)
Thrust washer thicknesses – mm (in):	
Standard	2.80 to 2.85 (0.1102 to 0.1122)
Oversize	2.99 to 3.04 (0.1177 to 0.1196)

Camshaft

Number of bearings	3
Drive	Chain and sprocket
Camshaft bearing diameter – mm (in)	39.615 to 39.635 (1.5596 to 1.5604)
Bearing bush inside diameter – mm (in)	39.662 to 39.682 (1.5615 to 1.5622)
Camshaft thrust plate thickness – mm (in)	4.457 to 4.508 (0.1754 to 0.1774)
Camshaft endfloat – mm (in)	0.062 to 0.193 (0.0024 to 0.0076)
Cam lift:	
Inlet valve – mm (in)	5.300 (0.208)
Exhaust valve – mm (in)	5.300 (0.208)
Cam length (heel to toe) – mm (in)	
Inlet	32.288 to 32.516 (1.2711 to 1.2801)
Exhaust	32.615 to 32.846 (1.2840 to 1.2931)

Pistons

Diameter – mm (in):	
Standard (1)	73.910 to 73.920 (2.9098 to 2.9102)
Standard (2)	73.920 to 73.930 (2.9102 to 2.9106)
Standard (3)	73.930 to 73.940 (2.9106 to 2.9110)
Standard (4)	73.940 to 73.950 (2.9110 to 2.9114)
Standard service	73.930 to 73.955 (2.9106 to 2.9116)
0.5 (0.02) oversize	74.460 to 74.485 (2.9314 to 2.9324)
1.0 (0.04) oversize	74.960 to 74.985 (2.9511 to 2.9521)
Piston-to-bore clearance – mm (in)	0.015 to 0.050 (0.0006 to 0.0020)
Piston ring gap (fitted) – mm (in)	
Top and 2nd rings	0.25 to 0.45 (0.0098 to 0.0177)
Bottom ring	0.20 to 0.40 (0.0078 to 0.0157)
Bottom (oil control) ring gap position	In line with gudgeon pin
2nd ring gap position	90° to oil control ring gap
Top ring gap position	180° to oil control ring gap

Gudgeon pins
Pin length – mm (in) .... 54.6 to 55.4 (2.1496 to 2.1810)
Pin diameters – mm (in):
    White .... 20.622 to 20.625 (0.8118 to 0.8120)
    Red .... 20.625 to 20.628 (0.8120 to 0.8121)
    Blue .... 20.628 to 20.631 (0.8121 to 0.8122)
    Yellow .... 20.631 to 20.634 (0.8122 to 0.8123)
Connecting rod interference at 21°C (70°F) .... 0.013 to 0.045 mm (0.0005 to 0.0017 in)
Pin-to-piston interference at 21°C (70°F) .... 0.005 to 0.011 mm (0.0002 to 0.0004 in)

Connecting rods
Big-end bore diameter – mm (in) .... 46.685 to 46.705 (1.8380 to 1.8388)
Small-end bore diameter – mm (in) .... 20.589 to 20.609 (0.8106 to 0.8114)
Bearing shell inside diameter (fitted) – mm (in):
    Standard .... 43.016 to 43.050 (1.6935 to 1.6948)
    0.254 (0.01) undersize .... 42.768 to 42.802 (1.6837 to 1.6851)
    0.508 (0.02) undersize .... 42.518 to 42.552 (1.6739 to 1.6752)
    0.762 (0.03) undersize .... 42.268 to 42.302 (1.6640 to 1.6654)
    1.016 (0.04) undersize .... 42.018 to 42.052 (1.6542 to 1.6555)
Journal-to-bearing shell clearance .... 0.006 to 0.060 (0.0002 to 0.0020)

Cylinder head
Valve seat angle (inlet and exhaust) .... 45°
Valve seat width – mm (in):
    Inlet and exhaust .... 1.20 to 1.75 (0.0472 to 0.0688)
Lower correction angle (inlet and exhaust) .... 30°
Upper correction angle (inlet and exhaust) .... 80°
Upper correction angle – service cutter .... 75°
Valve stem bore (inlet and exhaust) – mm (in):
    Standard .... 7.907 to 7.938 (0.3112 to 0.3125)
    0.381 (0.015) oversize .... 8.288 to 8.319 (0.3262 to 0.3275)

Valves
Clearances – mm (in)
  Inlet:
    At operating temperature 0.22 (0.009)
    Cold .... 0.20 to 0.25 (0.008 to 0.010)
  Exhaust:
    At operating temperature 0.59 (0.023)
    Cold .... 0.56 to 0.61 (0.022 to 0.024)
Tappet diameter – mm (in) .... 13.081 to 13.094 (0.5149 to 0.5155)
Tappet clearance in cylinder block – mm (in) ..... 20.25 to 20.75 (0.797 to 0.816)
Valve spring free length:
  Inlet and exhaust – mm (in) 42 (1.653)
Valve lift (excluding clearance) – mm (in):
  Inlet and exhaust 8.367 (0.3294)
Valve head diameter – mm (in):
  Inlet .... 32.89 to 33.15 (1.294 to 1.305)
  Exhaust .... 29.01 to 29.27 (1.142 to 1.152)
Valve stem diameter:
  Inlet valves – mm (in):
    Standard .... 7.868 to 7.886 (0.3098 to 0.3105)
    0.076 oversize .... 7.944 to 7.962 (0.3128 to 0.3135)
    0.381 (0.015) oversize .... 8.249 to 8.267 (0.3248 to 0.3255)
  Exhaust valves – mm (in):
    Standard .... 7.846 to 7.864 (0.3089 to 0.3096)
    0.076 oversize .... 7.922 to 7.940 (0.3119 to 0.3126)
    0.281 (0.015) oversize .... 8.227 to 8.245 (0.3239 to 0.3246)
Valve stem-to-guide clearance – mm (in):
  Inlet .... 0.021 to 0.070 (0.0008 to 0.0027)
  Exhaust .... 0.043 to 0.092 (0.0017 to 0.0036)
Valve timing:
  Inlet valve opens .... 14° BTDC
  Inlet valve closes .... 46° ABDC
  Exhaust valve opens .... 65° BBDC
  Exhaust valve closes .... 11° ATDC

Engine lubrication
Oil grade .... HD multigrade
Viscosity:
  -23 to 32°C (-9° to 90°F) .... SAE 10W/30, 10W/40 or 10W/50
  over -18°C (0°F) .... SAE 15W/40 or 15W/50
  Over -12°C (10°F) .... SAE 20W/40 or 20W/50
  Under -23°C (-9°F) .... SAE 5W/30
Oil change:
  Without filter change .... 2.75 litres (4.85 Imp pints)
  With filter change .... 3.25 litres (5.75 Imp pints)

Oil initial fill capacity (new or reconditioned engine)	3.40 litres (5.98 Imp pints)
Minimum oil pressure at 80°C (175°F)	0.6 kgf/cm^2 (8.5 lbf/in^2) at 750 rpm
Warning light operates at	0.32 to 0.53 kgf/cm^2 (4.5 to 7.5 lbf/in^2)
Relief valve opening pressure	2.41 to 2.75 kgf/cm^2 (34.3 to 39.1 lbf/in^2)
Oil pump clearances — mm (in)	
Outer rotor-to-housing	0.14 to 0.26 (0.005 to 0.010)
Inner-to-outer rotor	0.051 to 0.127 (0.02 to 0.005)
Rotors-to-cover endfloat	0.025 to 0.06 (0.001 to 0.002)

Torque wrench settings

	Nm	lbf ft
Main bearing cap bolts	95	70
Connecting rod (big-end) bolts	31	23
Rear oil seal retainer bolts	18	13
Flywheel bolts	68	50
Clutch pressure plate bolts	10	7
Chain tensioner bolts	8	6
Camshaft thrust plate bolts	4	3
Camshaft sprocket bolts	19	14
Timing cover bolts	10	7
Coolant pump bolts	10	7
Crankshaft pulley bolt	54	40
Coolant pump pulley bolts	10	7
Starter motor bolts	41	30
Fuel pump bolts	18	13
Oil pump bolts	19	14
Sump drain plug	25	18
Sump fixing bolts:		
Stage 1	8	6
Stage 2	11	8
Stage 3	11	8
Oil pressure sender	15	11
Coolant temperature sender	15	11
Rocker shaft pedestal bolts	42	31
Cylinder head bolts:		
Stage 1	15	11
Stage 2	48	35
Stage 3	88	65
Stage 4 (after 15 minutes delay)	109	80
Rocker cover screws	4	3
Exhaust manifold nuts and bolts	16	12
Intake manifold nuts and bolts	19	14
Carburettor flange nuts	19	14
Thermostat housing cover bolts	19	14
Spark plugs	19	14
Engine-to-transmission bolts	41	30
Transmission oil filler plug	25	18

Part B: CVH engine
General

Engine type	Four-cylinder, overhead cam, mounted transversely, water-cooled. CVH Compound Valve Hemispherical head

	1.3 litre	**1.6 litre**
Data:		
Code	JPC	LUB
Firing order (No 1 at timing cover end)	1-3-4-2	1-3-4-2
Bore	79.96 mm (3.15 in)	79.96 mm (3.15 in)
Stroke	64.52 mm (2.54 in)	79.52 mm (3.13 in)
Cubic capacity	1296 cc (79.09 cu in)	1597 cc (97.46 cu in)
Compression ratio	9.5:1	9.5:1
Compression pressure at starter speed	11.2 to 14.8 kgf/cm^2 (159 to 210 lbf/in^2)	11.2 to 14.8 kgf/cm^2 (159 to 210 lbf/in^2)
Idle speed (rpm)	775 to 825	775 to 825
Maximum continuous engine speed (rpm)	6450	6300
Engine output (DIN)	51kW at 6000 rpm	71 kW at 6000 rpm
Engine torque (DIN)	10.2 kgf m at 3500 rpm	13.5 kgf m at 4000 rpm

Cylinder block

Material	Cast iron
Number of main bearings	5
Cylinder bore diameter — mm (in):	
Standard (1)	79.94 to 79.95 (3.1472 to 3.1476)
Standard (2)	79.95 to 79.96 (3.1476 to 3.1480)
Standard (3)	79.96 to 79.97 (3.1480 to 3.1484)
Standard (4)	79.97 to 79.98 (3.1484 to 3.1488)
Oversize (A)	80.23 to 80.24 (3.1587 to 3.1590)
Oversize (B)	80.24 to 80.25 (3.1590 to 3.1594)
Oversize (C)	80.25 to 80.26 (3.1594 to 3.1598)

Main bearing shell inner diameter — mm (in):
    Standard ....   58.011 to 58.038 (2.2839 to 2.2850)
    Undersize 0.25 (0.01) ....   57.761 to 57.788 (2.2740 to 2.2751)
    Undersize 0.50 (0.02) ....   57.511 to 57.538 (2.2642 to 2.2653)
    Undersize 0.75 (0.03) ....   57.261 to 57.288 (2.2544 to 2.2554)

Crankshaft

Main bearing journal diameter — mm (in):
    Standard ....   57.98 to 58.00 (2.2827 to 2.2835)
    Undersize 0.25 (0.01) ....   57.73 to 57.75 (2.2728 to 2.2736)
    Undersize 0.50 (0.02) ....   57.48 to 57.50 (2.2630 to 2.2638)
    Undersize 0.75 (0.03) ....   57.23 to 57.25 (2.2531 to 2.2539)
Main bearing running clearance — mm (in) ....   0.011 to 0.058 (0.0004 to 0.0023)
Thrust washer thickness — mm (in):
    Standard ....   2.301 to 2.351 (0.0906 to 0.0926)
    Oversize ....   2.491 to 2.541 (0.0981 to 0.1000)
Crankshaft endfloat — mm (in) ....   0.09 to 0.30 (0.0035 to 0.0118)
Crankpin (big-end) diameter — mm (in):
    Standard ....   47.89 to 47.91 (1.8854 to 1.8862)
    Undersize 0.25 (0.01) ....   47.64 to 47.66 (1.8756 to 1.8764)
    Undersize 0.50 (0.02) ....   47.39 to 47.41 (1.8657 to 1.8665)
    Undersize 0.75 (0.03) ....   47.14 to 47.16 (1.8559 to 1.8567)
    Undersize 1.00 (0.04) ....   46.89 to 46.91 (1.8461 to 1.8468)
Big-end bearing running clearance — mm (in) ....   0.006 to 0.060 (0.0002 to 0.0024)

Camshaft

Number of bearings   5
Drive ....   Toothed belt
Belt tension:
    Setting up (torque wrench on camshaft sprocket):
        1.3 litre (colour code blue) ....   6.0 to 6.5 kgf m (43 to 47 lbf ft)
        1.6 litre (colour code yellow) ....   4.5 to 5.0 kgf m (33 to 36 lbf ft)
Final setting (using Ford tool 21-113):
    Used belt ....   4 to 5 on scale
    New belt ....   10 to 11 on scale
Note: *a used belt is one which has been in use for more than 30 minutes*
Camshaft thrust plate thickness — mm (in) ....   4.99 to 5.01 mm (0.1965 to 0.1972)
Cam lift — mm (in):
    1.3 litre 5.79 (0.2280)
    1.6 litre 6.09 (0.2398)
Cam length (heel to toe) — mm (in):
    Inlet:
        1.3 litre 38.305 (1.5081)
        1.6 litre 38.606 (1.5199)
    Exhaust:
        1.3 litre 37.289 (1.4681)
        1.6 litre 37.590 (1.4799)
Camshaft bearing diameter — mm (in):
    1 ....   44.75 (1.7618)
    2 ....   45.00 (1.7717)
    3 ....   45.25 (1.7815)
    4 ....   45.40 (1.7913)
    5 ....   45.75 (1.8012)
Camshaft endfloat — mm (in) ....   0.05 to 0.15 (0.0020 to 0.0059)

Pistons and piston rings

Diameter — mm (in):
    Standard 1 ....   79.910 to 79.920 (3.1461 to 3.1465)
    Standard 2 ....   79.920 to 79.930 (3.1465 to 3.1468)
    Standard 3 ....   79.930 to 79.940 (3.1468 to 3.1472)
    Standard 4 ....   79.940 to 79.950 (3.1472 to 3.1476)
    Standard service ....   79.930 to 79.955 (3.1468 to 3.1478)
    Oversize 0.29 (0.01) ....   80.210 to 80.235 (3.1579 to 3.1589)
    Oversize 0.50 (0.02) ....   80.430 to 80.455 (3.1665 to 3.1675)
Piston-to-bore clearance — mm (in):
    Production ....   0.020 to 0.040 (0.00079 to 0.00157)
    Service ....   0.010 to 0.045 (0.00039 to 0.00177)
Ring gap positions (when fitted) ....   120° apart
Piston ring gap — mm (in):
    Compression ....   0.30 to 0.50 (0.0118 to 0.0197)
    Oil control ....   0.4 to 1.4 (0.0175 to 0.0551)

Gudgeon pin

Pin length — mm (in) .... 66.20 to 67.00 (2.606 to 2.638)
Pin diameter — mm (in):
    White .... 20.622 to 20.625 (0.8119 to 0.8120)
    Red .... 20.625 to 20.628 (0.8120 to 0.8121)
    Blue .... 20.628 to 20.631 (0.8121 to 0.8122)
    Yellow .... 20.631 to 20.634 (0.8122 to 0.8124)
Play in piston — mm (in) .... 0.005 to 0.011 (0.0002 to 0.0004)
Interference fit in piston — mm (in) .... 0.013 to 0.045 (0.0005 to 0.0018)

Connecting rod

Big-end bore diameter — mm (in) .... 50.890 to 50.910 (2.0035 to 2.0043)
Small-end bore diameter — mm (in) .... 20.589 to 20.609 (0.8106 to 0.8114)
Big-end bearing shell inside diameter — mm (in):
    Standard .... 47.916 to 47.950 (1.8865 to 1.8878)
    Undersize 0.25 (0.01) .... 47.666 to 47.700 (1.8766 to 1.8779)
    Undersize 0.50 (0.02) .... 47.416 to 47.450 (1.8668 to 1.8681)
    Undersize 0.75 (0.03) .... 47.166 to 47.200 (1.8569 to 1.8583)
    Undersize 1.00 (0.04) .... 46.916 to 46.950 (1.8471 to 1.8484)
Big-end bearing running clearance — mm (in) .... 0.006 to 0.060 (0.0002 to 0.0024)

Cylinder head

Material .... Light alloy
Valve seat angle .... 45°
Valve seat width — mm (in) .... 1.75 to 2.32 (0.0689 to 0.0913)
Upper correction angle (production):
    Inlet and exhaust .... 30°
    Service correction cutter angle .... 15°
Lower correction angle (production):
    Inlet and exhaust .... 77°/70°
    Service correction cutter angle .... 75°/70°
Maximum cylinder head distortion permissible — mm (in):
    Over distance of 26 (1.02) 0.04 (0.0016)
    Over distance of 156 (6.14) 0.08 (0.0031)
    Over full length 0.15 (0.0059)
    Facing head mating surface 0.30 (0.0118)
Minimum combustion chamber depth (after refacing) — mm (in) 19.60 (0.7717)

Valves — general

	1.3 litre	1.6 litre
Inlet valve opens	13° ATDC	8° ATDC
Inlet valve closes	28° ABDC	36° ABDC
Exhaust valve opens	30° BBDC	34° BBDC
Exhaust valve closes	15° BTDC	6° BTDC
Valve lift — mm (in):		
Inlet	9.56 (0.3764)	10.09 (0.3972)
Exhaust	9.52 (0.3748)	10.06 (0.3961)
Valve spring free length — mm (in)	47.2 (1.8583)	47.2 (1.8583)

Inlet valve

Length — mm (in) .... 134.54 to 135.00 (5.2969 to 5.3150)
Head diameter — mm (in) .... 41.9 to 42.1 (1.6496 to 1.6575)
Stem diameter — mm (in):
    Standard .... 8.025 to 8.043 (0.3159 to 0.3167)
    Oversize 0.2 (0.008) .... 8.225 to 8.243 (0.3238 to 0.3245)
    Oversize 0.4 (0.016) .... 8.425 to 8.443 (0.3317 to 0.3324)
Valve stem-to-guide clearance — mm (in) .... 0.020 to 0.063 (0.0008 to 0.0025)

Exhaust valve

Length — mm (in):
    1.3 engines .... 131.17 to 131.63 (5.1642 to 5.1823)
    1.6 engines .... 131.57 to 132.03 (5.1800 to 5.1980)
Head diameter — mm (in):
    1.3 engines .... 33.9 to 34.1 (1.3346 to 1.3425)
    1.6 engines .... 36.9 to 37.1 (1.4528 to 1.4606)
Valve stem diameter — mm (in):
    Standard .... 7.999 to 8.017 (0.3149 to 0.3156)
    Oversize 0.2 (0.008) .... 8.199 to 8.217 (0.3228 to 0.3235)
    Oversize 0.4 (0.016) .... 8.399 to 8.417 (0.3307 to 0.3314)
Valve stem-to-guide clearance — mm (in) .... 0.046 to 0.089 (0.0018 to 0.0035)

Lubrication

Oil pump type .... Gear, driven by crankshaft
Minimum oil pressure at 80°C (175°F):
    At 750 rpm .... 1.0 kgf/cm² (14 lbf/in²)
    At 2000 rpm .... 2.8 kgf/cm² (41 lbf/in²)

Engine oil capacity:

Without filter change	3.50 litres (6.2 Imp pints)
With filter change	3.75 litres (6.6 Imp pints)
Initial fill capacity (new or reconditioned engine)	3.86 litres (6.8 Imp pints)
Oil grade	HD multigrade

Viscosity:

-23 to 32°C (-9 to 90°F)	SAE 10W/30, 10W/40 or 10W/50
Over -18°C (0°F)	SAE 15W/40 or 15W/50
Over -12°C (10°F)	SAE 20W/40 or 20W/50
Under -23°C (-9°F)	SAE 5W/30

Torque· wrench settings

	Nm	lbf ft
Main bearing cap bolts	95	70
Big-end bearing cap bolts	30	22
Oil pump mounting bolts	10	7
Oil pump pick-up tube bolt to block	20	15
Oil pump pick-up to pump	12	9
Rear oil seal carrier bolts	10	7
Sump bolts	10	7
Flywheel	85	63
Crankshaft pulley bolt	110	81
Cylinder head bolts:		
Stage 1	25	18
Stage 2	55	40
Stage 3	Tighten further 90°	Tighten further 90°
Stage 4	Tighten further 90°	Tighten further 90°
Camshaft thrust plate bolts	12	9
Camshaft sprocket bolt	55	41
Belt tensioner bolts	18	13
Coolant pump bolts	8	6
Rocker arm studs in head	12	9
Rocker arm nuts	24	18
Rocker cover screws	8	6
Timing cover screws	8	6
Exhaust manifold bolts	16	12
Intake manifold bolts	18	13
Carburettor mounting bolts	20	15
Thermostat housing bolts	8	6
Clutch pressure plate bolts	10	7
Spark plugs	27	20
Engine-to-transmission bolts	41	30
Transmission oil filler plug	25	18
Fuel pump nuts	14 to 18	10 to 13

PART A: OHV ENGINE

1 General description

The engine is of overhead valve type, based upon the 'Kent' design used in many earlier Ford models, including the Fiesta.

The engine is mounted transversely at the front of the vehicle together with the transmission to form a combined power train.

The engine is of water-cooled, four-cylinder in-line type, having overhead valves operated by tappets, pushrods and rocker arms.

The camshaft is located within the cylinder block and chain-driven from the crankshaft. A gear on the camshaft drives the oil pump and the distributor, while an eccentric operates the fuel pump lever.

The cylinder head is of crossflow type, having the exhaust manifold mounted on the opposite side to the intake manifold.

The crankshaft runs in three main bearings, with endfloat controlled by semi-circular thrust washers located on either side of the centre main bearing.

The oil pump is mounted externally on the cylinder block just below the distributor, and the full-flow type oil filter is screwed directly into the oil pump.

2 Routine maintenance – ohv engine

The following routine maintenance procedures must be carried out at the specified intervals given at the front of this manual.
1 Engine oil level check: check the engine oil level with the car parked on level ground, preferably after allowing the engine to cool down. The oil level must be kept between the minimum and maximum markings on the dipstick. Top up the oil level through the filler neck in the rocker cover.

2 Engine oil change and filter renewal: drain the old engine oil at the specified mileage intervals and at the same time renew the filter (see Section 11). Top up the engine oil level using oil of the specified grade.
3 Occasionally check the engine and associated components for signs of oil, coolant or fuel leakage.
4 Check and, if necessary, adjust the valve clearances, as described in Section 6, at the specified mileage intervals.
5 Clean the crankcase emission control orifice: detach the filler cap-to-intake manifold hose and remove the control orifice from the filler cap unit by pulling and rotating it free. Clean the orifice in a suitable solvent. Renew the orifice if it is damaged. Refit and connect the hose.
6 Renew the crankcase emission filter. Detach hose from base of air filter unit, remove the old emission filter valve, then insert a new one into position in the grommet. Reconnect the pipes.

3 Operations possible without removing engine from vehicle

The following work can be carried out without having to remove the engine:

(a) *Cylinder head – removal and refitting*
(b) *Valve clearances – adjustment*
(c) *Sump – removal and refitting*
(d) *Rocker gear – overhaul*
(e) *Crankshaft front oil seal – renewal*
(f) *Pistons/connecting rods – removal and refitting*
(g) *Engine mountings – renewal*
(h) *Oil filter – removal and refitting*
(j) *Oil pump – removal and refitting*

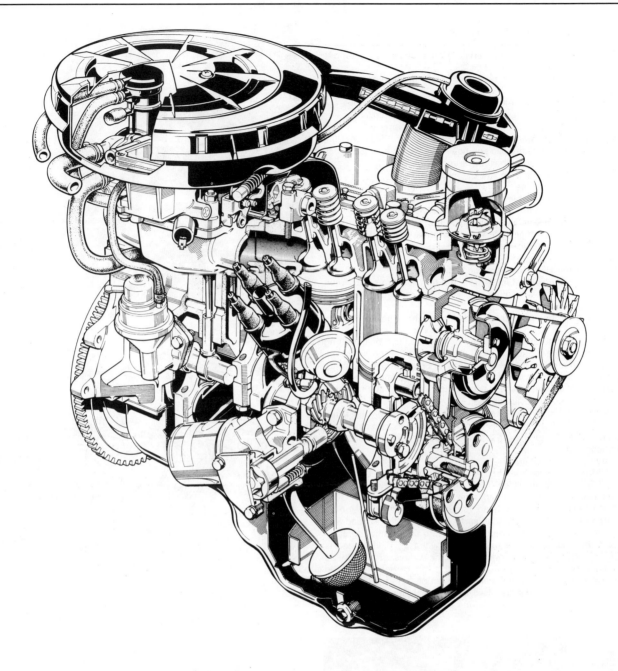

Fig. 1.1 Cutaway view of the ohv engine (Sec 1)

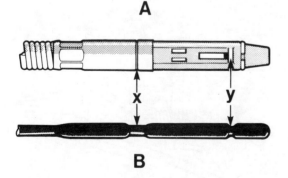

Fig. 1.2 Oil level markings on dipstick (Sec 2)

A Auxiliary warning system type
B Standard dipstick type

X Maximum level mark
Y Minimum level mark

4 Operations only possible with engine removed from vehicle

1   The following work should be carried out only after the engine has been removed from the vehicle.

    (a) *Crankshaft main bearings – renewal
    (b) Crankshaft – removal and refitting
    (c) **Flywheel – removal and refitting
    (d) **Crankshaft rear oil seal – renewal
    (e) Camshaft – removal and refitting
    (f) Timing gears and chain – removal and refitting

2   Although it is possible to undertake the job marked * without removing the engine, and those marked ** by removing the transmission (see Chapter 6), such work is not recommended and is unlikely to save much time over that required to withdraw the complete engine/transmission.

5   Cylinder head – removal and refitting

1   If the engine is in the vehicle, carry out the preliminary operations described in paragraphs 2 to 15.

2   Open the bonnet and fit protective covers to the front wing upper surfaces.

3   Disconnect the battery earth strap. It is as well to remove the battery, so that no metal objects are placed across its terminals.

4   Remove the air cleaner unit, as described in Chapter 3.

5   Drain the cooling system, as described in Chapter 2. Note that the coolant should have an antifreeze solution mix and can be used again, so drain into a suitable container for re-use.

6   Disconnect the hoses from the thermostat housing.

7   Detach the choke cable.

8   Release the throttle cable from the carburettor operating lever by moving the spring clip and removing the bracket fixing bolt.

9   Disconnect the fuel and vacuum pipes from the carburettor.

10   Disconnect the breather hose from the intake manifold.

11   On vehicles with servo-assisted brakes, disconnect the vacuum hose from the intake manifold.

12   Disconnect the HT leads from the spark plugs.

13   Disconnect the electrical leads from the temperature sender unit, the anti-run-on (anti-diesel) solenoid valve at the carburettor, and the radiator fan thermal switch.

14   Unbolt and remove the heated air box from the exhaust manifold (where fitted).

15   Disconnect the exhaust downpipe from the manifold by unbolting the connecting flanges. Support the exhaust system at the front end.

16   Pull free and remove the oil filler cap with breather hoses (photo).

17   Extract the four screws and remove the rocker cover.

18   Unscrew and remove the four fixing bolts and lift away the rocker shaft assembly from the cylinder head.

19   Withdraw the pushrods, keeping them in their originally fitted sequence. A simple way to do this is to punch holes in a piece of card and number them 1 to 8 from the thermostat housing end of the cylinder head (photo).

20   Remove the spark plugs.

21   Unscrew the cylinder head bolts progressively in the reverse order to that given for tightening (see Fig. 1.7). Remove the cylinder head.

22   To dismantle the cylinder head, refer to Section 18.

23   Before refitting the cylinder head, remove every particle of carbon, old gasket and dirt from the mating surfaces of the cylinder head and block. Do not let the removed material drop into the cylinder bores or waterways; if it does, remove it. Normally, when a cylinder head is removed, the head is decarbonised and the valves ground in as described in Section 19 to remove all traces of carbon. Clean the threads of the cylinder head bolts and mop out oil from the bolt holes in the cylinder block. In extreme cases, screwing a bolt into an oil-filled hole can cause the block to fracture due to hydraulic pressure.

5.19 Remove the pushrods

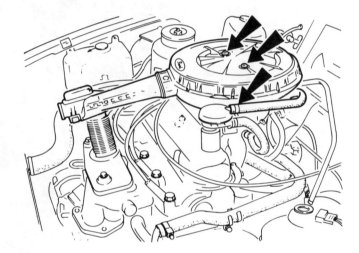

Fig. 1.3 Remove the air cleaner unit (Sec 5)

Release at points arrowed

5.16 Oil filler cap and breather hoses

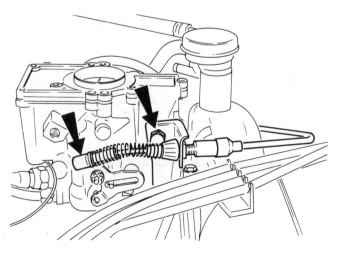

Fig. 1.4 Disconnect the throttle cable and bracket (Sec 5)

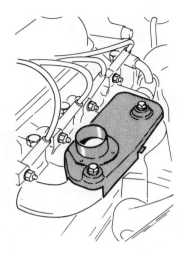

Fig. 1.5 Heated air box on exhaust manifold (Sec 5)

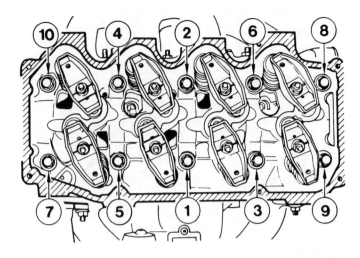

Fig. 1.7 Cylinder head bolt tightening sequence (Sec 5)

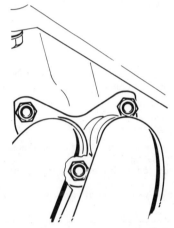

Fig. 1.6 Exhaust downpipe-to-manifold flange securing nuts (Sec 5)

Fig. 1.8 Refit the rocker shaft assembly; engaging the adjuster balls into the pushrod cups (sockets) (Sec 5)

24 If there is any doubt about the condition of the intake or exhaust gaskets, unbolt the manifolds and fit new ones to perfectly clean mating surfaces.

25 Locate a new cylinder head gasket on the cylinder block, making quite sure that the bolt holes, coolant passages and lubrication holes are correctly aligned.

26 Lower the cylinder head carefully into position on the block.

27 Screw in all the bolts finger tight and then tighten them in four stages, in the sequence shown in Fig. 1.7, to the specified torque.

28 Refit the pushrods in their original order.

29 Lower the rocker shaft assembly into position, making sure that the rocker adjusting screws engage in the sockets at the ends of the pushrods.

30 Screw in the rocker pedestal bolts finger tight. At this stage, some of the rocker arms will be applying pressure to the ends of the valve stems and some of the rocker pedestals will not be in contact with the cylinder head. The pedestals will be pulled down, however, when the bolts are tightened to the specified torque, which should now be done.

31 Adjust the valve clearances, as described in the next Section.

32 Refit the rocker cover. If the gasket is in anything but perfect condition, renew it.

33 Fit the oil filler cap and breather hose and the spark plugs. Tighten these to the specified torque. They are of tapered seat type, no sealing washers being used.

34 Connect the exhaust downpipe and fit the heated air box.

35 Reconnect all electrical leads, vacuum and coolant hoses.

36 Reconnect the cables. Refit the battery (if removed) and reconnect the battery terminals.

37 Fit the air cleaner.

38 Refill the cooling system, as described in Chapter 2.

6 Valve clearances – adjustment

1 This operation should be carried out with the engine cold and the air cleaner and rocker cover removed.

2 Using a ring spanner or socket on the crankshaft pulley bolt, turn the crankshaft in a clockwise direction until No 1 piston is at tdc on its compression stroke. This can be verified by checking that the pulley and timing cover marks are in alignment and that the valves of No 4 cylinder are rocking. When the valves are rocking, this means that the slightest rotation of the crankshaft pulley in either direction will cause one rocker arm to move up and the other to move down.

3 Numbering from the thermostat housing end of the cylinder head, the valves are identified as follows:

Valve No	Cylinder no
1 – Exhaust	1
2 – Inlet	1
3 – Exhaust	2
4 – Inlet	2
5 – Exhaust	3
6 – Inlet	3
7 – Exhaust	4
8 – Inlet	4

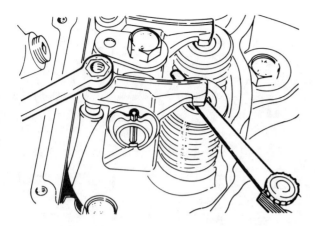

Fig. 1.9 Adjust the valve clearances (Sec 6)

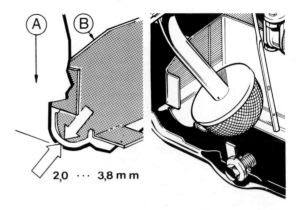

Fig. 1.11 Sump-to-baffle plate must be as shown (Sec 7)

A Sump   B Baffle

4   Adjust the valve clearances by following the sequence given in the following table. Turn the crankshaft pulley 180° (half a turn) after adjusting each pair:

Valves rocking	Valves to adjust
7 and 8	1 (Exhaust), 2 (Inlet)
5 and 6	3 (Exhaust), 4 (Inlet)
1 and 2	7 (Exhaust), 8 (Inlet)
3 and 4	5 (Exhaust), 6 (Inlet)

5   The clearances for the inlet and exhaust valves are different (see Specifications). Use a feeler gauge of the appropriate thickness to check each clearance between the end of the valve stem and the rocker arm. The gauge should be a stiff sliding fit. If it is not, turn the adjuster bolt with a ring spanner. These bolts are of stiff thread type and require no locking nut. Turn the bolt clockwise to reduce the clearance and anti-clockwise to increase it.
6   Refit the air cleaner and rocker cover on completion of adjustment.

7   Sump – removal and refitting

1   Disconnect the battery earth lead and drain the engine oil.
2   Unbolt and withdraw the starter motor. Support the motor to avoid straining the electrical wiring.
3   Unbolt and remove the clutch cover plate.
4   Extract the sump securing bolts and remove the sump. If it is stuck, prise it gently with a screwdriver, but do not use excessive leverage. If it is very tight, cut round the gasket joint using a sharp knife.
5   Before refitting the sump, remove the front and rear sealing strips

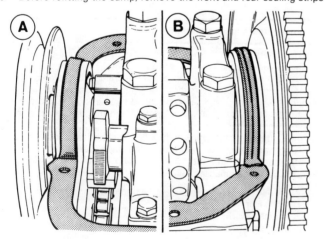

Fig. 1.10 Sump gaskets and sealing strips (Sec 7)

A Timing cover end   B Flywheel end

and gaskets. Clean the mating surfaces of the sump and cylinder block.
6   Stick new gaskets into position on the block using thick grease to retain them, then install new sealing strips into their grooves so that they overlap the gaskets.
7   Before offering up the sump, check that the gap between the sump and oil baffle is between 2.0 and 3.8 mm (0.08 and 0.15 in) – Fig. 1.11.
8   Screw in the sump bolts and tighten in three stages to the specified torque, in accordance with Fig. 1.12.

   Stage 1 – in alphabetical order
   Stage 2 – in numerical order
   Stage 3 – in alphabetical order

9   It is important to follow this procedure in order to provide positive sealing against oil leakage.
10   Refit the clutch cover plate and the starter motor and reconnect the battery.
11   Refill the engine with the correct grade and quantity of oil.

8   Rocker gear – dismantling and reassembly

1   With the rocker assembly removed, as described in Section 5, extract the split pin from one end of the rocker shaft.
2   Take off the spring and plain washers from the end of the shaft.
3   Slide off the rocker arms, support pedestals and coil springs, keeping them in their originally fitted order. Clean out the oil holes in the shaft.
4   Apply engine oil to the rocker shaft before reassembling and make sure that the flat on the end of the shaft is to the same side as the rocker arm adjuster screws. This is essential for proper lubrication of the components.
5   If a new rocker shaft is being fitted, check that the end plug is located (Fig. 1.15).

9   Crankshaft front oil seal – renewal

1   Disconnect the battery earth cable.
2   Slacken the alternator mounting and adjuster bolts and after pushing the alternator in towards the engine, slip off the drivebelt.
3   Unscrew and remove the crankshaft pulley bolt. To prevent the crankshaft turning while the bolt is being released, jam the teeth of the starter ring gear on the flywheel after removing the clutch cover plate or starter motor for accesss.
4   Remove the crankshaft pulley. This should come out using the hands, but, if it is tight, prise it carefully with two levers placed at opposite sides under the pulley flange.
5   Using a suitable claw tool, prise out the defective seal and wipe out the seat.
6   Install the new seal using a suitable distance piece, the pulley and its bolt to draw it into position. If it is tapped into position, the seal may be distorted or the timing cover fractured.
7   When the seal is fully seated, remove the pulley and bolt, apply

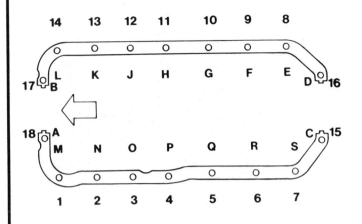

Fig. 1.12 Sump retaining bolt tightening sequence. Arrow indicates front of engine (Sec 7)

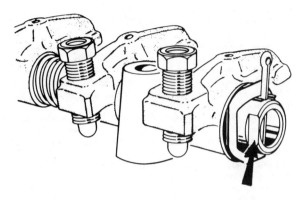

Fig. 1.13 Flat on rocker shaft (arrowed) and retaining pin (Sec 8)

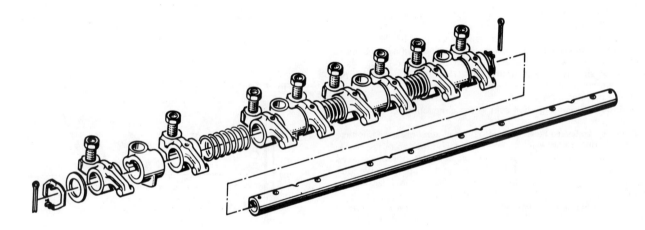

Fig. 1.14 Rocker components (Sec 8)

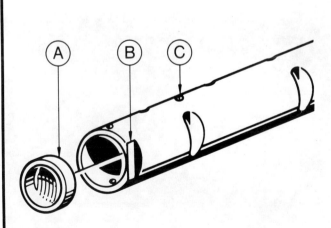

Fig. 1.15 Rocker shaft front end plug (A), flat (B) and oil hole (C) (Sec 8)

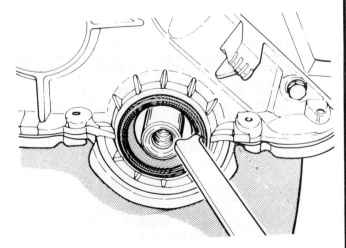

Fig. 1.16 Prising out the crankshaft front oil seal (Sec 9)

grease to the seal rubbing surface of the pulley, install it and tighten the securing bolt to the specified torque.

8   Refit the clutch cover or starter motor.

9   Fit and tension the drivebelt (Chapter 2) and reconnect the battery.

10 Piston/connecting rod – removal and refitting

1   Remove the cylinder head and the sump, as described in Sections 6 and 7 respectively. Do not remove the oil pick-up filter or pipe, which is an interference fit.

2   Note the location numbers stamped on the connecting rod big-ends and caps, and to which side they face. No 1 assembly is nearest the timing cover and the assembly numbers are towards the camshaft side of the engine.

3   Turn the crankshaft by means of the pulley bolt until the big-end cap bolts for No 1 connecting rod are in their most accessible position. Unscrew and remove the bolts and the big-end cap complete with bearing shell. If the cap is difficult to remove, tap it off with a plastic-faced hammer.

4   If the bearing shells are to be used again (refer to Section 18), keep the shell taped to its cap.

5   Feel the top of the cylinder bore for a wear ridge. If one is detected, it should be scraped off before the piston/rod is pushed out of the top of the cylinder block. Take care when doing this not to score the cylinder bore surfaces.

6   Push the piston/connecting rod out of the block, retaining the bearing shell with the rod if it is to be used again.

7   Dismantling the piston/rod is covered in Section 18.

8   Repeat the operations on the remaining piston/rod assemblies.

9   To install a piston/rod assembly, have the piston ring gaps staggered, as shown in the diagram (Fig. 1.18), oil the rings and apply a piston ring compressor. Compress the piston rings.

10   Oil the cylinder bores.

11   Wipe out the bearing shell seat in the connecting rod and insert the shell.

12   Lower the piston/rod assembly into the cylinder bore until the base of the piston ring compressor stands squarely on the top of the block.

13   Check that the directional arrow on the piston crown faces towards the timing cover end of the engine and then apply the wooden handle of a hammer to the piston crown. Strike the head of the hammer sharply to drive the piston into the cylinder bore.

14   Oil the crankpin and draw the connecting rod down to engage with the crankshaft. Check that the bearing shell is still in position in the connecting rod.

15   Wipe the bearing shell seat in the big-end cap clean and insert the bearing shell.

16   Fit the cap, screw in the bolts and tighten to the specified torque.

17   Repeat the operations on the remaining pistons/connecting rods.

18   Refit the sump (Section 7) and the cylinder head (Section 5). Refill with oil and coolant.

11 Oil filter and pump – removal and refitting

1   The oil pump is externally mounted on the forward-facing side of the crankcase (photo).

2   Using a suitable removal tool (strap wrench or similar), unscrew and remove the oil filter cartridge and discard it.

3   Unscrew the three mounting bolts and withdraw the oil pump from the engine.

4   Clean away the old gasket.

5   If a new pump is being fitted, it should be primed with engine oil before installation. Do this by turning its shaft while filling it with clean engine oil.

6   Locate a new gasket on the pump mounting flange, insert the pump shaft and bolt the pump into position.

7   Grease the rubber sealing ring of a new filter and screw it into position on the pump, using hand pressure only, **not** the removal tool.

8   Top up the engine oil to replenish any lost during the operations.

12 Lubrication system – description

1   Engine oil contained in the sump is drawn through a strainer and pick-up tube by an externally-mounted oil pump of twin rotor design.

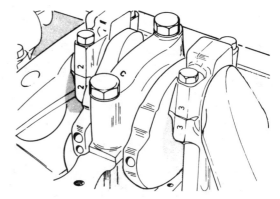

Fig. 1.17 Connecting rod big-end numbers (Sec 10)

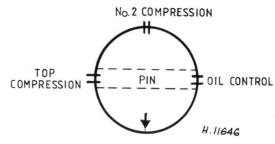

Fig. 1.18 Piston ring end gap positioning diagram (Sec 10)

Fig. 1.19 Installing a piston/connecting rod (Sec 10)

11.1 Oil filter and pump unit

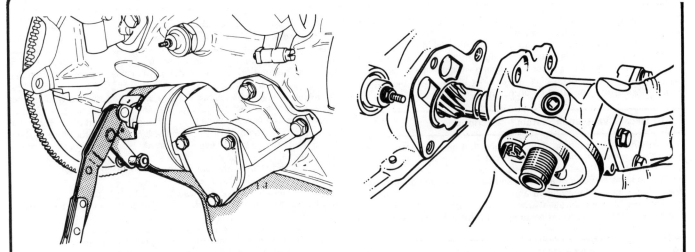

Fig. 1.20 Oil filter removal using strap wrench (Sec 11)

Fig. 1.21 Removing the oil pump (Sec 11)

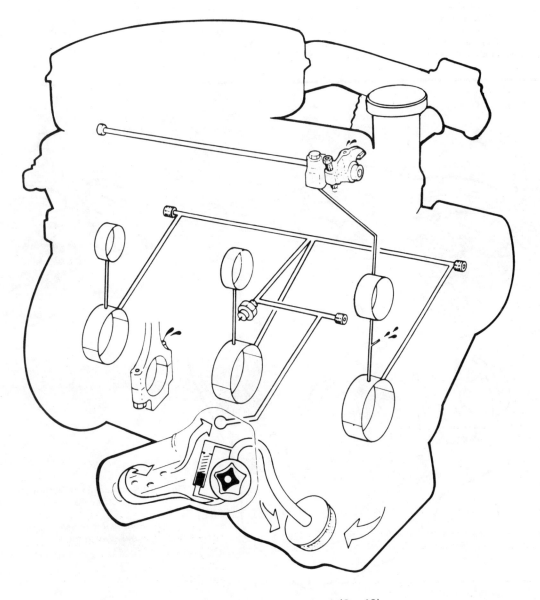

Fig. 1.22 Engine lubrication circuit (Sec 12)

2   The oil is then forced through a full-flow, throw-away type oil filter which is screwed onto the oil pump.

3   Oil pressure is regulated by a relief valve integral in the oil pump.

4   The pressurised oil is directed through the various galleries and passages to all bearing surfaces. A drilling in the big-end provides lubrication for the gudgeon pins and cylinder bores. The timing chain and sprockets are lubricated by an oil ejection nozzle.

13 Crankcase ventilation system – description

The system is of closed type, ensuring that blow-by gases which pass the piston rings and collect in the crankcase, also oil vapour, are drawn into the combustion chambers to be burnt.

The system consists of a vented engine oil filler cap connected by one hose to the intake manifold and by another to the air cleaner.

The gas flow is controlled by a calibrated port in the oil filler cap and by the manifold vacuum according to throttle setting.

14 Engine mountings – removal and refitting

The operations are as described in Section 34 of this Chapter.

15 Engine – method of removal

The engine should be removed from the vehicle complete with transmission (gearbox and final drive) in a downward direction.

16 Engine and transmission – removal

1   This procedure entails lowering the engine and gearbox, and removing the unit from beneath the car. For this reason, certain items of equipment are necessary. A suitable engine hoist should be employed to lower the engine. A more difficult alternative would be to use a good trolley jack. Secondly, if an inspection pit is not available, four strong axle jacks capable of supporting the weight of the car, must be used. In addition, a willing friend will make the procedure easier.

2   Select 4th gear, or reverse gear on 5-speed models, to make gearshift adjustment easier on reassembly.

3   Open and remove the bonnet, as described in Chapter 12.

4   Disconnect the battery leads.

5   Drain the engine coolant, as described in Chapter 2.

6   Remove the radiator and thermo-electric fan unit, as described in Chapter 2.

7   To drain any remaining coolant within the engine undo and remove the cylinder block drain plug from the left-hand side at the front (exhaust manifold face) and drain the remaining coolant into a suitable container.

8   Disconnect the crankcase ventilation hoses and remove the air cleaner unit, as described in Chapter 3.

9   Unclip and disconnect the heater hoses from the intake manifold connection and the lateral coolant pipe.

10   Refer to Section 5 and proceed as described in paragraphs 7 to 15 inclusive.

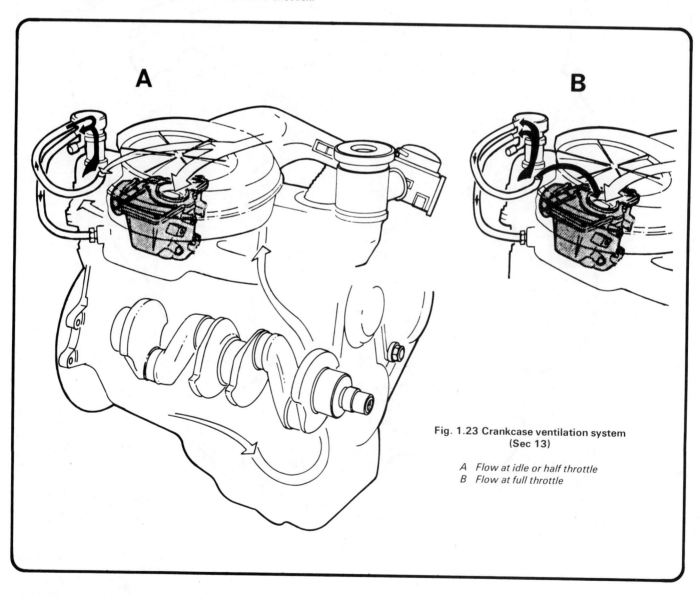

Fig. 1.23 Crankcase ventilation system (Sec 13)

A   Flow at idle or half throttle
B   Flow at full throttle

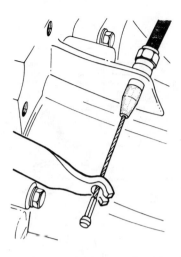

Fig. 1.24 Clutch cable connection (Sec 16)

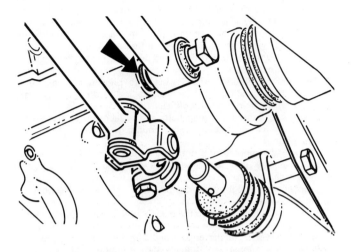

Fig. 1.26 Gearchange stabilizer rod connection. Arrow indicates washer location (Sec 16)

11 Disconnect the wiring connections from the alternator, the oil pressure switch, the reversing light switch and the engine oil dipstick (if applicable). Undo the securing bolt and disconnect the engine earth strap.

12 Disconnect the speedometer drive cable at the gearbox end.

13 Disconnect the clutch cable from the release lever and transmission support, referring to Chapter 5 for details.

14 Raise and support the vehicle on safety stands at the front and rear, ensuring that, when raised, the vehicle is level and there is sufficient clearance to lower and remove the engine and transmission from underneath.

15 Disconnect the starter motor leads.

16 Disconnect the gearchange rod from the gearbox selector shaft. Do this by releasing the clamp bolt and withdrawing the rod. Tie the rod to the stabilizer and then unhook the tension spring.

17 Unscrew the single bolt and disconnect the stabilizer from the gearbox. Note the washer which is located between the stabilizer trunnion and the gearbox casing (Fig. 1.26).

18 Drain the gearbox. As no drain plug is fitted, this is carried out by unscrewing the cap nut on the selector shaft locking assembly Take care not to lose the locking pin and spring.

19 Undo and remove the four nuts retaining the gearshift housing unit to the floor. Rotate the shift rod and stabilizer 180° and support them by tying them up with a length of cord or wire.

20 Unscrew and remove the pivot bolt and nut from the inboard end of the left side front suspension lower arm, then remove the bolt which secures the balljoint at the outboard end of the lower arm to the stub axle carrier. An Allen key can be used to prevent the bolt turning while the nut is unscrewed.

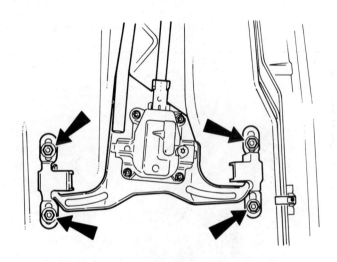

Fig. 1.27 Gearshift housing unit-to-floor bolts (arrowed) (Sec 16)

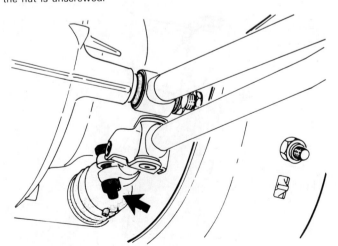

Fig. 1.25 Gearchange rod clamp bolt (arrowed) (Sec 16)

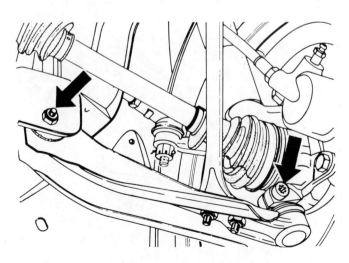

Fig. 1.28 Front suspension lower arm pivot bolt and nut locations (Sec 16)

21 The left-hand driveshaft must now be released from the transmission. Do this by inserting a lever between the inboard constant velocity (CV) joint and the transmission. With an assistant pulling the roadwheel outwards, strike the lever hard with the hand.

22 Tie the driveshaft up to the steering rack housing to prevent strain to the CV joints.

23 Restrain the differential pinion cage to prevent the cage from turning, using a plastic plug or similar. Failure to do this may make reconnection of the driveshafts difficult.

24 Remove the three retaining bolts and detach the tie-bar on the right-hand side, complete with mounting bracket, from the crossmember.

25 Release the inboard and outboard ends of the front suspension lower arm on the right-hand side of the vehicle, as described for the left-hand side.

26 Disconnect the right-hand driveshaft, as previously described for the left-hand one.

27 Connect a suitable hoist to the engine, preferably using a spreader bar and connecting lifting hooks to the engine; lifting lugs provided.

28 With the weight of the engine and transmission just supported, disconnect the engine and transmission mountings at the points shown in Figs. 1.31, 1.32, 1.33 and 1.34.

29 Unbolt the engine mounting (complete with coolant hose support bracket, where applicable) from the side-member and from the wing apron panel.

30 Carefully lower the engine/transmission and withdraw it from under the car. To ease the withdrawal operation, lower the engine/transmission onto a crawler board or a sheet of substantial plywood placed on rollers or lengths of pipe.

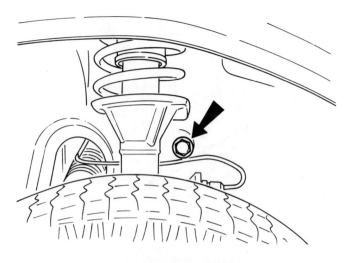

Fig. 1.31 Engine mounting bolt under right-hand wheel arch (Sec 16)

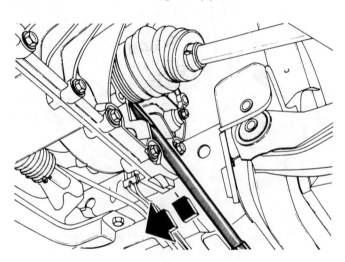

Fig. 1.29 Driveshaft removal from transmission (Sec 16)

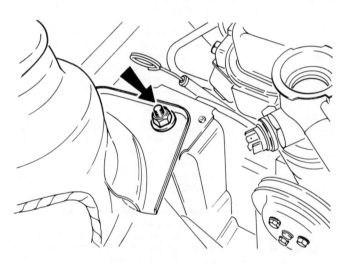

Fig. 1.32 Engine mounting nut on right-hand suspension strut retaining plate (arrowed) (Sec 16)

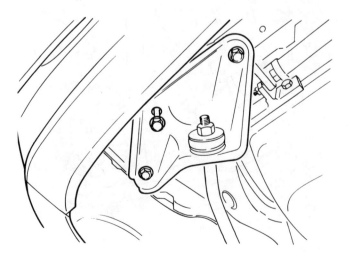

Fig. 1.30 Tie-bar mounting bolts. Note that XR2 variant differs (Sec 16)

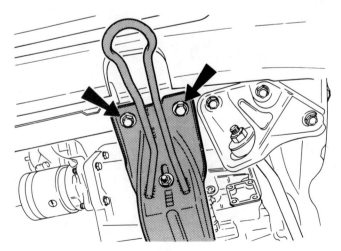

Fig. 1.33 Engine bearer retaining bolts – front (Sec 16)

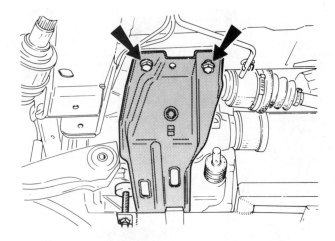

Fig. 1.34 Engine bearer retaining bolts – rear (Sec 16)

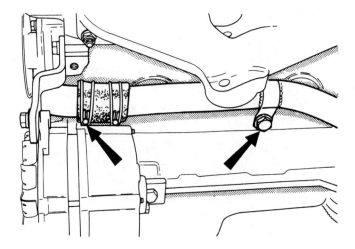

Fig. 1.35 Engine lateral coolant pipe connections (Sec 17)

Separation

31 Unscrew and remove the starter motor bolts and remove the starter.

32 Unbolt and remove the clutch cover plate from the lower part of the clutch bellhousing.

33 Unscrew and remove the bolts from the clutch bellhousing-to-engine mating flange.

34 Withdraw the transmission from the engine. Support its weight so that the clutch assembly is not distorted while the input shaft is still in engagement with the splined hub of the clutch driven plate.

17 Engine – complete dismantling

1 The need for dismantling will have been dictated by wear or noise in most cases. Although there is no reason why only partial dismantling cannot be carried out to renew such items as the timing chain or crankshaft rear oil seal, when the main bearings or big-end bearings have been knocking, and especially if the vehicle has covered a high mileage, then it is recommended that a complete strip down is carried out and every engine component examined as described in Section 18.

2 Position the engine so that it is upright on a bench or other convenient working surface. If the exterior is very dirty it should be cleaned before dismantling using paraffin and a stiff brush or a water-soluble solvent.

3 Remove the coolant pipe from the side of the engine by disconnecting the hose clips and the securing bolt.

4 If not already done, drain the engine oil.

5 Remove the dipstick and unscrew and discard the oil filter.

6 Disconnect the HT leads from the spark plugs, release the distributor cap and lift it away complete with leads.

7 Unscrew and remove the spark plugs.

8 Disconnect the breather hose from the intake manifold and remove it complete with the oil filler cap.

9 Disconnect the fuel and vacuum pipes from the carburettor and unbolt and remove the carburettor.

10 Unbolt the thermostat housing cover and remove it, together with the thermostat (refer to Chapter 2).

11 Remove the rocker cover.

12 Remove the rocker shaft assembly (four bolts).

13 Withdraw the pushrods, keeping them in their originally fitted order.

14 Remove the cylinder head, complete with manifolds, as described in Section 5.

15 Remove the bolt that holds the distributor clamp plate to the cylinder block and withdraw the distributor.

16 Unbolt and remove the fuel pump.

17 Remove the oil pump (Section 11).

18 Pinch the two runs of the coolant pump drivebelt together at the pump pulley to prevent the pulley rotating and release the pulley bolts.

19 Release the alternator mounting and adjuster link bolts, push the alternator in towards the engine and remove the drivebelt.

Fig. 1.36 Unbolt and remove the fuel pump (Sec 17)

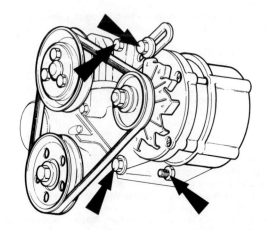

Fig. 1.37 Alternator retaining and drivebelt adjustment bolts (Sec 17)

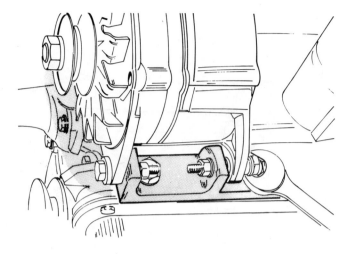

Fig. 1.38 Alternator mounting bracket (Sec 17)

17.22 Unscrew the crankshaft pulley retaining bolt

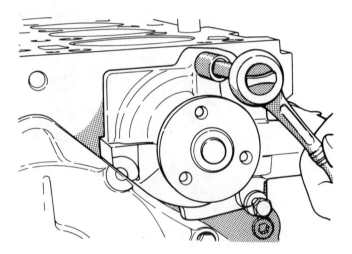

Fig. 1.39 Unbolt and remove the coolant pump (Sec 17)

17.25 Remove the timing chain cover

20 Unbolt the alternator bracket and remove the alternator.
21 Unbolt and remove the coolant pump.
22 Unscrew the crankshaft pulley bolt. To do this, the flywheel starter ring gear will have to be jammed to prevent the crankshaft from turning (photo).
23 Remove the crankshaft pulley. If this does not pull off by hand, carefully use two levers behind it placed at opposite points.
24 Place the engine on its side and remove the sump. Do not invert the engine at this stage, or sludge and swarf may enter the oilways.
25 Unbolt and remove the timing chain cover (photo).
26 Take off the oil slinger from the front face of the crankshaft sprocket.
27 Slide the chain tensioner arm from its pivot pin on the front main bearing cap.
28 Unbolt and remove the chain tensioner.
29 Bend back the lockplate tabs from the camshaft sprocket bolts and unscrew and remove the bolts.
30 Withdraw the sprocket complete with timing chain.
31 Unbolt and remove the camshaft thrust plate.
32 Rotate the camshaft until each cam follower (tappet) has been pushed fully into its hole by its cam lobe.
33 Withdraw the camshaft, taking care not to damage the camshaft bearings.
34 Withdraw each of the cam followers, keeping them in their

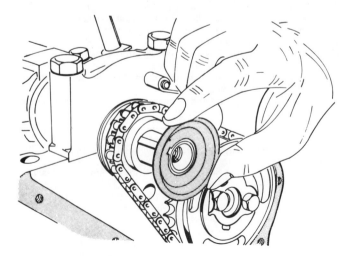

Fig. 1.40 Removing the crankshaft oil slinger (Sec 17)

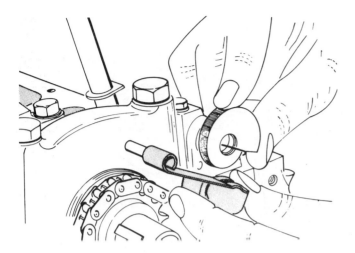

Fig. 1.41 Sliding off the chain tensioner arm (Sec 17)

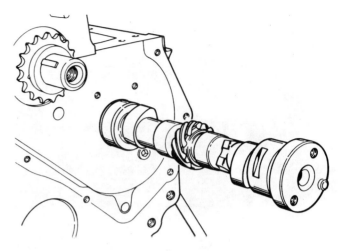

Fig. 1.44 Withdrawing the camshaft (Sec 17)

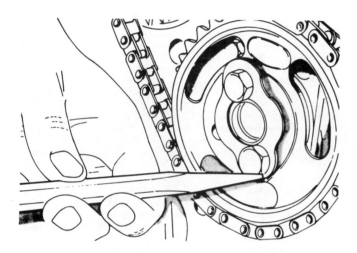

Fig. 1.42 Bending back the camshaft sprocket bolt locktabs (Sec 17)

17.34 Lift out the cam followers (tappets), using a valve grinding tool

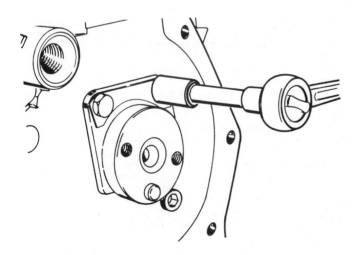

Fig. 1.43 Unbolting the camshaft thrust plate (Sec 17)

originally fitted sequence by marking them with a piece of numbered tape or using a box with divisions (photo).

35 From the front end of the crankshaft, draw off the sprocket using a two-legged extractor.

36 Check that the main bearing caps are marked F (Front), C (Centre) and R (Rear). The caps are also marked with an arrow which indicates the timing cover end of the engine, a point to remember when refitting the caps.

37 Check that the big-end caps and connecting rods have adjacent matching numbers facing towards the camshaft side of the engine. Number 1 assembly is nearest the timing chain end of the engine. If any markings are missing or indistinct, make some of your own with quick-drying paint (photo).

38 Unbolt and remove the big-end bearing caps. If the bearing shell is to be used again, tape the shell to the cap (photo).

39 Now check the top of the cylinder bore for a wear ridge. If one can be felt, it should be removed with a scraper before the piston/rod is pushed out of the cylinder.

40 Remove the piston/rod by pushing it out of the top of the block. Tape the bearing shell to the connecting rod.

41 Remove the remaining three piston/rod assemblies in a similar way.

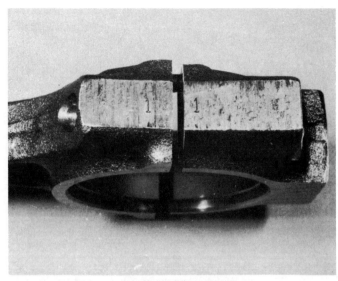

17.37 Connecting rod and big-end cap markings

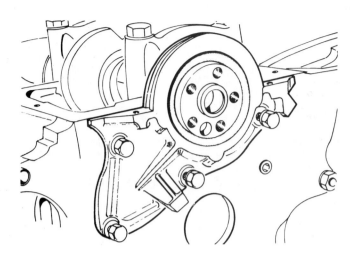

Fig. 1.45 Crankshaft rear oil seal retainer (Sec 17)

17.38 Removing the big-end cap

42 Unbolt the clutch pressure plate cover from the flywheel. Unscrew the bolts evenly and progressively until spring pressure is relieved, before removing the bolts. Be prepared to catch the clutch driven plate as the cover is withdrawn.

43 Unbolt and remove the flywheel. It is heavy, do not drop it. If necessary, the starter ring gear can be jammed to prevent the flywheel rotating. There is no need to mark the fitted position of the flywheel to its mounting flange as it can only be fitted one way. Take off the adaptor plate (engine backplate).

44 Unbolt and remove the crankshaft rear oil seal retainer.

45 Unbolt the main bearing caps. Remove the caps, tapping them off if necessary with a plastic-faced hammer. Retain the bearing shells with their respective caps if the shells are to be used again, although unless the engine is of low mileage this is not recommended (see Section 18).

46 Lift the crankshaft from the crankcase and lift out the upper bearing shells, noting the thrust washers either side of the centre bearing. Keep these shells with their respective caps, identifying them for refitting to the crankcase if they are to be used again.

47 With the engine now completely dismantled, each component should be examined, as described in the following Section before reassembling.

18 Engine – examination and renovation

1 Clean all components using paraffin and a stiff brush, except the crankshaft, which should be wiped clean and the oil passages cleaned out with a length of wire.

2 Never assume that a component is unworn simply because it looks all right. After all the effort which has gone into dismantling the engine, refitting worn components will make the overhaul a waste of time and money. Depending on the degree of wear, the overhauler's budget and the anticipated life of the vehicle, components which are only slightly worn may be refitted, but if in doubt it is always best to renew.

Crankshaft, main and big-end bearings

3 The need to renew the main bearing shells or to have the crankshaft reground will usually have been determined during the last few miles of operation when perhaps a heavy knocking has developed from within the crankcase or the oil pressure warning lamp has stayed on, denoting a low oil pressure probably caused by excessive wear in the bearings.

4 Even without these symptoms, the journals and crankpins on a high mileage engine should be checked for out-of-round (ovality) and taper. For this a micrometer will be needed to check the diameter of the journals and crankpins at several different points around them. A motor factor or engineer can do this for you. If the readings show that either out-of-round or taper is present, then the crankshaft should be reground by your dealer or engine reconditioning company to accept the undersize main and big-end shell bearings which are available. Normally, the company doing the regrinding will supply the necessary undersize shells.

5 If the crankshaft is in good condition, it is wise to renew the bearing shells as it is almost certain that the original ones will have worn. This is often indicated by scoring of the bearing surface or by the top layer of the bearing metal having worn through to expose the metal underneath.

6 Each shell is marked on its back with the part number. Undersize shells will have the undersize stamped additionally on their backs.

7 Standard size crankshafts having main bearing journal diameters at the lower end of the tolerance range are marked with a yellow spot on the front balance weight. You will find that with this type of crankshaft, a standard shell is fitted to the seat in the crankcase but a yellow colour-coded shell to the main bearing cap.

8 If a green spot is seen on the crankshaft then this indicates that 0.243 mm (0.01 in) undersize big-end bearings are used.

Cylinder bores, pistons, ring and connecting tubes

9 Cylinder bore wear will usually have been evident from the smoke emitted from the exhaust during recent operation of the vehicle on the

road, coupled with excessive oil consumption and fouling of spark plugs.

10 Engine lift can be extended by fitting special oil control rings to the pistons. These are widely advertised and will give many more thousands of useful mileage without the need for a rebore, although this will be inevitable eventually. If this remedy is decided upon, remove the piston/connecting rods as described in Section 10 and fit the proprietary rings in accordance with the manufacturer's instructions.

11 Where a more permanent solution is decided upon, the cylinder block can be rebored by your dealer or engineering works, or by one of the mobile workshops which now undertake such work. The cylinder bore will be measured both for out-of-round and for taper to decide how much the bores should be bored out. A set of matching pistons will be supplied in a suitable oversize to suit the new bores.

12 Due to the need for special heating and installing equipment for removal and refitting of the interference type gudgeon pin, the removal and refitting of pistons to the connecting rods is definitely a specialist job, preferably for your Ford dealer.

13 The removal and refitting of piston rings is however well within the scope of the home mechanic. Do this by sliding two or three old feeler blades round behind the top compression ring so that they are at equidistant points. The ring can now be slid up the blades and removed. Repeat the removal operations on the second compression ring and then the oil control ring. This method will not only prevent the rings from dropping onto empty grooves as they are withdrawn, but it will also avoid ring breakage.

14 Even when new piston rings have been supplied to match the pistons, always check that they are not tight in their grooves and also check their end gaps by pushing them squarely down their particular cylinder bore and measuring with a feeler blade. Adjustment of the end gap can be made by careful grinding to bring it within the specified tolerance.

15 If new rings are being fitted to an old piston, always remove any carbon from the grooves beforehand. The best tool for this job is the end of a broken piston ring. Take care not to cut your fingers, piston rings are sharp. The cylinder bores should be roughened with fine glass paper to assist the bedding-in of the new rings.

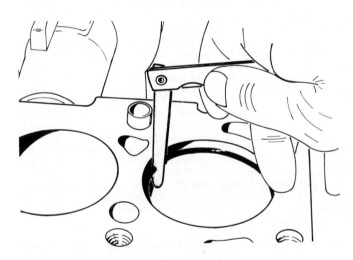

Fig. 1.46 Checking a piston ring end gap (Sec 18)

Timing sprockets and chain

16 The teeth on the timing sprockets rarely wear, but check for broken or hooked teeth even so.

17 The timing chain should always be renewed at time of major engine overhaul. A worn chain is evident if, when supported horizontally at both ends, it takes on a deeply bowed appearance.

18 Finally check the rubber cushion on the tensioner spring leaf. If grooved or chewed up, renew it.

Flywheel

19 Inspect the starter ring gear on the flywheel for wear or broken teeth. If evident, the ring gear should be renewed in the following way. Drill the ring gear with two holes, approximately 7 or 8 mm (0.3 in) diameter and offset as shown (Fig. 1.47). Make sure that you do not drill too deeply or you will damage the flywheel.

20 Tap the ring gear downward off its register and remove it.

21 Place the flywheel in the household refrigerator for about an hour and then heat the new ring gear to between 260 and 280°C (500 and 536°F) in a domestic oven. Do not heat it above 290°C (554°F) or its hardness will be lost.

22 Slip the ring onto the flywheel and gently tap it into position against its register. Allow it to cool without quenching.

23 The clutch friction surface on the flywheel should be checked for grooving or tiny hair cracks, the latter being caused by overheating. If these conditions are evident, it may be possible to surface grind the flywheel provided its balance is not upset. Otherwise, a new flywheel will have to be fitted – consult your dealer about this.

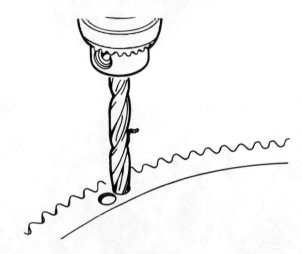

Fig. 1.47 Drilling the flywheel starter ring gear (Sec 18)

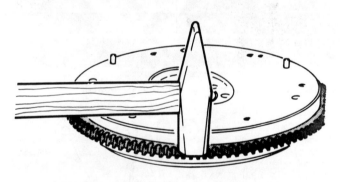

Fig. 1.48 Removing the ring gear from the flywheel (Sec 18)

Oil pump

24 The oil pump should be checked for wear by unbolting and removing the cover plate and checking the following tolerances (photo).

  (a) Outer rotor-to-pump body gap
  (b) Inner rotor-to-outer rotor gap
  (c) Rotor endfloat (use a feeler blade and straight-edge across pump body)

Use feeler blades to check the tolerances and if they are outside the specified values, renew the pump.

25 If the pump is serviceable, renew the O-ring and refit the cover (photo).

18.24 Check the oil pump rotor-to-body clearance at (a) and the inner-to-outer rotor clearance at (b)

18.25 Oil pump O-ring seal must be renewed (arrowed)

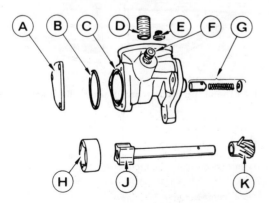

Fig. 1.49 Oil pump components (Sec 18)

A Cover	F Plug
B O-ring	G Relief valve
C Pump body	H Outer rotor
D Threaded insert	J Inner rotor
E Filter (relief valve)	K Drive pinion

Oil seals and gasket

26 Renew the oil seals on the timing cover and the crankshaft rear retainer as a matter of routine at time of major overhaul. Oil seals are cheap, oil is not! Use a piece of tubing as a removal and installing tool. Apply some grease to the oil seal lips and check that the small tensioner spring in the oil seal has not been displaced by the vibration caused during fitting of the seal.

27 Renew all the gaskets by purchasing the appropriate 'de-coke', short or full engine set. Oil seals may be included in the gasket sets.

Crankcase

28 Clean out the oilways with a length of wire or by using compressed air. Similarly clean the coolant passages. This is best done by flushing through with a cold water hose. Examine the crankcase and block for stripped threads in bolt holes; if evident, thread inserts can be fitted.

29 Renew any core plugs which appear to be leaking or which are excessively rusty.

30 Cracks in the casting may be rectified by specialist welding, or by one of the cold metal key interlocking processes available.

Camshaft and bearings

31 Examine the camshaft gear and lobes for damage or wear. If evident a new camshaft must be purchased, or one which has been 'built-up' such as are advertised by firms specialising in exchange components.

32 The bearing internal diameters should be checked against the Specifications if a suitable gauge is available; otherwise, check for movement between the camshaft journal and the bearing. Worn bearings should be renewed by your dealer.

33 Check the camshaft endfloat by temporarily refitting the camshaft and the thrust plate.

Cam followers

34 It is seldom that the cam followers wear in their bores, but it is likely that after a high mileage, the cam lobe contact surface will show signs of a depression or grooving

35 Where this condition is evident, renew the cam followers. Grinding out the wear marks will only reduce the thickness of the hardened metal of the cam follower and accelerate further wear.

Cylinder head and rocker gear

36 The usual reason for dismantling the cylinder head is to decarbonise and to grind in the valves. Reference should therefore be made to the next Section, in addition to the dismantling operations described here. First remove the manifolds.

37 Using a standard valve spring compressor, compress the spring on No 1 valve (valve nearest the timing cover). Do not overcompress the spring or the valve stem may bend. If it is found that, when screwing down the compressor tool, the spring retainer does not release from the collets, remove the compressor and place a piece of tubing on the retainer so that it does not impinge on the collets and strike the end of the tubing a sharp blow with a hammer. Refit the compressor and compress the spring.

38 Extract the split collets and then gently release the compressor and remove it.

39 Remove the valve spring retainer, the spring and the oil seal.

40 Withdraw the valve.

41 Repeat the removal operations on the remaining seven valves. Keep the valves in their originally fitted sequence by placing them in a piece of card which has holes punched in it and numbered 1 to 8 (from the timing cover end).

42 Place each valve in turn in its guide so that approximately one third of its length enters the guide. Rock the valve from side to side. If there is any more than an imperceptible movement, the guides will have to be reamed (working from the valve seat end) and oversize stemmed valves fitted. If you do not have the necessary reamer (tool 21-042 or 21-043), leave this work to your Ford dealer.

43 Examine the valve seats. Normally, the seats do not deteriorate but the valve heads are more likely to burn away in which case, new valves can be ground in as described in the next Section. If the seats require re-cutting, use a standard cutter available from most accessory or tool stores or consult your motor engineering works.

44 Renewal of any valve seat which is cracked or beyond recutting is definitely a job for your dealer or motor engineering works.

45 If the cylinder head mating surface is suspected of being distorted due to persistent leakage of coolant at the gasket joint, then it can be checked and surface ground by your dealer or motor engineering works. Distortion is unlikely under normal circumstances with a cast iron head.

46 Check the rocker shaft and rocker arms pads which bear on the valve stem end faces for wear or scoring, also for any broken coil springs. Renew components as necessary after dismantling, as described in Section 8. If the valve springs have been in use for 50 000 miles (80 000 km) or more, they should be renewed.

47 Reassemble the cylinder head by fitting new valve stem oil seals. Install No 1 valve (lubricated) into its guide and fit the valve spring with the closer coils to the cylinder head, followed by the spring retainer. Compress the spring and engage the split collets in the cut-out in the valve stem. Hold them in position while the compressor is gently released and removed.

48 Repeat the operations on the remaining valves, making sure that each valve is returned to its original guide or if new valves have been fitted, into the seat into which it was ground.

49 On completion, support the ends of the cylinder head on two wooden blocks and strike the end of each valve stem with a plastic or copper-faced hammer; just a light blow to settle the components.

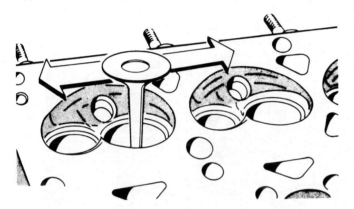

Fig. 1.50 Checking valve in guide for wear (Sec 18)

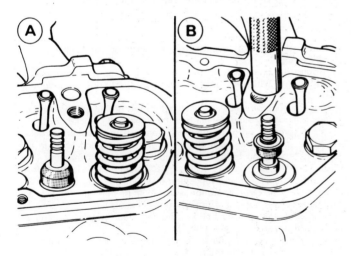

Fig. 1.51 Valve stem oil seals (Sec 18)

A   Exhaust valve type   B   Inlet valve type

19 Cylinder head and pistons – decarbonising

1 With the cylinder head removed, as described in Section 5, the carbon deposits should be removed from the combustion spaces using a scraper and a wire brush fitted into an electric drill. Take care not to damage the valve heads, otherwise no special precautions need be taken as the cylinder head is of cast iron construction.

2 Where a more thorough job is to be carried out, the cylinder head should be dismantled as described in the preceding Section so that the valves may be ground in and the ports and combustion spaces cleaned, brushed and blown out after the manifolds have been removed.

3 Before grinding-in a valve, remove the carbon and deposits completely from its head and stem. With an inlet valve, this is usually quite easy, simply scraping off the soft carbon with a blunt knife and finishing with a wire brush. With an exhaust valve the deposits are very much harder and those on the head may need a rub on coarse emery cloth to remove them. An old woodworking chisel is a useful tool to remove the worst of the head deposits.

4 Make sure that the valve heads are really clean, otherwise the rubber suction cup of the grinding tool will not stick during the grinding-in operations.

5 Before starting to grind in a valve, support the cylinder head so that there is sufficient clearance under for the valve stem to project fully without being obstructed.

6 Take the first valve and apply a little coarse grinding paste to the bevelled edge of the valve head. Insert the valve into its guide and apply the suction grinding tool to its head. Rotate the tool between the palms of the hands in a back-and-forth rotary movement until the gritty action of the grinding-in process disappears. Repeat the operation with the fine paste and then wipe away all traces of grinding paste and examine the seat and bevelled edge of the valve. A matt silver mating band should be observed on both components, without any sign of black spots. If some spots do remain, repeat the grinding-in process until they have disappeared. A drop or two of paraffin applied to the contact surfaces will increase the speed of grinding-in, but do not allow any paste to run down into the valve guide. On completion, wipe away every trace of grinding paste using a paraffin-moistened cloth.

7 Repeat the operations on the remaining valves, taking care not to mix up their originally fitted sequence.

8 The valves are refitted as described in Section 18.

9 An important part of the decarbonising operation is to remove the carbon deposits from the piston crowns. To do this, turn the crankshaft so that two pistons are at the top of their stroke and press some grease between these pistons and the cylinder walls. This will prevent carbon particles falling down into the piston ring grooves. Stuff rags into the other two bores.

10 Cover the oilways and coolant passages with masking tape and then using a blunt scraper remove all the carbon from the piston crowns. Take care not to score the soft alloy of the crown or the surface of the cylinder bore.

11 Rotate the crankshaft to bring the other two pistons to tdc and repeat the operations.

12 Wipe away the circle of grease and carbon from the cylinder bores.

13 Clean the top surface of the cylinder block by careful scraping.

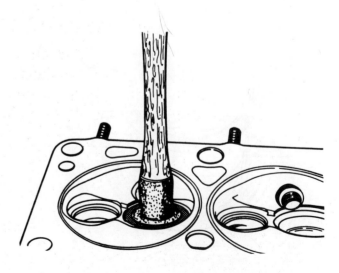

Fig. 1.52 Grinding-in a valve (Sec 19)

20.4 Fit the upper main bearing shell (with lubrication groove) and the thrust washers (centre bearing)

20.6 Lubricate the main bearing shells with engine oil

20.8 Tighten main bearing cap bolts progressively

20 Engine – reassembly

1   With everything clean, commence reassembly by oiling the bores for the cam followers and inserting them fully in their original sequence.

2   Lubricate the camshaft bearings and insert the camshaft from the timing cover end of the engine.

3   Fit the thrust plate and tighten the fixing bolts to the specified torque. The endfloat will already have been checked, as described in Section 18.

4   Wipe clean the main bearing shell seats in the crankcase and fit the shells, noting that the lower shells do not have the lubrication groove. Using a little grease, stick the semi-circular thrust washers on either side of the centre bearing so that the oil grooves are visible when the washers are installed (photo).

5   Check that the Woodruff key is in position on the front end of the crankshaft and tap the crankshaft sprocket into place using a piece of tubing.

6   Oil the bearing shells and lower the crankshaft into the crankcase (photo).

7   Wipe the seats in the main bearing caps and fit the bearing shells into them. Install the caps so that their markings are correctly positioned, as explained at dismantling in Section 17.

8   Screw in the cap bolts and tighten evenly to the specified torque (photo).

9   Now check the crankshaft endfloat. Ideally a dial gauge should be used, but feeler blades are an alternative if inserted between the face of the thrust washer and the machined surface of the crankshaft balance weight after having prised the crankshaft first in one direction and then the other. Provided the thrust washers at the centre bearing

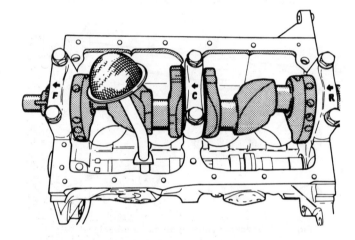

Fig. 1.54 Main bearing cap markings (Sec 20)

have been renewed, the endfloat should be with the specified tolerance. If it is not, oversize thrust washers are available (see Specifications).

10   Rotate the crankshaft so that the timing mark on its sprocket is directly in line with the centre of the crankshaft sprocket mounting flange.

11   Engage the camshaft sprocket within the timing chain and then engage the chain around the teeth of the crankshaft sprocket. Push the camshaft sprocket onto its mounting flange. The camshaft sprocket bolt holes should now be in alignment with the tapped holes in the camshaft flange and both sprocket timing marks in alignment (Fig. 1.56). Turn the camshaft as necessary to achieve this, also withdraw the camshaft sprocket and reposition it within the loop of the chain. This is a 'trial and error' operation which must be continued until exact alignment of bolt holes and timing marks is achieved.

12   Screw in the sprocket bolts to the specified torque and bend up the tabs of a new lockplate (photo).

13   Bolt the timing chain tensioner into position, retract the tensioner cam spring and then slide the tensioner arm onto its pivot pin. Release the cam tensioner so that it bears upon the arm.

14   Fit the oil slinger to the front of the crankshaft sprocket so that its convex side is against the sprocket.

15   Using a new gasket, fit the timing cover which will already have been fitted with a new oil seal (see Section 18). One fixing bolt should be left out at this stage as it also holds the coolant pump. Grease the oil seal lips and fit the crankshaft pulley. Tighten the pulley bolt to the specified torque.

16   Using a new gasket, bolt the crankshaft rear oil seal retainer into position. Tighten the bolts to the specified torque (photo).

17   Locate the engine adaptor (back) plate on its dowels and then fit the flywheel (photo).

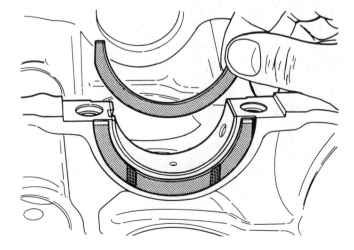

Fig. 1.53 Crankshaft endfloat half thrust washers (Sec 20)

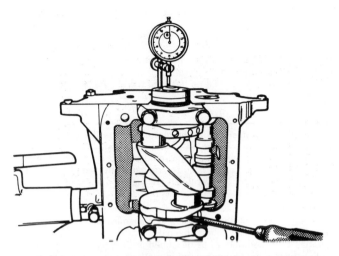

Fig. 1.55 Checking the crankshaft endfloat using the dial gauge method (Sec 20)

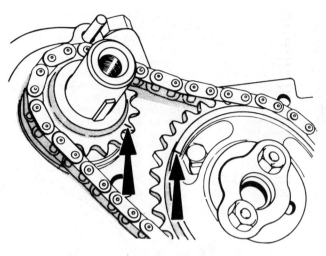

Fig. 1.56 Crankshaft and camshaft sprocket timing marks (arrowed) (Sec 20)

20.12 Secure the camshaft sprocket retaining bolts with the tab washer

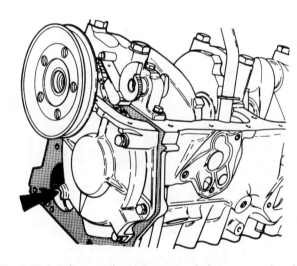

Fig. 1.57 Bolt (arrowed) which secures timing cover and coolant pump (Sec 20)

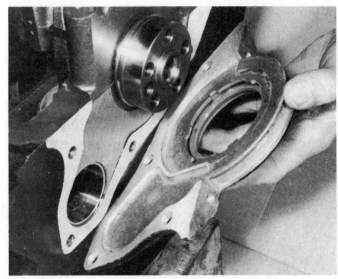

20.16 Refit the crankshaft rear oil seal retainer – note new gasket

20.17 Locate the engine backplate over the two dowels

18 Screw in and tighten the flywheel bolts to the specified torque. To prevent the flywheel turning, the starter ring gear can be jammed or a piece of wood placed between a crankshaft balance weight and the inside of the crankcase.

19 Install and centralise the clutch, as described in Chapter 5.

20 The pistons/connecting rods should now be installed. Although new pistons will have been fitted to the rods by your dealer or supplier (see Section 18), it is worth checking to ensure that with the piston crown arrow pointing to the timing cover end of the engine, the oil hole in the connecting rod is on the left as shown (Fig. 1.58). Oil the cylinder bores.

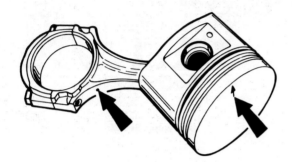

Fig. 1.58 Piston-to-connecting rod relationship. Lubrication hole and piston crown mark (arrowed) must align as shown (Sec 20)

21 Install the pistons/connecting rods, as described in Section 10.

22 Fit the sump, as described in Section 7.

23 Fit the oil pressure sender unit, if removed.

24 Turn the crankshaft until No 1 piston is at tdc (crankshaft pulley and timing cover marks aligned) and fit the oil pump complete with new gasket and a new oil filter, as described in Section 11.

25 Using a new gasket, fit the fuel pump. If the insulating block became detached from the crankcase during removal, make sure that a new gasket is fitted to each side of the block.

26 Fit the coolant pump using a new gasket.

27 Fit the cylinder head, as described in Section 5.

28 Refit the pushrods in their original sequence, and the rocker shaft, also as described in Section 5.

29 Adjust the valve clearances (Section 6) and refit the rocker cover using a new gasket.

30 Fit the intake and exhaust manifolds using new gaskets and tightening the nuts and bolts to the specified torque.

31 Refit the carburettor using a new flange gasket and connect the fuel pipe from the pump.

32 Screw in the spark plugs and the coolant temperature switch (if removed).

33 Refit the thermostat and the thermostat housing cover.

34 Fit the pulley to the coolant pump pulley flange.

35 Fit the alternator and the drivebelt and tension the belt, as described in Chapter 2.

36 Refit the distributor, as described in Chapter 4.

37 Refit the distributor cap and reconnect the spark plug HT leads.

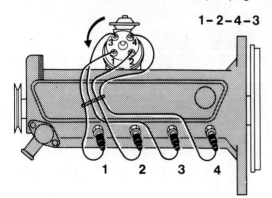

1- 2- 4- 3

Fig. 1.59 Distributor cap to spark plug HT lead connections (Sec 20)

38 Bolt on and connect the coolant pipe to the side of the cylinder block.

39 Fit the breather pipe from the oil filler cap to the intake manifold and fit the cap.

40 Check the sump drain plug for tightness. A new seal should be fitted at regular intervals to prevent leakage. Refit the dipstick.

41 Refilling with oil should be left until the engine is installed in the vehicle.

21 Engine/transmission – reconnection and refitting

1 This is a direct reversal of the removal and separation from the transmission. Take care not to damage the engine ancillary components and body panels when raising the unit into position.

Reconnection

2 Reconnection of the engine and transmission is a reversal of separation, but if the clutch has been dismantled, check that the driven plate has been centralised, as described in Chapter 5.

3 Locate the engine bearer and mountings and tighten the attachment bolts and nuts.

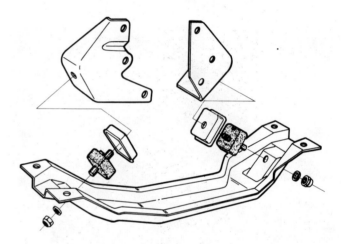

Fig. 1.60 Engine bearer and mountings (Sec 21)

Refitting

4 First check that the engine sump drain plug is tight and that the gearbox cap nut (removed to drain the oil) is refitted, together with its locking pin and spring.

5 Manoeuvre the engine/transmission under the vehicle and attach the lifting hoist. Raise the engine carefully until the engine mounting stud is engaged in the suspension strut retaining plate and the engine bearer is in contact with the floorpan. Align the engine bearer with the retaining bolt holes then fit and tighten the bolts. When tightening the bolts check that the mounting rubbers are not being twisted.

6 Refit the transmission bearer to the rubber insulator, fit the right-hand mounting retaining nut and washer, the side-mounted bolt and washer (under the wheel arch) and tighten.

7 With the engine and transmission fully secured, release the lifting hoist and remove it.

8 If some sort of plug was used to prevent the differential pinion cage from turning, remove the plug now. If a plug was not used, insert a finger in the driveshaft hole and align the cage ready to receive the driveshaft. If this is not done, the driveshaft cannot engage with the splined pinion gear. Use a new snap-ring and reconnect the right-hand driveshaft to the transmission by having an assistant apply pressure on the roadwheel. Check that the snap-ring has locked in position.

9 Relocate the right-hand tie-bar and bracket to the crossmember and refit the retaining bolts.

10 Reconnect the right-hand lower suspension arm. Tighten the bolts.

11 Refit the driveshaft and suspension lower arm to the opposite side in a similar way to that just described.

12 Rotate the gearchange housing back through 180° then loosely attach it to the floor panels with the retaining bolts.

13 Reconnect the transmission stabilizer rod, making sure to insert the washer between the rod and the transmission case (photo).
14 Check that the gearchange rod is still in 4th (4-speed gearbox) or reverse (5-speed gearbox).
15 Tighten the gearbox housing-to-floor attachment bolts.
16 Check that the contact faces of the gearchange rod and selector shaft are free of grease then reconnect them and adjust as follows, according to gearbox type.

Four-speed manual transmission
  (a) Pull downwards on the gearchange rod and slip it onto the selector shaft which projects from the transmission. The clamp should be loose on the gearchange rod (photo).
  (b) Using a 3.5 mm (0.14 in) diameter rod or pin, insert it as shown and pull the gear lever downwards to lock it in the selector slide. When inserting the rod, point up upward to 'feel' the cut-out in the gear lever before prising it downwards (photo). Now turn your attention to the gearbox.
  (c) Using a pin or rod, inserted into the hole in the end of the projecting selector shaft, turn the shaft clockwise to its stop and retain it in this position with a strong rubber band. Now tighten the clamp pinch-bolt (photo).
  (d) Remove the locking pins.

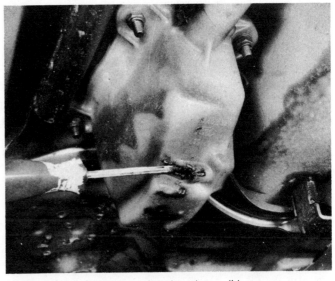
21.16B Locking the gear lever into the selector slide

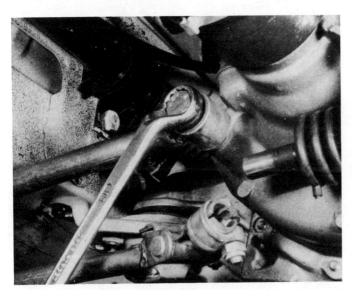
21.13 Connect the transmission stabilizer rod

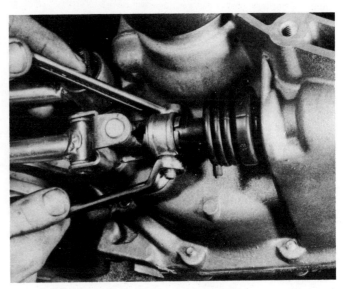
21.16C Tightening the gearchange rod clamp bolt

21.16A Sliding the clamp onto the transmission selector shaft

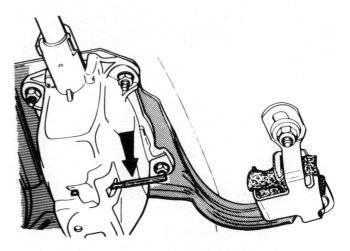
Fig. 1.61 Gearlever locked in selector housing by pin (arrowed) – four-speed transmission (Sec 21)

Five-speed manual transmission

(a) Use a lock tool similar to that shown, pull the gear lever down in its selector gate reverse gear position and set the tool to hold it against the stop (Fig. 1.62).

(b) Invert a suitable rod or draft into the hole in the selector shaft, rotate the shaft clockwise until it is felt to be against the stop then push it into the gearbox and retain it in this position while tightening the gearchange rod clamp bolt. Remove the drift and lock tool (Fig. 1.63).

17 Refit the clutch housing cover plate and secure with retaining bolts.

18 Refit the starter motor and reconnect its wiring.

19 Reconnect the engine earth strap underneath also the reversing light lead.

20 Refit the exhaust system and bolt the downpipe to the manifold. Refit the heated air box which connects with the air cleaner.

21 Reconnect the clutch operating cable.

22 Reconnect the electrical leads, the fuel pipe, the brake vacuum hose and the speedometer cable.

23 Reconnect the throttle cable and the heater hoses.

24 Reconnect the radiator coolant hoses.

25 Fill up with engine oil, transmission oil and coolant, then reconnect the battery (Fig. 1.64).

26 Refit the bonnet, bolting the hinges to their originally marked positions.

27 Fit the air cleaner and reconnect the hoses and the air cleaner intake spout.

28 Once the engine is running, check the dwell angle, timing, idle speed and mixture adjustment (refer to Chapters 3 and 4).

29 If a number of new internal components have been installed, run the vehicle at restricted speed for the first few hundred miles to allow time for the new components to bed in. It is also recommended that with a new or rebuilt engine, the engine oil and filter are changed at the end of the running-in period.

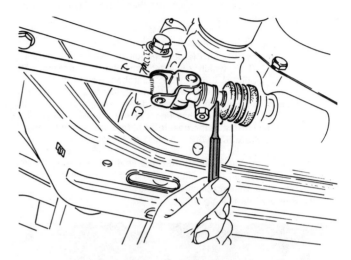

Fig. 1.63 Retain selector shaft when tightening clamp bolt (Sec 21)

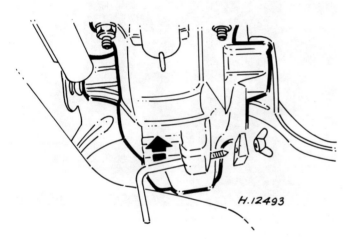

Fig. 1.62 Hold gear lever in position with lock tool – five-speed transmission (Sec 21)

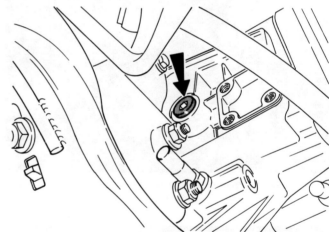

Fig. 1.64 Oil filler plug location on the transmission (Sec 21)

22 Fault diagnosis – ohv engine

Symptom	Reason(s)
Engine fails to turn over when starter operated	Discharged or defective battery Dirty or loose battery leads Defective starter solenoid or switch Engine earth strap disconnected Defective starter motor
Engine turns over but will not start	Ignition damp or wet Ignition leads to spark plugs loose Shorted or disconnected low tension leads Dirty, incorrectly set or pitted contact breaker points

Symptom	Reason(s)
	Faulty condenser
	Defective ignition switch
	Ignition LT leads connected wrong way round
	Faulty coil
	Contact breaker point spring earthed or broken
	No petrol in petrol tank
	Vapour lock in fuel line (in hot conditions or at high altitude)
	Blocked float chamber needle valve
	Fuel pump filter blocked
	Choked or blocked carburettor jets
	Faulty fuel pump
Engine stalls and will not start	Ignition failure — in severe rain or after traversing water splash
	No petrol in petrol tank
	Petrol tank breather choked
	Sudden obstruction in carburettor
	Water in fuel system
Engine misfires or idles unevenly	Ignition leads loose
	Battery leads loose on terminals
	Battery earth strap loose on body attachment point
	Engine earth lead loose
	Low tension lead to terminals on coil loose
	Low tension lead from distributor loose
	Dirty, or incorrectly gapped spark plugs
	Dirty, incorrectly set or pitted contact breaker points
	Tracking across distributor cap (oily or cracked cap)
	Ignition too retarded
	Faulty coil
	Mixture too weak
	Sticking engine valve
	Incorrect valve clearance
	Air leak in carburettor
	Air leak at inlet manifold to cylinder head, or inlet manifold to carburettor
	Weak or broken valve springs
	Worn valve guides or stems
	Worn pistons and piston rings
Lack of power and poor compression	Burnt out exhaust valves
	Sticking or leaking valves
	Worn valve guides and stems
	Weak or broken valve springs
	Blown cylinder head gasket (accompanied by increase in noise)
	Worn pistons and piston rings
	Worn or scored cylinder bores
	Ignition timing wrongly set
	Contact breaker points incorrectly gapped
	Incorrect valve clearances
	Incorrectly set spark plugs
	Mixture too rich or too weak
	Dirty contact breaker points
	Fuel filters blocked causing top end fuel starvation
	Distributor automatic advance weights or vacuum advance and retard mechanism not functioning correctly
	Faulty fuel pump giving top end fuel starvation
Excessive oil consumption	Badly worn, perished or missing valve stem oil seals
	Excessively worn valve stems and valve guides
	Worn piston rings
	Worn pistons and cylinder bores
	Excessive piston ring gap allowing blow-by
	Piston oil return holes choked
Oil being lost due to leaks	Leaking oil filter gasket
	Leaking rocker cover gasket
	Leaking timing case gasket
	Leaking sump gasket
	Loose sump plug
Unusual noises from engine	Worn valve gear (noisy tapping from top cover)
	Worn big-end bearings (regular heavy knocking)
	Worn main bearings (rumbling and vibration)
	Worn crankshaft (knocking, rumbling and vibration)

PART B: OHC ENGINE

23 General description

This engine, designated CVH (Compound Valve angle, Hemispherical combustion chamber) can be described in more conventional terms as a four-cylinder overhead cam (ohc) engine.

The engine is mounted, together with the transmission, transversely at the front of the vehicle and transmits power through open driveshafts to the front roadwheels.

The engine is available in two capacities, 1.3 and 1.6 litres.

The crankshaft is supported in five main bearings within a cast iron crankcase.

The cylinder head is of light alloy construction, supporting the overhead camshaft in five bearings. These bearings cannot be renewed and, in the event of wear occurring, the complete cylinder head must be changed. The fuel pump is mounted on the side of the cylinder head and is driven by a pushrod from an eccentric cam on the camshaft.

Fig. 1.65 Cutaway view of the CVH (ohc) engine (Sec 23)

The distributor is driven from the rear (flywheel) end of the camshaft.

The cam followers are of hydraulic type, which eliminates the need for valve clearance adjustment and also ensures that valve timing is always correct which is not the case if a mechanical type arrangement should be out of adjustment.

The cam followers operate in the following way: when the valve is closed, pressurized engine oil passes through a port in the body of the cam followers and four grooves in the plunger and into the cylinder feed chamber. From this chamber, oil flows through a ball-type non-return valve into the pressure chamber. The tension of the coil spring causes the plunger to press the rocker arm against the valve and to eliminate any free play.

As the cam lifts the cam follower, the oil pressure in the pressure chamber increases and causes the non-return valve to close the port feed chamber. As oil cannot be compressed, it forms a rigid link between the body of the cam follower, the cylinder and the plunger which then rise as one component to open the valve.

The clearance between the body of the cam follower and the cylinder is accurately designed to meter a specific quantity of oil as it escapes from the pressure chamber. Oil will only pass along the cylinder bore when pressure is high during the moment of valve opening. Once the valve has closed, the escape of oil will produce a small amount of free play and no pressure will exist in the pressure chamber. Oil from the feed chamber can then flow through the non-return valve into the pressure chamber so that the cam follower cylinder can be raised by the pressure of the coil spring, thus eliminating any play in the arrangement until the valve is operated again.

As wear occurs between rocker arm and valve stem, the quantity of oil which flows into the pressure chamber will be slightly more than the quantity lost during the expansion cycle of the cam follower. Conversely, when the cam follower is compressed by the expansion of the valve, a slightly smaller quantity of oil will flow into the pressure chamber than was lost.

If the engine has been standing idle for a period of time, or after overhaul, when the engine is started up valve clatter may be heard. This is a normal condition and will gradually disappear within a few minutes of starting up as the cam followers are pressurized with oil.

The coolant pump is mounted on the timing belt end of the cylinder block and is driven by the toothed belt.

A gear type oil pump is mounted on the timing belt end of the cylinder block and is driven by a gear on the front end of the crankshaft.

A full-flow oil filter of throw-away type is located on the side of crankcase nearer the front of the vehicle.

24 Routine maintenance – CVH engine

The routine maintenance procedures for the CVH engine closely follow those given for the ohv engine in Section 2. Note, however, that it is not necessary to check or adjust the valve clearances.

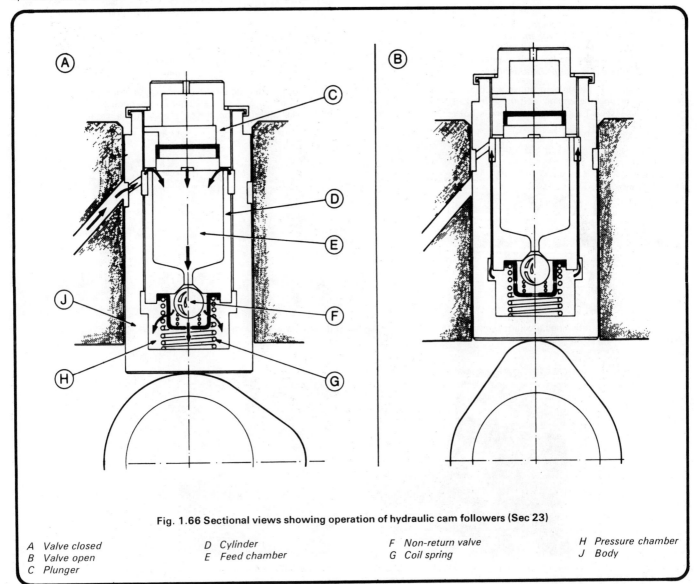

Fig. 1.66 Sectional views showing operation of hydraulic cam followers (Sec 23)

A Valve closed	D Cylinder	F Non-return valve	H Pressure chamber
B Valve open	E Feed chamber	G Coil spring	J Body
C Plunger			

25 Operations possible without removing engine from vehicle

The following work can be carried out without having to remove the engine:

(a) *Timing belt – renewal*
(b) *Camshaft oil seal – renewal*
(c) *Camshaft – removal and refitting*
(e) *Crankshaft front oil seal – renewal**
(f) *Sump – removal and refitting*
(g) *Piston/connecting rod – removal and refitting*
(h) *Engine/transmission mountings – removal and refitting*

*Note that replacement of the crankshaft front oil seal with the engine *in situ* is made difficult by restricted access. Accurate fitting of the new seal in this position will only be possible using Ford special tool number 21-093 (or a similar fabricated distance piece) used, together with the crankshaft timing belt pulley retaining bolt, to draw the new seal into position against the stop.

In view of the above, partial removal of the engine and transmission may well be necessary to renew this seal.

26 Operations only possible with engine removed from vehicle

1   The following work should be carried out only after the engine has been removed:

(a) *Crankshaft main bearings – renewal*
(b) *Crankshaft – removal and refitting*
(c) **Flywheel – removal and refitting*
(d) *** Crankshaft rear oil seal – renewal*
(e) **Oil pump – removal and refitting*

2   Although it is possible to undertake those operations marked * without removing the engine, and those marked ** by removing the transmission (see Chapter 6), such work is not recommended and is unlikely to save much time over that required to withdraw the complete engine/transmission.

27 Timing belt – inspection, removal and refitting

1   This is not a routine operation and will only normally be required after a very high mileage has been covered, or for removal of the coolant pump.
2   Disconnect the battery earth lead.
3   Release the alternator mounting and adjuster link bolts, push the alternator in towards the engine and slip the drivebelt from the pulleys.
4   Unscrew the four bolts and remove the timing belt cover (photo).
5   The timing belt can now be inspected for signs of excessive wear or damage; if found, the belt must be renewed. If the belt is damaged or has worn prematurely, a check must be made to find the cause. There are three main causes of timing belt failures and these are as follows:

(a) *If some of the teeth have sheared off and some are badly worn, check the surface of the crankshaft pulley teeth for signs of damage or defects and renew the pulley, if necessary*
(b) *If some belt teeth have sheared off and other are cracked at their roots, then this indicates an excessive torque loading on the belt, and the water pump, distributor, timing belt tensioner wheel and the camshaft must be checked for freedom of movement. In the case of the camshaft the rockers must be removed when checking it for freedom of rotation. Renew or repair as necessary before renewing the timing belt*
(c) *If some teeth have sheared from the belt whilst others are undamaged, the belt will have jammed in the belt pulley or the engine has possibly been over-revved. Check the items mentioned in (b) and renew as necessary*

6   To remove the timing belt, proceed as follows.
7   Using a ring or socket spanner on the crankshaft pulley bolt, turn the crankshaft until the timing mark on the camshaft sprocket is

27.4 Undo the four retaining bolts (arrowed) to remove the timing cover

27.7A Camshaft sprocket timing mark

27.7B Align the crankshaft sprocket with its timing mark

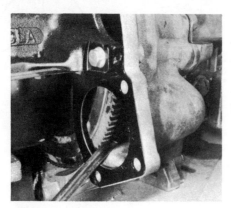

27.7C One method of jamming the flywheel ring gear

27.7D Another method of jamming the flywheel ring gear

opposite the tdc mark on the cylinder head and the small projection on the crankshaft belt sprocket front flange is in alignment with the tdc mark on the oil pump casing. Remove the starter, jam the flywheel ring gear and unbolt and remove the crankshaft pulley (photos).

8   Slacken the bolts which secure the belt tensioner and using a large screwdriver, prise the tensioner to one side to relieve spring tension on the belt. (Some tensioners do not incorporate a spring). Temporarily retighten the bolts.

9   If the original belt is to be refitted, mark it for direction of travel and also the exact tooth positions on all three sprockets.

10 Slip the timing belt from its sprockets (photo).

27.10 Removing the timing belt

11 Refit by reversing the removal operations, but before engaging the belt to the camshaft and crankshaft sprockets, check that they are set to tdc as previously described. Adjust the position of the sprockets slightly if necessary, but avoid any excessive movement of the sprockets while the belt is off, as the piston crowns and valve heads may make contact, with consequent damage to both components.

12 Engage the timing belt with the teeth of the crankshaft sprocket (slip the sprocket off the crankshaft if necessary to avoid kinking the belt), and then pull the belt vertically upright on its right-hand run. Keep it taut and engage it with the teeth of the camshaft sprocket. Check that the positions of the crankshaft and camshaft sprockets have not altered.

13 Wind the belt around the camshaft sprocket, around and under the tensioner idler pulley and over the coolant pump pocket (no set position for this) (photo).

14 Loosen the tensioner retaining bolts by half a turn each to allow the tensioner to snap into position against the timing belt.

15 With the crankshaft locked in position at tdc, fit a 41 mm socket and torque wrench onto the camshaft sprocket bolt and apply an anti-clockwise torque in accordance with the settings given in the Specifications. Whilst applying this torque setting to the camshaft, simultaneously tighten the tensioner retaining bolts, right-hand then left-hand bolt, to their specified torque wrench setting. This is an initial setting up procedure only – the belt tension should be checked with Ford tool 21-113; therefore the car will have to be taken to a dealer as soon as possible.

16 Refit the crankshaft pulley, the retaining bolt and washer, and tighten to the specified torque wrench setting (photo).

17 Refit the belt cover, refit and adjust the drivebelt, and reconnect the battery.

28 Camshaft oil seal – renewal

1   Disconnect the battery earth lead.

2   Release the timing belt from the camshaft sprocket, as described in the preceding Section.

27.13 Timing belt correctly located

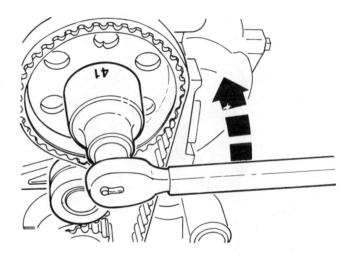

Fig. 1.67 Method used to initially tension the timing belt (Sec 27)

27.16 Crankshaft pulley, bolt and washer

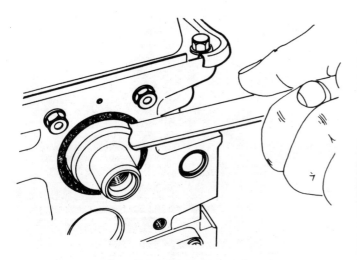

Fig. 1.68 Removing the camshaft oil seal (Sec 28)

28.5 Camshaft oil seal

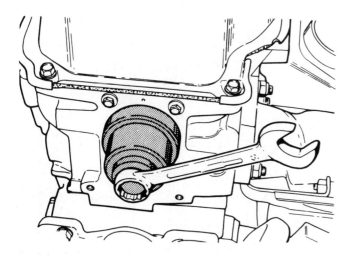

Fig. 1.69 Installing the camshaft oil seal (Sec 28)

distributor cap and secure it to the left-hand side of the engine compartment.

6   Unscrew the three bolts and withdraw the distributor from the cylinder head. Note that the distributor body is marked in relation to the cylinder head.

7   Unbolt and remove the fuel pump, complete with coil spring.

8   Withdraw the insulating spacer and operating pushrod.

9   Unbolt the throttle cable bracket at the carburettor and then disconnect the cable by sliding back the spring clip.

10 Remove the rocker cover (photo).

11 Unscrew the securing nuts and remove the rocker arms and guides. Keep the components in their originally installed sequence by marking them with a piece of numbered tape or by using a suitably sub-divided box.

12 Withdraw the hydraulic cam followers, again keeping them in their originally fitted sequence.

13 Slacken the alternator mounting and adjuster link bolts, push the alternator in towards the engine and slip the drivebelt from the pulleys.

14 Unbolt and remove the timing belt cover and turn the crankshaft to align the timing mark on the camshaft sprocket with the one on the cylinder head.

3   Pass a bar through one of the holes in the camshaft sprocket to anchor the sprocket while the retaining bolt is unscrewed. Remove the sprocket.

4   Using a suitable tool, hooked at its end, prise out the oil seal.

5   Apply a little grease to the lips of the new seal and draw it into position using the sprocket bolt and a suitable distance piece (photo).

6   Refit the sprocket, tightening the bolt to the specified torque wrench setting. Thread locking compound should be applied to the threads of the bolt.

7   Refit and tension the timing belt, as described in the preceding Section.

8   Reconnect the battery.

29 Camshaft – removal and refitting

1   Disconnect the battery earth lead.

2   Disconnect the crankcase ventilation hose from the intake manifold and the rocker cover.

3   Extract the two larger screws from the lid of the air cleaner, raise the air cleaner, disconnect the hoses and remove the cleaner.

4   Disconnect the pipes and remove the windscreen washer fluid reservoir from the engine compartment.

5   Disconnect the HT leads from the spark plugs, then remove the

29.10 Remove the rocker cover

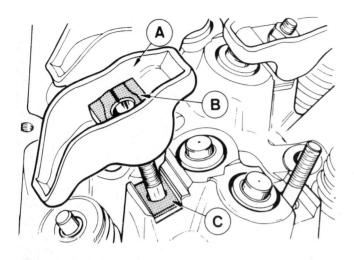

Fig. 1.70 Rocker arm components (Sec 29)

A *Rocker arm*   C *Spacer plate*
B *Guide*

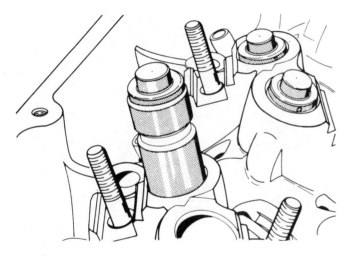

Fig. 1.71 Removing a cam follower (Sec 29)

29.16A Method used to loosen the camshaft sprocket bolt

29.16B Withdraw the camshaft sprocket

29.17A Unscrewing the camshaft thrust plate bolts

15 Slacken the bolts on the timing belt tensioner, lever the tensioner against the tension of its coil spring (if fitted) and retighten the bolts. With the belt now slack, slip it from the camshaft sprocket.
16 Pass a rod or large screwdriver through one of the holes in the camshaft sprocket to lock it and unscrew the sprocket bolt. Remove the sprocket (photos).
17 Extract the two bolts and pull out the camshaft thrust plate (photos).
18 Carefully withdraw the camshaft from the distributor end of the cylinder head (photo).
19 Refitting the camshaft is a reversal of removal, but observe the following points.
20 Lubricate the camshaft bearings before inserting the camshaft into the cylinder head.
21 It is recommended that a new oil seal is always fitted after the camshaft has been installed (see preceding Section). Apply thread locking compound to the sprocket bolt threads.
22 Fit and tension the timing belt, as described in Section 27.
23 Oil the hydraulic cam followers with hypoid type transmission oil before inserting them into their original bores.
24 Refit the rocker arms and guides in their original sequence, use **new** nuts and tighten to the specified torque. It is essential that before each rocker arm is installed and its nut tightened, the respective cam follower is positioned at its lowest point (in contact with cam base circle). Turn the camshaft (by means of the crankshaft pulley bolt) as necessary to achieve this.
25 Use a new rocker cover gasket.

29.17B Lift out the camshaft thrust plate

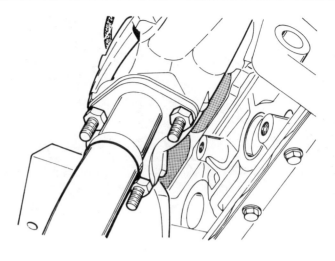

Fig. 1.72 Exhaust downpipe connection to manifold (Sec 30)

29.18 Withdraw the camshaft

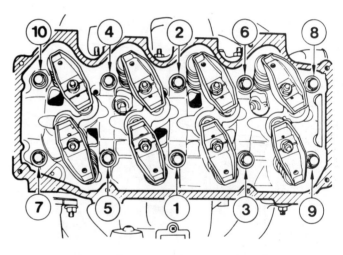

Fig. 1.73 Cylinder head bolt tightening sequence (Sec 30)

30 Cylinder head – removal and refitting

1 Disconnect the battery earth lead.
2 Remove the air cleaner and detach the connecting hoses.
3 Drain the cooling system (Chapter 2).
4 Disconnect the coolant hoses from the thermostat housing.
5 Disconnect the coolant hoses from the automatic choke (if necessary).
6 Disconnect the throttle cable from the carburettor.
7 Disconnect the fuel pipe from the fuel pump.
8 Disconnect the vacuum servo pipe from the intake manifold.
9 Disconnect the leads from the coolant temperature sender, the ignition coil, and the anti-run-on (anti-diesel) solenoid valve at the carburettor.
10 Unbolt the exhaust downpipe from the manifold by unscrewing the flange nuts. Support the exhaust pipe by tying it up with wire.
11 Release the alternator mounting and adjuster link bolts, push the alternator in towards the engine and slip the drivebelt from the pulleys.
12 Unbolt and remove the timing belt cover.
13 Slacken the belt tensioner bolts, lever the tensioner to one side against the pressure of the coil spring (if fitted) and retighten the bolts.

14 With the timing belt now slack, slip it from the camshaft sprocket.
15 Disconnect the leads from the spark plugs and unscrew and remove the spark plugs.
16 Remove the rocker cover.
17 Unscrew the cylinder head bolts, progressively and in the reverse sequence to that given for tightening (Fig. 1.73). Discard the bolts, as new ones must be used at reassembly.
18 Remove the cylinder head complete with manifolds. Use the manifolds, if necessary, as levers to rock the head from the block. Do not attempt to tap the head sideways off the block, as it is located on dowels, and do not attempt to lever between the head and the block, or damage will result.
19 Before installing the cylinder head, make sure that the mating surfaces of head and block are perfectly clean with the head locating dowels in position. Clean the bolt holes free from oil. In extreme cases it is possible for oil left in the holes to crack the block.
20 Turn the crankshaft to position No 1 piston about 20 mm (0.8 in) before it reaches tdc.
21 Place a new gasket on the cylinder block and then locate the cylinder head on its dowels. The upper surface of the gasket is marked OBEN-TOP (photos).

30.21A Locate the new cylinder head gasket ...

30.21B ... with the OBEN TOP mark uppermost

30.21C Refit the cylinder head

22 Install and tighten the **new** cylinder head bolts, tightening them in four stages (see Specifications). After the first two stages, the bolt heads should be marked with a spot of quick-drying paint so that the paint spots all face the same direction. Now tighten the bolts (Stage 3) through 90° (quarter turn) followed by a further 90° (Stage 4). Tighten the bolts at each stage only in the sequence shown (Fig. 1.73) before going on to the next stage. If all the bolts have been tightened equally, the paint spots should now all be pointing in the same direction (photo).

23 Fit the timing belt as described in Section 27.

24 Refitting and reconnection of all other components is a reversal of dismantling.

25 Refill the cooling system.

30.22 Cylinder head bolt alignment marks

31 Crankshaft front oil seal – renewal

If replacing the oil seal with the power unit in situ first refer to the cautionary notes concerning its renewal in Section 25.

1 Disconnect the battery earth lead.

2 Release the alternator mounting and adjuster link bolts, push the alternator in towards the engine and slip the drivebelt from the pulleys.

3 Unbolt and remove the timing belt cover and by using a spanner or socket on the crankshaft pulley bolt, turn the crankshaft until the timing mark on the camshaft sprocket is in alignment with the mark on the cylinder head.

4 Unbolt and withdraw the starter motor so that the flywheel ring

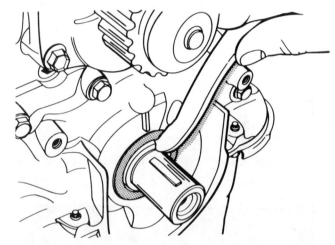

Fig. 1.74 Extracting the oil seal from the oil pump housing
(Sec 31)

gear can be jammed with a cold chisel or other suitable device and the crankshaft pulley unbolted and removed.

5 Slacken the belt tensioner bolts, lever the tensioner to one side and retighten the bolts. With the belt slack, it can now be slipped from the sprockets. Before removing the belt note its original position on the sprockets (mark the teeth with quick-drying paint), also its direction of travel.

6 Pull off the crankshaft sprocket. If it is tight, use a two-legged extractor.

7 Remove the dished washer from the crankshaft, noting that the concave side is against the oil seal.

8 Using a suitably hooked tool, prise out the oil seal from the oil pump housing.

9 Grease the lips of the new seal and press it into position using the pulley bolt and a suitable distance piece made from a piece of tubing.

10 Fit the thrust washer (concave side to oil seal), the belt sprocket and the pulley to the crankshaft.

11 Fit and tension the timing belt by the method described in Section 27.

12 Fit the timing belt cover

13 Refit and tension the alternator drivebelt.

14 Remove the starter ring gear jamming device, refit the starter motor and reconnect the battery.

32 Sump – removal and refitting

1 Disconnect the battery earth lead.

2 Drain the engine oil.

3 Unbolt and remove the starter motor.

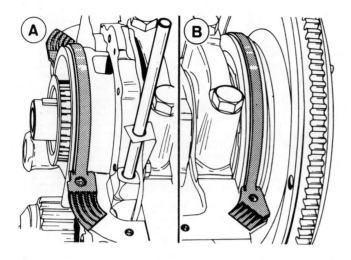

Fig. 1.75 Sump front (A) and rear (B) sealing strip locations
(Sec 32)

4   Unbolt and remove the cover plate from the clutch housing.
5   Unscrew the plastic timing belt guard from the front end of the engine (two bolts).
6   Unscrew the sump securing bolts progressively and remove them.
7   Remove the sump and peel away the gaskets and sealing strips.
8   Make sure that the mating surfaces of the sump and block are clean, then fit new end sealing strips into their grooves and stick new

side gaskets into position using thick grease. The ends of the side gaskets should overlap the seals (photos).
9   Offer up the sump, taking care not to displace the gaskets and insert the securing bolts. Tighten the bolts in two stages to the final torque given in the Specifications (photos). Fit the timing belt guard.
10 Refit the cover plate to the flywheel housing (photo).
11 Refit the starter motor
12 Fill the engine with oil and reconnect the battery.

33 Piston/connecting rods – removal and refitting

1   Remove the sump, as described in the preceding Section, and the cylinder head, as described in Section 30.
2   Check that the connecting rod and cap have adjacent numbers at their big-end to indicate their position in the cylinder block (No 1 nearest timing cover end of engine) (photo).
3   Bring the first piston to the lowest point of its throw by turning the crankshaft pulley bolt and then check if there is a wear ridge at the top of the bore. If there is, it should be removed using a scraper, but do not damage the cylinder bore.
4   Unscrew the big-end bolts and remove them.
5   Tap off the cap. If the bearing shell is to be used again, make sure that it is retained with the cap. Note the two cap positioning roll pins.
6   Push the piston/rod out of the top of the block, again keeping the bearing shell with the rod if the shell is to be used again.
7   Repeat the removal operations on the remaining piston/rod assemblies.
8   Dismantling a piston/connecting rod is covered in Sections 18 and 41.
9   To refit a piston/rod assembly, have the piston ring gaps staggered as shown in the diagram (Fig. 1.76). Oil the rings and apply a piston ring compressor. Compress the piston rings.
10 Oil the cylinder bores.

32.8A Locate the sump sealing strip

32.8B Sump gasket to overlap sealing strip

32.9A Fitting the sump

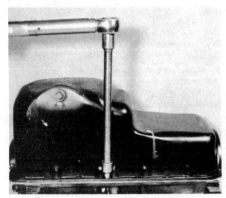

32.9B Tightening the sump bolts

32.10 Fit the flywheel housing cover plate

33.2 Connecting rod and big-end cap matching numbers

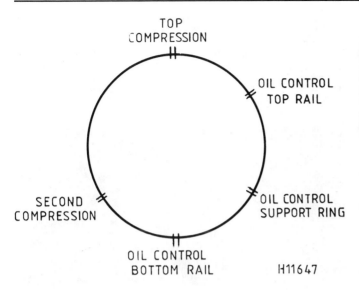

Fig. 1.76 Piston ring end gap positioning diagram (Sec 33)

33.13 Installing a piston/connecting rod

33.11 Fit the bearing shell to the connecting rod

33.15 Fit the bearing shell to the big-end cap

11 Wipe clean the bearing shell seat in the connecting rod and insert the shell (photo).

12 Insert the piston/rod assembly into the cylinder bore until the base of the piston ring compressor stands squarely on the top of the block.

13 Check that the directional arrow on the piston crown faces towards the timing cover end of the engine, then apply the wooden handle of a hammer to the piston crown. Strike the head of the hammer sharply to drive the piston into the cylinder bore and release the ring compressor (photo).

14 Oil the crankpin and draw the connecting rod down to engage with the crankshaft. Make sure the bearing shell is still in position.

15 Wipe the bearing shell seat in the big-end cap clean and insert the bearing shell (photo).

16 Fit the cap, screw in the bolts and tighten them to the specified torque (photos).

17 Repeat the operations on the remaining pistons/connecting rods.

18 Refit the sump (Section 32) and the cylinder head (Section 30). Refill the engine with oil and coolant.

33.16A Fit the big-end cap ...

33.16B ... and tighten the retaining bolts

34 Engine/transmission mountings – removal and refitting

The information below also applies to ohv engines

1   The engine mountings can be removed if the weight of the engine/transmission is first taken by one of the three following methods.

2   Either support the engine under the sump using a jack and a block of wood, or attach a hoist to the engine lifting lugs. A third method is to make up a bar with end pieces which will engage in the water channels at the sides of the bonnet lid aperture. Using an adjustable hook and chain connected to the engine lifting lugs, the weight of the engine can be taken off the mountings.

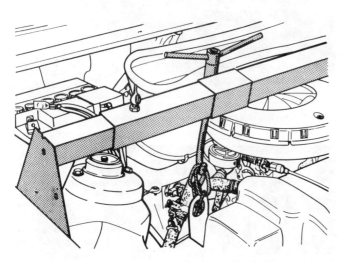

Fig. 1.77 Typical engine support bar (Sec 34)

Engine right-hand mounting

3   Unscrew and remove the mounting side bolt from under the right-hand wheel arch, just to the rear of and above the brake hose bracket (photo).

4   Unscrew and remove the mounting retaining nut and washer from the suspension strut cup retaining plate.

5   Undo the three bolts securing the mounting unit to the cylinder block (working from underneath). The mounting unit and bracket can then be lowered from the engine.

6   Unbolt and remove the mounting from its support bracket.

Engine bearer and mountings

7   Unscrew and remove the two nuts securing each mounting (front and rear) to the engine bearer.

8   Support the engine bearer, then undo and remove the four retaining bolts from the floorpan, two at the front and two at the rear (photo).

9   Unscrew the retaining nut to disconnect the rubber mounting from the transmission support.

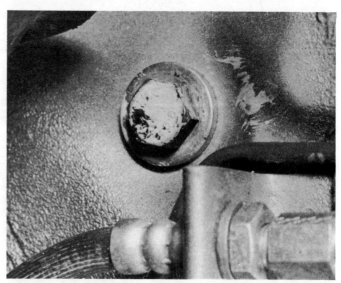

34.3 Right-hand engine mounting side retaining bolt

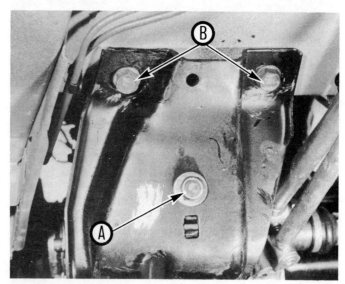

34.8 Engine bearer (rear end) showing mounting retaining nut (A) and retaining bolts to floor (B)

All mountings

10   Refitting of all mountings is a reversal of removal. Make sure that the original sequence of assembly of washers and plates is maintained.

11   Do not fully tighten all mounting bolts until they are all located. As the mounting bolts and nuts are tightened, check that the mounting rubbers do not twist.

35 Oil filter – removal and refitting

1   The oil filter is of throw-away screw-on cartridge type, mounted on the right-hand side of the crankcase (photo).

35.1 Oil filter location

35.2 Oil filter removal using a clamp wrench

36.1 Oil pressure relief valve

2   The filter should be unscrewed using a strap, clamp or chain wrench (photo).
3   When fitting a new filter, smear the rubber sealing ring with grease and screw it on as tightly as possible using hand pressure only, **not** a tool.
4   After starting the engine, the oil pressure warning light will stay on for a few seconds while the filter fills with oil. This is normal after fitting a new filter. Top up the engine oil.

36 Lubrication system – description

1   The oil pump draws oil from the sump through a pick-up pipe and then supplies pressurised oil through an oilway on the right-hand side of the engine into a full-flow oil filter. A pressure relief valve is incorporated inside the pump casing (photo).
2   Filtered oil passes out of the filter casing through the central threaded mounting stud into the main oil gallery.
3   Oil from the main gallery lubricates the main bearings, and the big-end bearings are lubricated from oilways in the crankshaft.

Fig. 1.79 Sectional view of the valve rocker assembly (Sec 36)

4   The connecting rods have an oil hole in the big-end on the side towards the exhaust manifold. Oil is ejected from this hole onto the gudgeon pins and cylinder bores.
5   The oil pressure warning switch is located next to the oil filter and connected by an internal passage to the main oil gallery. Oil from this passage is supplied to the centre camshaft bearing.
6   Oil is provided to the other camshaft bearings by means of a longitudinal drilling within the camshaft.
7   The hydraulic cam followers (tappets) are supplied with oil through the grooves in the camshaft bearing journals and oilways in the cylinder head.
8   The contact face of the rocker arm is lubricated from ports in the tappet guides, while the end faces of the valve stems are splash lubricated.

37 Crankcase ventilation system – description

1   The system is of closed type, in which oil and blow-by fumes are extracted from the crankcase and passed into the intake manifold, after which they are burnt during the normal combustion cycle.
2   At light throttle openings, the emissions are drawn out of the rocker cover, through a control orifice in the crankcase ventilation filter and into the intake manifold. Under full throttle conditions the gas flow routing is still as just described, but, in addition, the gases are drawn through a filter and pass into the air cleaner.
3   This arrangement offsets any tendency for the fuel/air ratio to be adversely affected at full throttle.

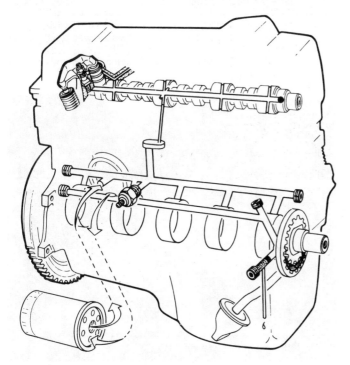

Fig. 1.78 Lubrication circuits in the CVH engine (Sec 36)

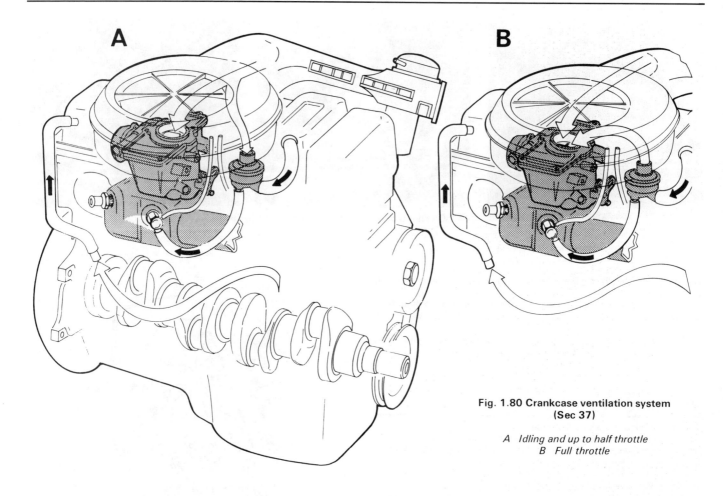

Fig. 1.80 Crankcase ventilation system (Sec 37)

A   Idling and up to half throttle
B   Full throttle

38 Engine – method of removal

The engine should be removed from the vehicle complete with transmission (gearbox and final drive) in a downward direction.

39 Engine/transmission – removal and separation

Proceed as described for the ohv engine in Section 16 of this Chapter, but note the following differences:

1   A lateral coolant pipe is not fitted to the side of the cylinder block on the CVH variants, but the heater hoses must be disconnected from the thermostat housing and distribution (photos).

2   When disconnecting the driveshafts, disregard paragraphs 20 to 26 as they can be detached by undoing the socket-head bolts. These can be loosened using a 6mm Allen key.

3   Disconnect the right-hand shaft just to the right of the intermediate shaft support bracket. Remove the bolts, together with the link washers, and detach the shaft, but do not let it hang freely; support it by suspending with a suitable length of wire. The right-hand intermediate shaft can be left in position during removal of the engine/transmission.

4   Disconnect the inner end of the left-hand driveshaft by unscrewing and removing the socket-head bolts and three link washers. Suspend the driveshaft with wire. Note that there is no need to disconnect the steering trackrod balljoint and lower suspension arm pivot or tie-rod to enable the engine/transmission to be removed and refitted.

5   Remove the intermediate shaft, as described in Chapter 7, once the engine/transmission is removed, to allow for their subsequent separation.

6   Support and lower the engine/transmission (photos).

40 Engine – complete dismantling

1   The need for dismantling will have been dictated by wear or noise in most cases. Although there is no reason why only partial dismantling cannot be carried out to renew such items as the oil pump or crankshaft rear oil seal, when the main bearings or big-end bearings

39.1A Thermostat housing hose connections on the CVH engine

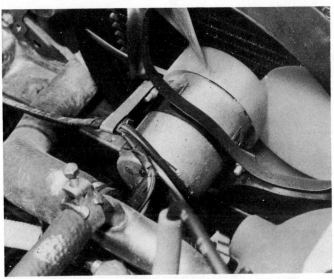

39.1B Radiator bottom hose and distribution piece on the CVH engine

39.6A Attach engine support sling to points indicated (arrowed)

39.6B Engine and transmission (CVH) lowered onto trolley for removal from underneath the car

have been knocking, and especially if the vehicle has covered a high mileage, it is recommended that a complete strip-down be carried out and every engine component examined as described in Section 41.

4   Unbolt and remove the engine bearer and mountings. Position the engine so that it is upright and safely chocked on a bench or other convenient working surface. If the exterior of the engine is very dirty it should be cleaned before dismantling, using paraffin and a stiff brush or a water-soluble solvent.

3   Remove the alternator, the mounting bracket and exhaust heat shield, and the adjuster link.

4   Disconnect the heater hose from the coolant pump.

5   Drain the engine oil and remove the filter.

6   Jam the flywheel starter ring gear to prevent the crankshaft from turning and unscrew the crankshaft pulley bolt. Remove the pulley.

7   Unbolt and remove the timing belt cover (4 bolts).

8   Slacken the two bolts on the timing belt tensioner, lever the tensioner against its spring pressure and tighten the bolts to lock it in position.

9   With the belt now slack, note its running direction and mark the mating belt and sprocket teeth with a spot of quick-drying paint. This is not necessary if the belt is being renewed.

10   Disconnect the spark plug leads and remove the distributor cap complete with HT leads.

11   Unscrew and remove the spark plugs.

12   Disconnect the crankcase ventilation hose from its connector on the crankcase.

13   Remove the rocker cover.

14   Unscrew the cylinder head bolts in the reverse order to tightening (Fig. 1.73) and discard them. New bolts must be used at reassembly.

15   Remove the cylinder head, complete with manifolds.

16   Turn the engine on its side. Do not invert it as sludge in the sump may enter the oilways. Remove the sump bolts, withdraw the sump and peel off the gaskets and sealing strips.

17   Remove the bolts from the clutch pressure plate in a progressive manner until the pressure of the assembly is relieved and then remove the cover, taking care not to allow the driven plate (friction disc) to fall to the floor.

18   Unbolt and remove the flywheel. The bolt holes are offset so it will only fit one way.

19   Remove the engine adaptor plate.

20   Unbolt and remove the crankshaft rear oil seal retainer.

21   Unbolt and remove the timing belt tensioner and take out the coil spring. (This spring is not used on all models.)

22   Unbolt and remove the coolant pump.

23   Remove the belt sprocket from the crankshaft using the hands or, if tight, a two-legged puller. Take off the dished washer.

24   Unbolt the oil pump and pick-up tube and remove them as an assembly.

25   Unscrew and remove the oil pressure switch (photo).

40.25 Unscrewing the oil pressure switch

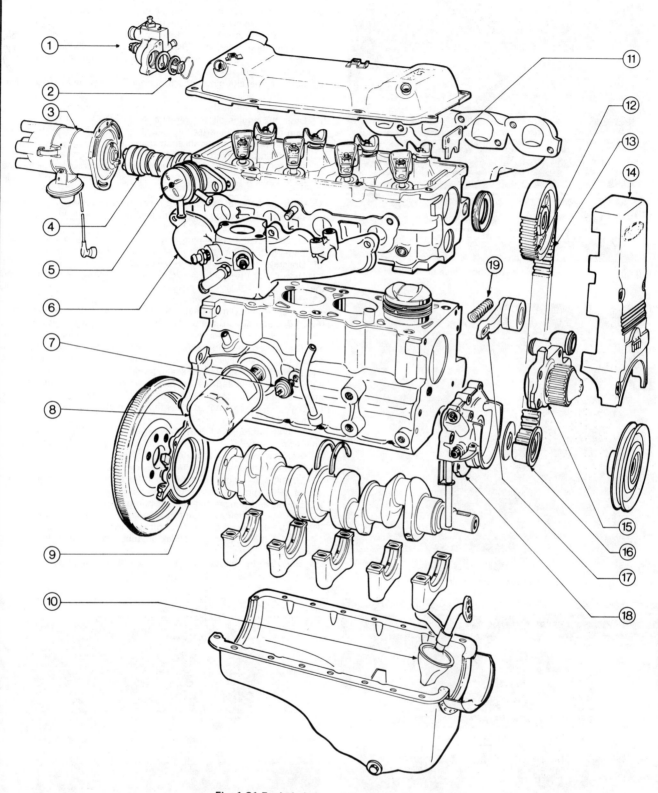

Fig. 1.81 Exploded view of the engine (Sec 40)

1	Thermostat housing	7	Oil pressure switch	11	Camshaft thrust plate	16
2	Thermostat	8	Oil filter	12	Camshaft belt sprocket	17
3	Distributor	9	Oil seal retainer	13	Timing belt	18
4	Camshaft	10	Oil pump intake pipe	14	Timing belt cover	19
5	Fuel pump		and strainer	15	Coolant pump	
6	Intake manifold					

1   Thermostat housing
2   Thermostat
3   Distributor
4   Camshaft
5   Fuel pump
6   Intake manifold

7   Oil pressure switch
8   Oil filter
9   Oil seal retainer
10 Oil pump intake pipe
     and strainer

11 Camshaft thrust plate
12 Camshaft belt sprocket
13 Timing belt
14 Timing belt cover
15 Coolant pump

16 Crankshaft belt sprocket
17 Timing belt tensioner
18 Oil pump
19 Belt tensioner spring (not
     fitted to all models)

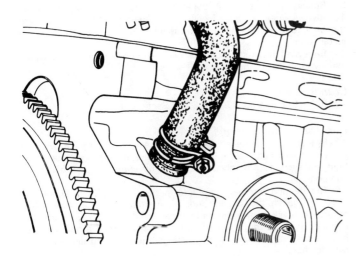

Fig. 1.82 Crankcase ventilation hose attachment (Sec 40)

Fig. 1.85 Remove the timing belt tensioner (Sec 40)

26 Turn the crankshaft so that all the pistons are half-way down the bores, and feel if a wear ridge exists at the top of the bores. If so, scrape the ridge away, taking care not to damage the bores.

27 Inspect the big-end and main bearing caps for markings. The main bearings should be marked 1 to 5 with a directional arrow pointing to the timing cover end. The big-end caps and connecting rods should have adjacent matching members towards the oil filter side of the engine. Number 1 is at the timing cover end of the engine. Make your own marks if necessary.

28 Unscrew the bolts from the first big-end cap and remove the cap. The cap is located on two roll pins, so if the cap requires tapping off make sure that it is not tapped in a sideways direction.

29 Retain the bearing shell with the cap if the shell is to be used again.

30 Push the piston/connecting rod out of the top of the cylinder block, again retaining the bearing shell with the rod if the shell is to be used again.

31 Remove the remaining pistons/rods in a similar way.

32 Remove the main bearing caps, keeping the shells with their respective caps if the shells are to be used again. Lift out the crankshaft.

33 Take out the bearing shells from the crankcase, noting the semi-circular thrust washers on either side of the centre bearing. Keep the shells identified as to position in the crankcase if they are to be used again.

34 Prise down the spring arms of the crankcase ventilation baffle and remove it from inside the crankcase just below the ventilation hose connection (Fig. 1.86).

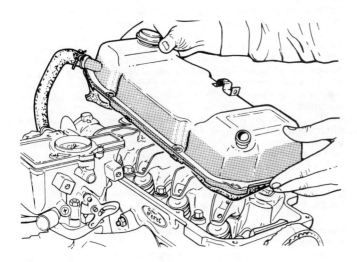

Fig. 1.83 Lift the rocker cover clear (Sec 40)

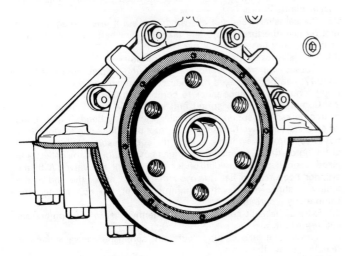

Fig. 1.84 Crankshaft rear oil seal retainer (Sec 40)

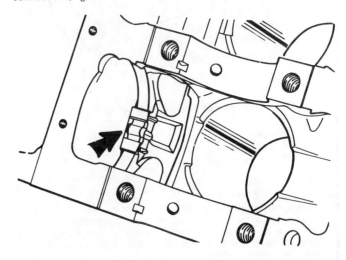

Fig. 1.86 Crankcase ventilation baffle (arrowed) (Sec 40)

35 The engine is now completely dismantled and each component should be examined, as described in the following Section, before reassembling.

41 Engine – examination and renovation

Crankshaft bearings, cylinder bores and pistons
1 Refer to paragraphs 1 to 15 of Section 18. The information applies equally to the CVH engine, except that standard sized crankshafts are unmarked and the following differences in the piston rings should be noted.
2 The top rings are coated with molybdenum. Avoid damaging the coating when fitting the rings to the pistons.
3 The lower (oil control) ring must be fitted so that the manufacturer's mark is towards the piston crown, or the groove towards the gudgeon pin. Take care that the rails of the oil control ring abut without overlapping.

Timing sprockets and belt
4 It is very rare for the teeth of the sprockets to wear, but attention should be given to the tensioner idler pulley. It must turn freely and smoothly, be ungrooved and without any shake in its bearing. Otherwise renew it.
5 Always renew the coil spring (if fitted) in the tensioner. If the engine has covered 50 000 miles (80 000 km) then it is recommended that a new belt be fitted, even if the original one appears in good condition.

Flywheel
6 Refer to paragraphs 19 to 23 of Section 18.

Oil pump
7 The oil pump is of the gear type, incorporating a crescent-shaped spacer. Although no wear limit tolerances are specified, if, on inspection, there is obvious wear between the gears or between the driven gear and the pump casing, the pump should be renewed. Similarly if a high mileage engine is being reconditioned, it is recommended that a new pump be fitted.

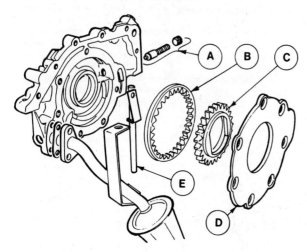

Fig. 1.87 Exploded view of the oil pump (Sec 41)

A *Relief valve*   D *Cover plate*
B *Driven gear*   E *Oil return pipe*
C *Drive gear*

Oil seals and gaskets
8 Renew the oil seals in the oil pump and in the crankshaft rear oil seal retainer as a matter of routine at time of major overhaul. It is recommended that the new seals should be drawn into these components using a nut and bolt and distance pieces, rather than tapping them into position, to avoid distortion of the light alloy castings.

9 Renew the camshaft oil seal after the camshaft has been installed.
10 Always smear the lips of a new oil seal with grease, and check that the small tensioner spring in the oil seal has not been displaced during installation.
11 Renew all gaskets by purchasing the appropriate engine set, which usually includes the necessary oil seals.

Crankcase
12 Refer to paragraphs 28 to 30 of Section 18.

Camshaft and bearings
13 Examine the camshaft gear and lobes for damage or wear. If evident, a new camshaft must be purchased, or one which has been built-up, such as are advertised by firms specializing in exchange components.
14 The bearing internal diameters in the cylinder head should be checked against the Specifications if a suitable gauge is available, otherwise check for movement between the camshaft journal and the bearing. If the bearings are proved to be worn, then a new cylinder head is the only answer as the bearings are machined directly in the cylinder head.
15 Check the camshaft endfloat by temporarily refitting the camshaft and thrust plate. If the endfloat exceeds the specified tolerance, renew the thrust plate.

Cam followers
16 It is seldom that the hydraulic type cam followers (tappets) wear in their cylinder head bores. If the bores are worn then a new cylinder head is called for.
17 If the cam lobe contact surface shows signs of a depression or grooving, grinding out the wear surface will only remove the hardened surface of the follower but may also reduce its overall length to a point where the self-adjusting capability of the cam follower is exceeded and the valve clearances are not taken up, with consequent noisy operation.
18 The cam follower can be dismantled for renewal of individual components after extracting the circlip, but after a high mileage it is probably better to renew the follower complete. After reassembly of a cam follower, do not attempt to fill it with oil but just smear the parts with a little hypoid oil during assembly.

Cylinder head and rocker arms
19 The usual reason for dismantling the cylinder head is to decarbonise and to grind in the valves. Reference should therefore be made to the next Section in addition to the dismantling operations described here.
20 Remove the intake and exhaust manifolds and their gaskets, also the thermostat housing (Chapter 2).
21 Unscrew the nuts from the rocker arms and discard the nuts. **New** ones must be fitted at reassembly.
22 Remove the rocker arms and the hydraulic cam followers, keeping them in their originally fitted sequence. Keep the rocker guide and spacer plates in order.
23 The camshaft need not be withdrawn but if it is wished to do so first remove the thrust plate and take the camshaft out from the rear of the cylinder head.
24 The valve springs should now be compressed. A standard type of compressor will normally do the job, but a forked tool (Part No 21-097) can be purchased or made up to engage on the rocker stud using a nut and distance piece to compress it (Fig. 1.88).
25 Compress the valve spring and extract the split collets. Do not overcompress the spring, or the valve stem may bend. If it is found when screwing down the compressor tool that the spring retainer does not release from the collets, remove the compressor and place a piece of tubing on the retainer so that it does not impinge on the collets and place a small block of wood under the head of the valve. With the cylinder head resting flat down on the bench, strike the end of the tubing a sharp blow with a hammer. Refit the compressor and compress the spring.
26 Extract the split collets and then gently release the compressor and remove it.
27 Remove the valve spring retainer, the spring and the valve stem oil seal. Withdraw the valve.
28 Valve removal should commence with No 1 valve (nearest timing cover end). Keep the valves and their components in their originally

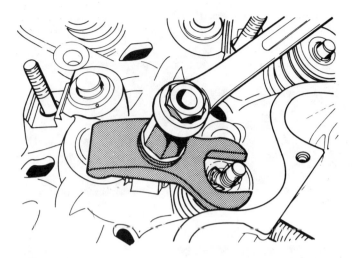

Fig. 1.88 Special valve spring compressing tool (Sec 41)

installed order by placing them in a piece of card which has holes punched in it and numbered 1 to 8.

29 To check for wear in the valve guides, place each valve in turn in its guide so that approximately one third of its length enters the guide. Rock the valve from side to side. If any more than the slightest movement is possible, the guides will have to be reamed (working from the valve seat end) and oversize stemmed valves fitted. If you do not have the necessary reamer (Tool No 21-071 to 21-074), leave this work to your Ford dealer.

30 Examine the valve seats. Normally the seats do not deteriorate, but the valve heads are more likely to burn away, in which case new valves can be ground in as described in the next Section. If the seats require recutting, use a standard cutter, available from most accessory or tool stores.

31 Renewal of any valve seat which is cracked or beyond recutting is definitely a job for your dealer or motor engineering works.

32 If the rocker arm studs must be removed for any reason, a special procedure is necessary. Warm the upper ends of the studs with a blow-lamp flame (**not** a welder) before unscrewing them. Clean out the cylinder head threads with an M10 tap and clean the threads of oil or grease. Discard the old studs and fit new ones, which will be coated with adhesive compound on their threaded portion. Screw in the studs without pausing, otherwise the adhesive will start to set and prevent the stud seating.

33 If the cylinder head mating surface is suspected of being distorted, it can be checked and surface ground by your dealer or motor engineering works. Distortion is possible with this type of light alloy head if the bolt tightening method is not followed exactly, or if severe overheating has taken place.

34 Check the rocker arm contact surfaces for wear. Renew the valve

springs if they have been in service for 50 000 miles (80 000 km) or more.

35 Commence reassembly of the cylinder head by fitting new valve stem oil seals (photo).

36 Oil No 1 valve stem and insert the valve into its guide (photo).

37 Fit the valve spring (closer coils to cylinder head), then the spring retainer (photos).

38 Compress the spring and engage the split collets in the cut-out in the valve stem (photo). Hold them in position while the compressor is gently released and removed.

39 Repeat the operations on the remaining valves, making sure that each valve is returned to its original guide or, if new valves have been fitted, into the seat into which it was ground.

40 Once all the valves have been fitted, support the ends of the cylinder head on two wooden blocks and strike the end of each valve stem with a plastic or copper-faced hammer, just a light blow to settle the components.

41 Fit the camshaft (if removed) and a new oil seal, as described in Section 28.

42 Smear the hydraulic cam followers with hypoid type transmission oil and insert them into their original bores (photo).

43 Fit the rocker arms with their guides and spacer plates, use new nuts and tighten to the specified torque. It is important that each rocker arm is installed only when its particular cam follower is at its lowest point (in contact with the cam base circle) (photos).

44 Refit the exhaust and intake manifolds and the thermostat housing, using all new gaskets.

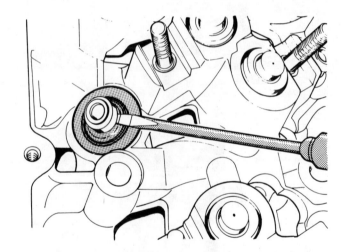

Fig. 1.89 Valve stem oil seal can be prised free (Sec 41)

41.35A Using a socket to install a valve stem oil seal

41.35B Valve stem oil seal fitted

41.35C Valve components

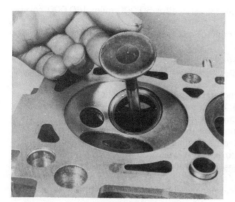

41.36 Insert valve into its guide

41.37A Locate the valve spring, ...

41.37B ... the valve spring retainer, ...

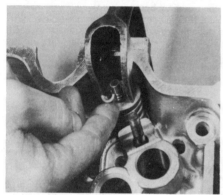

41.38 ... compress the spring and insert the split collet

41.42 Inserting a hydraulic cam follower

41.43A Fitting a rocker arm spacer plate

41.43B Fit the rocker arm and guide

41.43C Tighten rocker arm nut

42 Cylinder head and pistons – decarbonising

1   With the cylinder head removed, as described in Section 30, the carbon deposits should be removed from the combustion surfaces using a blunt scraper. Take great care as the head is of light alloy construction and avoid the use of a rotary (power-driven) wire brush.

2   Where a more thorough job is to be carried out, the cylinder head should be dismantled, as described in the preceding Section, so that the valve may be ground in, and the ports and combustion spaces cleaned and blown out after the manifolds have been removed.

3   Before grinding-in a valve, remove the carbon and deposits completely from its head and stem. With an inlet valve this is usually quite easy, simply a case of scraping off the soft carbon with a blunt knife and finishing with a wire brush. With an exhaust valve, the deposits are very much harder and those on the valve head may need a rub on coarse emery cloth to remove them. An old woodworking chisel is a useful tool to remove the worst of the valve head deposits.

4   Make sure that the valve heads are really clean, otherwise the rubber suction cup grinding tool will not stick during the grinding-in operations.

5   Before starting to grind in a valve, support the cylinder head so that there is sufficient clearance under it for the valve stem to project fully without being obstructed, otherwise the valve will not seat properly during grinding.

6   Take the first valve and apply a little coarse grinding paste to the bevelled edge of the valve head. Insert the valve into its guide and apply the suction grinding tool to its head. Rotate the tool between the palms of the hands in a back-and-forth rotary movement until the gritty action of the grinding-in process disappears. Repeat the

operation with fine paste and then wipe away all trace of grinding paste and examine the seat and bevelled edge of the valve. A matt silver mating band should be observed on both components, without any sign of black spots. If some spots do remain, repeat the grinding-in process until they have disappeared. A drop or two of paraffin applied to the contact surfaces will speed the grinding process, but do not allow any paste to run down into the valve guide. On completion, wipe away every trace of grinding paste using a paraffin-moistened cloth.

7   Repeat the operations on the remaining valves, taking care not to mix up their originally fitted sequence.

8   An important part of the decarbonising operation is to remove the carbon deposits from the piston crowns. To do this (engine in vehicle), turn the crankshaft so that two pistons are at the top of their stroke and press some grease between the pistons and the cylinder walls. This will prevent carbon particles falling down into the piston ring grooves. Plug the other two bores with rag.

9   Cover the oilways and coolant passages with masking tape and then using a blunt scraper, remove all the carbon from the piston crowns. Take great care not to score the soft alloy of the crown or the surface of the cylinder bore.

10 Rotate the crankshaft to bring the other two pistons to tdc and repeat the operations.

11 Wipe away the circles of grease and carbon from the cylinder bores.

12 Clean the top surface of the cylinder block by careful scraping.

43.1 Crankcase ventilation baffle

43 Engine – reassembly

1   With everything clean and parts renewed where necessary, commence reassembly by inserting the ventilation baffle into the crankcase. Make sure that the spring arms engage securely (photo).

2   Insert the bearing half shells into their seats in the crankcase, making sure that the seats are perfectly clean (photo).

3   Stick the semi-circular thrust washers on either side of the centre bearing with thick grease. Make sure that the oil channels face outwards (photo).

4   Oil the bearing shells and carefully lower the crankshaft into position (photos).

5   Insert the bearing shells into the main bearing caps, making sure that their seats are perfectly clean. Oil the bearings and install the caps to their correct numbered location and with the directional arrow pointing towards the timing belt end of the engine (photos).

43.2 Main bearing upper shell fitting

43.3 Locate the crankshaft thrust washer

43.4A Lubricate the main bearing shells ...

43.4B ... and install the crankshaft

43.5A Fit the bearing shells to the main bearing caps ...

43.5B ... then fit the caps, ...

43.5C ... ensuring that they are positioned correctly according to their markings ...

43.6 ... then tighten the cap bolts

43.7 Check crankshaft endfloat using a feeler gauge

6   Tighten the main bearing cap bolts to the specified torque (photo).
7   Check the crankshaft endfloat. Ideally a dial gauge should be used, but feeler blades are an alternative if inserted between the face of the thrust washer and the machined surface of the crankshaft balance web, having first prised the crankshaft in one direction and then the other (photo). Provided the thrust washers at the centre bearing have been renewed, the endfloat should be within specified tolerance. If it is not, oversize thrust washers are available (see Specifications).
8   The pistons/connecting rods should now be installed. Although new pistons will have been fitted to the rods by your dealer or supplier with the piston crown arrow or cast nipple in the piston oil cut-out pointing towards the timing belt end of the engine, the F mark on the connecting rod or the oil ejection hole in the rod big-end is as shown (Fig. 1.90).
9   Oil the cylinder bores and install the pistons/connecting rods, as described in Section 33.
10 Fit the oil pressure switch and tighten.
11 Before fitting the oil pump, action must be taken to prevent damage to the pump oil seal from the step on the front end of the crankshaft. First remove the Woodruff key and then build up the front end of the crankshaft using adhesive tape to form a smooth inclined surface to permit the pump seal to slide over the step without turning back its lip or displacing the seal spring during installation (photo).
12 If the oil pump is new, pour some oil into it before installation in order to prime it and rotate its driving gear a few turns (photo).
13 Align the pump gear flats with those on the crankshaft and install the oil pump, complete with new gasket. Tighten the bolts to the specified torque (photos).
14 Remove the adhesive tape and tap the Woodruff key into its groove (photo).

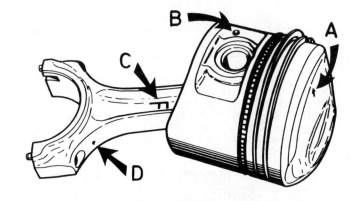

Fig. 1.90 Piston/connecting rod orientation (Sec 43)

A Arrow points towards timing belt end
B Cast nipple position
C Cast F mark on connecting rod
D Oil ejection hole

15 Bolt the oil pump pick-up tube into position (photos).
16 To the front end of the crankshaft, fit the dished thrust washer (belt guide) so that its concave side is towards the pump (photo).
17 Fit the crankshaft belt sprocket. If it is tight, draw it into position using the pulley bolt and a distance piece. Make sure that the belt

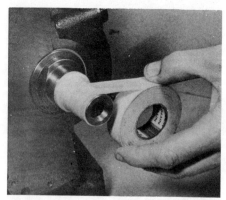

43.11 Tape the front end of the crankshaft to protect the oil pump seal when fitting

43.12 Prime the oil pump

43.13A Oil pump ready for fitting

43.13B Tighten the oil pump retaining bolts

43.14 Insert the crankshaft Woodruff key

43.15A Locate the oil pump pick-up tube ...

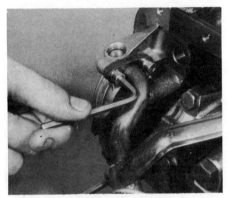
43.15B ... and fit the retaining bolts

43.16 Locate the thrust washer ...

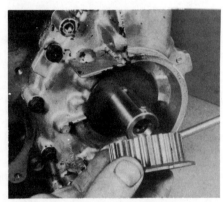
43.17 ... then the crankshaft timing belt sprocket

43.18A Fit the coolant pump ...

43.18B ... and tighten its retaining bolts

43.20 Locate the crankshaft rear oil seal and retainer

retaining flange of the sprocket is towards the front of the crankshaft and the nose of the shaft has been smeared with a little grease before fitting (photo).

18 Install the coolant pump using a new gasket and tightening the bolts to the specified torque (photos).

19 Fit the timing belt tensioner and its coil spring (where fitted). Lever the tensioner fully against the spring pressure and temporarily tighten the bolts.

20 Using a new gasket, bolt on the rear oil seal retainer, which will have been fitted with a new oil seal and the seal lips greased (photo).

21 Engage the engine adaptor plate on its locating dowels and then offer up the flywheel. It will only go on in one position as it has offset holes. Insert new bolts and tighten to the specified torque. The bolts are pre-coated with thread sealant (photos).

22 Fit the clutch and centralise it (refer to Chapter 5).

23 With the engine resting on its side (not inverted unless you are quite sure that the pistons are not projecting from the block), fit the sump, gaskets and sealing strips, as described in Section 32.

24 Fit the cylinder head, as described in Section 30, using **new** bolts. Refit the manifolds (photos).

25 Install and tension the timing belt, as described in Section 27.

26 Using a new gasket, fit the rocker cover. Tighten the cover retaining bolts to the specified torque.

27 Reconnect the crankcase ventilation hoses between the rocker cover and the crankcase.

28 Screw in a new set of spark plugs, correctly gapped, and tighten

43.21A Locate the engine adaptor plate ...

43.21B ... followed by the flywheel

43.21C Flywheel bolts are pre-coated with thread sealant

43.21D Tighten the flywheel bolts

43.24A Refit the exhaust manifold ...

43.24B ... and hot air ducting

43.24C Engine lift hook is fitted with the intake manifold

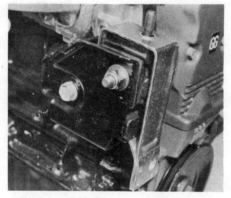

43.32 Engine mounting unit – right-hand rear

to the specified torque – this is important. If the specified torque is exceeded, the plugs may be impossible to remove.

29 Fit the timing belt cover.

30 Fit the crankshaft pulley (if not done already) and tighten the bolt to the specified torque while the flywheel ring gear is locked to prevent it from turning.

31 Smear the sealing ring of a new oil filter with a little grease, and screw it into position using hand pressure only.

32 Install the engine mounting brackets, if removed (photo).

33 Refit the ancillaries. The alternator bracket and alternator (Chapter 19), the fuel pump (Chapter 3), the thermostat housing (Chapter 2), and the distributor (Chapter 4).

34 Fit the distributor cap and reconnect the HT leads.

35 Check the tightness of the oil drain plug and insert the dipstick.

44 Engine/transmission – reconnection and refitting

1 This is a direct reversal of removal and separation of the engine from the transmission. Take care not to damage the radiator or front wings during installation.

Reconnection

2 Check that the clutch driven plate has been centralised, as described in Chapter 5.

3 Make sure that the engine adaptor plate is correctly located on its positioning dowels.

4 Smear the splines of the transmission input shaft with a little grease and then, supporting the weight of the transmission, connect it

to the engine by passing the input shaft through the splined hub of the clutch plate until the transmission locates on the dowels.

5   Refit the flange bolts and locate the engine bearer and mounting brackets with the stay rod (photos). Tighten the bolts.

6   Refit the intermediate driveshaft, as described in Chapter 7.

Refitting

7   The refitting procedures are similar to those given for the ohv engine in Section 21 of this Chapter.

8   Once the engine and transmission units are raised and their mountings are secured, the lift sling can be disconnected and the driveshaft reconnected. Insert the driveshaft socket-head securing bolts, together with the link washers, and tighten them to their specified torque wrench setting (Chapter 7).

9   Reconnect the gearchange rod and stabilizer rod, adjusting them as described in paragraphs 12 to 15 in Section 21 of this Chapter.

10   Once the engine is running, check the timing, idle speed and mixture adjustment (refer to Chapters 3 and 4).

44.5B Opposing engine/transmission mounting bracket

44.5A Engine/transmission bearer mounting bracket and stay rod

11   If a number of new internal components have been installed, run the vehicle at a restricted speed for the first few hundred miles to allow time for the new components to bed in. It is also recommended that, with a new or rebuilt engine, the engine oil and filter be changed at the end of the running-in period.

45   Fault diagnosis – CVH engine

Refer to Section 22 but ignore all reference to mechanical type contact breaker points

Rough engine idling or misfiring may also be caused on CVH engines by a slack or worn timing belt which has jumped a sprocket tooth.

A certain amount of 'chatter' is normal when starting an engine with hydraulic valve lifters, but the noise should disappear as the lifters fill with oil.

Chapter 2
Cooling, heating and ventilation systems

Contents

Coolant mixtures – general	4	Heater – removal and refitting	16
Coolant pump (CVH engine) – removal and refitting	9	Heater controls – adjustment	13
Coolant pump (ohv engine) – removal and refitting	8	Heater controls (Base and L) – removal and refitting	14
Cooling system – draining, flushing and refilling	3	Heater controls (Ghia and XR2) – removal and refitting	15
Drivebelt – removal, refitting and tensioning	10	Heating and ventilation system – description	12
Expansion tank – removal and refitting	11	Radiator – removal, repair and refitting	7
Fault diagnosis – cooling system	18	Radiator fan – removal and refitting	6
Fault diagnosis – heating and ventilating system	19	Routine maintenance – cooling system	2
General description	1	Thermostat – removal, testing and refitting	5
Heater – dismantling and reassembly	17		

Specifications

System type .... Radiator with expansion tank, belt-driven coolant pump and electric radiator fan. Semi-pressurised system on 1.0 and 1.1 engines; fully pressurised on 1.3 and 1.6 engines

Radiator

Type .... Crossflow, fin on tube
Pressure cap rating .... 0.9 kgf/cm^2 (13 lbf/in^2)

Thermostat

Type .... Wax
Opening temperature .... 85° to 89°C (185° to 192°F)
Fully open temperature .... 99° to 102°C (210° to 216°F)

Coolant pump

Type .... Centrifugal with vee belt drive (ohv) or driven from toothed timing belt (CVH)
Drivebelt tension (ohv) .... 12.5 mm (0.5 in) total deflection at centre of longest run

Capacity (including heater)

1.0 and 1.1 litre engines .... 5.5 litres (9.7 Imp pints)
1.3 litre engine .... 6.3 litres (11.1 Imp pints)
1.6 litre engine .... 8.0 litres (14.1 Imp pints)

Antifreeze

Recommended concentration (UK)	45% by volume
Type	To Ford specification SSM 97B 9103A

Torque wrench settings

	Nm	lbf ft
Coolant pump bolts	8	6
Radiator mounting bolts	8	6
Thermostat housing bolts:		
ohv	19	14
CVH	8	6
Coolant pump pulley bolts (ohv)	8	6
Fan shroud-to-radiator bolts	8	6
Fan motor-to-shroud nuts	4	3
Radiator drain plug	1.5	1.1

1 General description

The cooling system on all models consists of a radiator, a coolant pump, a thermostat and an electrically-operated radiator fan. The system is pressurised and incorporates an overflow container.

The system used on the ohv engine differs from that used on the CVH engine in layout and location of components. The coolant pump on the ohv engine is driven by the alternator drivebelt, while the pump on the CVH engines is driven by the toothed timing belt.

The cooling system operates in the following way. When the coolant is cold, the thermostat is shut and coolant flow is restricted to the cylinder block, cylinder head, intake manifold and the vehicle interior heater matrix.

As the temperature of the coolant rises the thermostat opens, allowing initially partial and then full circulation of the coolant through the radiator.

If the vehicle is in forward motion then the inrush of air cools the coolant as it passes across the radiator. If the coolant temperature rises beyond a predetermined level, due for example to ascending a gradient or being held up in a traffic jam, then the electric fan will cut in to supplement normal cooling.

The expansion tank is of the degas type and the necessary pressure/vacuum relief valve is incorporated in the tank cap.

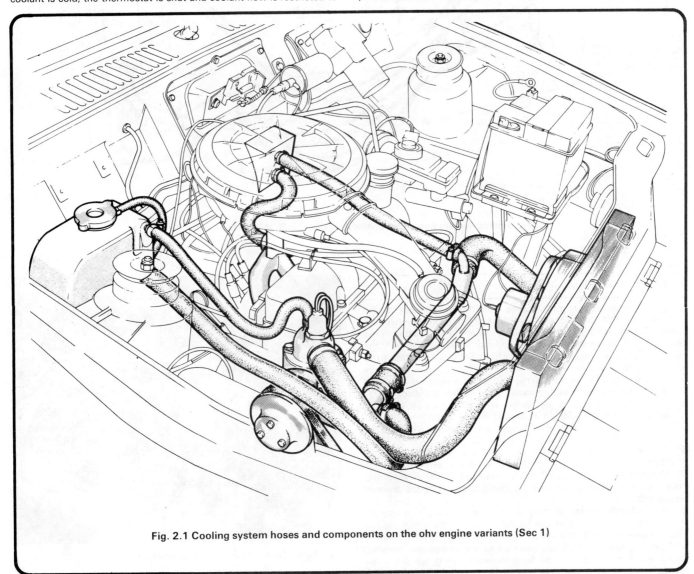

Fig. 2.1 Cooling system hoses and components on the ohv engine variants (Sec 1)

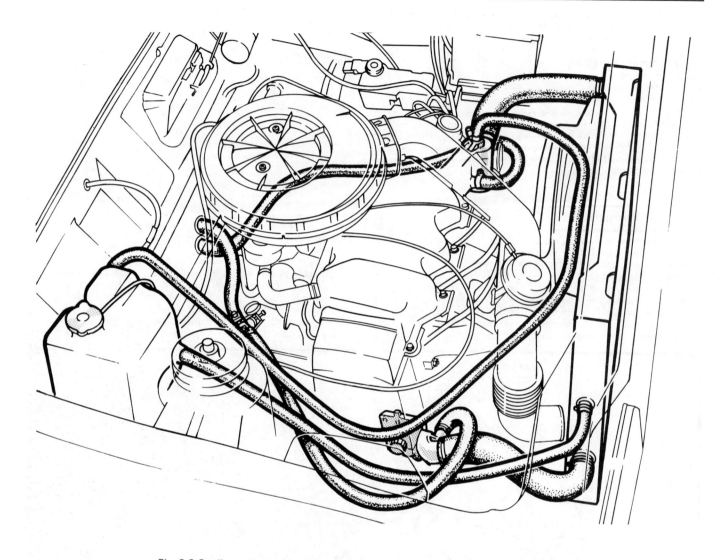

Fig. 2.2 Cooling system hoses and components on the CVH engine variants (Sec 1)

2   Routine maintenance – cooling

1   At the intervals recommended in Routine Maintenance at the beginning of this manual, visually check the coolant level in the expansion tank. If topping-up is required, use antifreeze mixture of the same strength as the original coolant used for filling the system. If the engine is hot, slowly unscrew the filler cap on the expansion tank to its safety notch position and allow the system to depressurise before fully removing the cap. Failure to observe this safety measure could result in steam escaping under high pressure and possible scalding.

2   Frequent topping-up of the system will indicate a leak, as under normal conditions the addition of coolant is a rare occurrence.

3   Regularly inspect all coolant hoses for security of clips and for evidence of deterioration of the hoses (photo).

4   At specified intervals check the tension of the coolant pump drivebelt (ohv engines only) and adjust if necessary (see Chapter 10).

5   On CVH engines, no attention will be needed to the coolant pump drive alone as on these engines the pump is driven by the toothed timing belt.

6   If the electric radiator cooling fan has not been heard to operate for some time, a simple test can be carried out to check that the fan motor is serviceable. Switch on the ignition and pull the lead from the temperature sensor which is screwed into the thermostat housing. Bridge the two contacts of the lead connecting plug, when the fan should operate. Although this test does not of course prove the

2.3 Check cooling system hoses for condition and security

function of the temperature switch, the switch is unlikely to be faulty if there has been an indication of normal temperature during the preceding period of motoring.

7 Renew the coolant (antifreeze) mixture at the intervals specified in Routine Maintenance.

Safety note

8 Take particular care when working under the bonnet with the engine running, or ignition switched on, on vehicles fitted with a temperature-controlled radiator cooling fan. As the coolant temperature rises the fan may suddenly actuate so make sure that ties, clothing, hair and hands are away from the fan. Remember that the coolant temperature will continue to rise for a short time after the engine is switched off.

3 Cooling system – draining, flushing, refilling

1 It is preferable to drain the system when the coolant is cold. If it must be drained when hot, release the pressure cap very slowly, having first covered it with a cloth to avoid any possibility of scalding.
2 Set the heater control to maximum heat position.
3 Place a container under the radiator and release the bottom hose or, where fitted, unscrew the radiator drain plug and allow the system to drain into the container. If the coolant mixture is known to be of the correct ratio and it is not due for renewal it can be saved for re-use.
4 Provided the coolant is of the correct antifreeze mixture then no flushing should be necessary and the system can be refilled immediately as described below.
5 Where the system has been neglected however, and rust or sludge is evident at draining, then the system should be flushed through with a cold water hose inserted into the thermostat housing (thermostat removed – see Section 5) until the water flows clean from the disconnected bottom hose and the radiator.
6 In severe cases, the drain plug on the cylinder block can be unscrewed to assist sludge removal and flushing. On CVH models there is no drain plug on the cylinder block so you will need to detach the bottom hose (photo).
7 If the radiator is suspected of being clogged, remove it and reverse flush it, as described in Section 7.
8 When the coolant is being changed, it is recommended that the overflow pipe is disconnected from the expansion tank and the coolant drained from the tank. If the interior of the tank is dirty, remove it and thoroughly clean it out. Evidence of oil within the expansion tank may indicate a leaking cylinder head gasket.
9 Reconnect the radiator and expansion tank hoses, and refit the cylinder block drain plug (if removed), or connect the bottom hose (CVH), as applicable.
10 Using the correct antifreeze mixture, fill the system through the thermostat housing filler neck slowly until the coolant is nearly overflowing. Wait a few moments for trapped air to escape and add more coolant. Repeat until the level does not drop and refit the cap.

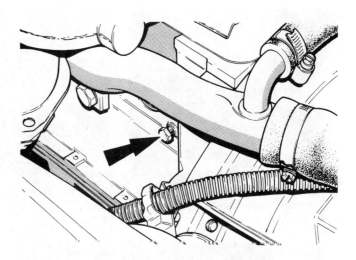

Fig. 2.4 Cylinder block drain plug location on the ohv engine (Sec 3)

3.6 Bottom hose connection to coolant pump – CVH engine

11 Pour similar strength coolant into the expansion tank up to the level marked and fit the cap. Start the engine and run it to normal operating temperature. Once it has cooled, check and carry out any final topping-up to the expansion tank **only**.

4 Coolant mixtures – general

1 Never operate the vehicle with plain water in the cooling system. Apart from the danger of freezing during winter conditions, an important secondary purpose of antifreeze is to inhibit the formation of rust and to reduce corrosion. This is particularly important with the CVH engine which has an alloy cylinder head.
2 Use a reliable brand of antifreeze with a glycol base – never one containing methanol which will evaporate during use.
3 Renew the coolant at the specified intervals. Although the antifreeze properties of the coolant will remain indefinitely, the effectiveness of the rust and corrosion will gradually weaken.
4 Even in climates where antifreeze is not required, never use plain water but use one of the branded inhibitors available.
5 A percentage of 45 to 50% antifreeze will protect the system adequately against all danger from frost, rust and corrosion.

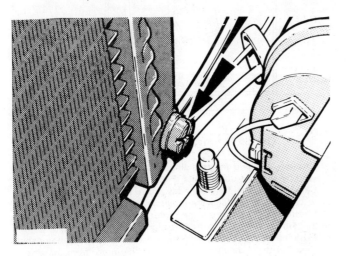

Fig. 2.3 Radiator drain plug (arrowed) (Sec 3)

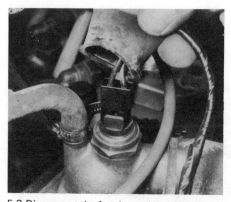

5.3 Disconnect the fan thermal switch lead – ohv engine

5.4A Thermostat housing and retaining bolts – CVH engine

5.4B Thermostat retaining clip – CVH engine

5.4C Remove the thermostat ...

5.4D ... and seal ring – CVH engine

5.7 Thermostat refitted (CVH engine) with new hoses and clips

5 Thermostat – removal, testing and refitting

1   Drain the cooling system, as described in Section 3.
2   Loosen the retaining clips and detach the degas and radiator top hoses from the thermostat housing. On the CVH engine, also detach the heater hoses.
3   Disconnect the lead from the thermal switch on the thermostat housing (photo).
4   Unscrew and remove the retaining bolts, then lift clear the thermostat housing.
5   Prise free and lift out the thermostat, noting its orientation. On the CVH engine, detach the circlip to allow the thermostat to be removed together with its O-ring (photos).
6   To test the thermostat, first check that in a cold condition its valve plate is closed. Suspend it in a pan of water and gradually heat the water; at or near boiling the valve plate should be fully open. A more accurate assessment of the opening and closing points of the thermostat can be made if a suitable thermometer is placed in the water and results compared with the temperatures given in the Specifications. Check that the thermostat closes again as the water cools down.
7   Refitting is a reversal of removal. Always use a new gasket and apply a little jointing compound to the threads of the thermostat housing bolts before screwing them in. Use new hoses and clips where necessary (photo).

6 Radiator fan – removal and refitting

1   Disconnect the battery.
2   Pull the wiring connector plug from the rear of the fan motor and unclip the wiring from the fan cowl.

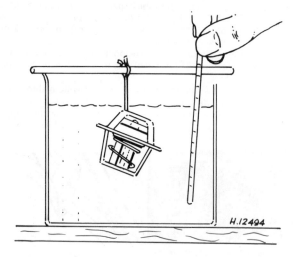

Fig. 2.5 Thermostat check method (Sec 5)

3   Unscrew the two fan retaining bolts from the base of the cowl, followed by the two upper bolts (Fig. 2.7).
4   Carefully lift the fan assembly from the engine compartment, taking care not to damage the radiator.
5   If removing the fan from the motor shaft, first mark their relative fitted positions to ensure correct realignment on assembly.
6   Extract the retaining clip and take off the fan from the motor shaft.
7   Unscrew the three nuts and separate the motor from the shroud.
8   Reassembly and refitting are reversals of the removal and dismantling operations.

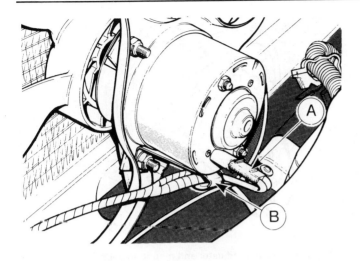

Fig. 2.6 Radiator fan wiring connector (A) and wire retaining clip (B) (Sec 6)

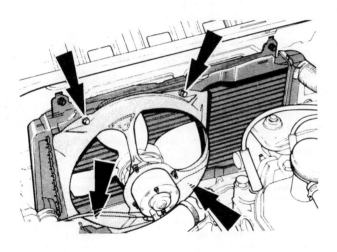

Fig. 2.7 Radiator fan shroud securing bolts (arrowed) (Sec 6)

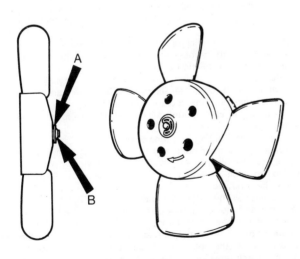

Fig. 2.8 Radiator fan retaining washer (A) and clip (B) (Sec 6)

7 Radiator – removal, repair and refitting

1   Drain the cooling system, as described in Section 3. Retain the coolant if it is fit for further service.

2   Release the retaining clips and disconnect all the hoses from the radiator (photos).

3   Disconnect the wiring plug from the rear of the radiator fan motor.

4   Unscrew and remove the two mounting bolts (photo) and carefully lift the radiator, complete with cowl and fan, from the engine compartment (photo). The base of the radiator is held in place by lugs.

5   If the purpose of removal was to thoroughly clean the radiator, first reverse flush it with a cold water hose. The normal coolant flow is from left to right (from the thermostat housing to the radiator) through the matrix and out of the opposite side.

6   If the radiator fins are clogged with flies or dirt, remove them with a soft brush or blow compressed air from the rear face of the radiator. It is recommended that the fan assembly is first removed, as described in the preceding Section. In the absence of a compressed air line, a strong jet from a water hose may provide an alternative method of cleaning.

7   If the radiator is leaking, it is recommended that a reconditioned or new one is obtained from specialists. Home repairs are seldom

7.2A Disconnect the radiator top hose, ...

7.2B ... the bottom hose and expansion tank hose

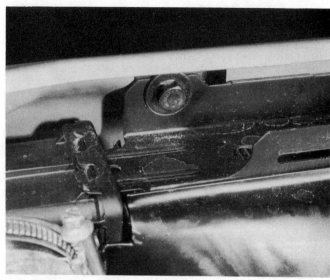

7.4A Radiator mounting bolt

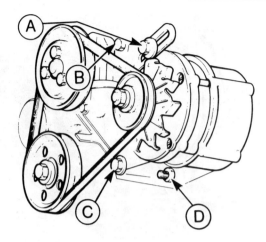

Fig. 2.9 Alternator adjuster and mounting bolts – ohv engine
(Sec 8)

A Adjuster link clamp bolt	C Lower front mounting bolt
B Adjuster link-to-block bolt	D Lower rear mounting bolt

4   Disconnect the coolant hose from the pump. Remove the previously slackened pulley bolts and take off the pulley.
5   Unbolt the coolant pump and remove it.
6   Peel away the old gasket from the engine block and clean the surface.
7   No provision is made for repair and if the pump is leaking or noisy it should be renewed.
8   Refitting is a reversal of removal. Use a new gasket, smeared with jointing compound, and apply the same compound to the threads of the fixing bolts. Tighten the bolts to the specified torque.
9   Adjust the drivebelt tension, as described in Section 10, and refill the cooling system.

9 Coolant pump (CVH engine) – removal and refitting

1   Drain the cooling system, as described in Section 3.
2   Release the alternator mountings and adjuster strap bolt, push the alternator in towards the engine and slip the drivebelt from the pulley.
3   Apply a spanner to the crankshaft pulley bolt and turn the crankshaft until the notch on the pulley is opposite the tdc mark on the belt cover scale.
4   Remove the timing belt cover and check that the camshaft and the crankshaft sprockets are aligned with their timing marks (see Chapter 1). This will prove that No 1 piston is at tdc, not No 4 piston. If the marks are not aligned, turn the crankshaft through another complete turn.
5   Using a spot of quick-drying paint, mark the teeth of the belt and their notches on the sprockets so that the belt can be re-engaged in its original position in relation to the sprocket teeth.
6   Slacken the belt tensioner bolts and slide the tensioner to relieve the tautness of the belt, then slip the belt from the crankshaft sprocket, tensioner pulley and the coolant pump sprocket.
7   Release the clamps and disconnect the hoses from the coolant pump.
8   Remove the timing belt tensioner.
9   Unscrew the four bolts and remove the coolant pump from the engine cylinder block.
10 No provision is made for repair and if the pump is leaking or noisy it must be renewed.
11 Clean away the old gasket and ensure that the mating surfaces of the pump and block are perfectly clean.
12 Position a new gasket (on the cylinder block) which has been smeared both sides with jointing compound. Offer up the coolant pump, screw in the bolts and tighten to the specified torque.
13 Fit the belt tensioner, but with the mounting bolts only screwed in loosely.
14 Reconnect and tension the timing belt as described in Chapter 1, Section 27.

7.4B Radiator and fan unit

successful. If the radiator, due to neglect, requires the application of chemical cleaners, then these are best used when the engine is hot and the radiator is in the vehicle. Follow the manufacturer's instructions precisely and appreciate that there is an element of risk in the use of most de-scaling products, especially in a system which incorporates alloy and plastic materials.
8   Refit the radiator by reversing the removal operations, but make sure that the rubber lug insulators at its base are in position.
9   Fill the system, as described in Section 3.

8 Coolant pump (ohv engine) – removal and refitting

1   Drain the cooling system, as described in Section 3.
2   Release the coolant pump pulley bolts now while the drivebelt is still in position. Any tendency for the pulley to turn as the bolts are unscrewed can be restrained by depressing the top run of the belt.
3   Release the alternator mounting and adjuster link bolts, push the alternator in towards the engine and slip the drivebelt from the coolant pump pulley.

15 Refit the timing belt cover.
16 Fit the alternator drivebelt and tension it, as described in the next Section.
17 Reconnect the coolant hoses to the pump and the bottom hose to the radiator.
18 Fill the cooling system, as described in Section 3.

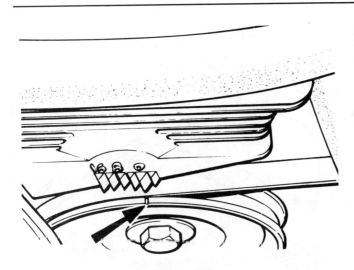

Fig. 2.10 Timing marks – CVH engine (Sec 9)

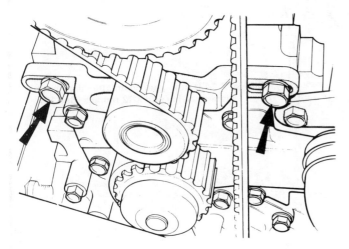

Fig. 2.11 Slacken the timing belt tensioner bolts (arrowed) (Sec 9)

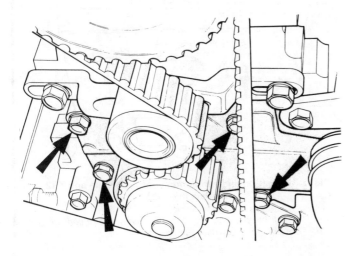

Fig. 2.12 Coolant pump unit retaining bolts (arrowed) (Sec 9)

10 Drivebelt – removal, refitting and tensioning

1 A conventional vee drivebelt is used to drive the alternator and coolant pump pulleys on ohv engines, and the alternator pulley on CVH engines, power being transmitted from a pulley on the front end of the crankshaft.
2 To remove a belt, slacken the alternator mounting bolts and the bolts on the adjuster link, push the alternator in towards the engine and slip the belt from the pulleys.
3 Fit the belt by slipping it over the pulley rims while the alternator is still loose on its mountings. Never be tempted to remove or fit a belt by pricing it over a pulley without releasing the alternator. Either the pulley will be damaged or the alternator or coolant pump will be distorted.
4 To retension the belt, pull the alternator away from the engine until the belt is fairly taut and nip up the adjuster strap bolt. Check that the total deflection of the belt is 12.5 mm (0.5 in) at the mid point of its longest run. A little trial and error may be required to obtain the correct tension. If the belt is too slack, it will slip and soon become glazed or burnt and the coolant pump (ohv) and alternator will not perform correctly, with consequent overheating of the engine and low battery charge. If the belt is too tight, the bearings in the alternator and/or coolant pump will soon be damaged.
5 **Do not** lever against the body of the alternator to tension the belt or damage may occur.

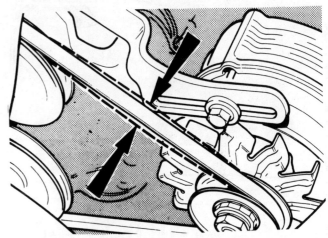

Fig. 2.13 Drivebelt tension checking point (Sec 10)

11 Expansion tank – removal and refitting

1 If the coolant in the system is hot, release the pressure cap slowly having covered it with a cloth to avoid any possibility of scalding.
2 Position a suitable container beneath the expansion (degas) tank then loosen the tank hoses and drain the coolant from the tank.
3 Disconnect the overflow pipe from the filler neck on the expansion tank.
4 Unscrew and remove the retaining screw and withdraw the expansion tank.
5 Refit in the reverse order to removal and top up the cooling system, as described in Section 3.

12 Heating and ventilation system – description

The heater is of the type which utilizes waste heat from the engine coolant. The coolant is pumped through the matrix in the heater casing

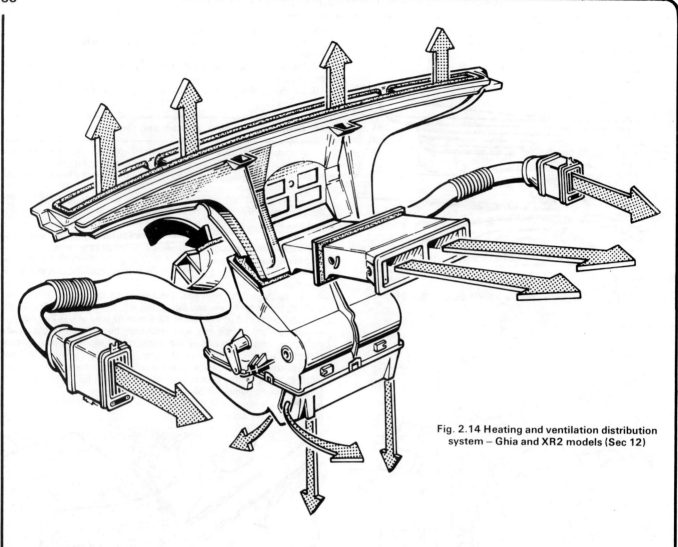

Fig. 2.14 Heating and ventilation distribution
system – Ghia and XR2 models (Sec 12)

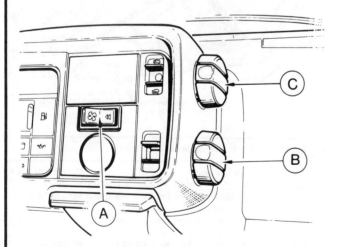

Fig. 2.15 Heating and ventilation controls – Base and L models
(Sec 12)

Left-hand drive shown

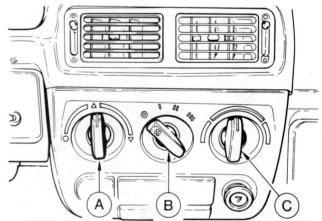

Fig. 2.16 Heating and ventilation controls – Ghia and XR2
models (Sec 12)

A *Air distribution control*   C *Temperature control*
B *Three-stage fan switch*

where air, force-fed by a duplex radial fan, disperses the heat into the vehicle interior.

Fresh air enters the heater or the ventilator ducts through the grille at the rear of the bonnet lid. Air is extracted from the interior of the vehicle through outlets at the rear edges of the doors.

There are differences between the heater used on Base and L models and other versions in the Fiesta range. On Base and L models, a two-speed fan switch is used instead of the three-position switch used on other versions. On all models, except the Base and L versions, central and side window vents are incorporated in the facia panel.

The heater/ventilator controls are of rotating knob type, operating through cables to flap valves which deflect the air flowing through the heater both to vary the temperature and to distribute the air between the footwell and demister outlets.

13 Heater controls – adjustment

1   The heater control cables are adjusted from the control unit.
2   Move the controls to their top and bottom stops to set the adjustment. When moving the controls to the stop positions, a considerable amount of resistance will be felt.

14 Heater controls (Base and L) – removal and refitting

1   Disconnect the battery earth lead.
2   From inside the vehicle, remove the dash lower trim panel on each side (left and right). The panels are secured by tags and clips.
3   Remove the retaining screws and withdraw the upper steering column shroud.
4   Withdraw the ashtray from the facia panel.
5   Pull free and remove the heater and ventilation control knobs.
6   Unscrew and remove the two screws from the lower section of the instrument cluster bezel then withdraw the bezel upper section from the guide slots. Lift it clear of the control unit at the side.
7   Detach the switch lead connectors at the rear of the bezel.

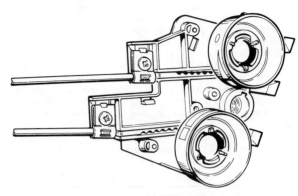

Fig. 2.18 Control unit and cable connections – Base and L models (Sec 14)

15 Heater controls (Ghia and XR2) – removal and refitting

1   Disconnect the battery earth lead.
2   Working inside the vehicle, remove the dash lower trim panel on each side (left and right). The panels are secured with clips and tags.
3   Pull and withdraw the control knobs from the three rotary switches on the control unit.
4   Unscrew and remove the four screws securing the control unit bezel and the control unit screws (Figs. 2.19 and 2.20). Carefully withdraw the control unit from the crash padding.

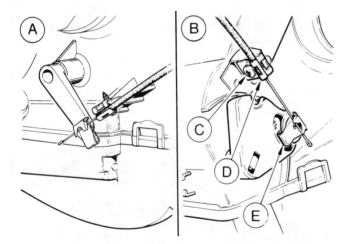

Fig. 2.17 Heater control cable connections (to heater casing) (Sec 14)

A   *Left side connection*
B   *Right side connection*
C   *Outer cable clamp screw*
D   *Plate nut*
E   *Clip*

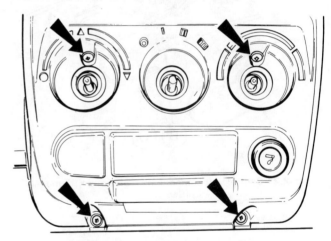

Fig. 2.19 Control unit bezel retaining screws (arrowed) – Ghia and XR2 models (Sec 15)

Fig. 2.20 Control unit retaining screws (arrowed) – Ghia and XR2 models (Sec 15)

8   At the heater casing remove the cable clamp screws and unclip the control cables.
9   Disconnect the control unit lights, then unscrew and remove the control unit, withdrawing complete with the Bowden cables.
10 Refitting is a reversal of the removal procedure. On completion adjust, as described in Section 13.

5   Disconnect the control cables from the heater unit casing by loosening the clamp screws and unclipping the cables.

6   Partially withdraw the control unit (with cables) from under the crash pad so that the fan control switch lead can be detached, then fully remove the control unit.

7   This control unit type can be dismantled by bending back the four securing lugs using a suitable screwdriver and then removing the cover. To release the Bowden cables, unscrew their clamp screws and disengage the cables from the toothed band guides. The pivots and toothed band guides can then be removed from the baseplate of the control unit.

8   Refit in the reverse order to removal and adjust the cables, as described in Section 13 when reconnecting them.

16 Heater – removal and refitting

1   Disconnect the battery earth lead.

2   To minimise the coolant loss, move the heater controls to the warm position then drain the engine coolant; saving it for re-use by emptying into a suitable container.

3   Working within the engine compartment, disconnect the coolant hoses from the heater pipe stubs at the rear bulkhead. Raise the ends of the hoses to minimise loss of any remaining coolant in the hoses.

4   The heater matrix may still contain coolant and should be drained by blowing into the upper heater pipe stub and catching the coolant which will be ejected from the lower one.

5   Remove the cover plate and gasket from around the heater pipe stubs. This is held to the bulkhead by two self-tapping screws.

6   Undo and remove the six screws retaining the cowl panel cover place in position. Move the cover plate and bonnet lock to one side, out of the way.

7   Reach through the cover plate aperture and detach the lead connector from the fan motor (Fig. 2.23).

8   Working inside the vehicle, remove the dash lower trim panels from both sides. The panels are held in position by clips and tags.

9   Disconnect the control cables from the heater casing and the flap arms.

10   Using a suitable screwdriver, unclip the cover from the heater unit, lower the cover, together with the heater matrix and remove rear end from the guide. The heater matrix can now be fully removed, but take care not to spill any remaining coolant over trim and carpets.

11   Disconnect the air distribution ducts from the heater case on the left- and right-hand sides.

12   Undo the two retaining nuts and lower the heater case unit to enable it to be withdrawn sideways from underneath the facia padding. Note that on models fitted with a central console it is first necessary to detach and remove the radial fan and console before the heater can be withdrawn.

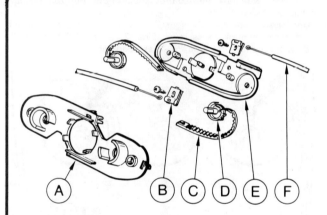

Fig. 2.21 Control unit components – Ghia and XR2 models (Sec 15)

A   Cover   D   Pivot
B   Plate nut   E   Baseplate
C   Toothed belt   F   Cable

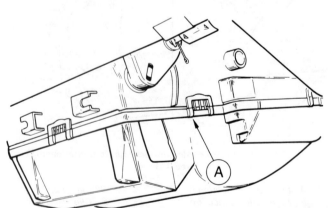

Fig. 2.23 Fan motor wiring connector (B) (Sec 16)

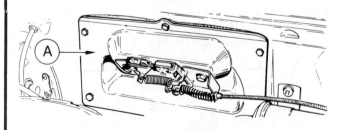

Fig. 2.22 Cowl panel cover plate (A) (Sec 16)

Fig. 2.24 Heater casing cover clips (A) (Sec 16)

13 Refitting is a reversal of removal. Check that the heater casing seal to the cowl is in good order, otherwise renew it. Adjust the heater controls on completion, as described in Section 13.

14 Top up the cooling system (Section 3) and reconnect the battery.

17 Heater – dismantling and reassembly

1 Use a sharp knife to cut through the casing gaskets in line with the casing half-joint flanges (Fig. 2.25).

2 Unclip and separate the half-casings.

3 Lift out the electric motor and fan unit.

4 If not already removed, unclip the retainers securing the matrix cover, withdraw the cover and lift the matrix from its heater case mounting.

5 The temperature and air distribution control valves can be removed by twisting them and pressing from the casing half.

6 Reassembly is a reversal of the removal procedure. When refitting the air distribution valve, rotate the operating lever so that the window and valve markings align. The valve can only be fitted in this position. (Fig. 2.27).

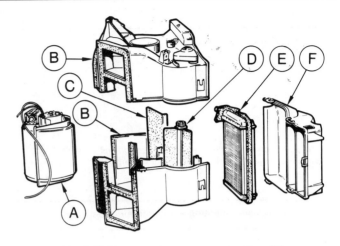

Fig. 2.26 Heater casing components (Sec 17)

A Fan
B Half-casings
C Temperature control valve
D Air distributor valve
E Matrix
F Cover

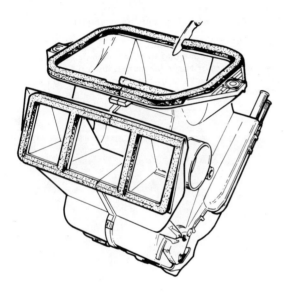

Fig. 2.25 Cut the heater casing seal gasket (Sec 17)

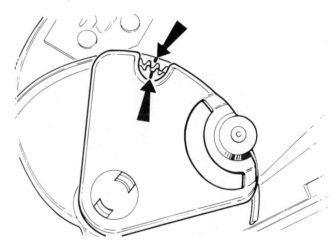

Fig. 2.27 Align the marks (arrowed) when fitting the distribution valve (Sec 17)

18 Fault diagnosis – cooling system

Symptom	Reason(s)
Heat generated in engine not being successfully disposed of by radiator	Insufficient water in cooling system Drivebelt slipping (accompanied by a shrieking noise on rapid engine acceleration) – ohv only Radiator core blocked or radiator grille restricted Bottom coolant hose collapsed, impeding flow Thermostat not opening properly Ignition timing incorrect or automatic advance malfunctioning (accompanied by loss of power and perhaps misfiring) Carburettor incorrectly adjusted (mixture too weak) Exhaust system partially blocked Oil level in sump too low Blown cylinder head gasket (water/steam being forced down the expansion tank overflow pipe under pressure) Engine not yet run-in Brakes binding
Too much heat being dispersed by radiator	Thermostat jammed open Incorrect grade of thermostat fitted allowing premature opening of valve Thermostat missing

Symptom	Reason(s)
Leaks in system	Loose clips on water hoses Top or bottom coolant hoses perished and leaking Radiator core leaking Thermostat gasket leaking Pressure cap spring worn or seal ineffective Blown cylinder head gasket (pressure in system forcing water/steam down expansion tank pipe) Cylinder wall or head cracked
Oil in expansion tank (may be ignored if slight oil deposit present initially after major overhaul or decarbonising)	Blown cylinder head gasket Cracked head or block

19 Fault diagnosis – heating and ventilating system

Symptom	Reason(s)
Lack of heat in vehicle interior, poor air distribution or demisting/defrosting capability	Thermostat faulty or of incorrect type Heater matrix blocked Coolant pump not operating due to slipping belt (ohv) or eroded impeller Incorrectly adjusted heater controls Blower motor inoperative due to blown fuse or other fault Disconnected ducts or hoses for air distribution Overcooling in cold weather by continuously running radiator fan Deteriorated seal at bonnet lid-to-air intake

Chapter 3
Fuel, exhaust and emissions control systems

Contents

Accelerator cable – removal, refitting and adjustment	9
Accelerator pedal – removal and refitting	10
Air cleaner – description	3
Air cleaner – removal and refitting	5
Air cleaner element – renewal	4
Carburettor – dismantling and reassembly (general)	12
Choke cable – removal, refitting and adjustment	11
Emissions control components – maintenance and testing	28
Emissions control components – removal and refitting	29
Emissions control system – description	27
Exhaust system – general	26
Fault diagnosis – fuel system	30
Ford IV carburettor – adjustments	14
Ford IV carburettor – description	13
Ford IV carburettor – dismantling and reassembly	16
Ford IV carburettor – removal and refitting	15
Ford VV carburettor – adjustments	18
Ford VV carburettor – description	17
Ford VV carburettor – dismantling and reassembly	20
Ford VV carburettor – removal and refitting	19
Fuel pump – testing, removal and refitting	6
Fuel tank – cleaning and repair	8
Fuel tank – removal and refitting	7
General description	1
Manifolds	25
Routine maintenance – fuel and exhaust system	2
Weber carburettor – adjustments	22
Weber carburettor – description	21
Weber carburettor – dismantling, inspection and reassembly	24
Weber carburettor – removal and refitting	23

Specifications

System type .... Rear-mounted fuel tank, mechanical fuel pump, thermostatically-controlled air cleaner and Ford or Weber carburettor

Fuel tank capacity
All models except XR2 .... 34 litres (7.5 gallons)
XR2 .... 38 litres (8.4 gallons)

Fuel grade requirement
1.0 litre .... 91 Octane (2-star)
1.1, 1.3 and 1.6 litre .... 97 Octane (4-star)

Fuel pump
Type .... Mechanical diaphragm type, camshaft driven, non-repairable

Air cleaner
Element type .... Paper, disposable
Heat sensor rating .... 26 to 30° C (79 to 86° F)

Carburettors
Ford IV .... Single venturi (IV), with manual choke, fixed jet
Ford variable venturi (VV) .... Downdraught with sonic idle circuit, coolant-heated automatic choke and anti-run-on valve

Weber dual venturi (2V) .... Fixed jet with electrically-heated automatic choke and anti-run-on valve

Application:

Engine	Carburettor number
Ford IV	
Ford VV	
1.0 litre	77BF-9510-KBA or KGA
1.1 litre	84BF-9510-KJA
1.3 litre	84SF-9510-KEA
Weber 2V	
1.6 litre	81SF-9510-AB

Ford IV carburettor timing data:
Idle speed .... 800 rpm
Idle mixture setting (CO level) 1.25%
Fast idle speed (manual choke) .... 1400 rpm
Float level setting .... 29 mm (1.14 in)
Accelerator pump stroke .... 2.0 mm (0.08 in)
Choke plate pull-down .... 3.5 mm (0.14 in)
Main jet 112

Ford VV carburettor timing data:
Idle speed (fan on) .... 750 to 850 rpm
Idle mixture setting (CO level) .... 1 to 2%
Weber 2V carburettor timing data:
Idle speed .... 775 to 825 rpm
Idle mixture setting (CO level) .... 1.0 to 1.50%
Fast idle speed (on high cam) .... 2675 to 2725 rpm
Float level setting .... 34.5 to 35.5 mm (1.35 to 1.40 in)
Choke plate pull-down .... 5.2 to 5.8 mm (0.20 to 0.23 in)
Choke phasing .... 1.5 to 2.5 mm (0.06 to 0.10 in)
Main jet 115/125
Air jet 160/150
Emulsion tube F30/F30
Idle jet 50/60

Torque wrench settings

	Nm	lbf ft
Exhaust manifold flange	35 to 40	26 to 30
Exhaust connecting flange	38 to 45	28 to 33
Carburettor flange nuts:		
Ford	19	14
Weber	20	15
Fuel pump	18	13

1 General description

The fuel system is composed of four basic components. These are the fuel tank with level indicator, the fuel pump, the carburettor and its controls, and the air cleaner.

The fuel tank is located under the floorpan beneath the rear seats. The filler neck protrudes through the left-hand side of the vehicle, while the combined outlet pipe and fuel level indicator sender unit is located on the right-hand side of the tank. A ventilation or breather pipe is located on the top of the tank.

The fuel pump on all models is a mechanical diaphragm type being driven from the camshaft. On ohv models it is mounted on the side of the cylinder block whilst on CVH models it is mounted on the side of the cylinder head and is actuated by a pushrod. The fuel pumps on both models are fully sealed units and no servicing or repairs are possible.

One of three carburettor types will be fitted: the Ford IV, Ford VV (variable venturi) or Weber.

On all models the air cleaner unit is of the disposable paper element type with an integral thermostatic air intake control. The thermostatic unit ensures that the air intake temperature is in accordance with that required, the warm air being drawn from a heat box mounted directly across the exhaust manifold; cool air being drawn through the intake in the engine compartment. The thermostat within the air cleaner body opens or closes an air control flap valve to regulate the air intake temperature as required.

A basic emission control system is fitted, and this is described in Section 27.

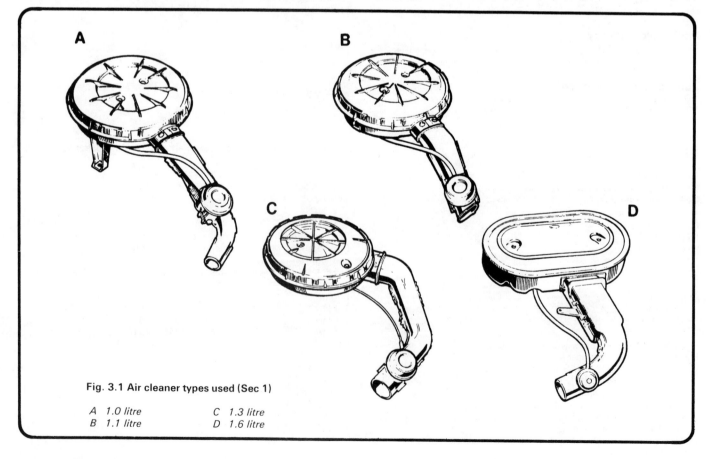

Fig. 3.1 Air cleaner types used (Sec 1)

A 1.0 litre
B 1.1 litre
C 1.3 litre
D 1.6 litre

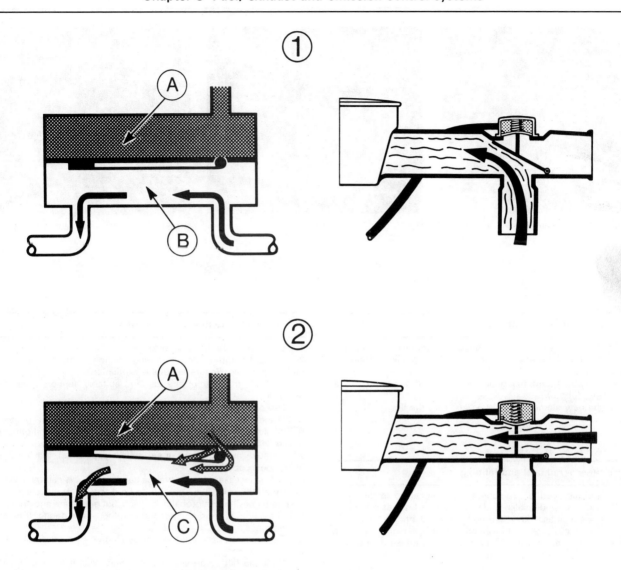

Fig. 3.2 Air cleaner intake sensor and diaphragm flap valve operating modes (Sec 1)

1 Sensor cold
2 Sensor hot

A Open to atmosphere
B Manifold vacuum

C Reduced vacuum (air bled through ball valve)

2 Routine maintenance – fuel and exhaust system

The following routine maintenance procedures must be undertaken at the specified intervals given at the start of this manual. Note that when making carburettor adjustments, the ignition system must be known to be in good condition and the timing adjustments correct as described in Chapter 4. On ohv engine variants it is also essential that the valve clearances are correctly adjusted, as described in Chapter 1.

1 **Air cleaner element:** Renew the air cleaner element at the specified intervals or sooner if the vehicle normally operates in a dirty environment. Refer to Section 4 for details.

2 **Engine idle speed:** With the engine warmed up to its normal operating temperature, connect up a tachometer and check the engine idle speed. If necessary adjust as described in the appropriate Section (14, 18 or 22 as applicable).

3 **Fuel system general check:** Make periodic checks to ensure that all fuel line connections are secure, that the fuel lines are in good condition and there are no signs of leaks from the lines, connections or the carburettor.

4 **Exhaust system general check:** Check the condition and security

of the exhaust system at the specified intervals. A leaky or severely corroded system must be repaired or renewed, as described in Section 26.

5 **Emission control system:** A basic emission control system is fitted and the system components must be checked, as described in Section 28.

3 Air cleaner – description

1 The air cleaner is of renewable paper element type, and is thermostatically-controlled to provide air at the most suitable temperature for combustion with minimum emission levels.

2 This is accomplished by drawing in both cold and hot air (from the exhaust manifold box) and mixing them. The proportion of hot and cold air is varied by the position of a deflector flap which itself is controlled by a vacuum diaphragm. The vacuum pressure is monitored by a heat sensor within the air cleaner casing to ensure that, according to the temperature requirements of the carburettor, the appropriate degree of intake manifold vacuum is applied to the air deflector flap to alter the volume of hot or cold air being admitted.

4.1 Remove the air cleaner lid screws

4.2 Air cleaner element

5.2 Air cleaner unit underside connections

4 Air cleaner element – renewal

1   To remove the air cleaner lid undo and remove the retaining screws and prise free the lid from its retaining clips around its periphery (photo).
2   Remove and discard the paper element and wipe out the air cleaner casing (photo).
3   Place the new element in position and refit the lid.

5 Air cleaner – removal and refitting

1   Undo and remove the two screws from the centre section of the cover. On 1.0 litre models also undo the support bracket screw.
2   The air cleaner assembly can now be lifted off the carburettor sufficiently far to be able to disconnect the vacuum hose, the crankcase (flame trap) emission hose and the air intake duct (photo).
3   Refit in the reverse order to removal.

6 Fuel pump – testing, removal and refitting

1   On ohv engines, the fuel pump is mounted on the cylinder block and is actuated by a lever which is in direct contact with an eccentric cam on the camshaft.
2   On CVH engines, the pump is mounted on the cylinder head and is actuated by a pushrod from an eccentric cam on the camshaft.
3   The fuel pump may be quite simply tested by disconnecting the fuel inlet pipe from the carburettor and placing its open end in a container.
4   Disconnect the LT lead from the negative terminal of the ignition coil to prevent the engine firing.
5   Actuate the starter motor. Regular well-defined spurts of fuel should be seen being ejected from the open end of the fuel inlet pipe.
6   Where this is not evident and yet there is fuel in the tank, the pump is in need of renewal. The pump is a sealed unit and cannot be dismantled or repaired.
7   To remove the pump, disconnect and plug the fuel inlet and outlet hoses at the pump and then unbolt it from the engine (photos).
8   Retain any insulating spacers and remove and discard the flange gaskets.
9   On CVH engines, withdraw the pushrod with coil spring.
10 Refitting is a reversal of removal, but use new flange gaskets. If crimped type hose clips were used originally, these will have been destroyed when disconnecting the fuel hoses. Renew them with conventional nut and screw or plastic ratchet type clips.

7 Fuel tank – removal and refitting

1   Disconnect the battery earth lead.
2   Using a length of flexible tubing, syphon as much fuel out of the tank as possible. Ensure adequate ventilation.
3   Jack up the rear of the car and suitably support it for access beneath.
4   Disconnect the flexible hoses from the sender unit.
5   Disconnect the electrical leads from the sender unit (photo).
6   While supporting the weight of the tank, unscrew and remove the four retaining nuts with flat washers (photo).
7   Remove the tank (and guard, where applicable), leaving the fuel filler pipe in position.
8   If it is necessary to remove the sender unit, this can be unscrewed from the tank using the appropriate Ford tool. Alternatively a suitable C-spanner or drift can probably be used, but great care should be taken that the flange is not damaged and that there is no danger from sparks if a hammer has to be resorted to.
9   Taking care not to damage the sealing washer, prise out the tank-to-filler pipe seal.
10 Refit the filler pipe seal, using a new seal, if there is any doubt about the condition of the old one.

6.7A Detaching hoses from fuel pump (CVH)

6.7B Fuel pump (ohv)

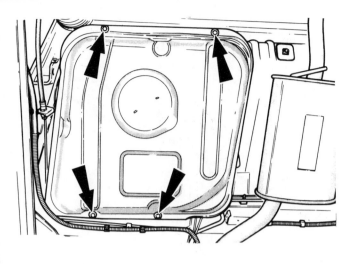

Fig. 3.3 Fuel tank retaining bolts (Sec 7)

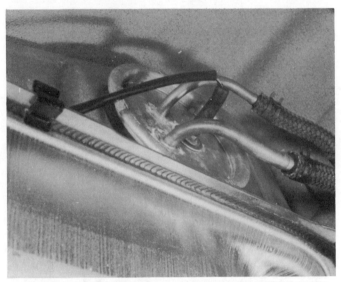

7.5 Fuel tank sender unit

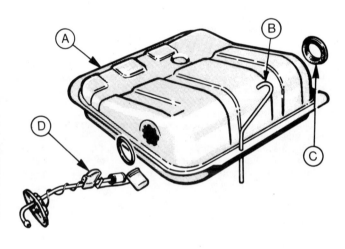

Fig. 3.4 Fuel tank components (Sec 7)

A   Tank   C   Fuel filler pipe seal
B   Ventilation hose   D   Sender unit

11   Refit the sender unit using a new seal as the original one will almost certainly be damaged.
12   The remainder of the refitting procedure is the reverse of removal. A smear of grease on the tank filler pipe exterior will aid its fitment.

8   Fuel tank – cleaning and repair

1   Remove the fuel tank from the vehicle.
2   If the tank contains sediment or water, it may be cleaned out using two or three rinses with paraffin. Shake vigorously using several changes of paraffin, but before doing so remove the sender unit (see Section 7). Allow the tank to drain thoroughly.
3   If removal of the tank was carried out in order to mend a leak, have it repaired professionally; radiator repairers will usually do this. *On no account attempt to weld or solder a fuel tank yourself.* To remove all trace of vapour requires several hours of steaming out.

9   Accelerator cable – removal, refitting and adjustment

1   Disconnect the earth lead from the battery.
2   From inside the car, detach and remove the lower dash trim panel on the driver's side.

7.6 Fuel tank retaining nut

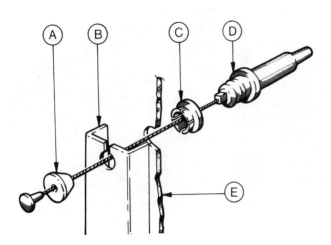

Fig. 3.5 Accelerator cable location at the pedal end (Sec 9)

A   Inner cable locating grommet   D   Outer cable
B   Pedal shaft   E   Bulkhead
C   Outer cable locating grommet

9.10 Accelerator cable adjusting sleeve (arrowed)

3   Pull the grommet from the accelerator pedal (Fig. 3.5), pull the inner cable through and unhook it from the accelerator pedal.
4   Using a suitable punch, knock out the bulkhead grommet. This will destroy the grommet, and release the outer cable.
5   Refer to Section 5 and remove the air cleaner.
6   Slide the clip from the inner cable end, and prise off the cable from the throttle shaft ball.
7   Using a suitable screwdriver, carefully prise out the cable retaining clip (Fig. 3.6). Depress the four pegs on the retainer, and pull the retainer from the mounting bracket.
8   Refitting is the reverse of this procedure.

Adjustment
9   With the air cleaner removed, jam the accelerator pedal in the fully open position, using a suitable length of wood against the seat, or a heavy weight.
10 Wind back the adjusting sleeve at the carburettor until the carburettor linkage is just in the fully open position (photo).
11 Release the pedal, then check to ensure that full throttle can be obtained.
12 Refit the air cleaner, as described in Section 5.

10 Accelerator pedal – removal and refitting

1   Disconnect the earth lead from the battery.
2   From inside the car, unclip and remove the lower dash trim panel on the driver's side.
3   Pull back the insulation panel and carpet from around the pedal.
4   Pull the grommet from the accelerator pedal, pull the inner cable through and unhook it from the accelerator pedal.
5   Unscrew and remove the pedal shaft bracket-to-bulkhead retaining bolt (Fig. 3.7).

Fig. 3.7 Pedal unit-to-bulkhead bolt (Sec 10)

6   On right-hand drive models, unscrew and remove the single retaining nut from under the wheel arch. On left-hand drive models this nut will be found on the engine side of the bulkhead. Remove the pedal.
7   Refitting is the reverse of this procedure, after which the accelerator cable adjustment should be checked, as described in Section 9.

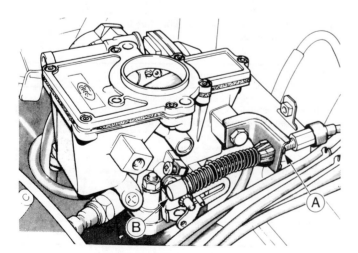

Fig. 3.6 Accelerator cable retaining clip (A) and linkage connection (B) to throttle shaft ball (Sec 9)

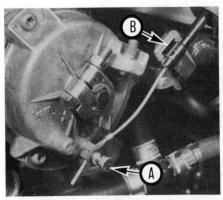

11.3 Choke cable retaining screw (A) and outer cable clip (B)

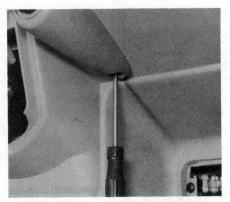

11.4A Choke control shroud screw removal

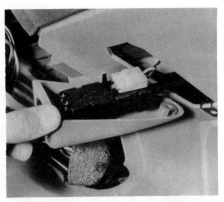

11.4B Choke control and shroud removal

11 Choke cable – removal, refitting and adjustment

1 Disconnect the earth lead from the battery.

2 Refer to Section 5 and remove the air cleaner.

3 Undo the screw securing the inner choke cable, and carefully prise out the spring clip retaining the outer cable (photo).

4 From inside the car, undo the single retaining screw and detach the cable switch mounting shroud (photos).

5 Prise free the choke cable control knob retaining clip, withdraw the knob (Fig. 3.8).

6 Extract the retaining bezel and pull the mounting shroud clear. Pull the cable and withdraw it through the engine compartment side of the bulkhead.

7 Refit in the reverse order of removal, but adjust as described below according to carburettor type.

Ford IV carburettor

8 Withdraw the choke knob to provide a clearance of 37 mm (1.45 in) between the bezel and the knob (Fig. 3.9). If possible make up a spacer to fit between the knob and bezel to maintain this distance.

9 Working at the carburettor end of the cable, measure and make a mark 22 mm (0.866 in) from the end of the inner cable using a pencil or tape. Some models have a kink or are fitted with a ferrule at this distance (Fig. 3.10).

10 Insert the cable through its location clamp so that the distance mark (kink or ferrule) butts against the inner cable clamp (photo). Hold

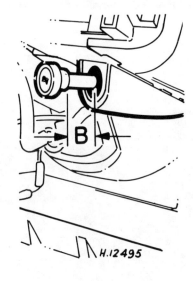

Fig. 3.9 Choke knob-to-bezel clearance during cable adjustment (Sec 11)

B = 37 mm (1.45 in)

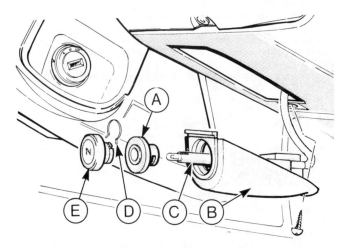

Fig. 3.8 Choke control knob components (Sec 11)

A Bezel	D Clip
B Shroud	E Knob
C Switch lever	

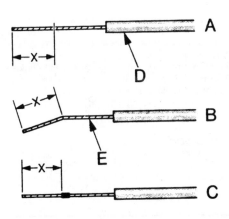

Fig. 3.10 Choke cable end types (Sec 11)

A Plain cable	D Outer cable
B Cable with kink	E Inner cable
C Cable with ferrule	X = 22 mm (0.866 in)

11.10A Locate the ferrule against clamp (arrowed) ...

11.10B ... and tighten retaining screw. Also shown is the fuel choke stop (A)

the clamp bolt with a spanner and tighten the retaining screw (photo).
11 Firmly pull on the outer cable to position the choke operating lever against the full choke stop (A in photo 11.10B) then secure the outer cable in the retaining clip.
12 With the operating lever held against the full choke stop, check that the spacer is still in position between the choke knob and bezel (or distance is as specified in paragraph 8).
13 Remove the spacer and check that the choke fully opens and closes using the choke knob.

Ford VV carburettor
14 Proceed as given in paragraphs 8 to 13 inclusive, but check that a small clearance (1.0 mm/0.04 in) exists between the choke operating lever and the off stop when the lever is released (in the off position).

12 Carburettor – dismantling and reassembly (general)

1 With time the component parts of the carburettor will wear and petrol consumption will increase. The diameter of the drillings and jets may alter due to erosion, and air and fuel leaks may develop around the spindles and other moving parts. Because of the high degree of precision involved, it is best to purchase an exchange rebuilt

carburettor. This is one of the few instances where it is better to take the latter course rather than rebuild the component itself.
2 It may be necessary to partially dismantle the carburettor to clear a blocked jet or renew a gasket. Providing care is taken there is no reason why the carburettor may not be completely reconditioned at home, but ensure a full repair kit can be obtained before you strip the carburettor down. **Never** poke out jets with wire to clean them – blow them out with compressed air or with air from a car tyre pump.

13 Ford IV carburettor – description

The carburettor is of the single venturi downdraught type, incorporating 'bypass' idling, main, power valve and accelerator pump systems. A manual, cable-operated choke is fitted, and the float chamber is externally vented.
Provision is made for throttle speed adjustment, but the mixture control screw is protected by a 'tamperproof' plastic plug which has to be destroyed to be removed. Replacement plugs can only be obtained by authorized workshops. The reason for this is to prevent adjustment of the mixture setting being carried out by persons not equipped with the necessary CO meter (exhaust gas analyser). The mixture is carefully set during production, to give the specified CO level after the initial running-in period.
The carburettor consists of two castings, the upper and lower bodies. The upper body incorporates the float chamber cover and pivot brackets, fuel inlet components, choke plate and the main and power valve system, idling system and accelerator pump discharge nozzle.
The lower body incorporates the float chamber, the throttle barrel and venturi, throttle valve components, adjustment screws, accelerator pump and distributor vacuum connections.
An anti-dieseling valve is fitted to some models, and its purpose is to shut off the idle fuel supply directly the ignition is turned off and so prevent any possibility of engine run-on.

14 Ford IV carburettor – adjustments

1 With the exception of the slow and fast idle adjustments, all of the following items can be carried out with the carburettor either on the bench or in the car.

Idle speed and mixture adjustment
2 Before carrying out the following adjustments ensure that all other engine variables ie contact breaker points gap, ignition timing, spark plug gap, valve clearances etc, have been checked and, where necessary, adjusted to their specified settings. The air cleaner must be fitted during adjustments.
3 With the engine at normal operating temperature, adjust the idle speed screw (Fig. 3.12) to obtain the specified idle speed. If available use a tachometer for this operation to ensure accuracy.
4 Adjustment of the idle mixture setting should not be attempted in territories where this may cause a violation of exhaust emission regulations. Where these regulations are less stringent the following procedure may be used.
5 Using a small screwdriver, prise out the tamperproof plug (if fitted) over the idle mixture screw.
6 If a CO meter is to be used, connect the unit according to the manufacturer's instructions.
7 Adjust the idle speed, as described in paragraph 3.
8 Run the engine at 3000 rpm for 30 seconds to clear the inlet manifold of excess fuel. Repeat this operation every 30 seconds during the adjustment procedure.
9 Turn the idle mixture screw in the desired direction to achieve the fastest possible engine speed consistent with smooth, even running; or the correct specified CO reading on the meter scale.
10 If necessary, readjust the idle speed setting.

Fast idle adjustment
11 Check and adjust the slow idle speed, then remove the air cleaner unit and check the choke plate pull-down, below.
12 With the engine warmed up, hold the choke plate fully open, operate the choke linkage as far as possible (about 1/3 of its travel) and check the fast idle speed.
13 To adjust the fast idle, bend the tag (Fig. 3.13) the required amount.

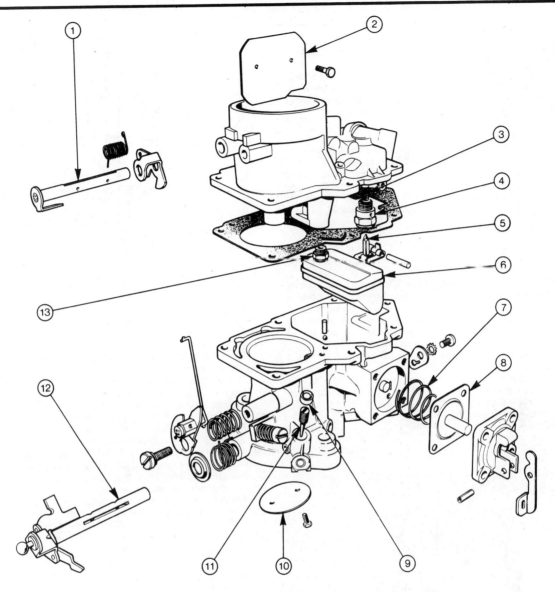

Fig. 3.11 Ford carburettor components (Secs 13 and 16)

1	Choke spindle	5 Needle valve	8 Accelerator pump diaphragm	11 Mixture screw
2	Choke plate	6 Float	9 Tamperproof plug	12 Throttle spindle
3	Fuel inlet filter	7 Pump return spring	10 Throttle plate	13 Main jet
4	Needle valve housing			

Note: *Some carburettors may have an anti-dieselling valve (idle cut-off) fitted*

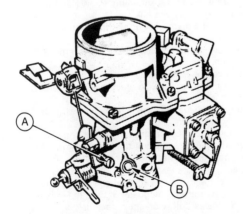

Fig. 3.12 Ford carburettor idle speed screw (A) and idle mixture screw tamperproof plug (B) (Sec 14)

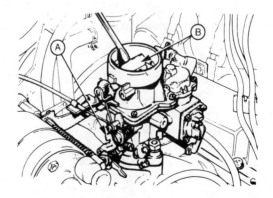

Fig. 3.13 Hold open choke plate (B) and adjust fast idle tag (A) (Sec 14)

Choke plate pull-down

14 Rotate the choke lever on the carburettor until the choke plate is fully closed.

15 Open the choke plate against the spring pressure up to its stop, then insert a gauge rod or twist drill of the specified size, as shown in Fig. 3.14. Bend the adjusting tag as necessary to give the correct dimension between the choke plate and the carburettor.

Accelerator pump stroke

16 Unscrew the throttle speed screw until it clears the linkage.

17 Depress the accelerator pump diaphragm plunger fully and then check the clearance between the end of the plunger and the operating lever (Fig. 3.15) using a gauge rod or twist drill of the specified size.

18 If necessary, bend the operating rod at the U-bend to give the correct clearance. Reset the slow idle speed, item (a) above.

Float level

19 Remove the air cleaner and disconnect the choke cable.

20 Disconnect the fuel inlet pipe and the vent pipe from the carburettor.

21 Remove the upper body securing screws, lift the upper body away, disengaging the choke link at the same time. As the upper body is withdrawn, the accelerator pump discharge valve will be exposed and, if the throttle linkage is actuated, it is possible for the valve and weight to be ejected. These components will cause serious damage to the engine if they should fall down the carburettor throat.

22 Hold the carburettor upper body vertically so that the float hangs downward.

23 Measure the distance between the bottom of the float to the mating face of the upper body (Fig. 3.16). The distance should be as specified. Note that the gasket **must** be removed.

24 Adjust as required by bending the tag A.

25 Reassembly is the reverse of dismantling.

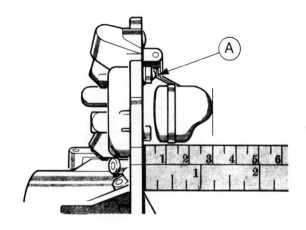

Fig. 3.16 Adjust float level by bending tag (A) (Sec 14)

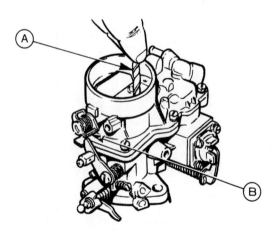

Fig. 3.14 Insert twist drill (A) and adjust pull down tag (B) (Sec 14)

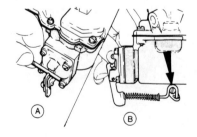

Fig. 3.15 Insert twist drill (A) and bend U-link – arrowed (B)
(Sec 14)

15 Ford IV carburettor – removal and refitting

1 Open the bonnet, disconnect the earth lead from the battery and remove the air cleaner, as described in Section 5.

2 Pull off the retaining clip and prise the accelerator cable off the throttle lever ball.

3 Slacken the inner choke cable clamp screw and prise out the outer cable retaining clip. Free the choke cable from the carburettor.

4 Pull off the distributor vacuum pipe and the fuel vent pipe.

5 If a crimp type clamp is fitted to the fuel inlet pipe, it should be cut off, and a screw type clamp fitted. If a screw type clamp is fitted, slacken the screw, then pull off the fuel feed pipe.

6 Remove the two nuts that secure the carburettor flange and remove the nuts and spring washers.

7 Carefully lift away the carburettor and its gasket, remembering that the float chamber is still full of petrol.

8 Refitting is the reverse of this procedure noting the following points:

    (a) Remove all traces of the old carburettor gasket, clean the mating flanges and fit a new gasket

    (b) Check for correct adjustment of the accelerator and choke cables, as described in Sections 9 and 11

16 Ford IV carburettor – dismantling and reassembly

1 Clean the exterior of the carburettor with a water soluble solvent. Clear a suitable area of the workbench in order to lay out the components as they are removed. Refer to Fig. 3.11 as necessary.

2 Unscrew the seven retaining screws and lift off the upper body, disconnecting the choke link.

3 Remove the pivot pin and withdraw the float and fuel inlet needle valve assembly (Fig. 3.17).

4 Unscrew the needle valve seat and remove it, together with the filter screen.

5 Remove the main jet.

6 Invert the lower body to eject the accelerator pump ball valve and weight.

7 Do not dismantle the choke valve plate or spindle unless absolutely necessary.

8 Remove the accelerator pump cover and disengage the cover from the operating link. Withdraw the diaphragm and return spring.

9 Do not dismantle the throttle valve plate unless absolutely essential.

10 Unscrew and remove the throttle speed screw.

11 It is not normally suggested that the mixture control screw is removed unless full workshop facilities including an exhaust gas analyser are available, and a new tamperproof plug can be obtained.

12 To remove the tamperproof plug, obtain a long self-tapping screw of suitable diameter to screw through the centre of the plug. The screw should bottom on the mixture screw, and then force out the plug.

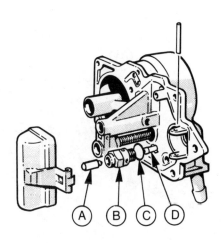

Fig. 3.17 Needle valve components (Sec 16)

A Needle valve   C Sealing washer
B Valve housing   D Intake filter

13 With the carburettor now completely dismantled, wash all components in clean fuel and renew any components which are worn. Should the choke or throttle valve plate spindles have worn in the carburettor body, then the carburettor should be renewed complete.
14 Blow through all jets and passages with air from a foot pump.

Never probe jets with a piece of wire since this will damage the jet.
15 Obtain a repair kit which will contain all the necessary gaskets for reassembly.
16 Reassembly is the reverse of the above procedure, noting the following points:

(a)   *The accelerator pump spring has its smaller diameter outwards*
(b)   *Check and adjust the float level, as described in Section 14*
(c)   *When refitting the upper body, hold the choke mechanism fully closed. The cranked end of the choke link should be at the bottom*
(d)   *Check and adjust the choke plate pull-down, as described in Section 14*
(e)   *Check and adjust the accelerator pump stroke, as described in Section 14*
(f)   *Check and adjust the idle speed and mixture, as described in Section 14*

17 Ford VV carburettor – description

1 Because of the anti-pollution regulations introduced in various countries, Ford developed a variable choke carburettor of their own design in order to comply with such regulations. The unit known as the Ford VV (variable venturi) carburettor, provides improved fuel atomisation and air/fuel mixture ratio under normal operating conditions.
2 The UK market models dealt with in this manual that have the Ford VV carburettor fitted have a manual choke operation for cold starting. The choke control is by means of a cable attached to the choke linkage in the lever housing, but the choke itself is activated by the pull-down piston. Some overseas models are fitted with an automatic choke (bi-metal coil type), but no details are given for this.

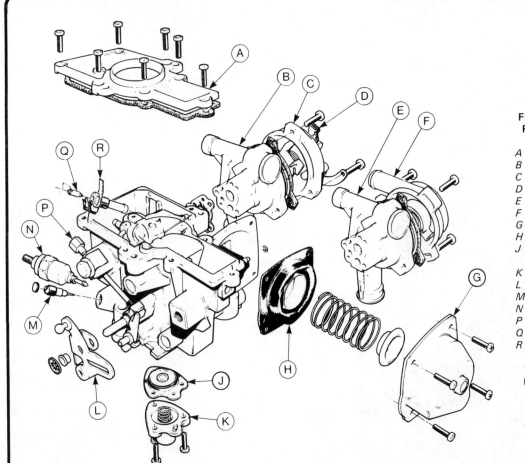

Fig. 3.18 Exploded view of the Ford VV carburettor (Sec 17)

A Top cover
B Manual choke
C Lever housing
D Choke cable bracket
E Auto-choke*
F Bi-metal housing*
G Control diaphragm cover
H Control diaphragm
J Accelerator pump diaphragm
K Accelerator pump cover
L Progressive throttle cam
M Mixture screw
N Anti-dieselling valve
P Idle speed screw
Q Needle valve
R Float bracket

*Certain overseas models only (manual choke for UK models)

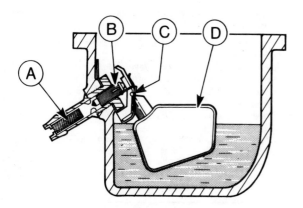

Fig. 3.19 The fuel intake components (Sec 17)

A *Fuel intake filter* C *Float pivot*
B *Needle valve* D *Float*

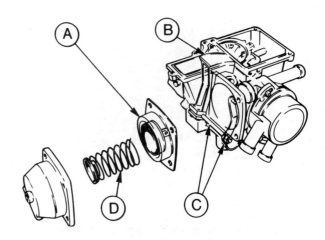

Fig. 3.20 The air control system unit components (Sec 17)

A *Vacuum diaphragm* C *Operating linkage*
B *Air valve* D *Return spring (diaphragm)*

3   The fuel inlet is controlled by a 'Viton' tipped needle valve and a float. No adjustment is provided for. The float chamber is vented into the carburettor air intake (Fig. 3.19).

4   The air control system is based upon a pivot type air valve which opens or closes the venturi in accordance with the engine air requirements (photo). The valve is actuated by a vacuum-controlled diaphragm. At idle, the valve is held in its almost closed position by the diaphragm return spring. Once the accelerator pedal is depressed, the demand for air increases as does the vacuum level in the venturi which actuates the diaphragm and air valve until the forces of return spring and vacuum are in balance.

5   The sonic idle system achieves very low emission levels. This is largely due to the method of atomisation of the fuel droplets, which utilise the speed of the airstream at the discharge tube. This airstream is at supersonic level and produces a shock wave which atomises the fuel droplets as they pass through (Fig. 3.21).

6   The main fuel control system consists of a pick-up tube, main and secondary jets and a tapered metering rod. Fuel is drawn through the system by reason of the vacuum created in the venturi.

7   The accelerator pump is vacuum-controlled to enrich the mixture in the venturi as soon as a fall in vacuum is sensed in the intake manifold. During prolonged idle, when the under-bonnet temperature rises, the fuel in the accelerator pump reservoir is liable to boil and

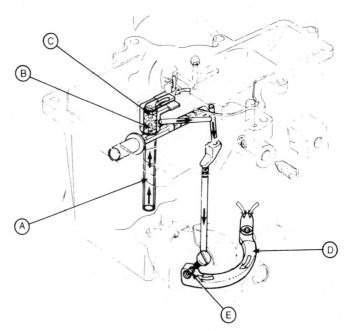

Fig. 3.21 Sonic idle system (Sec 17)

A *Main pick-up tube* D *Bypass gallery*
B *Idle fuel jet* E *Sonic discharge tube*
C *Idle air jet*

17.4 Ford VV carburettor air valve (arrowed)

vaporise. To offset this condition, which could cause enrichment of the idle mixture, a pump back bleed is fitted to bleed this vapour back into the float chamber. A vacuum break hole is incorporated in the system to obviate any tendency for high vacuum conditions at the fuel outlet to pull fuel through the accelerator pump circuit (Figs. 3.22 and 3.23).

8   An anti-dieseling valve is fitted into the carburettor (photo). Its purpose is to block the idle system when the ignition is switched off to prevent any tendency for the engine to run-on.

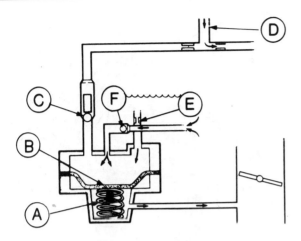

Fig. 3.22 Accelerator pump intake system (Sec 17)

A Return spring (compressed)
B Diaphragm
C One-way valve
D Vacuum break air hole
E Back bleed
F One-way valve

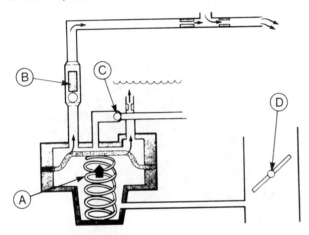

Fig. 3.23 Accelerator pump outlet system (Sec 17)

A Return spring
   (uncompressed)
B Outlet valve (open)
C Intake valve (closed)
D Throttle plate (open)

17.8 Ford VV carburettor, fuel anti-dieselling valve (arrowed)

18 Ford VV carburettor – adjustment

1   The following adjustments can be carried out without having to remove the carburettor from the engine.

Idle speed
2   With the engine at normal operating temperature, connect a tachometer in accordance with the manufacturer's instructions. Do not remove the air cleaner.
3   Start the engine, run it at 3000 rpm for 30 seconds and then let it idle. Turn the idle speed adjusting screw in or out as necessary to bring the speed to that given in the Specifications (Fig. 3.24).
4   Switch off the engine and remove the tachometer.

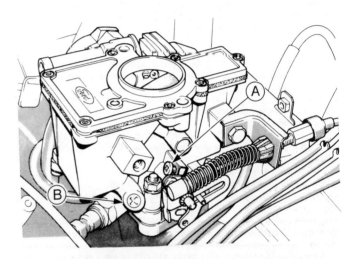

Fig. 3.24 Idle adjuster screw (A) and mixture screw (B) (Sec 18)

Idle mixture
5   This is set during production and the adjusting screw is sealed with a plug in order to conform to emission control regulations operating in certain countries.
6   The mixture may be in need of adjustment under one of the following conditions:

   (a) After carburettor overhaul
   (b) After a high mileage when engine characteristics may have changed slightly due to carbon build-up, wear or other factors

7   To adjust the mixture accurately, a CO (exhaust gas) analyser should be connected to the vehicle in accordance with the manufacturer's instructions. Also connect a tachometer.
8   Have the engine at normal operating temperature.
9   Using a thin, sharp screwdriver, prise out the tamperproof plug which covers the mixture screw.
10 Start the engine and run it at 3000 rpm for 30 seconds, then allow it to return to idle. Turn the mixture screw in (weak) or out (rich) until the CO level is within the specified range as indicated on the analysing equipment. The adjustment must be carried out within 30 seconds; otherwise, again increase the engine speed for 30 seconds before continuing with the adjustment.
11 Once the mixture is correct, adjust the idle speed as previously described, then recheck the mixture.
12 Switch off the engine and remove the tachometer and the exhaust gas analyser. Fit a new tamperproof plug to the mixture screw.
13 In the absence of a suitable exhaust gas analyser, an approximate setting of the mixture screw may be made by turning the screw inwards (engine idling) until the idle screw just begins to drop. Unscrew the screw the smallest amount necessary to achieve smooth idle. The CO level of the exhaust gas should be checked by your dealer at the earliest opportunity and further adjustment carried out as may be necessary.
14 Manual choke adjustment is normally made by setting the choke cable, as described in Section 11. After the cable is adjusted, ensure

that there is a 1.0 mm (0.04 in) clearance between the lever and stop when the choke is returned to the OFF position.

Choke pull-down/fast idle

15 This semi-automatic unit in the choke housing controls the air fuel mixture under warm-up conditions, when the engine is under light load or cruise controls. The checking and adjustment of this unit is best entrusted to your Ford dealer.

19 Ford VV carburettor – removal and refitting

1   Remove the air cleaner, as described earlier in this Chapter.
2   If the engine is hot, depressurise the cooling system by carefully removing the pressure cap, as described in Chapter 2.
3   Disconnect the choke cable from the operating lever on the choke housing, as described in Section 11.
4   Pull off the electrical lead from the anti-run-on valve on the carburettor.
5   Disconnect the distributor vacuum pipe.
6   Disconnect the throttle cable by pulling the spring clip to release the end fitting from the ball-stud and then unscrewing the cable bracket fixing bolt.
7   Disconnect and plug the fuel inlet hose from the carburettor. If crimped type hose clips are used, cut them off and fit screw type clips at reassembly.
8   Unscrew the two carburettor mounting flange nuts and lift the carburettor from the intake manifold. Remove the idle speed screw if necessary for access to the nut.
9   Refitting is a reversal of removal, but make sure that a new flange gasket is used on perfectly clean mating surfaces.
10 Reconnect and adjust the choke cable, as described in Section 11.

20 Ford VV carburettor – dismantling and reassembly

1   Complete overhaul of the carburettor is seldom required. It will usually be found sufficient to remove the top cover and mop out fuel, dirt and water from the fuel bowl and then blow through the accessible jets with air from a tyre pump or compressed air line. Do not direct air pressure into the accelerator pump air bleed or outlet, or the air valve vent, as diaphragm damage may occur.
2   To completely dismantle the carburettor, carry out the following operations, but remember that for a unit which has been in service for a high mileage it may be more economical to purchase a new or reconditioned one rather than to renew several individual components.
3   Remove the carburettor from the engine, as described in Section 19, and clean away external dirt.
4   Extract the seven screws and lift off the top cover and gasket.
5   Drain the fuel from the float bowl.
6   Using a thin sharp screwdriver, prise out the metering rod tamperproof plug.
7   Unscrew and withdraw the main metering rod, making sure to keep the air valve closed during the process (Fig. 3.26).
8   Extract the four cross-head screws and detach the main jet body and gasket. Take out the accelerator pump outlet one-way valve ball and weight by inverting the carburettor and allowing the components to drop out.
9   Lift out the float, the float spindle and the fuel inlet needle valve.
10 Extract the four cross-head screws and remove the air control vacuum diaphragm housing, the return spring and the spring seat. The diaphragm can be removed after the circlip is extracted.
11 Invert the carburettor, remove the three cross-head screws and detach the accelerator pump diaphragm, taking care not to lose the return spring.
12 Clean out all drillings, jets and passages in the carburettor with compressed air – **never** by probing with wire. Examine all components for wear or damage; renew gaskets and diaphragms as a matter of routine. Many necessary components will be supplied in repair kit form. The throttle linkage and air valve mechanism are particularly subject to wear, as are the diaphragm return springs to compression. Renew as necessary.
13 Commence reassembly by making sure that the metering rod bias spring is correctly installed to the air valve (Fig. 3.27).
14 Fit the accelerator pump assembly, making sure that the gasket-faced side of the diaphragm is towards the cover.

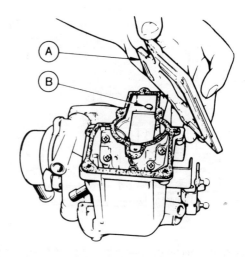

Fig. 3.25 Removing the top cover from the carburettor (Sec 20)

A   Top cover   B   Metering rod tamperproof
                                      plug

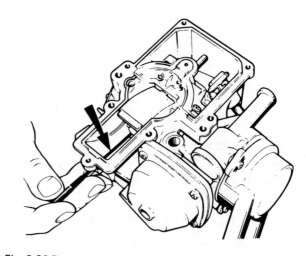

Fig. 3.26 Removing the main metering rod (arrowed) from the carburettor (Sec 20)

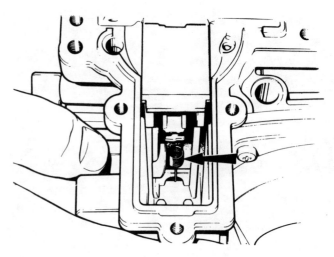

Fig. 3.27 Metering rod bias spring (arrowed) correctly located on air valve (Sec 20)

15 Reconnect and refit the air valve control vacuum diaphragm housing, making sure that the vacuum hole in the diaphragm is in alignment with the gallery in the carburettor body and the housing. As it is fitted, hold the air valve in the full open position until the housing is secured to ensure that the diaphragm is not trapped.

16 Fit the fuel inlet needle valve, the float and the float pivot pin. The needle valve should be so installed that the spring-loaded plunger on the valve will be in contact with the float once fuel has entered the float bowl (Figs. 3.28 and 3.29).

17 Insert the accelerator pump ball and weight into the pump discharge passage.

18 Use a new gasket and fit the main jet body.

19 Very carefully slide the metering rod into position, hold the air valve closed and screw in the rod until its shoulder is aligned with the vertical face of the main jet body. If the rod binds when screwing it in, do not force it, but check the reason. Do not overtighten it.

20 Fit a new tamperproof plug to the metering rod hole.

21 Fit the top cover with a new gasket.

22 Once the carburettor has been fitted to the engine, the idle speed and mixture must be checked and adjusted, as described in Section 18. If by any chance the mixture screw was removed at overhaul, screw it in very gently until it seats and then unscrew it three full turns. This will provide a basic setting to get the engine started.

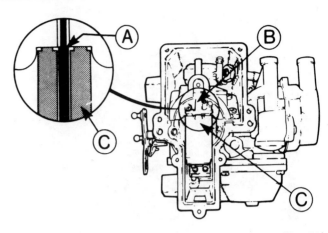

Fig. 3.30 Main metering rod adjustment on carburettor (Sec 20)

A Shoulder on rod
B Main jet body
C Air valve

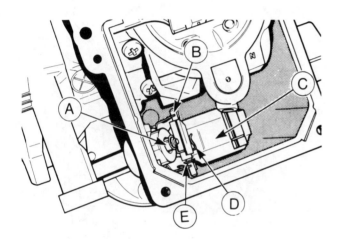

Fig. 3.28 Needle valve detail on the carburettor (Sec 20)

A Needle valve
B Float pin
C Float
D Spring clip
E Spacer washer

21 Weber carburettor – description

The carburettor is of the dual venturi downdraught type, incorporating bypass idling, main, power valve and accelerator pump systems. The float chamber is internally vented. An automatic choke is fitted and is electrically-operated, power being taken from the alternator.

A connection for the distributor vacuum pipe is provided. Provision is made for throttle speed adjustment, but the mixture control screw is protected by a tamperproof plastic plug which has to be destroyed to be removed. Replacement plugs can only be obtained by authorised workshops. The reason for this is to prevent adjustment of the mixture setting being carried out by persons not equipped with the necessary CO meter (exhaust gas analyser). The mixture is carefully set during production, to give the specified CO level after the initial running-in period.

The carburettor body consists of two castings which form the upper and lower bodies. The upper incorporates the float chamber cover, float pivot brackets, fuel inlet union, gauze filter, spring-loaded needle valve, twin air intakes, choke plates and the section of the power valve controlled by vacuum.

Incorporated in the lower body is the float chamber, accelerator pump, two throttle barrels and integral main venturis, throttle plates, spindles, levers, jets and the petrol power valve.

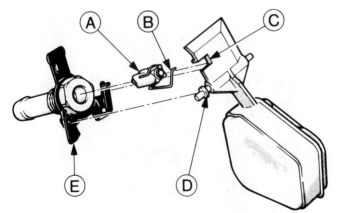

Fig. 3.29 Arrange needle valve clip and float cut-out (Sec 20)

A Needle valve
B Valve clip
C Float cut-out
D Spacer washer
E Pivot pin bracket

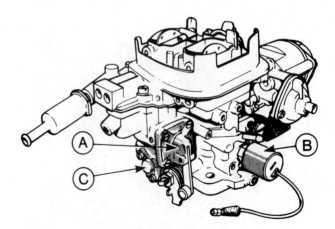

Fig. 3.31 The Weber carburettor (Sec 21)

A Accelerator pump unit
B Anti-dieselling solenoid
C Power valve unit

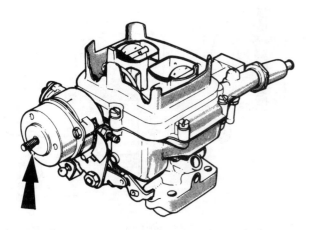

Fig. 3.32 Electric choke unit (arrowed) — Weber carburettor (Sec 21)

The throttle plate opening is in a preset sequence so that the primary starts to open first and is then followed by the secondary in such a manner that both plates reach full throttle position at the same time.

All the carburation systems are located in the lower body and the main progression systems operate in both barrels, whilst the idling and the power valve systems operate in the primary barrel only and the full load enrichment system in the secondary barrel.

The accelerator pump discharges fuel into the primary barrel.

A connection for the vacuum required to control the distributor advance/retard vacuum unit is located on the lower body.

22 Weber carburettor – adjustments

1   With the exception of the slow and fast idle adjustments, all of the following items can be carried out with the carburettor either on the bench or fitted to the engine.

Idle speed adjustment
2   Refer to Section 14 for details, and Fig. 3.33 for the adjusting screw. Ensure that the engine fan is operating by pulling the two wires from the sensor, and connecting the wires with a jumper lead.

Fast idle adjustment
3   Open the bonnet and remove the air cleaner, as described in Section 5.

4   Run the engine until the normal running temperature is reached. Hold the throttle partly open, then close the choke plates by hand and release the throttle (Fig. 3.34).
5   The throttle mechanism will hold the choke mechanism at the fast idle position. Release the choke plates, which should return to the open position.
6   If the choke plates do not fully open, then either the engine has not fully warmed up, or the electric choke is faulty.
7   **Without** touching the throttle, start the engine and check the fast idle speed against the figure given in the Specifications.
8   To adjust the fast idle speed, slacken the locknut and screw the adjuster (Fig. 3.35) in or out as required.
9   Tighten the locknut and refit the air cleaner.

Vacuum pull-down
10 With the air cleaner removed, as described in Section 5, pull the wire off the electric choke.
11 Remove the three retaining screws and lift off the automatic choke outer housing with the bi-metallic spring. Lift off the internal heat shield.
12 Fit an elastic band to the choke plate lever, and position it to hold the choke plates closed (Fig. 3.36). Open the throttle to allow the choke plates to close fully.

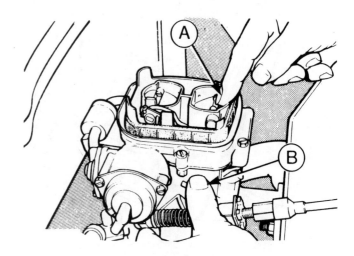

Fig. 3.34 Choke pull-down/fast idle setting (Sec 22)

A Hold choke plate shut   B Hold throttle partly open

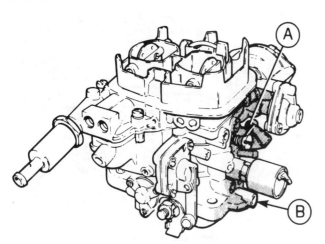

Fig. 3.33 Weber carburettor idle speed adjuster (A) and mixture adjuster (B) (with tamperproof plug) (Sec 22)

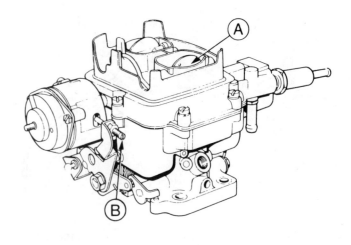

Fig. 3.35 Fast idle adjustment showing choke plates open (A) and fast idle adjustment screw (B) (Sec 22)

13 Using a suitable screwdriver, push the choke diaphragm open (Fig. 3.36), then measure the clearance between the choke plate and the carburettor body, using a gauge rod or twist drill of the specified size (Fig. 3.37).
14 To adjust the opening, remove the plug and screw the adjusting screw in or out as required.
15 Adjust the choke phasing, below.
16 Refit the heat shield and the choke housing. Reconnect the electric choke wire and the air cleaner, as described in Section 5.

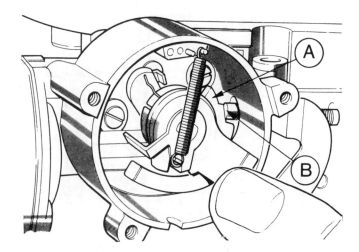

Fig. 3.38 Checking the choke phasing (Sec 22)

A Fast idle cam   B Fast idle adjuster screw

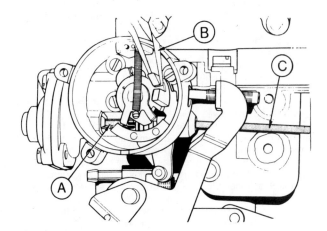

Fig. 3.36 Hold choke open with a rubber band (B) and push the diaphragm rod (A) with a small screwdriver (C) (Sec 22)

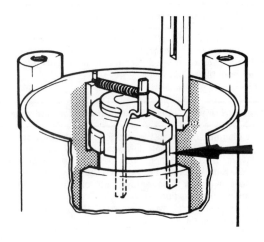

Fig. 3.39 Choke phase adjusting tag (arrowed) (Sec 22)

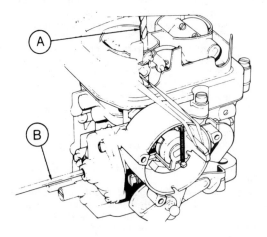

Fig. 3.37 Insert a twist drill (A) and adjust pull-down (B) (Sec 22)

22 Refit the heat shield and the choke housing. Reconnect the electric choke wire and the air cleaner, Section 5.

Float level
23 Refer to Section 5 and remove the air cleaner assembly.
24 Detach the fuel supply pipe and plug the end to stop dirt ingress.
25 If a crimp type clamp is fitted to the fuel inlet pipe, it should be cut off and a screw type clamp used for refitting.
26 Pull off the electric choke cable.
27 Undo and remove the screws and spring washers that secure the upper body to the lower body. Lift away the upper body, holding the fast idle adjusting screw clear of the choke housing.
28 Carefully examine the float for signs of puncture which may be tested by inserting in warm water and watching for air bubbles.
29 Inspect the float arm for signs of fracture, damage or bending and, if satisfactory, hold the upper body in the vertical position with the float hanging down, as shown in Fig. 3.40.
30 Measure the distance between the bottom of the float and the gasket on the upper body and adjust if necessary, to the dimensions given in the Specifications at the beginning of this Chapter. Adjustment is made at the tab which rests against the needle valve.
31 Reassemble the carburettor upper body, which is the reverse sequence to removal.

Choke phasing
17 Adjust the vacuum pull-down, above.
18 Hold the throttle partly open, and position the fast idle adjusting screw on the centre step of the fast idle cam. Release the throttle to hold the cam in this position.
19 Push the choke plates down until the cam jams against the fast idle screw (Fig. 3.38).
20 Measure the clearance between the choke plate and the carburettor body, using a gauge rod or twist drill of the specified size, as shown in Fig. 3.37.
21 Bend the tag (Fig. 3.39) as required to give the correct clearance.

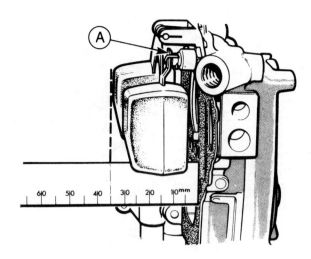

Fig. 3.40 Adjust float level by bending tag (A) (Sec 22)

23 Weber carburettor – removal and refitting

The procedure is very similar to that described for the Ford IV carburettor, Section 15, except that the manual choke cable is replaced by an electric choke wire, and four nuts are used to secure the unit to the manifold.

24 Weber carburettor – dismantling, inspection and reassembly

1   Before dismantling, wash the exterior of the carburettor and wipe dry using a non-fluffy rag. Select a clean area of workbench and lay several layers of newspaper on the top. Obtain several small containers for putting some of the small parts in, which could be easily lost. Whenever a part is to be removed look at it first so that it may be refitted in its original position. As each part is removed place it in order along one edge of the newspaper so that by using this method reassembly is made easier.
2   All parts of the carburettor are shown in Fig. 3.41.
3   Unscrew and remove the fuel filter from the upper body.
4   Undo and remove the six screws and spring washers that retain the upper body to the lower body. Hold the fast idle adjusting screw clear of the automatic choke housing and lift away the upper body and gasket.
5   Carefully extract the float pivot pin and lift out the float assembly, followed by the needle valve.
6   Using a box spanner, unscrew the needle valve carrier.
7   Undo and remove the three screws and spring washers that secure the spring-loaded power valve diaphragm cover. Lift away the cover and spring.
8   Undo and remove the four screws and spring washers that secure the accelerator pump cover to the lower body. Lift away the cover gasket, diaphragm and spring.
9   Undo the two screws that secure each choke plate to the shaft. Lift away the choke plates. Remove the burrs from the threaded holes and then withdraw the shafts.
10   Obtain a selection of screwdrivers with the ends in good condition and square so that the jets may be removed without damage.
11   Unscrew the idling jets and combined main/air correction jets from the lower body, noting the respective sizes and locations of each jet (Fig. 3.42). Remove the accelerator pump jet and its O-ring.
12   It is not normally suggested that the mixture control screw be removed unless full workshop facilities, including an exhaust gas analyser are available, and a new tamperproof plug can be obtained.
13   To remove the tamperproof plug, obtain a long self-tapping screw of suitable diameter to screw through the centre of the plug .The screw should bottom on the mixture screw, and then force out the plug.
14   Unhook the secondary throttle return spring from the secondary throttle control lever and then unscrew the nut from the primary

throttle shaft. Remove the throttle control lever, fast idle lever, washer, secondary throttle control lever, secondary throttle return spring, slow running stop lever, spring and washer from the spindle.
15   Unscrew and remove the nut, spring washer and plain washers from the secondary throttle shaft.
16   Undo the two screws that secure each throttle plate to the shaft. Lift away the two throttle plates. Remove the burrs from the threaded holes and then withdraw the shafts.

Automatic choke housing
17   Remove the three screws and detach the automatic choke housing with the bi-metallic spring. Lift off the internal heat shield.
18   Undo and remove the three screws securing the automatic choke to the carburettor. Disconnect the choke link from the housing and lift off the housing.
19   Remove the three screws securing the pull-down diaphragm cover (refer to Fig. 3.41) and lift off the cover, spring and diaphragm and operating rod assembly.

Inspection (general)
20   Dismantling is now complete and all parts should be thoroughly washed and cleaned in petrol. Remove any sediment in the float chamber and drillings, but take care not to scratch the fine drillings whilst doing so. Remove all traces of old gaskets using a sharp knife.
21   Clean the jets and passageways using clean, dry compressed air. Check the float assembly for signs of damage or leaking. Inspect the power valve and pump diaphragms and gaskets for splits or deterioration. Examine the mixture screw, needle valve seat and throttle spindle for signs of wear. Renew parts as necessary.
22   Insert the choke spindle in its bore, locate the choke plate in the shaft with the minus (–) sign uppermost. Secure the choke plates in position with two screws each. Peen over the threaded ends to lock.

Automatic choke reassembly
23   Refit the pull-down diaphragm and operating rod assembly, spring and cover. Ensure the diaphragm is flat and tighten the three securing screws.
24   Reconnect the automatic choke link, position the O-ring, refit the choke housing and secure it with three screws.
25   Refer to Section 22 and adjust the vacuum pull-down and choke phasing.
26   Refit the internal heat shield with the peg located in the notch in the housing. Connect the bi-metallic spring to the choke lever and loosely fit the three retaining screws. Align the mark on the outer housing with the centre (Index) mark on the choke housing (Fig. 3.43), then tighten the screws.
27   Slide the throttle shafts into their appropriate bores and fit the throttle plates into the shafts so that the angled degree marking is towards the base of the lower body. Secure the throttle plates with two screws each and peen over the ends to stop them from working loose.
28   Fit the plain and spring washers to the secondary throttle shaft and secure with the nut.
29   Refit the washer, primary spring, throttle stop lever, secondary spring, spring, secondary throttle lever, washer, fast idle lever and throttle operating lever to the primary throttle shaft and secure with the nut. Reconnect the secondary throttle spring.
30   If removed, refit the mixture control screw.
31   Refit the O-ring and accelerator pump jet (discharge tube) to the lower body.
32   Refit the idling jets and the combined main/air correction jets to the lower body in their original positions, noting that the secondary jets are located nearest the choke housing and throttle linkage.
33   Refit the accelerator pump and power valve diaphragm components, ensure the diaphragms are flat and tighten the screws.
34   Using a box spanner, screw in the needle valve housing. A new fibre washer should always be fitted under the housing.
35   Fit the needle valve into the housing (make sure it is the correct way up). Offer up the float to the pivot bracket and retain in position with the pivot pin.
36   Refer to Section 22 and check the float level setting.
37   Hold the fast idle adjusting screw clear and refit the upper body to the lower body. Release the fast idle lever and tighten the six screws.
38   Refit the fuel inlet filter.
39   When the carburettor has been refitted to the engine refer to Section 22 and carry out the necessary adjustments.

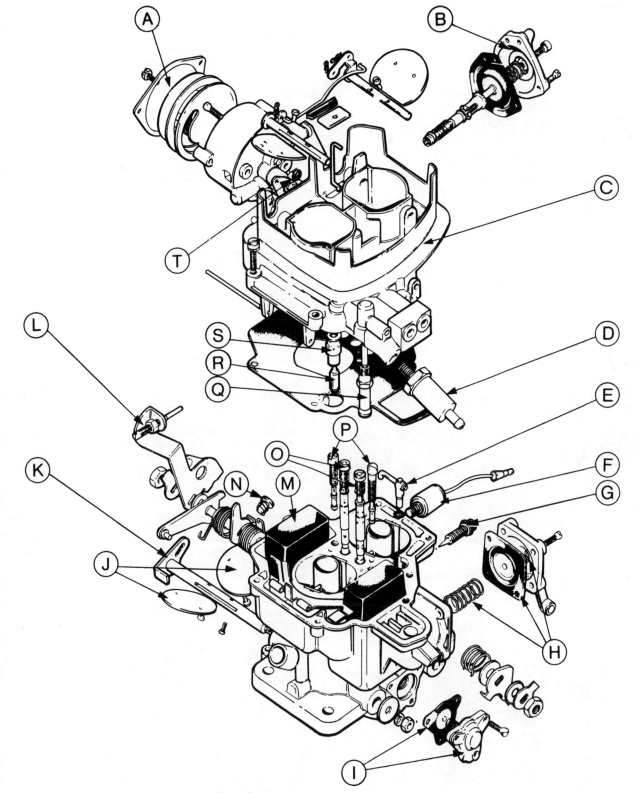

Fig. 3.41 Exploded view of the Weber (2V) carburettor (Sec 24)

A Electric choke housing
B Choke pull-down diaphragm
   unit
C Upper body
D Intake filter
E Accelerator discharge
   tube

F Anti-dieselling solenoid
G Mixture screw
H Accelerator pump unit
I Power valve diaphragm
   unit
J Throttle plates
K Secondary throttle
   spindle

L Fast idle adjuster
M Float
N Idle speed adjusting
   screw
O Combined emulsion tube,
   air correction and
   main jets

P Idle jets
Q Fuel return correction
R Needle valve
S Needle valve housing
T Rubber seal

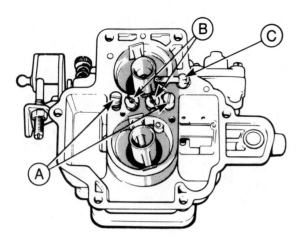

Fig. 3.42 Remove the idle jets (A), main jets (B) and accelerator pump jet (C) (Sec 24)

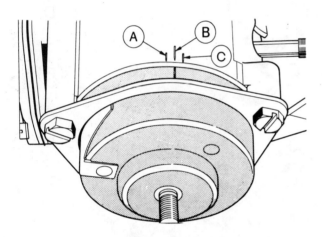

Fig. 3.43 Align index mark with centre mark (B) (Sec 24)

A is the rich position, C the lean position

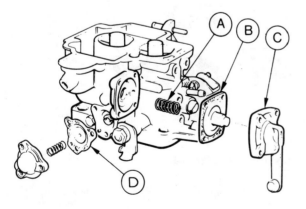

Fig. 3.44 Refit the accelerator pump spring (A) diaphragm (B) and cover (C) and the power valve diaphragm (D) spring and cover (Sec 24)

25 Manifolds

1   Removal and refitting of the manifolds is described in Chapter 1.

Intake

2   The intake manifold is of light alloy construction and is coolant-heated to improve the atomization of the fuel/air mixture.

Exhaust

3   The exhaust manifold is of cast iron construction and incorporates a heated air box as part of the air intake system for the thermostatically-controlled air cleaner (photo).

26 Exhaust system – general

1   The exhaust system fitted to all models is of two-piece construction, but there are three different system types fitted, according to model.
2   The system can be renewed in sections, as coupling sleeves are supplied so that an old section can be cut out and a new one inserted without the need to renew the entire system at the same time.
3   It is recommended, when working on an exhaust system, that the complete assembly be removed from under the vehicle by releasing the downpipe from the manifold and unhooking the flexible suspension hangers (photo).
4   Assemble the complete system, but do not fully tighten the joint clips until the system is back in the vehicle. Use a new exhaust manifold/flange gasket and check that the flexible mountings are in good order.
5   Set the silencer and expansion box in their correct attitudes in relation to the rest of the system before finally tightening the joint clips.
6   Check that with reasonable deflection in either direction, the exhaust does not knock against any adjacent components.

27 Emissions control system – description

1   An emissions control system is fitted in order to reduce the level of noxious gases that would otherwise be emitted from the vehicle exhaust. The system fitted can vary according to model, but whatever system is used it should be realised that, for optimum reduction of exhaust gas CO level, the good tune of the engine (carburettor and ignition) and the efficiency of the temperature-controlled air cleaner are essential requirements.

Positive crankcase ventilation (PCV)

2   The PCV system operates by drawing in air and mixing it with the vapours which have escaped past the piston rings (blow-by vapours). This mixture is then drawn into the combustion chamber through an oil separator and PCV valve. Refer also to Chapter 1, Section 13 (ohv) or 37 (CVH).

Thermostatically-controlled air cleaner

3   This type of air cleaner ensures a constant temperature of the intake air so that fuel atomization within the carburettor takes place using air at the correct temperature. This is effected by a duct system which draws in fresh air, or pre-heated air from a heat shroud around the engine exhaust manifold.
4   Operation of the system can be summarized as follows: when the engine is cold, heated air is directed from around the exhaust manifold into the air cleaner, but as the engine warms up cold air is progressively mixed with this warm air to maintain a suitable carburettor air temperature. At high ambient temperatures the hot air intake is closed off completely.
5   The mixing of air is regulated by a vacuum-operated valve on the air cleaner inlet duct, which is controlled by a bi-metal temperature sensor inside the air cleaner.

25.3 Exhaust manifold and heated air box (ohv shown)

26.3A Exhaust manifold-to-downpipe flange connection

26.3B Exhaust system flexible hanger

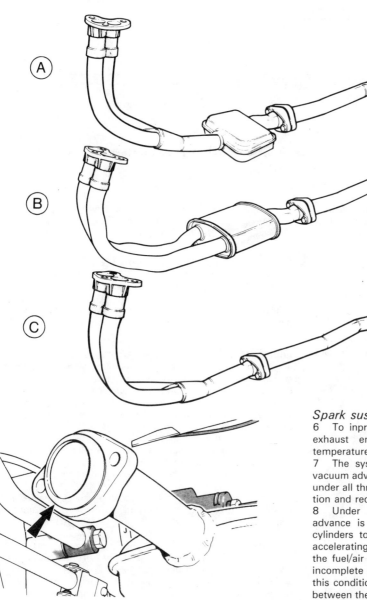

Fig. 3.45 Exhaust systems (Sec 26)

A *ohv models*
B *CVH models*
C *XR2 models*

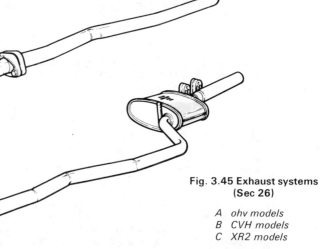

Fig. 3.46 Ensure that the flange joint faces are clean before assembling (Sec 26)

Spark sustain systems

6   To inprove driveability during warm-up conditions and to keep exhaust emission levels to a minimum, a vacuum-operated, temperature-sensitive emission control system is fitted.

7   The system is designed to ensure that the rate of distributor vacuum advance is compatible with the change in fuel/air mixture flow under all throttle conditions, thus resulting in more complete combustion and reduced exhaust emissions.

8   Under part throttle cruising conditions, distributor vacuum advance is required to allow time for the fuel/air mixture in the cylinders to burn. When returning to a part throttle opening after accelerating or decelerating, the distributor vacuum increases before the fuel/air mixture has stabilized. This can lead to short periods of incomplete combustion and increase of exhaust emission. To reduce this condition a spark delay valve is incorporated in the vacuum line between the carburettor and distributor to reduce the rate at which the distributor advances. Under certain conditions, particularly during the period of engine warm-up, some models may suffer from a lack of throttle response. To overcome this problem a spark sustain valve may

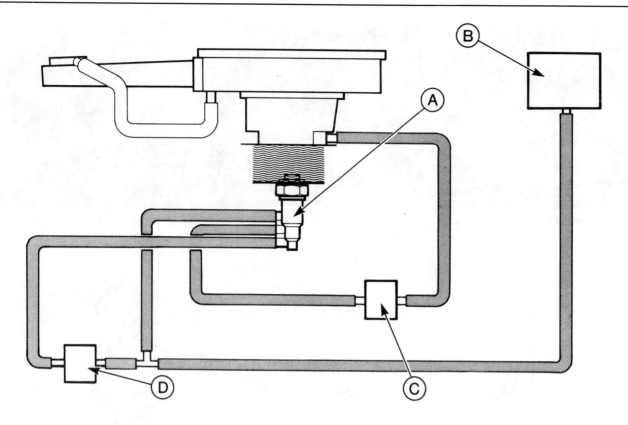

Fig. 3.47 Schematic diagram of the spark sustain system – CVH engine layout (Sec 27)

be fitted in the vacuum line either individually or in conjunction with the spark delay valve. This valve is used to maintain distributor vacuum under transient throttle conditions, thus stabilizing the combustion process.

9   The operation of the valves is controlled by a ported vacuum switch (PVS) which has the vacuum lines connected to it. The PVS operates in a similar manner to that of the thermostat in the cooling system. A wax-filled sensor is attached to a plunger which operates a valve. The PVS is actuated by the engine coolant and is sensitive to changes in engine operating temperature. When the engine is cold the sensor moves the plunger to open the upper and middle ports of the PVS. Therefore vacuum applied to the middle port is directed to the distributor via the upper port. As the engine warms up and coolant temperature increases, the wax expands and the plunger closes the upper port and opens the lower port. Vacuum applied to the centre port is now directed to the distributor via the lower port. In this way the spark sustain or delay valves can be activated or bypassed, according to engine operating temperature. The vacuum applied to the middle port of the PVS is taken from a connection on the carburettor through a fuel trap. The fuel trap prevents fuel or fuel vapour from being drawn into the distributor vacuum unit.

10 Testing of the various components of the system is not within the scope of the home mechanic due to the need for a vacuum pump and gauge, but if a fault has been diagnosed by a garage having the necessary equipment, the renewal of a defective component can be carried out.

28 Emissions control components – maintenance and testing

1   In view of the special test equipment and procedures there is little that can be done in the way of maintenance and testing for the emissions control system. In the event of a suspected malfunction of the system, check the security and condition of all vacuum and electrical connections then, where applicable, refer to the following paragraphs for further information.

2   In addition, whenever working on any of these systems, make a **careful** note of any electrical or vacuum line connections before removing to, to ensure correct refitting.

Positive crankcase ventilation (PCV)

3   Remove all the hoses and components of the system and clean them in paraffin or petrol. Ensure that all hoses are free from any obstruction and are in a serviceable condition. Where applicable, similarly clean the crankcase breather cap and shake it dry. Renew parts as necessary then refit them to the car.

Thermostatically-controlled air cleaner

4   The air cleaner must have its filter element renewed at the specified intervals. Refer to Section 4 for details.

5   The air cleaner unit air temperature control unit can be checked for operation, but the engine must be cold when starting this check. Look into the air intake spout and check that the air control flap valve is in the shut position.

6   Now start the engine and allow it to idle. The flap valve should open fully to allow the warm air to be drawn into the cleaner unit from the exhaust manifold ducting. As the engine warms up to its normal operating temperature the flap valve should progressively close to allow cooler air to enter the cleaner unit.

7   If the valve is stuck in the shut position, check the vacuum lines for condition and security. If these are in order then the heat sensor or diaphragm unit is at fault.

8   Detach the diaphragm-to-heat sensor vacuum pipe (at the sensor end) and connect up a vacuum pump to the diaphragm. Pump and apply a vacuum up to 100 mm (4.0 in) of mercury and retain this whilst checking the air flap.

9   If the flap opens, the heat sensor is defective and must be renewed, but if it remains shut then the diaphragm or control flap is faulty.

10 Disconnect the vacuum pump and reconnect the vacuum pipe to the sensor unit.

29 Emissions control components – removal and refitting

Spark delay/sustain valve – removal and refitting

1   Disconnect the vacuum lines at the valve and remove the valve from the engine.

2   When refitting a spark delay valve it must be positioned with the black side (marked CARB) towards the carburettor and the coloured side (marked DIST) towards the distributor. When refitting a spark sustain valve the side marked VAC must be towards the carburettor and the side marked DIST towards the distributor.

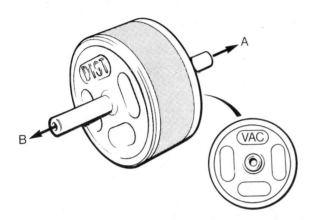

Fig. 3.48 Spark sustain valve is marked for direction of fitting (Sec 29)

A   to PVS   B   to distributor

Ported vacuum switch – removal and refitting

3   Remove the filler cap from the expansion tank to reduce pressure in the cooling system. If the engine is hot, remove the cap slowly using a rag to prevent scalding.

4   Disconnect the vacuum lines and, if necessary, the water hoses, then unscrew the valve from the intake manifold or adaptor.

5   When refitting the valve, note that the vacuum line from the carburettor is connected to the middle outlet on the PVS, the vacuum line from the spark delay valve (where fitted) is connected to the outlet nearest to the threaded end of the PVS, and the vacuum line from the spark sustain valve is connected to the outlet furthest from the threaded end of the PVS.

6   Reconnect the water hoses and, if necessary, top up the cooling system.

Fuel trap – removal and refitting

7   Disconnect the vacuum lines and remove the fuel trap from the engine.

8   When refitting, make sure that the fuel trap is positioned with the black side (marked CARB) towards the carburettor and the white side (marked DIST) towards the PVS.

Fig. 3.49 Fuel trap is marked for direction of fitting (Sec 29)

---

30 Fault diagnosis – fuel system

Symptom	Reason(s)
Fuel consumption excessive	Air cleaner choked giving rich mixture
	Leak from tank, pump or fuel lines
	Float chamber flooding due to incorrect level or worn needle valve
	Carburettor incorrectly adjusted
	Idle speed too high
	Incorrect valve clearances (ohv)
Lack of power, stalling or difficult starting	Faulty fuel pump
	Leak on suction side of pump or in fuel line
	Intake manifold or carburettor flange gaskets leaking
	Carburettor incorrectly adjusted
Poor or erratic idling	Weak mixture (screw tampered with)
	Leak in intake manifold
	Leak in distributor vacuum pipe
	Leak in crankcase extractor hose
	Leak in brake servo hose (if fitted)

Note: *High fuel consumption and poor performance are not necessarily due to carburettor faults. Make sure that the ignition system is properly adjusted, that the brakes are not binding and that the engine is in good mechanical condition before tampering with the carburettor.*

Chapter 4 Ignition system

Contents

Part A: Mechanical ignition system

Condenser − renewal 9
Contact breaker gap − adjustment 3
Contact breaker points − renewal 4
Distributor − overhaul 10
Distributor − removal and refitting 7
Distributor advance − checking 6
Distributor vacuum unit − removal and refitting 8
Fault diagnosis − mechanical ignition system 12
General description 1
Ignition timing − checking and adjustment 5
Routine maintenance − mechanical ignition system 2
Spark plugs, HT leads and distributor cap − general 11

Part B: Breakerless (electronic) ignition system

Distributor − removal and refitting 15
Fault diagnosis − electronic ignition system 20
General description 13
Ignition amplifier module − description, removal and refitting 16
Ignition coil − general 18
Ignition lock cylinder − removal and refitting 19
Routine maintenance − electronic ignition system 14
Spark plugs, HT leads and distributor cap − general 17

Specifications

Part A: Mechanical ignition system

General

System type .... Battery, coil and distributor with mechanical contact breaker
Polarity .... Negative earth
Firing order .... 1−2−4−3 (No 1 at timing cover end)

Ignition timing (initial)

1.0 litre .... 12° BTDC
1.1 litre .... 6° BTDC

Distributor

Make .... Bosch
Drive .... Gear on camshaft
Automatic advance method .... Mechanical and vacuum control
Rotation .... Anti-clockwise (viewed from cap)
Condenser capacity .... 0.20 ± 15% microfarad
Contact breaker points gap .... 0.40 to 0.50 mm (0.016 to 0.020 in)
Dwell angle .... 48° to 52°
Dwell variation (from idle to 2000 rpm) .... 4° maximum
Dwell overlap (lobe-to-lobe variation) .... 3° maximum
Advance characteristics * at 2000 rpm (engine) no load:

	Mechanical	Vacuum	Total
1.0 litre	-1.0° to 4.0°	6° to 12°	5° to 16°
1.1 litre	3° to 9°	13° to 21°	16° to 30°

Crankshaft degrees; initial advance not included

Coil
Type .... Low voltage with 1.5 ohm ballast resistor
Output .... 23kV (minimum)
Secondary resistance .... 5000 to 9000 ohms

Spark plugs
Type .... Motorcraft AGRF 22 or equivalent
Electrode gap .... 0.75 mm (0.030 in)

Part B: Breakerless (electronic) ignition system
General
System type .... Battery, coil and distributor incorporating electronic module
Polarity .... Negative earth
Firing order .... 1–3–4–2 (No 1 at timing cover end)

Ignition timing (initial)
1.3 and 1.6 litre .... 12° BTDC

Distributor
Make .... Bosch
Type .... Breakerless
Automatic advance method .... ESC module
Drive .... Dog or camshaft
Rotation .... Anti-clockwise (viewed from top)
Dwell angle .... Non-adjustable (governed by electronic module)
Advance characteristics (total) at 2000 rpm (engine speed):
    1.3 litre .... 18° to 34°
    1.6 litre .... 17° to 30.2°

Coil
Type .... High output breakerless ignition coil
Output (open circuit condition) .... 25 kV (minimum)
Primary resistance .... 0.72 to 0.88 ohm
Secondary resistance .... 4000 to 7000 ohm

Spark plugs
Make ....

Type:	Motorcraft	
	Production	**Service**
1.3 litre	AGPR 22 C	AGRF 22C
1.6 litre	AGPR 12C	AGPR 22C/AGPR 12C
Electrode gap	0.75 mm (0.30 in)	
HT lead resistance (per lead)	30 000 ohms (minimum)	

All system types
Torque wrench settings

Spark plugs:	Nm	lbf ft
ohv engines	13 to 20	10 to 15
CVH engines	19	14
Distributor clamp pinch-bolt (ohv)	4	3
Distributor clamp plate bolt (ohv)	10	7
Distributor mounting bolts (CVH)	7	5

PART A: MECHANICAL IGNITION SYSTEM

1 General description

A conventional ignition system is used on the 1.0 and 1.1 litre engine models marketed in the UK. The system consists of a coil, a distributor with mechanical contact breaker, a ballast resistor and spark plugs.

The distributor is mounted on the cylinder block and is driven from a skew gear on the camshaft. It incorporates both mechanical and vacuum advance capability.

The coil is mounted on the bulkhead panel and is of the oil-filled type.

The ballast resistor is a grey coloured wire, built into the loom which runs between the ignition switch and the coil. Its purpose is to limit the battery voltage to the coil during normal running to seven volts. During starting, the ballast resistor is bypassed to give full battery voltage at the coil to facilitate quick starting of the engine.

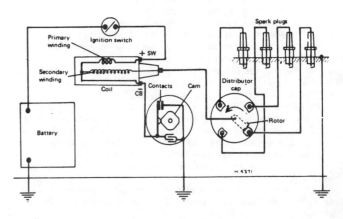

Fig. 4.1 Ignition system theoretical wiring diagram (Sec 1)

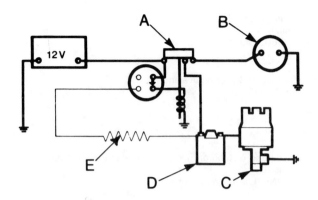

Fig. 4.2 Ignition switch in 'start' position (Sec 1)

A   Starter solenoid   D   Ignition coil
B   Starter motor   E   Ballast resistor wire
C   Distributor

The spark plugs are of small diameter and require a long reach 16 mm ($\frac{5}{8}$ in AF) socket to remove them instead of a conventional spark plug spanner; they are of the taper seat type.

The HT leads are of suppressed type, of carbon cored construction. Always pull them from the spark plugs by gripping the terminal rubber insulator, not the cable itself. The leads are numbered, No 1 being at the spark plug nearest the timing cover end of the engine.

Removal and refitting of the ignition lock cylinder on cars with a mechanical ignition system is identical to the procedure for breakerless ignition system models (Section 19).

2   Routine maintenance – mechanical ignition system

1   Routine maintenance of the ignition system is most important in ensuring engine reliability and efficiency. Check, adjust or renew as necessary those items listed in the Routine Maintenance Section at the start of this manual. Refer to the applicable Section in this Chapter for details on the item in question. In addition to those items listed, also make the following periodic ignition system checks.
2   Periodically check the rotor arm and distributor cap for cracks and renew them if evident.
3   Wipe the HT leads free from oil and grease and check the security of all ignition system connections.
4   Make sure that all earth connections from the battery, engine and transmission are tight and that the contact is being made between the surfaces of clean metal – not rusted or corroded.

3   Contact breaker gap – adjustment

1   This will normally only be required after new contact breaker points have been fitted, but it is worthwhile checking the adjustment at about halfway through the service interval in case the gap has altered due to wear on the contact breaker cam follower heel.
2   Access to the distributor is improved by removing the air cleaner unit, as described in Chapter 3.
3   Prise down the retaining clips or remove the securing screws, as appropriate, and remove the distributor cap and rotor.
4   Apply a spanner to the crankshaft pulley bolt and turn the crankshaft until the distributor points are fully open, with the heel of the cam follower on the highest point of one of the lobes of the cam.
5   Using feeler blades, check the points gap. If the blade is not a sliding fit, release the screw at the fixed contact so that the contact will move and adjust the gap. Retighten the screw, refit the rotor and cap. Take care not to contaminate the points with oil from the feeler gauges (photo).
6   This method of adjustment should be regarded as 'second best' as on modern engines, setting the points gap is usually carried out by measuring the dwell angle.
7   The dwell angle is the number of degrees through which the

3.5 Checking the contact breaker points gap

distributor cam turns during the period between the instants of closure and opening of the contact breaker points. Checking the dwell angle not only gives a more accurate setting of the contact breaker gap, but this method also evens out any variations in the gap which could be caused by pitting of the points, wear in the distributor shaft or its bushes, or difference in height of any of the cam peaks.
8   The dwell angle should be checked with a dwell meter connected in accordance with the maker's instructions. Refer to the Specifications for the correct dwell angle. If the dwell angle is too large, increase the points gap. If it is too small, reduce the gap.
9   The dwell angle should always be adjusted before checking and adjusting the ignition timing (see Section 5).

4   Contact breaker points – renewal

1   Disconnect the leads from the spark plugs, prise down the distributor cap clips or remove the screws, and place the cap and leads to one side.
2   Remove the rotor arm.
3   Pull off the contact breaker LT lead from the points.
4   Unscrew and remove the screw from the fixed contact arm. Take great care not to drop the screw into the interior of the distributor; if

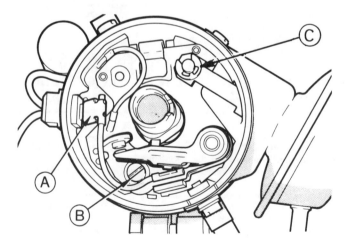

Fig. 4.3 Contact breaker points removal (Sec 4)

A   LT lead connector   C   Vacuum advance strut
B   Securing screw   circlip

necessary, cover the openings in the baseplate with rag before starting to remove the screw. If the screw is dropped, retrieve it before proceeding any further by removing the distributor (Section 7) and inverting it.

5   With the screw removed, lift out the contact breaker assembly.
6   Dressing the points on a strip of emery cloth is not recommended, and they should be renewed if they are in poor condition or they have completed their specified period of service (see Routine Maintenance at the front of this manual).
7   Fit the new contact breaker set, but leave the securing screw loose at this stage until the gap has been set using feeler blades, as described in the preceding Section.
8   Apply a little high melting-point grease to the distributor cam. (Grease may be supplied with the new contact breaker set).
9   Refit the rotor arm and the distributor cap and reconnect the spark plug leads.
10 Check and adjust the dwell angle (Section 3) and the ignition timing (next Section).

---

5   Ignition timing – checking and adjustment

1   This will be required whenever one of the following operations has been carried out.

(a)   Contact breaker points adjusted or renewed
(b)   Distributor removed and refitted
(c)   Change of fuel octane rating

2   Before checking the timing, check and adjust the dwell angle as described in Section 3, with the engine at normal operating temperature.
3   Increase the contrast of the notch in the crankshaft pulley and the appropriate mark on the timing index (refer to Specifications) by applying quick-drying white paint.
4   Connect a timing light (stroboscope) in accordance with the manufacturer's instructions.
5   Start the engine and allow it to idle.
6   Disconnect the vacuum pipe from the distributor and plug the pipe with a piece of rod.
7   If the timing light is now directed at the engine timing marks, the pulley notch will appear to be stationary and opposite the specified mark on the scale. If the marks are not in alignment, release the distributor clamp pinch-bolt and turn the distributor in whichever direction is necessary to align the marks.
8   Retighten the pinch-bolt, switch off the engine, remove the timing light and reconnect the vacuum pipe.
9   It may now be necessary to check and adjust the engine idle speed if the distributor setting has to be varied to any extent.

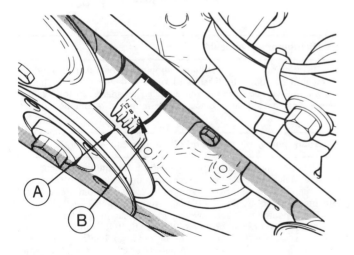

Fig. 4.4 Ignition timing marks (Sec 5)

A   Crankshaft pulley notch   B   Timing cover scale

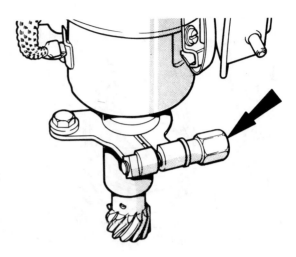

Fig. 4.5 Distributor clamp plate pinch-bolt (arrowed) (Sec 5)

---

6   Distributor advance – checking

1   A secondary use of a timing light is to check that the centrifugal and vacuum advance functions of the distributor are working.
2   The tests are not precise, as would be the case if sophisticated equipment were used, but will at least indicate the serviceability of the unit.
3   With the engine idling, timing light connected and vacuum pipe disconnected and plugged, as described in the preceding Section, increase the engine speed to 2000 rpm and note the approximate distance which the pulley mark moves out of alignment with the mark on the scale.
4   Reconnect the vacuum pipe to the distributor and repeat the test when for the same increase in engine speed, the alignment differential of the timing marks should be greater than previously observed. Refer to the Specifications for typical figures.
5   A further check of the vacuum advance can be made by removing the distributor cap after the engine has been switched off, disconnecting the distributor vacuum pipe at its suction end, and sucking the pipe. The suction should be sufficient to move the distributor baseplate slightly.
6   If these tests do not prove positive renew the vacuum unit, as described in Section 8.
7   Some models are equipped with a spark delay/sustain valve in the vacuum line from carburettor to distributor, the purpose of which is to delay vacuum advance under certain part throttle conditions. If such a valve is suspected of malfunctioning, it should be tested by substitution, or taken to a Ford dealer for specialized checking. The main effect of the valve is to reduce exhaust emission levels and it is unlikely that malfunction would have a noticeable effect on engine performance.
8   If a ported vacuum switch (PVS) is fitted in the vacuum line, its purpose is to bypass the spark sustain valve when normal engine operating temperature (as sensed by the temperature of the coolant flowing round the inlet manifold) has been reached.

---

7   Distributor – removal and refitting

1   Remove the air cleaner unit, as described in Chapter 3.
2   Disconnect the leads from the spark plugs, remove the distributor cap and place the cap with the leads to one side.
3   Disconnect the LT lead from the coil negative terminal and disconnect the distributor vacuum pipe.
4   Using a ring spanner or socket on the crankshaft pulley bolt, turn the crankshaft until No 1 piston is at tdc. Verify this by checking that the timing cover mark is aligned with the notch on the crankshaft pulley and that the rotor arm (contact end) is pointing to the No 1

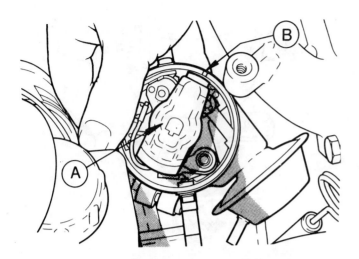

Fig. 4.6 Rotor arm (A) with rim alignment mark (B) (Sec 7)

spark plug lead contact in the distributor cap when fitted. Do not turn the crankshaft again until after the distributor has been refitted.
5   Mark the position of the rotor arm on the rim of the distributor body.
6   Mark the position of the distributor body in relation to the cylinder block.
7   Remove the bolt which holds the distributor clamp plate to the cylinder block, **do not** remove the distributor by releasing the clamp pinch-bolt.
8   Withdraw the distributor.
9   To install the original distributor, hold it over its hole in the cylinder block so that the body mark made before removal is aligned with the one on the cylinder block (No 1 piston still at tdc).
10 When the distributor is installed, the meshing of the drive and driven gears will cause the rotor arm to rotate in an anti-clockwise direction. This must be anticipated by positioning the rotor arm a few degrees in advance of its final marked position.
11 Install the distributor and check that the rotor arm and distributor body marks are aligned with the marks made before removal. Tighten the clamp plate bolt.
12 If the distributor was removed without marking its position, or if a new distributor is being fitted, install the distributor in the following way.
13 Set No 1 piston to tdc. To do this, remove No 1 spark plug and place the finger over the plug hole. Turn the crankshaft pulley bolt until compression can be felt, which indicates that No 1 piston is rising on its firing stroke. Continue turning until the timing marks for tdc are in alignment.
14 Hold the distributor over its hole in the cylinder block so that the vacuum unit is aligned with the engine oil dipstick guide tube.
15 Set the rotor arm to anticipate its rotation as the gears mesh on installation, remembering that the arm will turn in an anti-clockwise direction and should take up a final position with its contact end opposite No 1 spark plug lead contact (as if the distributor cap is fitted).
16 Release the clamp plate pinch-bolt and install the distributor. Check that the body and rotor arm are correctly positioned, then swivel the clamp plate as necessary to be able to screw in the clamp plate bolt. Tighten the clamp plate pinch-bolt.
17 Fit the distributor cap and reconnect the HT and LT leads.
18 Check the timing as described in Section 5 and then reconnect the vacuum pipe to the distributor.

8   Distributor vacuum unit – removal and refitting

1   This will normally only be required if a new unit is to be fitted because a fault has been diagnosed in the old one.
2   Remove the distributor cap and the rotor arm. Disconnect the vacuum pipe from the unit.

3   Extract the circlip which holds the vacuum advance actuating rod to the pivot post.
4   Extract the two screws which hold the unit to the distributor body, tilt the unit downwards to release the actuating rod from the pivot post and then withdraw the unit.
5   Refitting is a reversal of removal, but apply a little grease to the pivot post. Refitting may be made easier if the distributor baseplate is rotated slightly with the fingers.

9   Condenser – renewal

1   If the condenser is suspected of being faulty as a result of reference to the Fault Diagnosis chart at the end of this part of the Chapter, it may be removed and a new one fitted without having to remove the distributor.
2   Release the HT leads from the spark plugs, take off the distributor cap and place the cap and the leads to one side. Remove the rotor arm.
3   Disconnect the LT lead from the coil negative terminal.
4   Mark the position of the distributor body in relation to the clamp plate and then release the clamp plate pinch-bolt.
5   Turn the distributor approximately 120° in a clockwise direction to expose the condenser and extract its securing screw. Pull off its lead connecting block and remove the condenser.
6   Refitting is a reversal of removal.
7   Check the ignition timing on completion (Sec 5).

Fig. 4.7 Condenser location on distributor body – arrow indicates retaining screw (Sec 9)

10   Distributor – overhaul

1   Dismantling of the distributor should not be taken beyond the renewal of components described in earlier Sections of this Chapter.
2   Internal components are not supplied as spares. In the event of severe wear having taken place, obtain a new or reconditioned unit.

11   Spark plugs, HT leads and distributor cap – general

1   The spark plugs should be removed at the intervals described in Routine Maintenance. Before unscrewing the plugs, pull off the leads and brush out any grit from the plug recesses to avoid dropping any into the cylinders as the spark plugs are unscrewed.
2   The appearance of a removed spark plug can give some indication of the condition or state or tune of the engine, but as modern engines run on a weaker fuel/air mixture in order to conform to current emission control regulations, a rather whiter appearance of the spark plug electrode area must be expected than was the case on older cars. As the mixture control is preset during production, a black appearance of the plug electrode will normally be due to oil passing worn piston rings or valve stem oil seals, unless the carburettor has been tampered with.

Measuring plug gap. A feeler gauge of the correct size (see ignition system specifications) should have a slight 'drag' when slid between the electrodes. Adjust gap if necessary

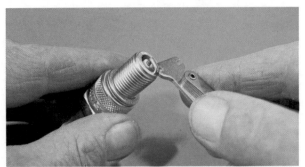

Adjusting plug gap. The plug gap is adjusted by bending the earth electrode inwards, or outwards, as necessary until the correct clearance is obtained. Note the use of the correct tool

Normal. Grey-brown deposits, lightly coated core nose. Gap increasing by around 0.001 in (0.025 mm) per 1000 miles (1600 km). Plugs ideally suited to engine, and engine in good condition

Carbon fouling. Dry, black, sooty deposits. Will cause weak spark and eventually misfire. Fault: over-rich fuel mixture. Check: carburettor mixture settings, float level and jet sizes; choke operation and cleanliness of air filter. Plugs can be re-used after cleaning

Oil fouling. Wet, oily deposits. Will cause weak spark and eventually misfire. Fault: worn bores/piston rings or valve guides; sometimes occurs (temporarily) during running-in period. Plugs can be re-used after thorough cleaning

Overheating. Electrodes have glazed appearance, core nose very white – few deposits. Fault: plug overheating. Check: plug value, ignition timing, fuel octane rating (too low) and fuel mixture (too weak). Discard plugs and cure fault immediately

Electrode damage. Electrodes burned away; core nose has burned, glazed appearance. Fault: pre-ignition. Check: as for 'Overheating' but may be more severe. Discard plugs and remedy fault before piston or valve damage occurs

Split core nose (may appear initially as a crack). Damage is self-evident, but cracks will only show after cleaning. Fault: pre-ignition or wrong gap-setting technique. Check: ignition timing, cooling system, fuel octane rating (too low) and fuel mixture (too weak). Discard plugs, rectify fault immediately

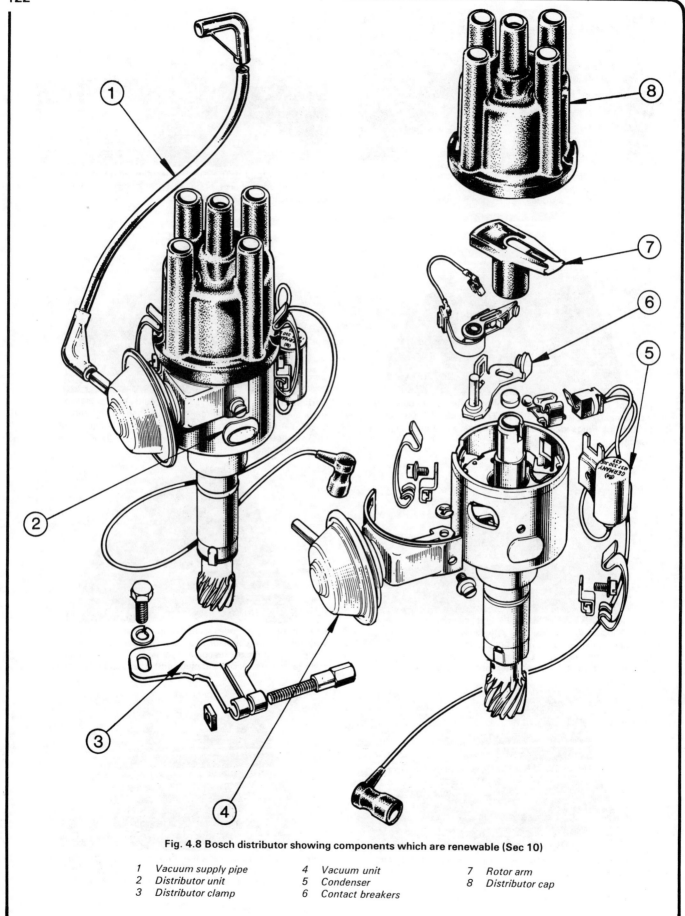

Fig. 4.8 Bosch distributor showing components which are renewable (Sec 10)

1	Vacuum supply pipe	4	Vacuum unit	7	Rotor arm
2	Distributor unit	5	Condenser	8	Distributor cap
3	Distributor clamp	6	Contact breakers		

3   Either clean the spark plugs and re-gap them or renew them, according to mileage interval. Cleaning the electrodes with a wire brush may leave conductance paths so an abrasive type cleaning device is to be preferred, but wash the plugs thoroughly in petrol to remove any abrasive powder, particularly from the threads if they were oily.

4   Always bend the outer electrode with a proper spark plug gapping tool to set the gaps to the specified clearance.

5   When installing the plugs use a long reach socket, apply a little grease to the threads of the plugs and tighten them only to the specified torque wrench setting. Overtightening may damage the plug or its seat.

6   Periodically wipe over the HT leads with a fuel-moistened cloth. Only pull the leads off by their rubber connectors.

7   The sockets on the distributor cap should be cleaned if they appear corroded when a lead is detached. A smear of petroleum jelly (not grease) applied to the ferrule on the end of the HT lead will help to prevent corrosion.

8   Never cut a carbon cored type of HT lead in order to insert a radio suppressor. Apart from being unnecessary, the cable will be ruined.

9   Examine the inside of the distributor cap. If the contacts are corroded or are excessively burnt, or if the carbon centre contact is worn away, renew the cap. Make sure that the leads are installed in their correct firing order (Fig. 4.11).

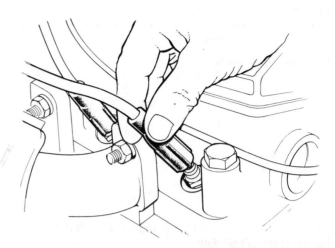

Fig. 4.10 Pull on HT lead terminal insulator when detaching (Sec 11)

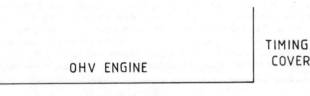

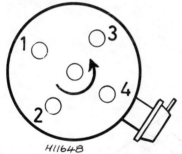

Fig. 4.9 HT lead connecting diagram on the ohv engine (Sec 11)

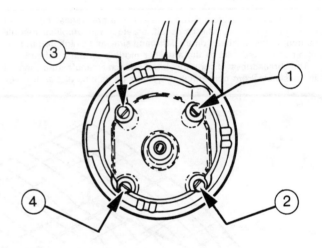

Fig. 4.11 Check inside of distributor cap for damage or cracks – plug lead positions are shown (Sec 11)

12 Fault diagnosis – mechanical ignition system

Symptom	Reason(s)
Engine fails to start	Discharged battery
	Loose battery connections
	Oil on contact points
	Disconnected ignition leads
	Faulty condenser
	Damp HT leads or distributor cap
	Faulty coil
	Mechanical fault (eg distributor drive)
	Ignition timing grossly incorrect (after overhaul)
Engine starts and runs but misfires	Faulty spark plug
	Cracked distributor cap
	Cracked rotor arm
	Worn advance mechanism
	Incorrect spark plug gap
	Incorrect contact breaker points gap
	Faulty condenser
	Faulty coil
	Incorrect timing
	Poor earth connections

Symptom	Reason(s)
Engine fires but will not run	Ballast resistor or associated component defective
Engine overheats and lacks power	Seized advance weights in distributor Perforated or disconnected vacuum pipe Incorrect ignition timing
Engine pinks	Timing too advanced Advance mechanism stuck Broken centrifugal weight spring Low fuel octane rating
Contact points badly burnt	Poor earth connections at battery or engine/body earth straps Faulty condenser

PART B: BREAKERLESS (ELECTRONIC) IGNITION SYSTEM

13 General description

1   The electronic system fitted consists of a breakerless distributor driven from the end of the camshaft, an electronic amplifier module mounted on the bulkhead on the left-hand side, and a high output type ignition coil, fitted next to the amplifier module on the bulkhead.
2   The breakerless distributor is of Bosch manufacture and is distinguishable from conventional systems by its blue distributor cap.

The unit has no mechanical contact breaker or condenser, these components being replaced by a trigger wheel, a trigger coil and a stator. The action of the distributor is to provide a pulse to the electronic module which in turn actuates the ignition coil to ignite the fuel/air mixture via the HT leads and spark plugs.
3   The electronic amplifier module is a sealed unit located on the left-hand side of the engine compartment bulkhead. The function of the module is to sense the trigger pulse from the distributor and amplify its voltage sufficiently to operate the module's output transistor. On receipt of this amplified voltage the module shuts off the ignition coil primary circuit allowing HT voltage to build up within the coil in the conventional manner and fire the appropriate spark plug via the distributor and HT leads. On completion of the firing cycle the primary

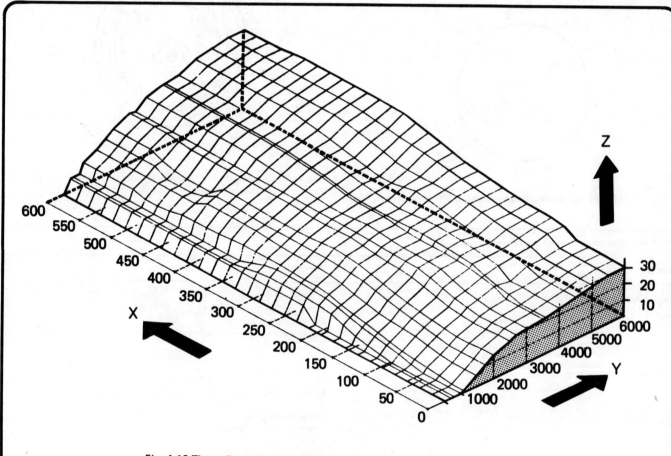

Fig. 4.12 Three dimensional ignition chart for the CVH engine (Secs 13 and 16)

| X | Inlet manifold vacuum | Y | Engine speed (rpm) | Z | Spark advance (crankshaft degrees) |

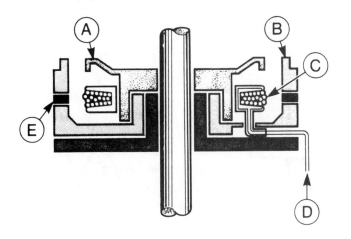

Fig. 4.13 Schematic diagram of the distributor signal
generating system components (Sec 13)

A   Trigger wheel
B   Stator arm
C   Magnetic trigger coil
D   Wires to module
E   Permanent magnet

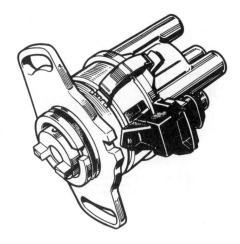

Fig. 4.14 The Bosch 'Hall Effect' distributor used on CVH
engined models (Sec 13)

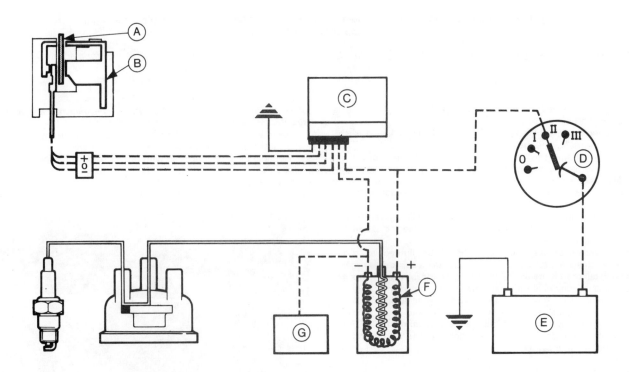

Fig. 4.15 Breakerless ignition system diagram showing current flow (dotted line) between firing
pulses (Sec 13)

A   Trigger vane segment in line sensor
    pick-up
B   Distributor 'Hall Effect' sensor
C   Module
D   Ignition key in running position
E   Battery
F   Coil primary circuit in operation
G   Tachometer

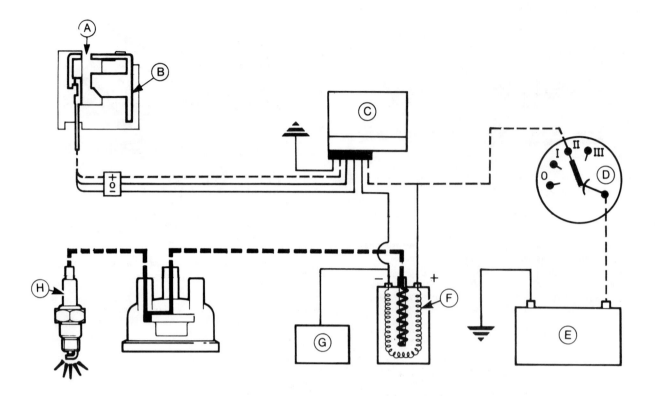

Fig. 4.16 Breakerless ignition system diagram showing current flow (dotted line) at start of firing pulse (Sec 13)

A   Trigger vane 'air gap' in line with pick-   C   Module   F   Coil HT voltage (primary circuit cut)
     up   D   Ignition key in running position   G   Tachometer
B   Distributor 'Hall Effect' sensor   E   Battery   H   Spark plug firing

circuit is then switched on again by the module and the cycle is repeated for the next cylinder.

4   The ignition coil, which is also located on the bulkhead in the engine compartment, operates on conventional principles, but with a higher output voltage. The unit is rated at 8 volts and is supplied via a ballast resistor wire during normal running. When starting the engine the ballast resistor wire is bypassed and the coil receives full battery voltage. The coil used on electronic breakerless systems is distinguished by a yellow label on the case.

5   The spark plugs used are the copper cored resistor type with a metric thread form. Only this type of plug is suitable for use in the electronic ignition system.

6   Repair and overhaul operations should be limited to those described in this Chapter as only the distributor cap, rotor arm, HT leads and vacuum unit are available as repair parts, all other items are sealed and only renewable as complete units. Should a fault in the system develop or be suspected, the advice of your dealer should be sought. Fault diagnosis procedures are lengthy and must follow a systematic approach using sophisticated test equipment. For these reasons fault diagnosis and repair are considered to be beyond the scope of the average owner.

Safety note

7   The voltage produced by the HT circuit on an electronic ignition system is approximately 25% greater than that from a conventional system. In consequence take extra precautions when handling the HT leads with the ignition switched on or the engine running. Although not lethal, the shock could be severe.

14 Routine maintenance – electronic ignition system

Very little is required in the way of servicing for the electronic ignition system, but that is not to say that it should be ignored. The

following items must be checked at the specified mileage intervals (see Routine Maintenance at the front of this manual).

1   Remove, clean and check the spark plug electrode settings. Adjust if necessary to the gap given in the Specifications.

2   Remove the distributor cap with the HT leads and wipe them clean and dry. Also wipe the coil tower and make sure that the plastic safety cover is fitted securely. Remove the rotor arm (photo) then visually inspect the distributor cap, rotor arm and HT leads for hairline cracks

14.2 Rotor arm removal from the breakerless distributor

and signs of arcing. If cracks or any signs of damage are visible renew the defective component. When refitting the distributor cap ensure that the HT leads are securely fitted to the cap, plugs and coil. Also ensure that the carbon brush and HT segments are not excessively worn.

3   At the specified mileage intervals remove and renew the spark plugs, as described in Section 17.

4   Dwell angle adjustment is unnecessary with a breakerless system and ignition timing once set should not require further attention.

15 Distributor – removal and refitting

1   The distributor is precisely positioned for optimum ignition timing during production and marked accordingly with a punch mark on the distributor mounting flange and the cylinder head (photo).

2   Disconnect the HT leads from the spark plugs.

3   Disconnect the wiring harness multi-plug from the distributor.

4   Release the distributor cap retaining clips, lift off the cap and position it, with the HT leads, to one side (photo).

5   Unscrew and remove the two distributor flange mounting bolts and withdraw the distributor from the cylinder head.

6   Check the distributor spindle for side-to-side movement. If excessive movement is found, the distributor must be renewed as it is not possible to obtain individual components for overhaul.

15.1 Distributor and cylinder head alignment marks (arrowed)

15.4 Distributor cap removal

7   Before refitting the distributor, check the condition of the oil seal beneath the mounting flange and renew it if necessary.

8   Hold the distributor so that the punch marks on the distributor body and the offset drive dog are in approximate alignment, then insert the distributor into its recess.

9   Check that the drive components have engaged and then rotate the distributor until the punch marks on flange and head are in alignment. Insert the bolts and tighten to the specified torque.

10   Reconnect all the disconnected components.

New unit

11   Where a new distributor is being installed, its flange will obviously not have a punch mark and it must therefore be fitted in the following way.

12   Hold the distributor in approximately its fitted position and also ensure that the drive dog is in approximately the correct alignment to engage with the offset segments of the camshaft dog.

13   Locate the distributor on the cylinder head. When you are sure that the drive dogs are fully engaged, screw in the flange bolts so that they are not only positioned centrally in the flange slots, but still allow the distributor to be rotated stiffly.

14   Reconnect the distributor cap, the spark plug leads and the LT multi-plug.

15   Using a little quick-drying white paint, increase the contrast of the timing notch in the crankshaft pulley and the appropriate mark (see Specifications) on the timing belt cover scale (photo).

16   Connect a timing light (stroboscope) in accordance with the manufacturer's instructions.

17   Start the engine, allow it to idle and point the timing light at the timing marks. They should appear stationary and in alignment. If they are not, rotate the distributor as necessary to bring them into line and then tighten one of the distributor bolts.

18   Switch off the engine, remove the timing light and then tighten all the distributor mounting bolts to the specified torque.

19   Punch mark the distributor flange at a point exactly opposite the mark on the cylinder head. Future installation can then be carried out as described in paragraphs 1 to 10 of this Section.

15.15 Ignition timing marks (CVH engine)

15 Ignition amplifier module – description, removal and refitting

1   The function of this device is to assess the mechanical and vacuum advance requirements under the varying operating conditions. The module contains a transducer which converts engine vacuum, transferred to it by a hose from the engine inlet manifold, to an electrical voltage. The unit also gauges input pulses fed to it from the distributor to obtain the engine speed. It is then able to give the exact

spark advance requirement for the engine speed and loading. The three dimensional graph shown in Fig. 4.12 illustrates the range of ignition advance characteristics regulated by the module.

2   The ignition amplifier cannot be repaired and, if damaged or known to be defective, it must be renewed as a unit. The vacuum advance characteristics of the module can be checked, but this is a task best entrusted to your Ford dealer.

3   To remove the module unit first disconnect the battery earth lead.

4   Detach the wiring loom connector from the module by pulling on the connector, not the leads.

5   Detach the vacuum hose from the module, undo and remove the single retaining screw and remove the module.

6   Refitting is a reversal of the removal procedure.

17 Spark plugs, HT leads and distributor cap – general

1   In general, the same remarks apply as were made in Section 11. Note, however, that a different type of plug is used, and that its electrode gap and tightening torque are different (photos).

2   Only remove plugs from the CVH engine when it is warm or cold – never when it is hot.

3   Note that the firing order on the CVH engine is different from the ohv engine.

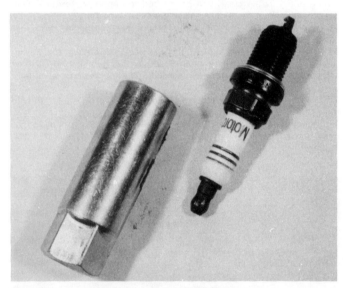

17.1A Miniature type spark plug and socket wrench

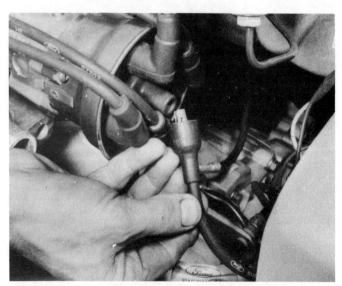

17.1B Connecting a spark plug HT lead

18 Ignition coil – general

1   The LT connections to the coil used with electronic ignition cannot be confused as the terminals are of different size.

2   **Never** fit a coil from a conventional ignition system into an electronic ignition system otherwise the amplifier module may be damaged.

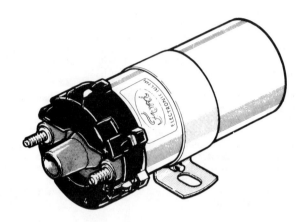

Fig. 4.17 The Bosch ignition coil which must be used with the breakerless ignition system (Sec 18)

19 Ignition lock cylinder – removal and refitting

This operation also applies to cars with mechanical ignition systems.

1   Disconnect the battery earth terminal, then remove the steering column lower shroud.

2   Insert the ignition key into the lock and turn to position 1.

3   Using a screwdriver, depress the cylinder retaining clip and withdraw the lock cylinder by pulling on the key (Fig. 4.18).

4   Refit by simply pushing the cylinder into position with the key held in position 1.

5   It should be noted that the steering column lock and tube are a combined unit and the lock cannot be renewed separately. For column tube and lock removal refer to Chapter 9.

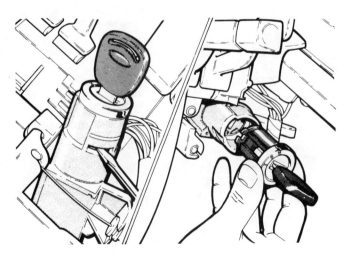

Fig. 4.18 Ignition lock cylinder removal method (Sec 19)

20 Fault diagnosis – electronic ignition system

Symptom	Reason(s)
Engine fails to start	Discharged battery
	Loose battery connections
	Disconnected ignition leads
	Crack in distributor cap or rotor
	Faulty amplifier module
Engine starts and runs but misfires	Faulty spark plug
	Crack in distributor cap
	Cracked rotor arm
	Faulty coil
	Poor earth connections
Engine overheats and lacks power	Perforated or disconnected vacuum pipe
Engine pinks	Low fuel octane rating

Note: *Any of the foregoing symptoms could be caused by incorrect timing, but unless the distributor mounting bolts have become slack this is unlikely as the timing is preset during production with the distributor flange and cylinder head punch marks aligned.*

Chapter 5   Clutch

Contents

Clutch – inspection 3
Clutch – refitting 5
Clutch – removal 2
Clutch cable – renewal 6

Clutch pedal – removal and refitting 7
Clutch release bearing – renewal 4
Fault diagnosis – clutch 8
General description 1

Specifications

Type .... Single plate, diaphragm spring

Actuation .... Cable (self-adjusting)

Pedal stroke (nominal) .... 145 mm (5.7 in)

Disc (driven plate)
Diameter:
   1.0 and 1.1 litre .... 165 mm (6.5 in)
   1.3 and 1.6 litre .... 190 mm (7.5 in)
Lining thickness .... 3.20 mm (0.126 in)

Torque wrench settings
Pressure plate to flywheel:

	Nm	lbf ft
165 mm diameter	9 to 11	7 to 8
190 mm diameter	16 to 20	12 to 15

1   General description

The clutch is of single dry plate type with a diaphragm spring pressure plate.

Actuation is by cable and the pendant-mounted pedal incorporates a self-adjusting mechanism.

The release bearing is of ball type and is kept in constant contact with the fingers of the diaphragm spring by the action of the pedal self-adjusting mechanism. In consequence, there is no pedal free movement adjustment required.

When the clutch pedal is released, the adjustment pawl is no longer engaged with the teeth on the pedal quadrant, the cable being tensioned, however, by the spring which is located between the pedal and the quadrant. When the pedal is depressed the pawl engages in the nearest vee between the teeth. The particular tooth engagement position will gradually change as the components move to compensate for wear in the clutch disc (driven plate) and stretch in the cable.

The size of the clutch varies according to engine capacity (see Specifications).

2   Clutch – removal

1   To remove the clutch it is necessary to disconnect the engine and transmission assembly. This can be done by either removing the engine and transmission complete, and then separating them on the bench (Chapter 1), or by removing the transmission only (Chapter 6).

2   Remove the clutch assembly by unscrewing the six bolts holding the pressure plate assembly to the rear face of the flywheel. Unscrew the bolts diagonally, half a turn at a time, to prevent distortion to the cover flange.

3   With all the bolts and spring washers removed lift the clutch

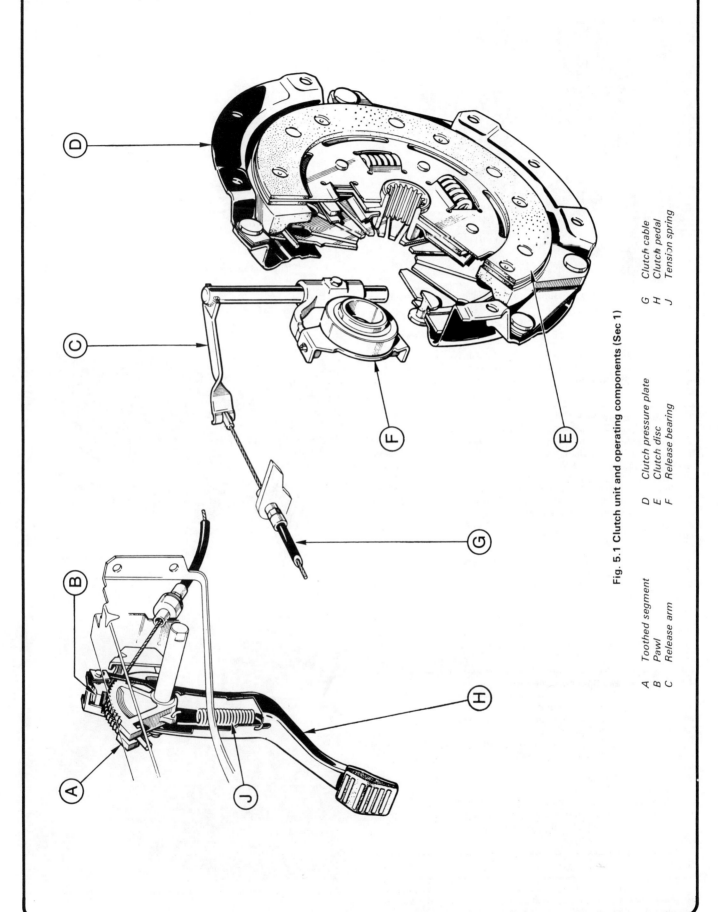

Fig. 5.1 Clutch unit and operating components (Sec 1)

A Toothed segment
B Pawl
C Release arm

D Clutch pressure plate
E Clutch disc
F Release bearing

G Clutch cable
H Clutch pedal
J Tension spring

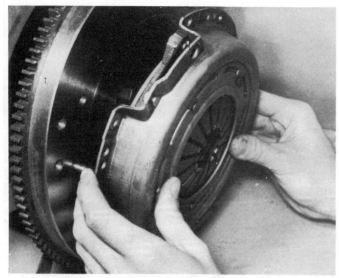

2.3 Withdraw the clutch pressure plate and disc from the flywheel. Note location dowels

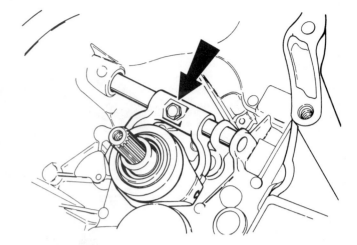

Fig. 5.2 Clutch release arm securing bolt – arrowed (Sec 4)

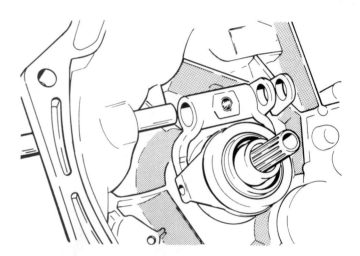

Fig. 5.3 Withdraw the shaft and remove the release bearing unit (Sec 4)

assembly off the locating dowels (photo). The clutch disc (driven plate) may fall out at this stage as it is not attached to either the clutch cover assembly or the flywheel.

3   Clutch – inspection

1   Examine the clutch disc friction lining for wear and loose rivets and the disc for rim distortion, cracks, broken hub springs, and worn splines. The surface of the friction linings may be highly glazed, but as long as the clutch material pattern can be clearly seen this is satisfactory. Compare the amount of lining wear with a new clutch disc at the stores in your local garage, and if the linings are more than three quarters worn renew the disc.
2   It is always best to renew the clutch as an assembly to preclude further trouble; an exchange unit will have been accurately set up and balanced to very fine limits.
3   Check the machined faces of the flywheel and the pressure plate. If either is grooved it should be machined until smooth or renewed.
4   If the pressure plate is cracked or split it is essential that an exchange unit is fitted, also if the pressure of the diaphragm spring is suspect.
5   Check the release bearing for smoothness of operation. There should be no harshness and no slackness in it. It should spin reasonably freely bearing in mind it has been pre-packed with grease.

4   Clutch release bearing – renewal

1   With the gearbox and engine separated to provide access to the clutch, attention can be given to the release bearing located in the bellhousing, over the input shaft.
2   The release bearing is an important component and unless it is nearly new it is a mistake not to renew it during an overhaul of the clutch.
3   To remove the release bearing, first remove the bolt securing the release arm (Fig. 5.2) and pull out the shaft.
4   The release fork and bearing can then be pulled off the input shaft.
5   To free the bearing from the release fork, simply unhook it (photo).
6   Refitting is a reversal of this procedure.

5   Clutch – refitting

1   It is important that no oil or grease gets onto the clutch disc friction linings, or the pressure plate and flywheel faces. It is advisable to refit the clutch with clean hands and to wipe down the pressure

4.5 Clutch release bearing attachment to fork (roll pin arrowed)

plate and flywheel faces with a clean dry rag before reassembly begins.

2   Place the clutch (driven plate) against the flywheel, ensuring that it is the correct way round. The flywheel side of the disc is smooth. If the disc is fitted the wrong way round, it will be quite impossible to operate the clutch (photo).

3   Refit the clutch cover assembly loosely on the dowels. Refit the six bolts and spring washers, and tighten them finger tight so that the disc is gripped but can still be moved (photo).

4   The clutch disc must now be centralised so that when the engine and gearbox are mated, the gearbox input shaft splines will pass through the splines in the centre of the disc.

5   Centralisation can be carried out quite easily by inserting a round bar or long screwdriver through the hole in the centre of the clutch, so that the end of the car rests in the small hole in the end of the crankshaft. Ideally an old input shaft should be used.

6   Using the hole in the end of the crankshaft as a fulcrum, moving the bar sideways or up and down will move the disc in the necessary direction to achieve centralisation.

7   Centralisation is easily judged by removing the bar and viewing the disc hub in relation to the hole in the centre of the clutch cover diaphragm spring. When the hub appears exactly in the centre of the hole all is correct. Alternatively, the input shaft will centre the clutch hub exactly obviating the need for visual alignment.

5.2 Clutch disc (driven plate) marking

5.8 Tightening the clutch cover (pressure) plate bolts. Note clutch disc centralising tool

8   Tighten the clutch bolts firmly in a diagonal sequence to ensure that the cover plate is pulled down evenly and without distortion of the flange. Finally tighten the bolts down to the specified torque.

6   Clutch cable – renewal

1   Raise the clutch pedal and position a suitable block of wood underneath it to support it.

2   Raise and support the bonnet then grip the clutch inner cable as shown and disengage it from the clutch release lever (photo).

3   Unclip and detach the dash lower insulating panel for access to the clutch pedal.

4   With the pedal raised, detach the pawl from the toothed segment, pivoting the segment forward.

5   Pivot the segment rearwards then remove the cable, passing it through the space between the pedal and the automatic adjustment unit. Withdraw the cable through the engine compartment (photo)

6   To refit the cable, first raise and support the clutch pedal, as described in paragraph 1. Check that the adjustment unit pawl is

5.3 Refit the clutch cover assembly

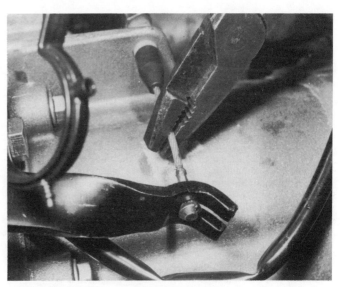

6.2 Detach cable from clutch release lever fork

6.5 Withdraw cable from engine compartment side

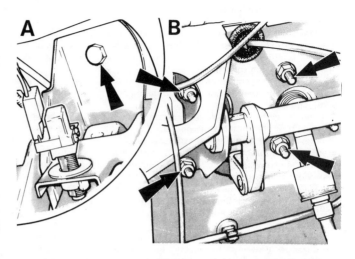

Fig. 5.5 Clutch/brake pedal bracket retaining bolt (A) to crash panel and bulkhead bolts (B) – right-hand drive (Sec 7)

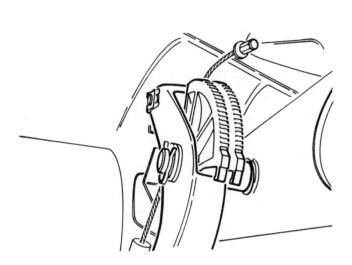

Fig. 5.4 Reattach the clutch cable to the segment unit (Sec 6)

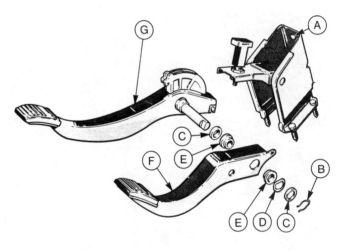

Fig. 5.6 Brake and clutch pedal assembly components (Sec 7)

A	Mounting bracket	E	Bush
B	Circlip	F	Brake pedal
C	Spacer	G	Clutch pedal
D	Washer		

disengaged from the segment then refit the clutch cable reversing the removal procedure.

7   When the cable is fitted, extract the support block from under the pedal then slowly operate the clutch to readjust the cable.

8   Refit the lower dash insulating panel to complete.

7   Clutch pedal – removal and refitting

1   Disconnect the clutch cable from the release lever and the pedal/self-adjustment unit, as described in Section 6.

2   On left-hand drive models, extract the spring clip from the pedal pivot shaft and withdraw the washers; keeping them in order for refitting. The pedal can then be removed sideways from the shaft.

3   On right-hand drive models the pedal is removed complete with the clutch/brake pedal support bracket. Detach the brake stop-light switch wire multi-connector plug then unscrew and remove the four support bracket-to-bulkhead retaining nuts and the single bolt to the upper crash panel (Fig. 5.5). The pedal box support bracket can now be renewed and the clutch pedal removed, as described in paragraph 2. If the brake pedal is to be removed, prise free the remove the bushes.

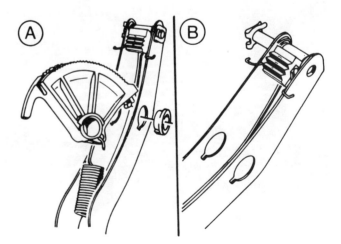

Fig. 5.7 Clutch adjuster segment (A) and pawl (B) removal (Sec 7)

4   To remove the adjuster mechanism, extract the pedal shaft bushes, remove the segment and detach it from the spring. To remove the adjuster pawl, extract its pivot shaft retaining clip on one side, withdraw the shaft and disengage the pawl and spring, noting their orientation (Fig. 3.7).

5   Reassembly of the pedal and adjuster mechanism is a reversal of the removal procedure. Lubricate the pivot shafts prior to assembly with molybdenum grease.

6   When the pawl and segment are refitted to the pedal, lever up the pawl and turn the segment so that the pawl can be positioned clear of the segment teeth on the smooth section of the segment (Fig. 5.8).

7   Refit the clutch pedal to the pivot shaft, locate the washers and securing clip and then attach the cable.

8   On right-hand drive models relocate the clutch/brake pedal bracket and secure with the retaining nuts and bolt.

9   Reconnect the clutch cable and adjust it, as described in Section 6.

10 Refit the dash lower insulating panel to complete, then check that the clutch operation is satisfactory.

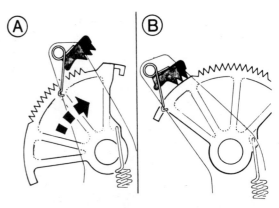

Fig. 5.8 Segment refitting: lift pawl (A) and rotate segment to position pawl as shown (B) (Sec 7)

8   Fault diagnosis – clutch

Symptom	Reason(s)
Judder when taking up drive	Loose engine/transmission mountings Worn friction linings Oil saturated linings Worn splines on input shaft or clutch disc
Clutch spin (failure to disengage) so that gears cannot be meshed	Disc sticking on input shaft splines due to rust. May occur after standing idle for long periods Damaged or misaligned pressure plate assembly
Clutch slip (increase in engine speed does not result in comparable increase in road speed – particularly on gradients)	Friction surfaces worn or oil contaminated Weak clutch engagement due to fault in automatic cable adjuster or weak diaphragm spring
Noise evident on depressing clutch pedal	Dry, worn or damaged release bearing Play between clutch disc and input shaft splines
Noise evident as clutch pedal released	Distorted clutch disc Weak or broken clutch disc torsion springs Distorted or worn input shaft Release bearing loose on mounting hub

Chapter 6 Transmission

Contents

Differential unit (four- and five-speed transmission) – overhaul ... 11
Fault diagnosis – transmission 18
Gearchange mechanism – adjustment 3
Gearchange mechanism (five-speed) – removal, overhaul and
refitting 15
Gearchange mechanism (four-speed) – removal, overhaul and
refitting 4
General description 1
Input shaft (four-speed) – overhaul 10
Mainshaft (four-speed) – overhaul 9
Routine maintenance – transmission 2

Speedometer driven gear (four- and five-speed transmission) –
removal and refitting 13
Transmission (five-speed) – dismantling and overhaul of major
assemblies 16
Transmission (five-speed) – dismantling (general) 14
Transmission (five-speed) – reassembly 17
Transmission (four- and five-speed) – removal and refitting 5
Transmission (four-speed) – dismantling (general) 7
Transmission (four-speed) – reassembly 12
Transmission (four-speed) – removal of major assemblies 6
Transmission housing and selector mechanism (four-speed) –
overhaul 8

Specifications

Transmission type .... Four or five forward speeds and one reverse, synchromesh on all forward gears

Lubrication

Lubricant type .... SAE 80 EP gear oil to Ford spec SQM-2C9008-A
Lubricant capacity:
   Four-speed gearbox .... 2.8 litre (4.9 Imp pints)
   Five-speed gearbox .... 3.1 litre (5.4 Imp pints)
Grease type (assembly only – see text):
   Four-speed .... To Ford specification SM1C-1020-B
   Five-speed:
      Gears, contact and thrust faces .... Molybdenum Disulphide paste to Ford spec SM1C-4505-A
      Synchroniser cones and mainshaft assemblies .... Colloidal Molybedenum Disulphide in oil to Ford spec SM1C-4504-A
      5th gear on input shaft .... Ford grease type ESEA-MIC-1014-A
      Selector shaft locking assembly sealer .... Anaerobic retaining and sealing compound to Ford spec SM4G-4645-AA or AB

Ratios

Four-speed gear ratios:	1.0 litre	1.1 litre
1st	3.58	3.58
2nd	2.04	2.04
3rd	1.35	1.30
4th	0.95	0.88
Reverse	3.77	3.77
Final drive ratio	4.06	3.58

Five-speed gear ratios:
1st	3.58
2nd	2.04
3rd	1.35
4th	0.95
5th	0.76
Reverse	3.62

Final drive ratio:
1.0 litre	4.29
1.1 litre	3.84 or 4.06
1.3 litre	3.84
1.6 litre	3.84

Snap-ring (circlip) thicknesses available
Mainshaft:
Gear synchronisers (not 5th) and ball-bearing inner race	1.52 mm (0.060 in)
	1.55 mm (0.061 in)
	1.58 mm (0.062 in)
	1.61 mm (0.063 in) and
	1.64 mm (0.065 in)
Fifth gear synchroniser	1.48 mm (0.058 in)
	1.53 mm (0.060 in) and
	1.58 mm (0.062 in)
Tolerance allowance	0 to −0.25 mm (0 to −0.0098 in)
Ball-bearing outer race	1.89 mm (0.0744 in)
	1.97 mm (0.0776 in) and
	2.04 mm (0.0804 in)
Tolerance allowance	0 to −0.030 mm (0 to −0.0012 in)

Input shaft:
Ball-bearing outer race	As mainshaft ball-bearing outer race
Fifth gear driving dog	1.65 mm (0.065 in)
	1.70 mm (0.066 in) and
	1.75 mm (0.068 in)
Tolerance allowance	0 to −0.025 mm (0 to −0.0010 in)

Torque wrench settings

	Nm	lbf ft
Four-speed gearbox		
Transmission-to-engine bolts	40	30
Starter motor bolts	40	30
Transmission bearer	52	38
Transmission bearer to transmission	90	66
Spindle carrier to balljoint	80	59
Gearshift stabilizer to transmission	55	41
Shift rod to selector shaft clamp bolt	15	11
Final drivegear to differential housing	115	85
Small to large housing	25	18
Housing cover	13	10
Selector shaft detent cap nut	27	20
Gearshift unit to floorpan	18	13
Oil filler plug	27	20
Reverse light switch	27	20
Selector gate stabilizer	6	4
Gearshift gaiter to body	2	1.5
Five-speed gearbox		
Transmission-to-engine bolts	40	30
Starter motor bolts	40	30
Transmission bearer (to transmission)	90	66
Transmission bearer (to floor)	52	38
Spindle carrier to balljoint	80	59
Gearshift stabilizer to transmission	55	41
Shift rod to selector shaft clamp bolt	16	12
Selector block to main selector shaft	14	10
Final drivegear to differential housing	115	85
Clutch housing to transmission housing	25	18
Intermediate to transmission housing	13	9
Fifth gear selector pin clamp bolt	17	13
Fifth gear selector plate to housing	30	22
Housing cover to intermediate housing	10	7
Selector shaft detent mechanism cap nut	30	22
Gearshift stabilizer to floor	18	13
Oil filler plug	27	20
Reverse light switch	27	20

1 General description

Four-speed gearbox

The gearbox and differential are housed in a two section light alloy casting which is bolted to a transversely mounted engine.

Drive from the engine/transmission is transmitted to the front roadwheels through open driveshafts.

The engine torque is transmitted to the gearbox input shaft. Once a gear is selected, power is then transmitted to the main (output) shaft. The helically cut forward speed gears on the output shaft are in constant mesh with the corresponding gears on the input shaft.

Synchromesh units are used for 1st/2nd and 3rd/4th gear selection and operate as follows.

When the clutch pedal is depressed and the gearchange lever is moved to select a higher gear, the synchro baulk ring is pressed onto the gear cone. The friction generated causes the faster rotating gear on the input shaft to slow until its speed matches that of the gear on the output shaft. The gears can then be smoothly engaged.

When changing to a lower gear, the principle of operation is similar except that the speed of the slower rotating gear is increased by the action of the baulk ring on the cone.

Reverse gear is of the straight-cut tooth type and is part of the 1st/2nd synchro unit. A sliding type reverse idler gear is used.

The torque from the gearbox output shaft is transmitted to the crownwheel which is bolted to the differential cage and thence through the differential gears to the driveshafts.

Any need for adjustment to the differential and its bearings has

been obviated by the inclusion of two diaphragm springs which are located in the smaller half of the transmission housing. Any tolerances which may exist are taken up by the sliding fit of the outer bearing ring in the smaller section of the housing.

Gear selection is obtained by rotary and axial movements of the main selector shaft (transmitted through a selector dog bolted to the selector shaft) and two guide levers to the guide shaft which also carries a selector dog.

Rotary movement of the main selector shaft engages a cam on the guide shaft selector dog either in the cut-out of the 1st/2nd or 3rd/4th gear selector fork or in the aperture in the reverse gear guide lever.

Axial movement of the selector shaft moves the appropriate selector fork on the guide shaft or reverse idler gear through the medium of the guide lever, so engaging the gear.

The selected gear is locked in engagement by a shift locking plate which is carried on the guide shaft selector dog and a spring-loaded interlock pin located in the smaller housing section.

Five-speed gearbox

The transmission is basically the same as the four-speed version with the exception of a modified selector mechanism, and an additional gear and synchro-hub contained in a housing attached to the side of the main transmission casing.

2 Routine maintenance – transmission

1   The only maintenance required is to check and top up, if necessary, the oil level in the transmission at the intervals specified in Routine Maintenance at the beginning of this manual.
2   A combined level/filler plug is fitted and the correct oil level is established when the oil is just seen to be running out of the plug hole when the vehicle is on level ground.
3   Regular oil changing is not specified by the manufacturers, but the oil can be drained if necessary (prior to removal of the unit or after traversing a flooded road for example) by removing the selector shaft locking mechanism (Fig. 6.4).

3 Gearchange mechanism – adjustment

1   This is not a routine operation and will normally only be required after dismantling, to compensate for wear or to overcome any 'notchiness' evident during gear selection.
2   To set the linkage correctly, refer to Chapter 1, Section 21.

4 Gearchange mechanism (four-speed) – removal, overhaul and refitting

1   Before commencing removal operations, engage 4th gear.
2   Unscrew the gear lever knob, slide the rubber gaiter up to the lever and remove it.
3   If the vehicle is not over an inspection pit, jack it up and fit axle stands.
4   Unhook the tension spring which runs between the gearchange rod and the side-member.
5   Slacken the clamp bolt and pull the gearchange rod from the selector shaft which projects from the transmission.
6   Unbolt the end of the stabilizer from the transmission housing. Note the washer between the stabilizer trunnion and the transmission.
7   Still working under the vehicle, unbolt the gearchange housing from the floor. Withdraw the housing/stabilizer from the vehicle.
8   To dismantle, unbolt the housing from the stabilizer and detach the gearchange lever with plastic cover and the stabilizer from the slide block.
9   Detach the gearchange rod from the slide block. This is done by unclipping the upper guide shell and withdrawing the rod.
10   The gear lever can be removed by prising off the rubber spring retaining clip and withdrawing the spring, half shell and plastic cover.
11   Renew any worn components and reassemble by reversing the dismantling procedure, but observe the following points.
12   If the stabilizer bush is in poor condition it can cause engine and transmission noises to be transmitted to the vehicle interior. To renew the bush press it out using a suitable bolt, nut and two washers, used

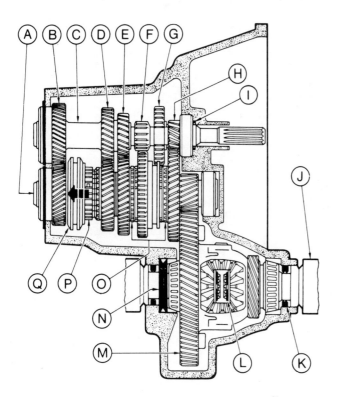

Fig. 6.1 Cutaway view of the four-speed transmission (Sec 1)

A	Mainshaft	K	Oil seal
B	4th gear	L	Driveshaft snap-ring
C	Input shaft	M	Crownwheel
D	3rd gear	N	Diaphragm springs
E	2nd gear	O	1st/2nd synchro with
F	Reverse gear		reverse gear
G	Reverse idler gear	P	3rd/4th synchro sleeve
H	1st gear	Q	3rd/4th synchro sleeve
I	Input shaft oil seal		(4th gear engaged)
J	Driveshaft inboard		
	CV joint		

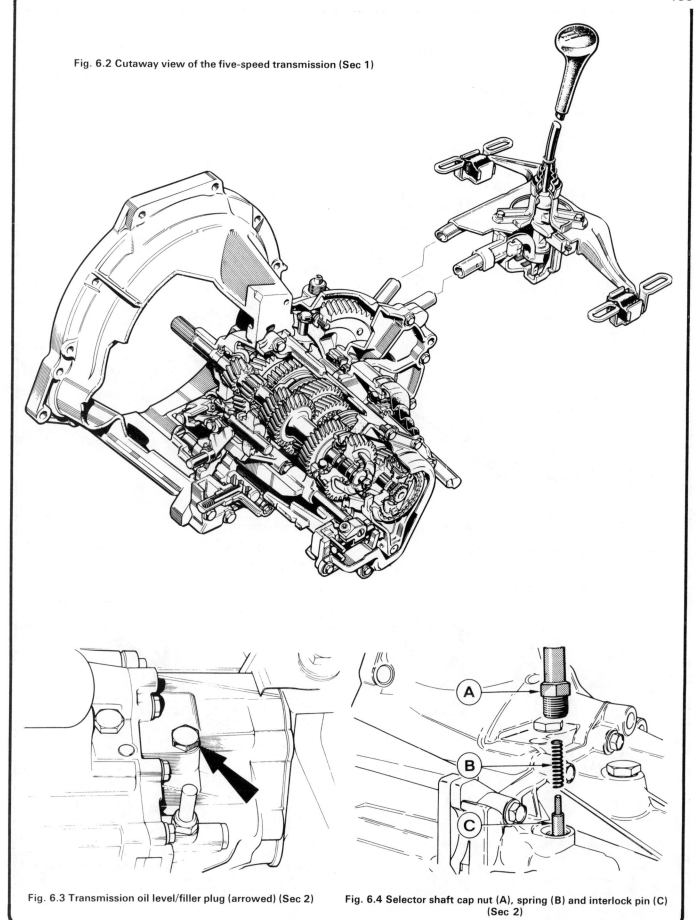

Fig. 6.2 Cutaway view of the five-speed transmission (Sec 1)

Fig. 6.3 Transmission oil level/filler plug (arrowed) (Sec 2)

Fig. 6.4 Selector shaft cap nut (A), spring (B) and interlock pin (C) (Sec 2)

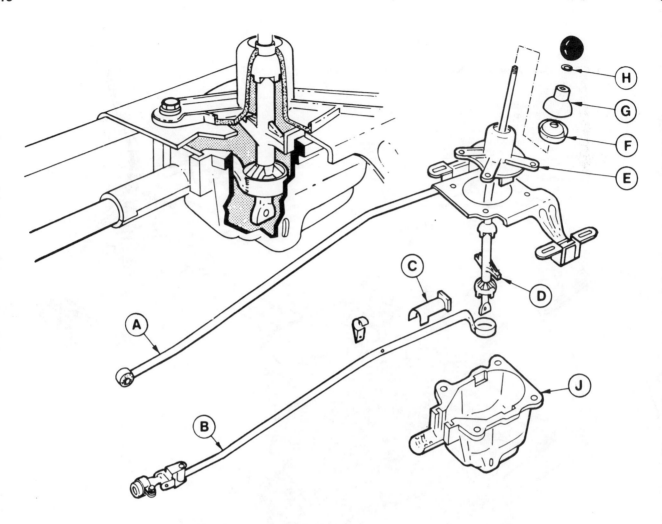

Fig. 6.5 Gearchange mechanism components (external) (Sec 4)

A	Stabilizer	D	Gear lever	G	Rubber spring
B	Shift rod	E	Housing	H	Circlip
C	Guide shell	F	Spring carrier	J	Selector gate

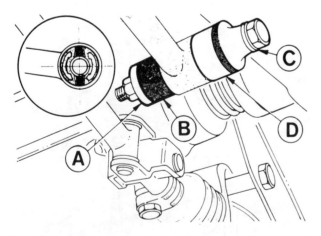

Fig. 6.6 Gearshift stabilizer bush fitting method. Note the void positions in bush (inset) (Sec 4)

A	Washer	C	Washer
B	Bush	D	Socket

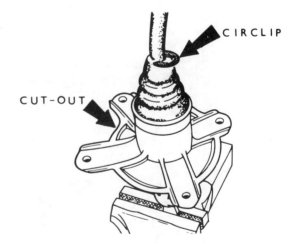

Fig. 6.7 Circlip location and cut-out section of cover (Sec 4)

together with a pair of suitable diameter sockets. During bush removal and refitting do not pull down excessively on the stabilizer bar. Use sockets of different diameters so that one is the same as that of the bush housing and one the same diameter as the fitted bush.

13 Having withdrawn the old bush, insert the new one drawing it into position using the sockets, bolt, washers and nut. Position the voids in the bush as shown in the inset in Fig. 6.6 and take care during fitting not to damage or distort the bush.

14 Make sure that the cut-out at the edge of the plastic cover is aligned with the curve in the gearchange lever as shown (Fig. 6.7).

15 The gear lever must locate in the shift rod cut-out.

16 To install the gearchange mechanism to the vehicle, offer it up from below and loosely attach it to the floorpan (photo).

17 Reconnect the stabilizer to the gearbox, remembering to fit the washer between the trunnion and the gearbox (Fig. 6.8).

18 The mechanism should now be secured to the floorpan by tightening the nuts to the specified torque.

19 Reconnect the gearchange rod to the shaft at the gearbox, as described in Chapter 1, Section 21.

20 Working inside the vehicle, refit the gaiter and the knob to the gear lever.

21 Lower the vehicle to the ground.

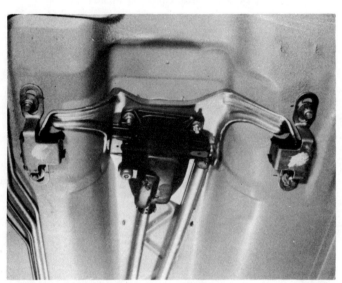

4.16 Gearchange mechanism to floorpan

5 Transmission (four- and five-speed) – removal and refitting

1 Disconnect the battery earth lead connector.

2 To ensure correct engagement of the selector mechanism during later operations, engage 4th gear on four-speed models or reverse gear on five-speed models.

3 Disconnect the speedometer cable from the transmission after unscrewing the retaining nut.

4 Unhook the clutch cable from the release lever, as described in Chapter 5.

5 Unscrew and remove the top four bolts which hold the gearbox flange to the engine.

6 Release the gearbox breather tube from the side rail.

7 If the vehicle is not over an inspection pit, raise its front end and fit axle stands.

8 Support the weight of the engine either by using a jack and block of wood under the sump or by attaching a hoist (refer to Chapter 1, Section 16).

9 Working under the vehicle, disconnect the leads from the starter motor and the reversing lamp switch.

10 Unbolt and remove the starter motor.

11 Unbolt and remove the cover plate from the lower face of the clutch housing (Fig. 6.10).

12 Disconnect the gearchange rod from the gearbox selector shaft by releasing the clamp pinch-bolt and pulling the rod towards the rear of

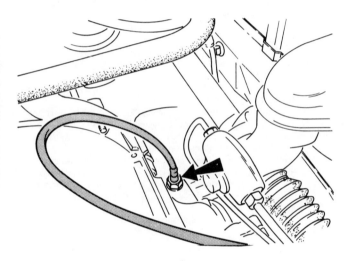

Fig. 6.9 Speedometer drive cable retaining nut (Sec 5)

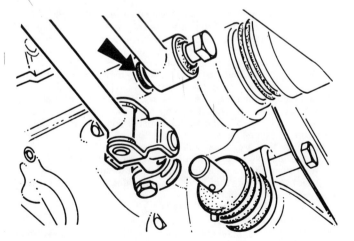

Fig. 6.8 Locate washer (arrowed) when connecting the stabilizer (Sec 4)

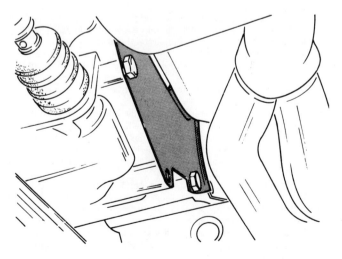

Fig. 6.10 Unbolt and remove the clutch cover plate (Sec 5)

the vehicle. On four-speed models, unhook the tension spring from the gearchange rod.

13 Unbolt the stabilizer rod from the side of the transmission, noting that there is a washer between the trunnion of the rod and the transmission casing.

14 Tie the gearchange rod and the stabilizer rod to the steering rack using a piece of wire.

15 Drain the oil from the transmission into a suitable container. As a drain plug is not fitted, unscrew the selector shaft locking assembly which includes the nut, cap, spring and interlock pin (Fig. 6.4).

16 On ohv engined models proceed as described in paragraphs 17 to 20 inclusive. On CVH engined models with driveshafts connected at their inner ends by socket-head bolts proceed as described in paragraphs 21 to 23 inclusive.

OHV engined models

17 Unscrew and remove the balljoint retaining bolt from the outboard end of the right- and left-hand suspension arms. The bolt is of Torx type, having a socket head, and, in the absence of the correct tool, an Allen key may be used to stop the bolt turning while the nut is unscrewed. Unbolt and detach the suspension arms from their body mountings.

18 Unbolt and disconnect the left-hand side tie-bar, together with its bracket, from the body.

19 Disconnect the right- and left-hand driveshafts from the transmission. Do this by inserting a lever between the constant velocity joint and the transmission. With an assistant pulling the roadwheel outwards, strike the end of the lever to release the joint from the differential. In order to prevent the differential pinions from turning and obstructing the driveshaft holes, insert a plastic plug or similar.

20 Tie up the disconnected driveshaft to avoid putting any strain on the joints. When supported out of the way, the maximum angle imposed on the joints must not exceed 45° for the outer and 20° for the inner joint (photo).

CVH engined models

21 Disconnect the inner end of the left-hand assembly by unscrewing the socket-head bolts and removing them, together with the link washers. Suspend the driveshaft with wire so that it is out of the way observing the cautionary notes in paragraph 20.

22 The right-hand intermediate shaft can be left in position during the removal of the transmission. It is only necessary to unscrew and remove the socket-head bolts with link washers and to suspend the driveshaft with wire out of the way, again observing the cautionary notes in paragraph 20.

23 If subsequently it is necessary to remove the intermediate driveshaft, refer to Chapter 7.

All models

24 Unscrew and remove the four bolts securing the engine/transmission bearer to the body (two at the front and two at the rear).

25 Lower the engine as much as possible without overstraining the ancillary fittings and attachments (coolant hoses etc) so that the transmission lower flange bolts can be unscrewed and removed. You may also need to loosen the engine mountings (see Chapter 1).

26 Withdraw the transmission unit from the engine and carefully lower it (together with the bearer) and remove it from underneath the vehicle.

27 Unbolt and detach the bearer from the transmission, as described in Chapter 1 (Section 34).

28 Before refitting the transmission, lightly smear the splined part of the input shaft with a little grease, also the thrust bearing guide sleeve.

29 If the clutch has been dismantled, make sure that the disc (driven plate) has been centralised, as described in Chapter 5.

30 Refit the engine bearer to the underside of the transmission, as described in Chapter 1 (Section 34).

31 Check that the engine adaptor plate is correctly located on its dowels.

32 With the transmission positioned on the floor below the vehicle, lift it up and engage the input shaft in the splined hub of the clutch driven plate. Obtain the help of an assistant for this work as the weight of the gearbox must not hang upon the input shaft while it is engaged in the driven plate.

33 Push the transmission into full engagement with the engine and check that the unit sits on its locating dowels and that the adaptor

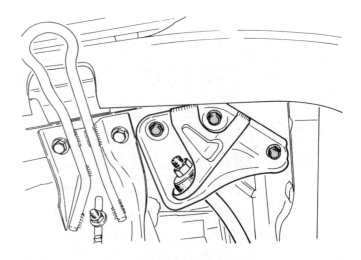

Fig. 6.11 Tie-bar bracket and retaining bolts (Sec 5)

5.20 Support the driveshafts once disconnected

plate has not been displaced. Any reluctance for the transmission to mate with the engine may be due to the splines of the input shaft and clutch driven plate not engaging. Try swivelling the transmission slightly, or have your assistant rotate the crankshaft by applying a spanner to the crankshaft pulley bolt.

34 Once the transmission is fully engaged, screw in the lower retaining bolts to hold it to the engine.

35 Align the engine transmission bearer bolt holes with the bolt holes in the body and fit the four retaining bolts. A trolley jack will be of assistance here to raise the engine/transmission unit and support it whilst the bolts are inserted. Tighten the bolts to the specified torque setting once they are all located.

36 If the engine mounting bolts were loosened during removal retighten them and remove the engine hoist or support device.

37 Insert the selector shaft interlock pin, spring and cap bolt, having smeared the threads of the bolt with jointing compound.

OHV engined models

38 Remove the temporary plastic plugs used to prevent displacement of the pinion gears in the differential. If plugs were not used, insert a finger into each driveshaft hole and align the pinion gear splined hole ready to accept the driveshaft. A mirror will assist in correct alignment (photo).

5.38 Pinion gear displaced in differential

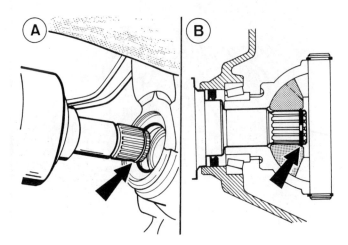

Fig. 6.12 Snap-ring location on driveshaft (A) and when fitted (B) (Sec 5)

39 Fit a new snap-ring to the splined end of the left-hand driveshaft and insert the shaft into the transmission. Turn the shaft as necessary to engage the splines with those on the pinion gear. Once engaged, have an assistant push hard on the roadwheel until the snap-ring engages, with the shaft fully home. Any reluctance to engage may be due to the driveshaft not being in a sufficiently horizontal attitude. In this event, remove the roadwheel in order to reduce the weight while the hub assembly is lifted.
40 Reconnect the suspension track control arm.
41 Repeat all the operations and refit the right-hand driveshaft.
42 Reconnect the left-hand tie-bar and bracket to its body mounting and tighten the three retaining bolts.
43 Reconnect the suspension arms to the body location on the inboard side, then reconnect the balljoint on the outer end of each arm to the spindle cover.

CVH engined models
44 If removed, reconnect the intermediate driveshaft assembly, as described in Chapter 7. Reconnect the left- and right-hand driveshafts by aligning the bolt holes and fitting the socket-head bolts with the link washers.

All models
45 Connect the stabilizer rod to the transmission, making sure to insert the washer between the trunnion of the rod and the transmission casing.
46 Reconnect and adjust the gearchange rod, as described in Chapter 1, Section 21.
47 Refit the gearchange rod tension spring (where applicable).
48 Refit the starter motor.
49 Connect the leads to the starter motor and to the reversing lamp switch.
50 Fit the cover plate to the clutch housing.
51 Lower the vehicle to the ground.
52 Fit the upper bolts to the clutch housing/engine flange (attaching the engine earth strap).
53 Reconnect the clutch operating cable.
54 Connect the speedometer drive cable to the transmission.
55 Fill the unit with the correct quantity and grade of oil.
56 Reconnect the battery earth lead.
57 Locate the transmission breather hole in the aperture in the longitudinal member.
58 Check the selection of all gears, and check the torque wrench settings of all nuts and bolts which were removed now that the weight of the vehicle is again on the roadwheels.

---

6 Transmission (four-speed) – removal of major assemblies

1 With the gearbox removed from the vehicle, clean away external dirt and grease using paraffin and a stiff brush or a water-soluble solvent. Take care not to allow water to enter the transmission.
2 Unscrew the lockbolt which holds the clutch release fork to the shaft and remove the shaft, followed by the fork and release bearing (Fig. 6.43).
3 If not removed for draining, unscrew the selector shaft cap nut spring and interlock pin.
4 Unbolt and remove the transmission housing cover.
5 Remove the snap-rings from the main and input shaft bearings (Fig. 6.15).
6 Unscrew and remove the connecting bolts and lift the smaller housing from the transmission. If it is stuck, tap it off carefully with a plastic-headed mallet.
7 Extract the swarf collecting magnet and clean it. Take care not to drop the magnet or it will shatter (Fig. 6.16).
8 Withdraw the selector shaft, noting that the longer portion of smaller diameter is at the bottom as the shaft is withdrawn.
9 Remove the selector shaft coil spring, the selector forks and the shift locking plate. Note the roll pin located in the locking plate cut-out (Fig. 6.18).
10 Withdraw the mainshaft, the input shaft and reverse gear as one assembly from the transmission housing (Fig. 6.19).
11 Lift the differential assembly from the housing.
12 The transmission is now dismantled into its major assemblies.

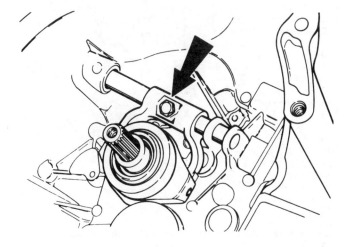

Fig. 6.13 Clutch release bearing fork lockbolt (arrowed) (Sec 6)

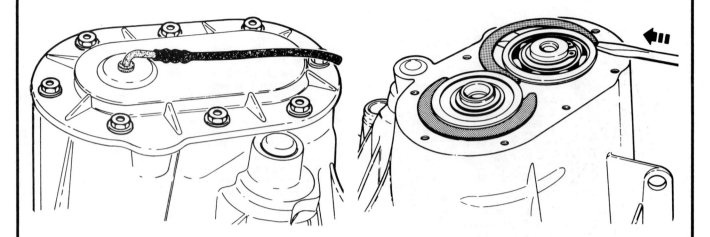

Fig. 6.14 Four-speed transmission cover plate (Sec 6)

Fig. 6.15 Removing the shaft snap-rings (Sec 6)

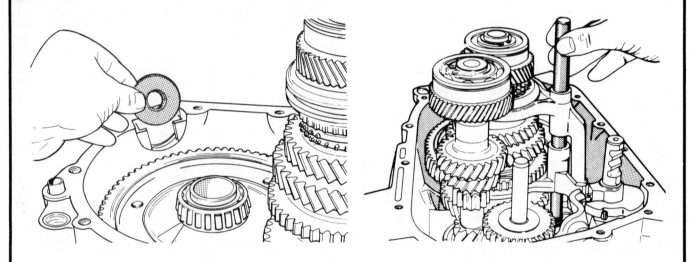

Fig. 6.16 Extract the magnetic disc (Sec 6)

Fig. 6.17 Withdrawing the selector shaft (Sec 6)

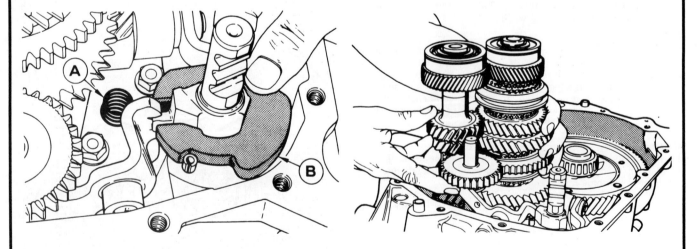

Fig. 6.18 Selector shaft coil spring (A) and shift lockplate (B)
(Sec 6)

Fig. 6.19 Withdrawing the geartrains (Sec 6)

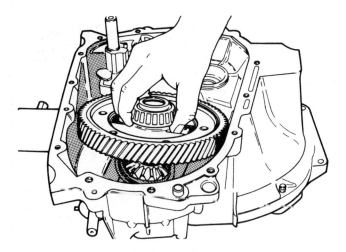

Fig. 6.20 Lifting out the differential unit (Sec 6)

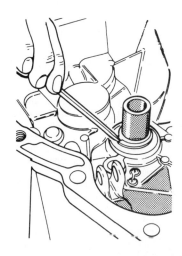

Fig. 6.22 Removing the input shaft oil seal (Sec 8)

7 Transmission (four-speed) – dismantling (general)

1 The need for further dismantling will depend upon the reasons for removal of the transmission in the first place.

2 A common reason for dismantling will be to renew the synchro units. Wear or malfunction in these components will have been obvious when changing over by the noise or by the synchro being easily beaten.

3 The renewal of oil seals may be required as evident by pools of oil under the vehicle when stationary.

4 Jumping out of gear may mean renewal of the selector mechanism, forks or synchro sleeves.

5 General noise during operations on the road may be due to worn bearings, shafts or gears and when such general wear occurs, it will probably be more economical to renew the transmission complete.

6 When dismantling the geartrains, always keep the components strictly in their originally installed order.

8 Transmission housing and selector mechanism (four-speed)

1 To remove the mainshaft bearing, break the plastic roller cage with a screwdriver. Extract the rollers and the cage, the oil slinger and retainers. Remove the bearing outer track.

2 When fitting the new bearing, also renew the oil slinger.

3 When renewing the input shaft oil seal, drive the old seal out by applying the drift inside the bellhousing (photos).

8.3A Transmission housing oil seal

Fig. 6.21 Breaking the mainshaft bearing plastic cage (Sec 8)

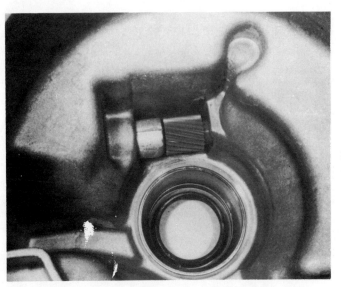

8.3B Transmission housing oil seal and speedometer driven gear

4   The constant velocity (CV) joint oil seals should be renewed at time of major overhaul.

5   The differential bearing tracks can be removed, using a drift inserted from the large housing section.

6   The differential bearing outer track and the diaphragm adjustment springs can be driven out of the smaller housing section using a suitable drift such as a piece of tubing.

7   Refit the input shaft oil seal so that its lips are as shown (Fig. 6.24). Apply grease to all the oil seal lips and check that the lip retaining spring has not been displaced during installation of the seal.

8   When installing the differential diaphragm springs and bearing track to the smaller housing section, note that the spring convex faces are towards each other. Stake the track with a light blow from a punch. This is only to hold the track during assembly of the remainder of the transmission.

9   If the selector mechanism is worn, sloppy or damaged, dismantle it by extracting the circlip and taking off the reverse selector lever (photo).

10   Remove the guide lever retaining plate and the guide shaft. Two bolts hold these components in place.

11   Extract the two circlips and detach the guide lever from the retaining plate (Fig. 6.30).

12   To remove the main selector shaft, pull the rubber gaiter up the shaft and then extract the single socket screw which secures the selector dog. Withdraw the shaft.

13   The selector shaft plastic bushes and oil seal should be renewed.

14   Reassembly is a reversal of dismantling, but when fitting the rubber gaiter make sure that its drain tube will point downward when installed in the vehicle. Use new circlips at reassembly.

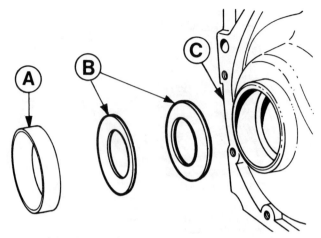

Fig. 6.25 Differential bearing preload diaphragm springs (Sec 8)

A   *Bearing track*   C   *Small housing section*
B   *Diaphragm springs*

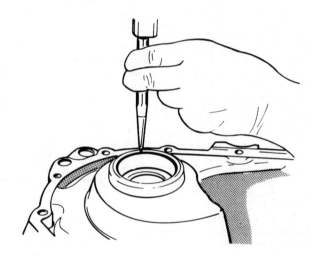

Fig. 6.26 Staking bearing track in small housing section (Sec 8)

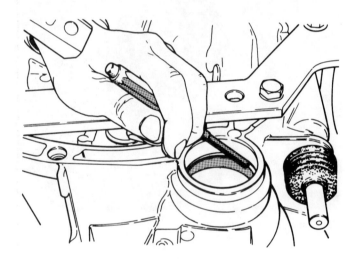

Fig. 6.23 Differential bearing track removal (Sec 8)

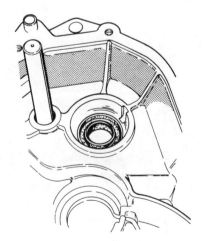

Fig. 6.24 Correctly installed input shaft oil seal (Sec 8)

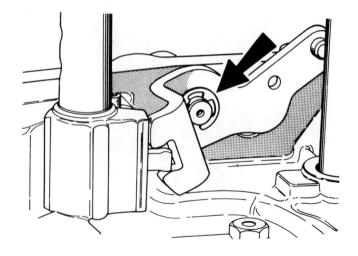

Fig. 6.27 Reverse selector lever retaining clip (arrowed) (Sec 8)

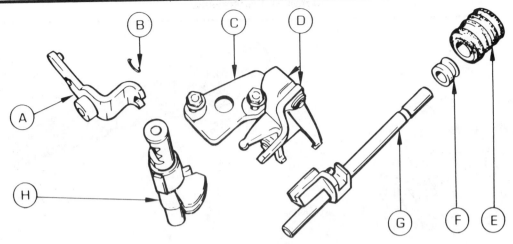

Fig. 6.28 Exploded view of the selector mechanism (Sec 8)

A	Reverse selector lever	C	Guide lever retaining plate
B	Circlip		
		D	Guide levers
		E	Flexible gaiter
		F	Oil seal
		G	Selector shaft with dog
		H	Guide shaft with dog

8.9 Selector mechanism

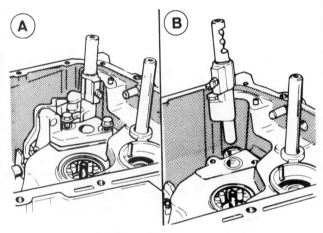

Fig. 6.29 Dismantling selector mechanism (Sec 8)

A   Removing retaining plate   B   Removing guide shaft

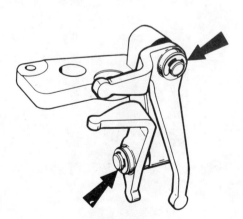

Fig. 6.30 Guide lever retaining circlips (Sec 8)

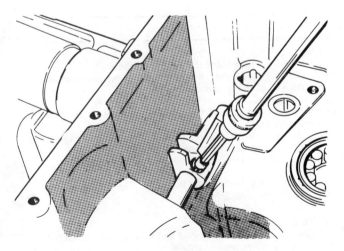

Fig. 6.31 Extracting lockscrew which secures dog to selector shaft (Sec 8)

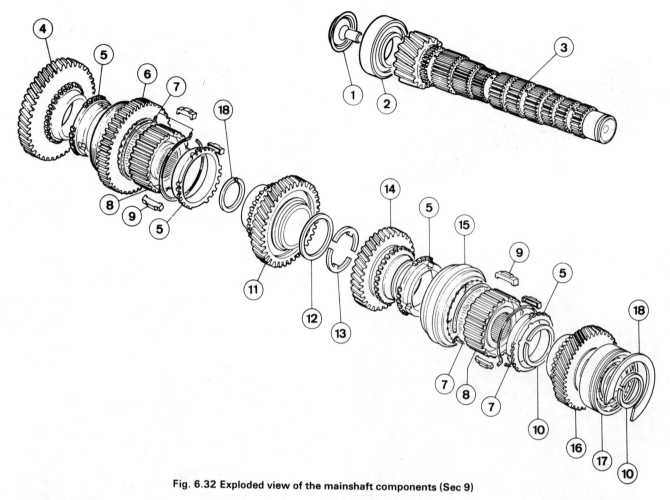

Fig. 6.32 Exploded view of the mainshaft components (Sec 9)

1	Oil thrower		
2	Roller bearing		
3	Mainshaft		
4	1st gear		
5	Synchroniser ring		

6 1st/2nd gear synchro
   with reverse gear
7 Retaining spring
8 Synchroniser hub
9 Blocker bar

10 Circlip
11 2nd gear
12 Retaining ring
13 Thrust half ring (segments)
14 3rd gear

15 3rd/4th gear synchro
16 4th gear
17 Ball-bearing
18 Snap-ring

9 Mainshaft (four-speed) – overhaul

Dismantling

1   Extract the circlip which holds the bearing to the shaft.
2   Using a puller, engaged behind 4th gear, draw off the gear and the bearing from the end of the mainshaft (photo).
3   Discard the bearing.
4   Extract the circlip and remove the 3rd/4th synchro with 3rd gear using hand pressure only.
5   Remove the anchor ring and the two thrust semi-circular segments, then take 2nd gear from the mainshaft.
6   Extract the circlip and take off 1st/2nd gear synchro unit with 1st gear.
7   The mainshaft is now completely dismantled. Do not attempt to remove the drive pinion gear (photo).

Synchronisers

8   The synchro units can be dismantled and new components fitted after extracting the circular retaining springs.
9   When reassembling the hub and sleeve, align them so that the cut-outs in the components are in alignment ready to receive the sliding keys.
10   The two springs should have their hooked ends engaged in the

9.2 Removing 4th gear and bearing from mainshaft

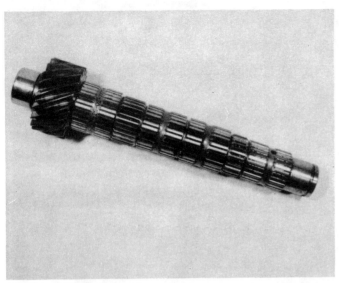

9.7 Mainshaft stripped

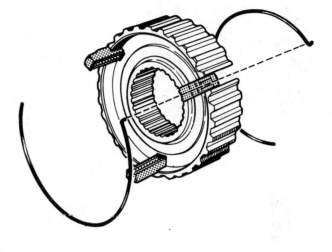

Fig. 6.33 Fitting direction of synchro retaining springs (Sec 9)

same sliding key, but must run in opposing directions as shown in Fig. 6.33.

11 The baulk rings should be renewed if they do not 'stick' when pressed and turned onto the gear covers, or if a clearance no longer exists between the baulk ring and the gear when pressed onto its cone.

Reassembly

12 With all worn or damaged components renewed, commence reassembly by oiling the shaft and then sliding 1st gear onto the shaft so that the gear teeth are next to the pinion drivegear (photo).

13 Fit 1st/2nd synchro baulk ring (photo).
14 Fit 1st/2nd synchro so that reverse gearteeth on the unit are furthest from 1st gear (photo).
15 Fit the circlip to secure the synchro to the mainshaft (photo).
16 Slide on the synchro baulk ring (photo).
17 Slide on 2nd gear (photo).
18 Fit 2nd gear so that the cone is towards the baulk ring.
19 Fit the thrust semi-circular segments and their anchor ring (photos).
20 To the shaft fit 3rd gear so that its teeth are towards 2nd gear (photo).

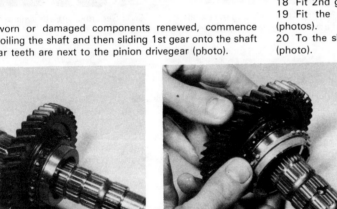

9.12 Fitting 1st gear to mainshaft

9.13 Fitting 1st/2nd baulk ring

9.14 Fitting 1st/2nd synchro with reverse gear

9.15 Fitting synchro securing circlip to mainshaft

9.16 Fitting 1st/2nd synchro baulk ring

9.17 Fitting 2nd gear to mainshaft

9.19A Thrust segments installed

9.19B Thrust segment anchor ring installation

9.20 Fitting 3rd gear to mainshaft

9.21 Fitting 3rd/4th synchro baulk ring

9.22 Fitting 3rd/4th synchro to mainshaft. Note that serrated edge is downwards

9.23 Securing 3rd/4th synchro with circlip

9.24 Fitting last (4th) synchro baulk ring to mainshaft

9.25 Fitting 4th gear to mainshaft

9.26A Fitting the mainshaft bearing

9.26B Using tube drift to fit the mainshaft bearing

9.27A Fitting mainshaft bearing circlip

9.27B Mainshaft fully assembled (four-speed transmission)

21 Fit the baulk ring (photo).
22 Slide on 3rd/4th synchro so that its serrated edge is towards the shaft drive pinion gear (photo).
23 Secure the synchro to the mainshaft with the circlip (photo).
24 Fit the baulk ring (photo).
25 Fit 4th gear (photo).
26 Fit the bearing so that its circlip groove is nearer the end of the shaft. Apply pressure only to the bearing centre track, using a press or a hammer and a piece of suitable diameter tubing (photos).
27 Fit the circlip to secure the bearing to the shaft. The mainshaft is now fully assembled (photos).

10 Input shaft (four-speed) – overhaul

1 The only components which can be renewed are the two ball-bearing races (photo).
2 Remove the securing circlip from the larger one and extract both bearings with a two-legged extractor or a press (photos).
3 When fitting the new bearings, apply pressure to the centre track only, using a press or a piece of suitable diameter tubing and a hammer. When installing the larger bearing, make sure that the circlip groove is nearer the end of the shaft.

11 Differential unit (four- and five-speed transmission) – overhaul

1 With the differential removed from the transmission housing, twist both drive pinions out of the differential case.
2 Extract one of the circlips from the end of the differential shaft, press the shaft out of the differential case and extract the pinions and the cage.
3 The differential tapered roller bearings can be drawn off using a two-legged extractor.
4 The crownwheel can be separated from the differential case after removing the six securing bolts. Tap the components apart using a plastic mallet.
5 If the crownwheel is to be renewed, then the gearbox mainshaft should be renewed at the same time, as the gearteeth are matched and renewal of only one component will give rise to an increase in noise during operation on the road.
6 Reassembly is a reversal of dismantling, but make sure that the deeply chamfered edge of the inside diameter is against the differential case. Tighten all bolts.
7 The pinion gears should be held in position by inserting plastic plugs or similar so that they will be in correct alignment for eventual installation of the driveshafts, refer to Section 5 of this Chapter.

10.1 Input shaft (four-speed transmission)

10.2A Input shaft large bearing and retaining circlip

10.2B Input shaft small bearing

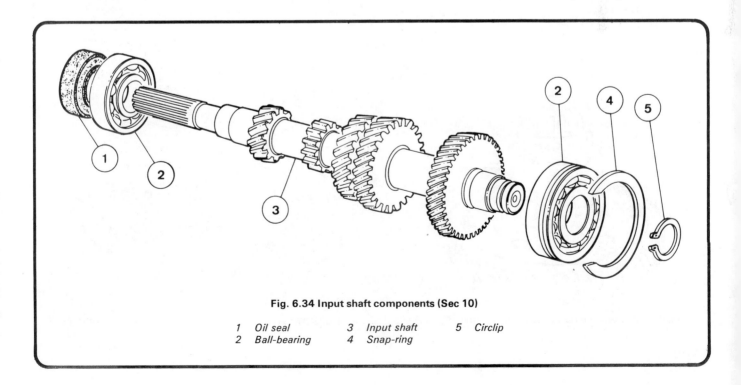

Fig. 6.34 Input shaft components (Sec 10)

1	Oil seal	3	Input shaft	5	Circlip
2	Ball-bearing	4	Snap-ring		

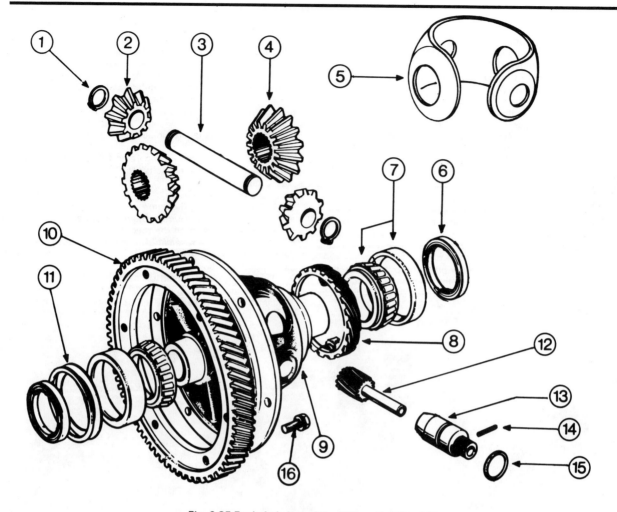

Fig. 6.35 Exploded view of the differential (Sec 11)

1	Circlip	6	Oil seal	10	Crownwheel	14	Roll pin
2	Pinion gear	7	Tapered roller bearing	11	Diaphragm springs	15	O-ring
3	Shaft	8	Speedometer worm	12	Speedometer drive	16	Crownwheel retaining
4	Drive pinion gear		drivegear		pinion		bolt
5	Thrust cage	9	Differential case	13	Bearing		

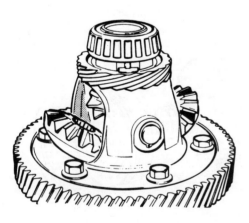

Fig. 6.36 Drive pinion removal from differential (Sec 11)

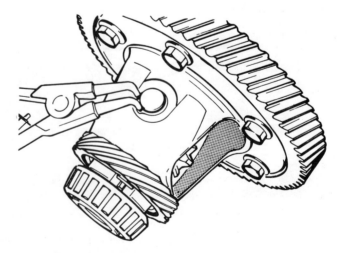

Fig. 6.37 Extracting differential case shaft circlip (Sec 11)

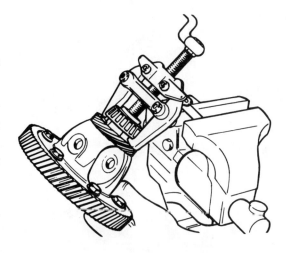

Fig. 6.38 Differential bearing removal (Sec 11)

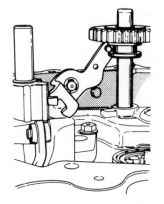

Fig. 6.40 Reverse selector lever supported on roversing lamp switch plunger ball (Sec 12)

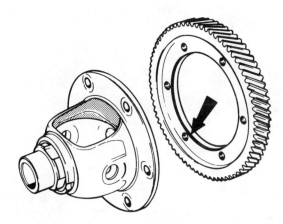

Fig. 6.39 Crownwheel chamfered edge (arrowed) (Sec 11)

12 Transmission (four-speed) – reassembly

1   With the larger housing section on the bench, lubricate the differential bearings with gear oil and insert the differential assembly into the housing (photo).
2   Slide reverse idler gear onto its shaft, at the same time engaging the selector lever in the groove of the gear which should be pointing downward (photo).
3   In order to make installation of the mainshaft and input shaft easier, lift the reverse idler gear so that its selector lever is held by the reversing lamp switch spring-loaded ball (photo).

4   Mesh the gears of the mainshaft and the input shaft and install both geartrains into the transmission housing simultaneously (photo).
5   Lower the reverse idler gear and its selector lever.
6   Fit the shift locking plate (photo).
7   Engage 1st/2nd selector fork with the groove in the mainshaft synchro sleeve. This fork has the shorter actuating lever (photo).
8   Engage 3rd/4th selector fork with the groove in its synchro sleeve. Make sure that the end of this fork actuating lever is engaged with the shift locking plate (photo).
9   Insert the coil spring in the selector shaft hole and pass the shaft downwards through the holes in the forks. Make sure that the longer section of the reduced diameter of the rod is pointing downward (photos).
10 Actuate the appropriate selector fork to engage 4th gear. Do this by inserting a rod in the hole in the end of the selector shaft which projects from the transmission casing and turning the shaft fully clockwise to its stop, then pushing the shaft inwards (photo).
11 Insert the magnetic swarf collector in its recess, taking care not to drop it (photo).
12 Locate a new gasket on the housing flange, install the smaller housing section and screw in and tighten the bolts (photos).
13 Fit the snap-rings to the ends of the main and input shafts. Cutouts are provided in the casing so that the bearings can be levered upwards to expose the snap-ring grooves. Snap-rings are available in three thicknesses and the thickest possible ring should be used which will fit into the groove. If any difficulty is experienced in levering up the bearing on the input shaft, push the end of the shaft from within the bellhousing (photos).
14 Tap the snap-rings to rotate them so that they will locate correctly in the cut-outs in the cover gasket which should now be positioned on the end of the housing. Fit a new gasket (photo).
15 Fit the cover plate, screw in the bolts and tighten them to the specified torque (photos).
16 Fit the interlock pin, spring and cap nut for the selector shaft locking mechanism. The threads should be coated with jointing compound before installation.

12.1A Interior of transmission larger housing

12.1B Installing the differential

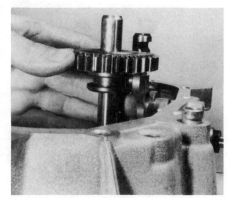

12.2 Fitting reverse idler gear

12.3 Reverse idler gear supported in raised position

12.4 Installing the geartrains

12.6 Fitting the shift locking plate

12.7 Fitting 1st/2nd selector fork

12.8 Fitting 3rd/4th selector fork

12.9A Inserting the selector shaft coil spring

12.9B Installing the selector shaft

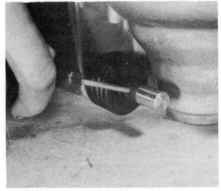

12.10 Turning the selector shaft to stop

12.11 Magnetic swarf collector

12.12A Locate the housing flange gasket ...

12.12B ... then fit the transmission smaller housing

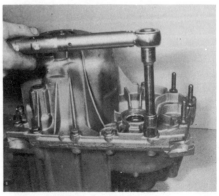

12.12C Tightening housing section connecting bolts

12.13A Raising bearing for snap-ring installation

12.13B Fitting the bearing snap-ring

12.14 Bearing snap-rings and gasket in position

12.15A Fit the transmission cover plate and gasket

12.15B Tighten cover plate bolts. Note breather tube

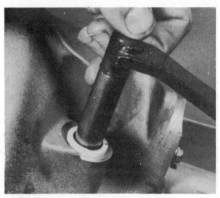

12.17A Insert clutch release shaft

12.17B Tighten the clutch release shaft fork bolt

13.6 Speedometer driven gear unit located with new roll pin (arrowed)

17 Refit the clutch release shaft, lever and bearing into the bellhousing (photos).

18 The transmission is now ready for installation in the vehicle. Wait until it is installed before filling with oil.

13 Speedometer driven gear (four- and five-speed transmission) – removal and refitting

1 This work may be done without having to remove the transmission from the vehicle.

2 Using a pair of side cutting pliers, lever out the roll pin which secures the speedometer drive pinion bearing in the transmission housing.

3 Withdraw the pinion bearing, together with the speedometer drive

cable. Separate the cable from the pinion by unscrewing the knurled ring.

4 Slide the pinion out of the bearing.

5 Always renew the O-ring on the pinion bearing before refitting.

6 Insert the pinion and bearing into the transmission housing using a back-and-forth twisting motion to mesh the pinion teeth with those of the drivegear. Secure with the roll pin (photo).

7 Reconnect the speedometer cable.

14 Transmission (five-speed) – dismantling (general)

1 As stated previously, the five-speed transmission is virtually identical to the four-speed unit, with the exception of an additional gear and synchro-hub, and a modified selector mechanism.

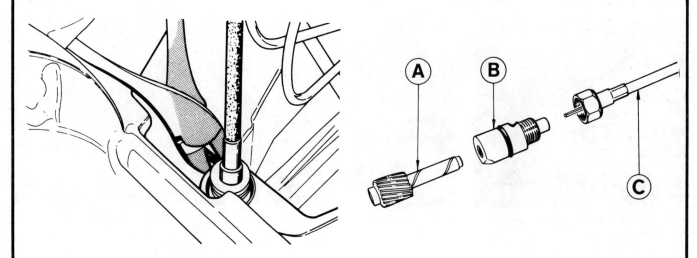

Fig. 6.41 Extracting speedometer pinion retaining roll pin (Sec 13)

Fig. 6.42 Speedometer driven gear (A), bearing (B) and drive cable (C) (Sec 13)

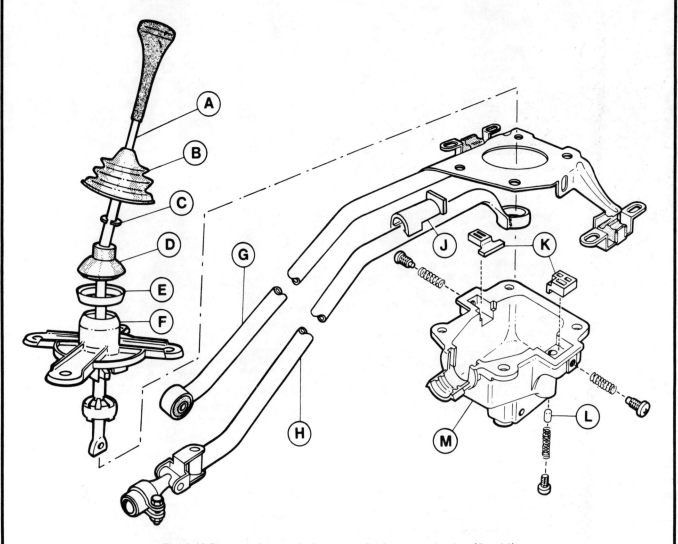

Fig. 6.43 Five-speed transmission external selector mechanism (Sec 14)

A	Gear lever	D	Rubber spring	G	Stabilizer	K	Guide elements
B	Gaiter	E	Spring carrier	H	Shift rod	L	Locking pin
C	Circlip	F	Housing cover	J	Guide shell	M	Selector housing

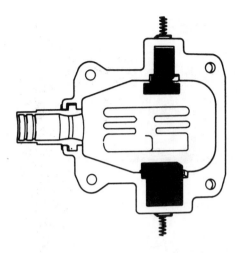

Fig. 6.44 Guide shells and springs fitting (Sec 14)

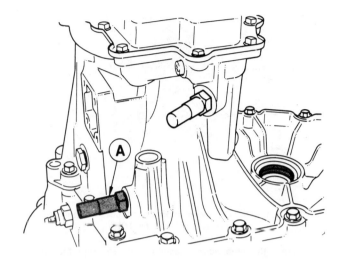

Fig. 6.45 Selector shaft locking mechanism – five-speed transmission (Sec 16)

A = 1st/4th and reverse gear cap nut

2   The overhaul procedures described in Sections 9, 10, 11 and 13 are therefore applicable to the five-speed unit with the exception of the following Sections. Note however, that if any new components are to be fitted to the mainshaft they must be lubricated with special grease, as given in the Specifications, during assembly.

3   When referring to previous Sections for overhaul procedures, it should be noted that all photos, except where indicated are of the four-speed transmission. Due to the close resemblance of the two transmissions, the photos shown can also be used in most instances for pictorial guidance when working on the five-speed transmission.

15 Gearchange mechanism (five-speed) – removal, overhaul and refitting

1   Proceed as described in paragraphs 1, 2 and 3 of Section 4, but engage reverse gear instead of 4th.

2   Disconnect the exhaust pipe from the rubber mountings at the rear.

3   Proceed as given in paragraphs 5, 6 and 7 of Section 4.

4   To dismantle, unscrew and remove the three guide element spring retaining screws, one from each side of the selector housing, and one underneath (which also holds a lockpin). Extract the three springs and the lockpin.

5   Unscrew and remove the four selector housing-to-stabilizer mounting frame and gear lever housing cover bolts. Lift the gearlever and cover away.

6   Unclip the upper guide shell and lift the shift rod out of the selector housing.

7   To dismantle the gearlever prise off the rubber spring securing ring using a screwdriver and withdraw the rubber spring, the spring carrier and housing cover.

8   Clean and inspect the dismantled components. Renew any showing signs of excessive wear. Reassemble by reversing the dismantling procedure but note the following points.

9   Make sure that the cut-out at the edge of the plastic cover is aligned with the curve in the gearchange lever.

10   Position the guide shells as shown (Fig. 6.44) and check that the gear lever is located in the ring of the shift rod as it is assembled.

11   Refit the gearchange mechanism to the vehicle, as described in paragraphs 16 to 21 in Section 4, and adjust as given for the five-speed transmission in Section 21 in Chapter 1.

16 Transmission (five-speed) – dismantling and overhaul of major assemblies

1   With the gearbox removed from the vehicle, clean away external dirt and grease using paraffin and a stiff brush, or a water-soluble grease solvent. Take care not to allow water to enter the transmission.

2   Drain off any residual oil in the transmission through a driveshaft opening.

3   Unscrew the lockbolt which holds the clutch release fork to the shaft and remove the shaft, followed by the fork and release bearing.

4   If not removed for draining, unscrew the selector shaft cap nut, spring and interlock pin. Now remove the additional 5th gear selector shaft cap nut, spring and interlock pin.

5   Unbolt and remove the transmission housing cover (photo).

16.5 Five-speed transmission housing cover

6   Unscrew the clamp bolt and lift the 5th gear selector pin assembly off the shift rod (Fig. 6.46).

7   Using circlip pliers, extract the 5th gear retaining snap-ring, then lift off the 5th gear, complete with synchro assembly and selector fork from the mainshaft.

8   Extract the circlip securing the 5th gear driving gear to the input shaft. Using a two-legged puller, draw the gear off the input shaft. *Do not re-use the old circlip when reassembling; a new one must be obtained.*

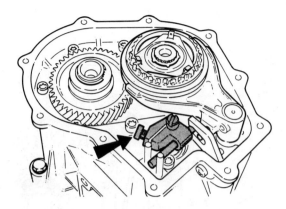

Fig. 6.46 5th gear selector pin clamp bolt – five-speed transmission (Sec 16)

9   Unscrew the nine socket-headed bolts securing the 5th gear casing to the main casing and carefully lift it off.

10 Remove the snap-rings from the main and input shaft bearings.

11 Unscrew and remove the connecting bolts then lift the smaller housing from the transmission casing. If it is stuck, tap it off carefully with a plastic-headed mallet.

12 Extract the swarf-collecting magnet and clean it. Take care not to drop the magnet or it will shatter.

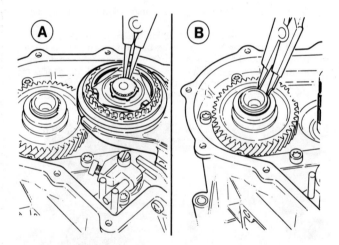

Fig. 6.47 5th gear retaining snap-ring (A) and input shaft circlip (B) locations – five-speed transmission (Sec 16)

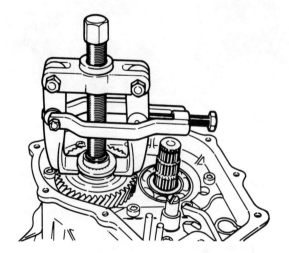

Fig. 6.48 Removal of 5th gear from input shaft with puller – five-speed transmission (Sec 16)

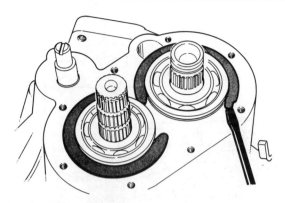

Fig. 6.49 Bearing snap-rings removal – five-speed transmission (Sec 16)

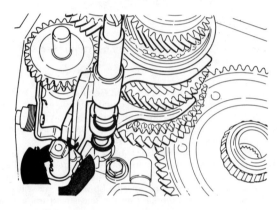

Fig. 6.50 Selector shaft guide sleeve and 1st/2nd gear selector fork circlip locations – five-speed transmission (Sec 16)

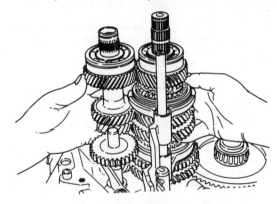

Fig. 6.51 Removal of mainshaft and input shaft as complete assembly – five-speed transmission (Sec 16)

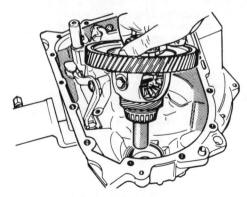

Fig. 6.52 Lifting out the differential unit – five-speed transmission (Sec 16)

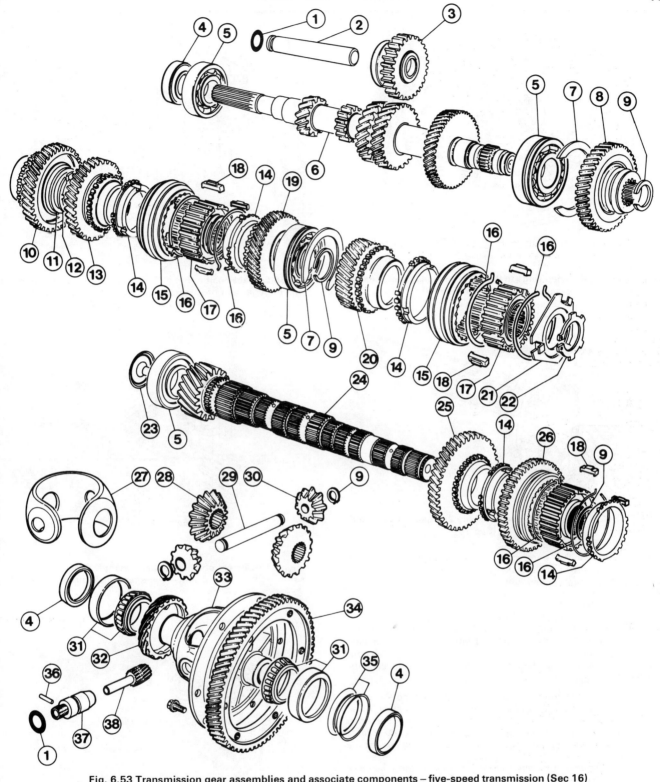

Fig. 6.53 Transmission gear assemblies and associate components – five-speed transmission (Sec 16)

1	O-ring	11	Supporting ring
2	Reverse idler gear shaft	12	Semi-circular thrust segment
3	Reverse idler gear	13	3rd gear (driven)
4	Radial oil seal	14	Synchroniser ring
5	Bearing	15	Selector ring
6	Input shaft	16	Retaining spring
7	Snap-ring	17	Synchroniser hub
8	5th gear	18	Blocker bar
9	Circlip	19	4th gear (driven)
10	2nd gear (driven)		

20	5th gear (driven)
21	Retaining plate
22	Circlip
23	Oil slinger
24	Mainshaft
25	1st gear (driven)
26	Selector ring with reverse gear
27	Thrust cage
28	Axleshaft pinion

29	Differential shaft
30	Differential pinion
31	Taper roller bearing
32	Speedometer drive worm
33	Differential housing
34	Final drivegear
35	Spring washers (2)
36	Locking pin
37	Speedometer drive pinion bearing
38	Speedometer drive pinion

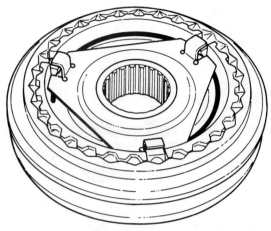

Fig. 6.54 Fitting the snap-rings to the main and input shaft bearing – five-speed transmission (Sec 16)

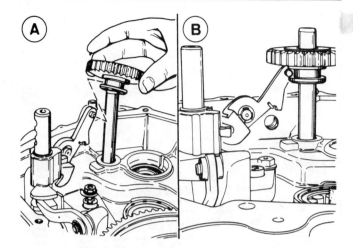

Fig. 6.56 Correct positioning of reverse gear on reverse shaft (A) and engagement of selector lever with groove in gear (B) – five-speed transmission (Sec 17)

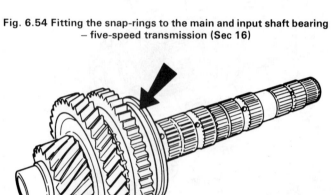

Fig. 6.55 Selector groove (arrowed) to face 2nd gear – five-speed transmission (Sec 16)

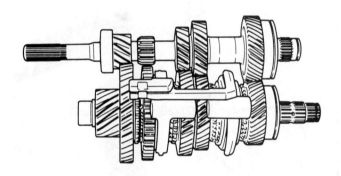

Fig. 6.57 Correct positioning of mainshaft and input shaft assemblies prior to refitting – five-speed transmission (Sec 17)

13 Release the circlips from the selector shaft guide sleeve and 1st/2nd gear selector fork. Carefully withdraw the guide sleeve.

14 Lift out the complete mainshaft assembly, together with the input shaft, selector forks and reverse gear as a complete unit from the transmission housing.

15 Remove the selector shaft and the shift locking plate.

16 Finally lift the differential assembly from the housing.

17 The transmission is now dismantled into its major assemblies, which can be further dismantled if necessary, as described in Sections 9, 10 and 11, but note the following differences when overhauling the mainshaft.

   (a) If overhauling the fifth gear synchroniser unit, note that the blocker bars are secured by means of a retaining plate. When assembling the unit proceed as described for the other synchro units, but ensure that the retaining spring located between the hub and retaining plate is pressing against the blocker bars

   (b) When reassembling the mainshaft, fit the 1st/2nd synchro so that the reverse gear teeth on the unit are positioned towards 1st gear, with the selector groove facing 2nd gear

   (c) If the input shaft and/or 5th gear are found to be in need of replacement it should be noted that they can only be renewed as a matching pair

17 Transmission (five-speed) – reassembly

1 With the larger housing section on the bench, lubricate the differential bearings with gear oil and insert the differential assembly into the housing.

2 Slide the reverse idler gear onto its shaft, at the same time

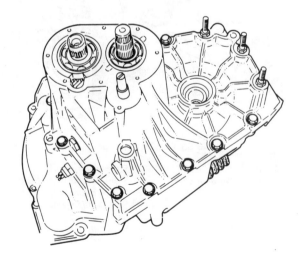

Fig. 6.58 Small housing section in position on main casing – five-speed transmission (Sec 17)

engaging the selector lever in the groove of the gear which should be pointing downwards.

3   Refit the selector shaft and shift locking plate.

4   Refit the mainshaft and input shaft as an assembly complete with selector forks. Guide the selector forks past the shift locking plate, noting that the plate must be turned clockwise to bear against the dowel.

5   Install the selector shaft guide sleeve and secure the 1st/2nd gear selector fork on the guide sleeve using new circlips.

6   Refit the swarf-collecting magnet to its location in the housing.

7   Locate a new gasket on the housing flange and place the small housing section in position. Refit and tighten the retaining bolts to the specified torque.

8   Fit the snap-rings to the ends of the main and input shafts. Cut-outs are provided in the casing so that the bearings can be levered upwards to expose the snap-ring grooves. Snap-rings are available in three thicknesses, and the thickest possible ring should be used which will fit into the groove. If any difficulty is experienced in levering up the bearing on the input shaft, push the end of the shaft from within the bellhousing.

9   Tap the snap-rings to rotate them so that they will locate correctly in the cut-outs in the 5th gear housing gasket, which should now be placed in position.

10 Fit the 5th gear housing and tighten the retaining bolts to the specified torque.

11 Coat the splines of 5th gear and the input shaft with the special grease (see Specifications). Before fitting the 5th gear, check that the marks on the input shaft and gear web are the same colour.

12 Heat 5th gear to approximately 80°C (176°F), and then drift it into place on the input shaft. Fit a new circlip to the input shaft using a tube of suitable diameter as a drift.

13 Fit 5th gear, complete with synchro assembly and selector fork, onto the mainshaft and secure with the snap-ring.

14 Coat the threads of the 5th gear selector shaft locking mechanism cap nut with sealer (see Specifications). Fit the interlock pin, spring and cap nut, then tighten the nut to the specified torque.

15 Fit the 1st/4th and reverse gear selector shaft interlock pin, spring and cap nut after first coating the threads of the cap nut with sealer. Tighten the nut to the specified torque.

16 Refit the 5th gear selector pin assembly to the shift rod, but do not tighten the clamp bolt at this stage.

17 Engage 5th gear with the selector shaft by turning the shaft clockwise as far as it will go from the neutral position, and then pulling it fully out.

18 Slide the selector ring and selector fork onto 5th gear.

19 Rotate the shift rod clockwise as far as the stop using a screwdriver and retain it in this position. Coat the clamp bolt threads with a locking compound then fit and tighten it to the specified torque wrench setting.

20 Place a new gasket in position and refit the housing cover, tightening the retaining bolts to the specified torque.

21 Fit the 1st/4th and reverse gear selector shaft interlock pin, spring

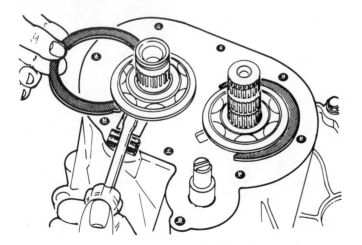

Fig. 6.59 Fitting the snap-rings to the main and input shaft bearing – five-speed transmission (Sec 17)

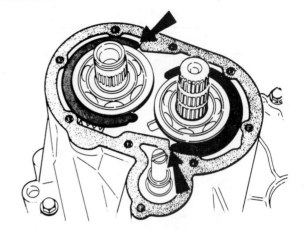

Fig. 6.60 Snap-rings correctly aligned to locate with cut-outs in gasket – five-speed transmission (Sec 17)

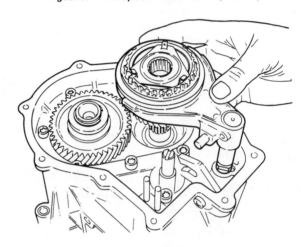

Fig. 6.61 Refitting 5th gear synchro assembly and selector fork – five-speed transmission (Sec 17)

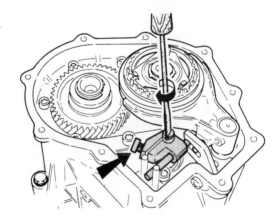

Fig. 6.62 Turning the shift rod clockwise with a screwdriver prior to tightening selector pin clamp bolt – five-speed transmission (Sec 17)

and cap nut after first coating the threads of the cap nut with sealer. Tighten the nut to the specified torque.

22 At this stage check the operation of the selector mechanism by engaging all the gears with the selector shaft.

23 Refit the clutch release shaft, lever and bearing into the bellhousing.

24 The transmission is now ready for installation in the vehicle. Wait until it is installed before filling with oil.

18 Fault diagnosis – transmission

Symptom	Reason(s)
Weak or ineffective synchromesh	Synchronising cones worn, split or damaged Baulk ring synchromesh dogs worn or damaged
Jumps out of gear	Broken selector shaft interlock spring Gearbox coupling dogs badly worn Selector fork rod groove badly worn
Excessive noise	Incorrect grade of oil in gearbox or oil level too low Bush or needle roller bearings worn or damaged Gear teeth excessively worn or damaged Shaft bearing circlips allowing excessive endplay
Noise when cornering	Driveshaft or wheel bearing worn Differential bearing worn

Chapter 7 Driveshafts

Contents

Description and maintenance 1
Driveshaft – overhaul 8
Driveshaft – removal and refitting 7
Driveshaft inboard joint bellows – renewal 4
Driveshaft inboard oil seal (1.0 and 1.1 litre) – renewal 2

Driveshaft inboard oil seal (1.3 and 1.6 litre) – renewal 3
Driveshaft outboard joint bellows – renewal 5
Fault diagnosis – driveshafts 9
Intermediate driveshaft (1.3 and 1.6 litre) – removal and
refitting 6

Specifications

Type .... Tubular, three section with inner and outer constant velocity (CV) joints. Additional intermediate driveshaft on 1.3 and 1.6 litre models on right-hand side

Lubricant
CV joints .... Grease to Ford specification SA - 1C - 4515 - A

Torque wrench settings

	Nm	lbf ft
Driveshaft hub nut	230	170
Lower suspension arm pivot bolt	45	33
Lower suspension arm balljoint pinch-bolt	30	22
Tie-rod to mounting bracket	50	37
Driveshaft coupling flange bolts (1.3 and 1.6 models only)	40	30
Intermediate driveshaft bearing housing to support bracket	20	15
Intermediate driveshaft support bracket to engine	68	50

1 Description and maintenance

Each driveshaft unit consists of three sections: the inboard end, namely a splined output shaft and constant velocity joint, the outboard end, being the splined front hub spindle and constant velocity joint, and a centre shaft with splined ends.

The inboard ends of the driveshaft are retained in the differential gears by the engagement of snap-rings. The outboard ends are secured to the hub by a nut which is staked after tightening. The 1.3 and 1.6 litre models differ from outer models in that they have driveshafts which are bolted at their inner ends to the transmission stub shaft on the left-hand side and the intermediate driveshaft on the

right-hand side. The intermediate shaft is a sliding fit into the right-hand transmission stub shaft and is supported on its outer end by a bearing and support bracket attached to the engine crankcase. The outboard end of the intermediate shaft and the inboard end of the right-hand driveshaft are attached by socket-head bolts.

The constant velocity joints are lubricated and sealed by flexible gaiters. The only maintenance required is a visual inspection, for splits in the gaiter or an oil leak from the inboard oil seal. A leakage of grease from the hub seal will indicate that the hub bearing oil seal is in need of renewal, and this is described in Section 3 of Chapter 10.

Where a driveshaft gaiter is split, it must be renewed immediately to avoid the entry of dirt and grit (see Section 4 or 5).

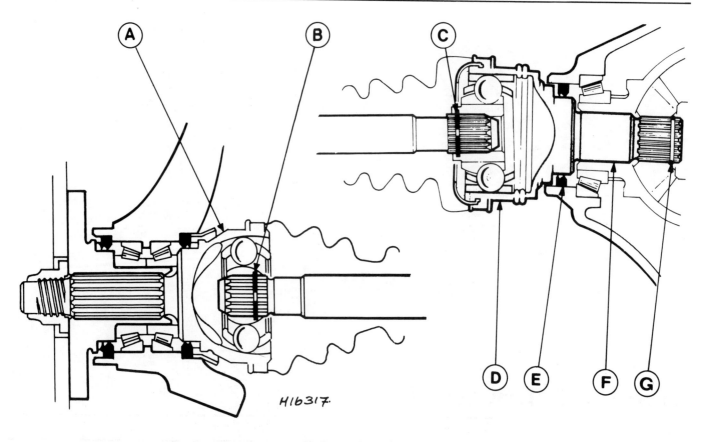

H16317

Fig. 7.1 Sectional view of driveshaft constant velocity (CV) joints (Sec 1)

A	Outboard joint	C	Circlip
B	Circlip	D	Inboard joint

E	Oil seal	G	Snap-ring
F	Inboard driveshaft		

2   Driveshaft inboard oil seal (1.0 and 1.1 litre) – renewal

1   Raise and support the car at the front on safety stands.
2   Drain the transmission oil by unscrewing the cap nut from the selector shaft locking mechanism, taking care not to lose the spring and interlock pin as they are ejected.
3   Disconnect the steering tie-rod balljoint by extracting the split pin and undoing the castellated nut. Release the tapered joint using a separator.
4   Unbolt and remove the pivot bolt from the inboard end of the suspension arm.
5   At the outboard end of the suspension arm, disengage the arm from the hub carrier by unscrewing and removing the pinch-bolt.
6   When the suspension arm is disconnected take care not to strain the tie-bar at its body mounting at the front.
7   With an assistant pulling the roadwheel, insert a lever between the inboard constant velocity joint and the transmission. Strike the end of the lever, so prising the driveshaft out of the transmission. Tie the driveshaft to the steering rack housing to avoid strain on the CV joints caused by excessive deflection of the driveshaft.
8   Insert a suitable plug (an old driveshaft stud is ideal) into the transmission casing to prevent the differential gears being dislodged if both driveshafts are being removed.
9   Using a tool with a hook at its end, prise out the oil seal from the differential housing. Take care not to damage the seal housing.
10 Wipe out the oil seal seat, apply grease to the lips of a new oil seal and tap it into position using a piece of tubing or similar as a drift.
11 Using a mirror, check that the pinion gear within the differential is in correct alignment to receive the driveshaft. If not, insert the finger to align it.
12 Fit a new snap-ring to the driveshaft and then offer it up to engage it in the transmission.
13 Have your assistant push inwards on the roadwheel until the

snap-ring is fully engaged. If any difficulty is experienced in pushing the driveshaft fully home, remove the roadwheel to reduce weight and lift the hub assembly until the driveshaft is in a more horizontal attitude.
14 Reconnect the suspension arm and tie-rod balljoint. Tighten the nuts and bolts to the specified torque when the weight of the car is again on its roadwheels.
15 Refit the interlock pin, spring and cap nut then top up the transmission oil level (see Chapter 6, Section 2).

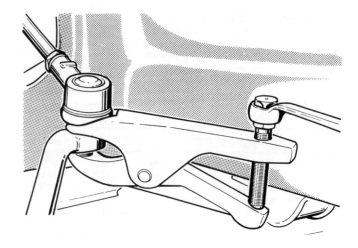

Fig. 7.2 Balljoint separator detaching the steering tie-rod joint (Sec 2)

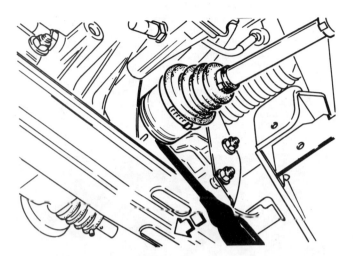

Fig. 7.3 Lever the driveshaft free from the transmission (Sec 2)

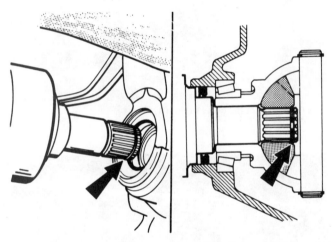

Fig. 7.4 Inserting driveshaft into transmission (left) and driveshaft snap-ring fully engaged with differential pinion gear (arrowed right) (Sec 2)

3 Driveshaft inboard oil seal (1.3 and 1.6 litre) renewal

1   Raise the front of the car and support on safety stands.

2   Drain the transmission oil by unscrewing the cap nut from the selector shaft locking mechanism. Take care not to lose the spring and interlock pin which will be ejected.

3   **Left-hand side seal:** Undo the six socket-head bolts and remove them, together with the three link washers from the driveshaft/stub shaft joint (photo). Separate the driveshaft and support it by suspending out of the way with a length of wire or cord, but not at too great an angle.

4   **Right-hand side seal:** Refer to Section 6 and remove the intermediate driveshaft.

5   The stub shaft on the side concerned can now be removed from the transmission housing by prising it out with a suitable lever or, if this proves difficult, it may be necessary to attach a slide hammer to the stub shaft to release it. The stub shaft is secured in the housing by a snap-ring and, once removed, this must be renewed. Note that if both the right- and left-hand stub shafts are to be removed at the same time, insert a suitable plug, tube or, if available, an old stub shaft into the transmission casing to prevent the differential gears being dislodged.

6   Using a tool with a hook at its end, prise out the oil seal from the differential housing. Take care not to damage the seal housing.

7   Wipe out the oil seal seat, apply grease to the lips of a new oil seal and tap it into position using a piece of tubing or similar as a drift.

8   Using a mirror, check that the pinion gear within the differential is in correct alignment to receive the stub shaft. If not, insert a finger to align it.

9   Fit a new snap-ring to the stub shaft and then offer it up to engage it in the transmission and tap it home with a tube drift so that the snap-ring is felt to engage (photo).

10 Reconnect the intermediate driveshaft on the right-hand side (see Section 6), then reconnect the driveshafts reversing the removal procedure.

11 Refit the interlock pin, spring and cap nut and top up the transmission oil level (see Chapter 6, Section 2).

3.3 Driveshaft flange joint socket-head bolts and link washers (1.3 and 1.6 litre)

3.9 Right-hand stub shaft location in transmission (1.3 and 1.6 litre)

4 Driveshaft inboard joint bellows – renewal

1   For 1.0 and 1.1 litre models, refer to Section 2 and proceed as described in paragraphs 1 to 6 inclusive. On 1.3 and 1.6 litre models refer to Section 3 and proceed as described in paragraphs 1 and 3 to

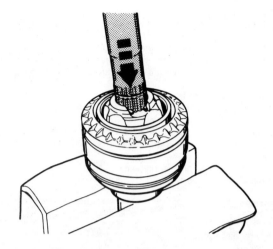

Fig. 7.5 Inserting the driveshaft into the CV joint (Sec 4)

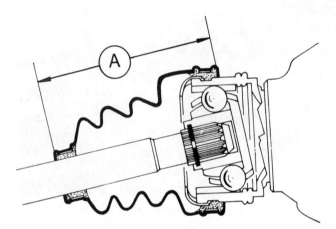

Fig. 7.6 Driveshaft bellows fitting (Secs 4 and 5)

A on inner joint of shaft angle of 10° to 20° = 80 to 90 mm (3.1 to 3.5 in)
A on outer joint with shaft horizontal = 98 to 102 mm (3.8 to 4.0 in)

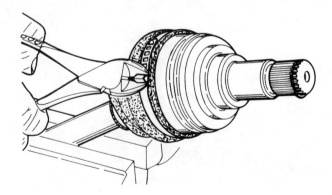

Fig. 7.7 Securing the bellows clamp with crimping pliers (Sec 4)

5   Fit the new bellows into position on the shaft and repack the CV joint with grease. Insert the driveshaft back through the joint unit, pushing through until the circlip is felt to engage and secure it.
6   Locate the new bellows into position over the CV joint. The bellows positioning is important. Check that, when in position with the inner joint fully contracted and at an angle of 10° to 20°, the full length of the bellows clamps is as shown in Fig. 7.6.
7   Fit and fasten the bellows clamps by holding them round the bellows finger tight, then clamp the pin into the next engagement hole. Crimp the clamp to secure it (photos).
8   Reconnect the tie-rod joint and suspension arm or driveshaft flange joint (as applicable), referring to Section 2 or 3.

4.7A Inboard joint bellows (1.0 and 1.1 litre)

4.7B Inboard joint bellows (1.3 and 1.6 litre)

5   Driveshaft outboard joint bellows – renewal

1   Unless the driveshaft is to be removed completely for other repair work to be carried out (refer to Section 7), the following method of bellows renewal is recommended to avoid having to disconnect the driveshaft from the hub carrier.
2   Remove the inboard joint bellows as described in the preceding Section.
3   On the right-hand driveshaft, mark the relative position of the

disconnect the right or left-hand driveshaft at the inner end (leaving the intermediate shaft in position).
2   Unclip and remove the bellows retaining clamps by prising open the looped section of the clamp with a screwdriver, then slide the bellows along the shaft to expose the CV (constant velocity) joint.
3   Wipe the surplus from the CV joint, then prise open the securing circlip and pull the shaft from the joint.
4   The bellows can now be withdrawn from the shaft.

torsional damper on the shaft then unbolt and remove the damper unit.

4   Release the clamps on the outboard joint bellows and slide the bellows along the driveshaft until they can be removed from the inboard end of the shaft.

5   Thoroughly clean the driveshaft before sliding on the new bellows. Replenish the outboard joint with specified lubricant and slide the bellows over the joint, setting its overall length to the appropriate dimension shown in Fig. 7.6.

6   Fit and tighten the bellows clamps, but make sure that the crimped part of the clamp nearest the hub does not interfere with the hub carrier as the driveshaft is rotated.

7   Refit the inboard bellows and connect the driveshaft to the transmission as described in the preceding Section.

8   Refit the torsional damper to the right-hand driveshaft and set it in the original position marked during removal or refer to Fig. 7.8 for its setting before fully tightening the retaining bolts.

6.3 Release the gaiter clamp (intermediate/stub shaft joint)

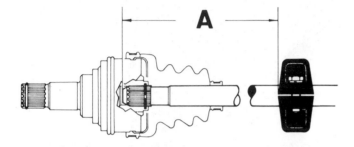

Fig. 7.8 Torsional damper location on shaft (Sec 5)

A = 308 to 312 mm (12.1 to 12.3 in)

6   Intermediate driveshaft (1.3 and 1.6 litre) – removal and refitting

1   Raise and support the front of the car on safety stands.

2   Using an Allen key, unscrew and remove the socket-head bolts and washers securing the constant velocity joint to the intermediate driveshaft. Tie the outer driveshaft away from the work area.

3   Prise free and release the clamp securing the intermediate driveshaft-to-stub shaft gaiter (photo).

4   Supporting the intermediate shaft, unscrew the socket-head bolts and detach the bearing housing from the support bracket.

5   Carefully slide the intermediate driveshaft from the differential stub shaft (photo).

6   Unbolt the support bracket from the engine.

7   Before refitting the driveshaft, check that the support bracket holes in the block are clear to a depth of 16.0 mm (0.63 in), and if necessary, re-tap them.

8   Refit the support bracket to the engine and insert the two bolts hand-tight.

9   Smear the intermediate driveshaft splines with a molybdenum disulphide grease, and insert the driveshaft into the differential.

10   Position the bearing housing on the support bracket, insert the two socket-head bolts and tighten them to the specified torque.

11   Tighten the upper support bracket bolt to the specified torque, followed by the lower bolt. **Note**: *It is important to tighten them in this order (photo).*

12   Pack the end flange of the intermediate driveshaft with 30 grams (1 oz) of molybdenum disulphide grease.

13   Mate the intermediate and outer driveshafts, insert the socket-head bolts, and tighten them *in diagonal sequence* to the specified torque.

14   Note that if either of the support bracket or bearing housing bolts is subsequently loosened, the complete tightening sequence described in paragraphs 8 to 11 must be followed in order to ensure correct position of the components.

15   Refit the intermediate shaft-to-stub shaft gaiter then locate the securing clamp, pushing it together finger tight, then clamp the pin into the next engagement hole. Crimp the clamp to secure it. Check that the gaiter is not twisted or stretched (photo).

6.5 Withdrawing the intermediate shaft from the stub shaft

6.11 Intermediate shaft support bracket

6.15 Intermediate shaft-to-stub axle gaiter refitted

7   Driveshaft – removal and refitting

1   Slacken the roadwheel bolts and then raise the front of the vehicle.
2   Remove the roadwheel.
3   Refit two of the roadwheel bolts as a means of anchoring the disc when the hub nut is unscrewed (the disc retaining screw is not strong enough to prevent the disc from rotating).
4   Have an assistant apply the footbrake and then unscrew the staked hub nut and remove it, together with the plain washer The hub nut is particularly tight, and if you are unsure of the stability of the car on its stands it is wise to refit the roadwheel(s) and slacken the hub nut when the car is on the ground.
5   Remove the temporary wheel bolts.
6   Unbolt the caliper and tie it up to the suspension strut to prevent strain on the flexible hose.
7   Disconnect the inboard end of the driveshaft, as described in Section 2 or 3.
8   Support the driveshaft on a jack or by tying it up.
9   Extract the small retaining screw and withdraw the brake disc from the hub.
10 It may now be possible to pull the hub from the driveshaft. If it does not come off easily, use a two-legged puller.
11 Withdraw the driveshaft, complete with CV joints. If both drive-shafts are being removed at the same time then the differential pinion gears must be retained in alignment with their transmission casing holes by inserting pieces of plastic tubing or, if available, an old stub shaft, but take care not to damage the oil seal within the transmission housing.
12 On 1.3 and 1.6 litre models the left-hand side driveshaft inboard CV joint/stub shaft unit can be removed from the transmission, as described in Section 3. On the right-hand side the intermediate shaft assembly and inboard stub shaft can be removed if necessary by referring to Sections 6 and 3 respectively.
13 To refit the driveshaft, first engage it in the splines of the hub carrier while supporting the shaft in a horizontal attitude to avoid strain on the CV joints.
14 Using the original nut and distance pieces of varying lengths, draw the driveshaft into the hub carrier.
15 Remove the old nut and distance pieces and fit the washer and a new nut, but only finger tight at this stage.
16 Fit the brake disc and caliper.
17 Connect the inboard end of the driveshaft and the suspension components as described in Section 2 or 3.
18 Temporarily screw in two wheel bolts and then have an assistant apply the footbrake.
19 Tighten the hub nut to the specified torque. It is safer to leave the final tightening of the hub nut until the weight of the car is on the

roadwheels. In the absence of a suitable torque wrench with a high enough range, full pressure on a knuckle bar or pipe extension about 457 mm (18 in) in length should give approximately the correct torque. Once tight, stake the nut into the shaft groove. Fit the roadwheel and lower the vehicle.
20 Tighten the roadwheel bolts and then check the torque wrench settings of the other front suspension attachments now that the weight of the vehicle is on the roadwheels.

Fig. 7.9 Brake caliper mounting bolts (arrowed) (Sec 7)

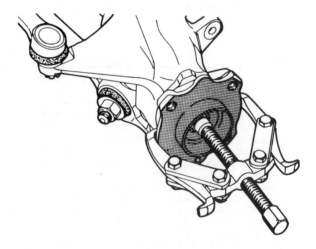

Fig. 7.10 Hub withdrawal from driveshaft using a puller (Sec 7)

Fig. 7.11 Tightening the hub nut (Sec 7)

Fig. 7.12 Stake the hub nut to secure (Sec 7)

8.4 Torsional damper on right-hand driveshaft – mark position before removing

8 Driveshaft – overhaul

1   Remove the driveshaft, as described in the preceding Section.
2   Clean away external dirt and grease, release the bellows clamps and slide the bellows from the CV joint.
3   Wipe away enough lubricant to be able to extract the circlip and then separate the CV joint with its splined shaft section from the main member of the driveshaft.
4   If removing the torsional damper from the right-hand driveshaft, mark its relative position on the shaft before unbolting it (photo).
5   Thoroughly clean the joint components and examine for wear or damage to the balls, cage, socket or splines. A repair kit may provide a solution to the problem, but, if the socket requires renewal, this will of course include the splined section of shaft and will prove expensive.

If both joints require renewal of major components, then a new driveshaft or one which has been professionally reconditioned may prove to be more economical.
6   If the torsional damper was removed from the right-hand driveshaft, refit it in the position marked during its removal.
7   Reassemble the joint by reversing the dismantling operations. Use a new circlip if necessary and pack the joint with the specified quantity of lubricant. When fitting bellows, set their length in accordance with the information given in Section 4 or 5 according to which joint (inboard or outboard) is being worked upon.
8   Refit the driveshaft as described in Section 7.

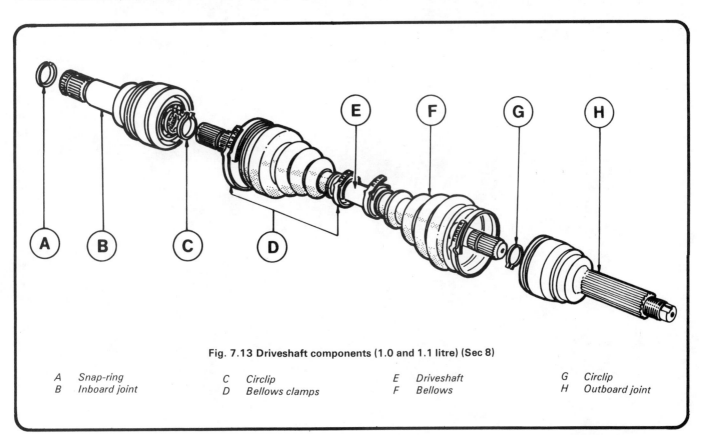

Fig. 7.13 Driveshaft components (1.0 and 1.1 litre) (Sec 8)

A	Snap-ring	C	Circlip	E	Driveshaft	G	Circlip
B	Inboard joint	D	Bellows clamps	F	Bellows	H	Outboard joint

9 Fault diagnosis – driveshafts

Symptom	Reason(s)
Knock when taking up drive	Wear in joint Wear in shaft splines Loose roadwheel bolts
Noise, especially on turns	Lack of lubrication Wear in joint Loose hub retaining nut
Leakage of lubricant	Split bellows or loose retaining clamp Faulty oil seal at differential end of shaft Faulty oil seal at roadwheel end of shaft (refer to Chapter 10)

Chapter 8 Braking system

Contents

Brake disc – examination, removal and refitting 5
Brake drum – inspection and renewal 8
Brake pressure control valve – removal and refitting 10
Brake warning lamps – description and renewal 17
Caliper piston assembly – removal, overhaul and refitting 4
Disc pads – inspection and renewal 3
Fault diagnosis – braking system 18
Flexible and rigid hydraulic pipes – removal and refitting 11
General description 1

Handbrake – adjustment 14
Handbrake cables – renewal 15
Handbrake lever – removal and refitting 16
Hydraulic system – bleeding 12
Master cylinder – removal, overhaul and refitting 9
Rear brake linings – inspection and renewal 6
Rear wheel cylinder – removal, overhaul and refitting 7
Routine maintenance – braking system 2
Vacuum servo unit – removal and refitting 13

Specifications

System type ....

Hydraulic, dual-circuit, discs at front, drums at rear. Servo assistance. Mechanical handbrake to rear wheels only

Front (disc) brakes

Caliper type	Single piston, sliding type
Disc diameter (outer):	
Standard	221 mm (8.71 in)
XR2 only	239 mm (9.42 in)
Disc thickness (new):	
Standard	10 mm (0.39 in)
XR2 only	20 mm (0.79 in)
Minimum allowable disc thickness:	
Standard	8.7 mm (0.34 in)
XR2 only	18.5 mm (0.73 in)
Allowable disc run-out	0.15 mm (0.006 in)
Minimum allowable pad thickness:	
Standard	1.5 mm (0.059 in)
XR2 only	1.5 mm (0.059 in)

Rear brakes

Drum diameter:	
Standard	177.8 mm (7.00 in)
XR2 only	177.8 mm (7.00 in)
Shoe width:	
Standard	30.0 mm (1.18 in)
XR2 only	38.0 mm (1.16 in)
Wheel cylinder diameter:	
Standard	17.5 mm (0.69 in)
XR2 only	19.0 mm (0.75 in)

Brake fluid ....

To Ford specification SAM - 6C - 9103A Amber

Torque wrench settings

	Nm	lbf ft
Disc caliper bracket to suspension unit	56	41
Caliper piston housing to bracket	23	17
Servo mounting nuts	23	17
Master cylinder-to-servo retaining nuts	24	18
Large bracket to bulkhead	23	17
Carrier plate to axle housing	23	17
Pressure control valve bracket (to chassis)	23	17
Hydraulic unions	14	10
Bleed valves	10	7

1 General description

The braking system is of four-wheeled hydraulic type, with discs at the front and drums at the rear.

The hydraulic system is of dual-circuit type, each circuit controls one front brake and one rear brake linked diagonally.

The calipers are of single piston, sliding piston housing type.

The rear brakes are of leading and trailing shoe design with a self adjusting mechanism. To compensate for the greater lining of wear of the leading shoe, its friction lining is thicker than that on the trailing shoe.

The master cylinder incorporates a reservoir cap which has a fluid level switch connected to a warning lamp on the instrument panel.

A vacuum servo is standard on certain models. When fitted to RHD versions, because of the location of the servo/master cylinder on the left-hand side of the engine compartment, the brake pedal is operated through a transverse rod on the engine compartment rear bulkhead.

A brake pressure regulating control valve is fitted into the hydraulic circuit to prevent rear wheel locking under conditions of heavy braking.

The floor-mounted handbrake control lever operates through cables to the rear wheels only.

2.1 Check/top up the brake fluid reservoir when necessary

2 Routine maintenance – braking system

1   At weekly intervals check the fluid in the translucent reservoir on the master cylinder (photo). The fluid will drop very slowly indeed over a period of time to compensate for lining wear, but any sudden drop in level or the need for frequent topping-up should be investigated immediately.

2   Always top up with hydraulic fluid which meets the specified standard and has been left in an airtight container. Hydraulic fluid is hygroscopic (absorbs moisture from the atmosphere) and must not be stored in an open container. **Do not** shake the tin prior to topping-up. Fluids of different makes can be intermixed provided they all meet the specification.

3   Inspect the thickness of the friction linings on the disc pads and brake shoes, as described in the following Sections, at the intervals specified in Routine Maintenance (photos).

4   The rigid and flexible hydraulic pipes and hoses should be inspected for leaks or damage regularly. Although the rigid lines are plastic coated to preserve them against corrosion, check for damage which may have occurred through flying stones, careless jacking or the traversing of rough ground.

5   Bend the hydraulic flexible hoses sharply with the fingers and examine the surface of the hose for signs of cracking or perishing of the rubber. Renew if evident.

6   Renew the brake fluid at the specified intervals and examine all rubber components (including master cylinder and piston seals) with a critical eye, renewing where necessary.

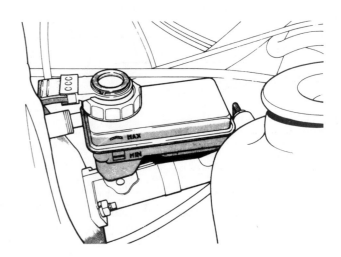

Fig. 8.1 Brake fluid level and markings in reservoir (Sec 2)

2.3A Front brake disc pad inspection aperture in caliper housing

2.3B Remove the rubber cover from the rear brake backplate ...

2.3C ... to inspect the brake linings for wear

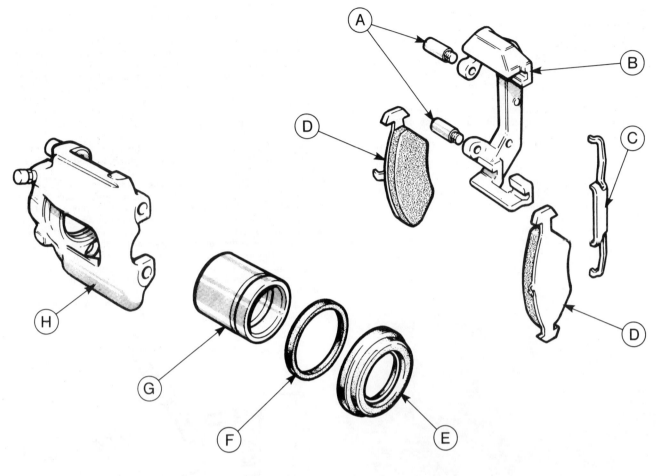

Fig. 8.2 Front brake caliper components (Sec 3)

| A | Anchor bracket bolts | C | Clip | E | Dust seal | G | Piston |
| B | Anchor bracket | D | Pads | F | Piston seal | H | Housing |

3 Disc pads – inspection and renewal

1   At the intervals specified in Routine Maintenance, place a mirror between the roadwheel and the caliper and check the thickness of the friction material of the disc pads. If the material has worn down to 1.5 mm (0.059 in) or less, the pads must be renewed as an axle set (four pads).

2   Slacken the roadwheel bolts, raise the front of the vehicle, support with safety stands and remove the roadwheel(s).

3   Using a screwdriver as shown, prise free the retaining clip from the caliper (photo).

4   Using a 7 mm Allen key, unscrew the bolts until they can be withdrawn from the caliper anchor brackets (photo).

5   Withdraw the piston housing and tie it up with a length of wire to prevent strain on the flexible hose (photo).

6   Withdraw the inboard pad from the piston housing; the pad being secured to the piston by means of a coil spring.

7   Withdraw the outer pad which is secured in position by the shim which has adhesive on both faces.

8   Clean away all residual dust or dirt, **taking care not to inhale the dust** as, being asbestos based, it is injurious to health.

9   Using a piece of flat wood, a tyre lever or similar, push the piston

3.3 Prise free the retaining clip

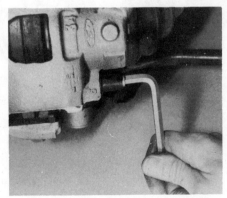
3.4 Undo the caliper anchor bracket bolts

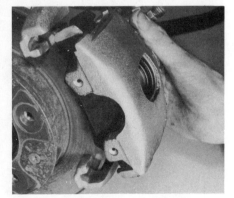
3.5 Remove the caliper piston housing

squarely into its bore. This is necessary in order to accommodate the new thicker pads when they are fitted.

10 Depressing the piston will cause the fluid level in the master cylinder reservoir to rise, so anticipate this by syphoning out some fluid using an old hydrometer or poultry baster. Take care not to drip hydraulic fluid onto the paintwork, it acts as an effective paint stripper.

11 Commence reassembly by fitting the inboard pad into the piston housing. Make sure that the spring on the back of the pad fits into the piston (photo).

12 Peel back the protective paper covering from the surface of the new outboard pad and locate it in the jaws of the caliper anchor bracket.

13 Locate the caliper piston housing and screw in the Allen bolts to the specified torque.

14 Fit the retaining clip (photo).

15 Repeat the operations on the opposite brake.

16 Apply the footbrake hard several times to position the pads against the disc and then check and top up the fluid in the master cylinder reservoir.

17 Fit the roadwheel(s) and lower the vehicle.

18 Avoid heavy braking (if possible) for the first hundred miles or so when new pads have been fitted. This is to allow them to bed in and reach full efficiency.

3.11 Inboard pad assembly to piston

3.14 Retaining clip refitted

4 Caliper piston assembly – removal, overhaul and refitting

1   Proceed as described in paragraphs 2 to 8 in the previous Section.

2   Disconnect the brake flexible hose from the caliper. This can be carried out in one of two ways. Either disconnect the flexible hose from the rigid hydraulic pipeline at the support bracket by unscrewing the union, or, once the caliper is detached, hold the end fitting of the hose in an open-ended spanner and unscrew the caliper from the hose. Do not allow the hose to distort an excessive amount.

3   Brush away all external dirt and pull off the piston dust-excluding cover.

4   Apply air pressure to the fluid inlet hole and eject the piston. Only low air pressure is needed for this, such as is produced by a foot-operated tyre pump.

5   Using a suitable hooked instrument, pick out the piston seal from the groove in the cylinder bore. Do not scratch the surface of the bore.

6   Examine the surfaces of the piston and the cylinder bore. If they are scored or show evidence of metal-to-metal rubbing, then a new piston housing will be required. Where the components are in good condition, discard the seal and obtain a repair kit.

7   Wash the internal components in clean brake hydraulic fluid or methylated spirit only, nothing else.

8   Using the fingers, manipulate the new seal into its groove in the cylinder bore.

9   Dip the piston in clean hydraulic fluid and insert it squarely into its bore.

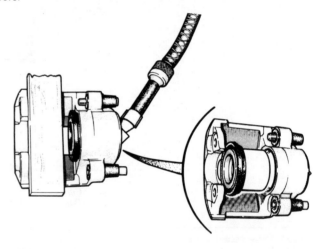

Fig. 8.3 Caliper piston removal method with compressed air. Note wooden block fitted to avoid damaging the piston (Sec 4)

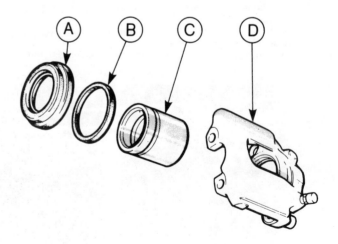

Fig. 8.4 Caliper and piston components (Sec 4)

A	Piston cover	C	Piston
B	Seal	D	Housing

10 Connect the rubber dust excluder between the piston and the piston housing and then depress the piston fully.

11 Refit the caliper by reversing the removal operations (see previous Section, paragraphs 11 to 14).

12 When reconnecting the brake hose check that it is fitted and secured so that it is not distorted and will not interfere with any adjacent steering or suspension components.

13 Bleed the hydraulic circuit, as given in Section 12, then refit the roadwheel(s) and lower the vehicle.

14 If new pads have been fitted, heavy braking should be avoided where possible for the first hundred miles or so to allow them to bed in and reach full efficiency.

5 Brake disc – examination, removal and refitting

1   Raise the front of the vehicle and remove the roadwheel.

2   Examine the surface of the disc. If it is deeply grooved or scored or if any small cracks are evident, it must either be refinished or renewed. Any refinishing must not reduce the thickness of the disc to below a certain minimum (see Specifications). Light scoring on a brake disc is normal and should be ignored.

3   If disc distortion is suspected, the disc can be checked for run-out using a dial gauge or feeler blades located between its face and a fixed point as the disc is rotated (Fig. 8.5).

4   Where run-out exceeds the specified figure, renew the disc.

5   To remove a disc, unbolt the caliper, withdraw it and tie it up to the suspension strut to avoid strain on the flexible hose.

6   Extract the small disc retaining screw and pull the disc from the hub.

7   If a new disc is being installed, clean its surfaces free from preservative before refitting the caliper. It will also be necessary to depress the piston and inner brake pad a small amount to accommodate the new thicker disc when assembling, see paragraphs 9 and 10 in Section 3.

9   Refit the caliper and the roadwheel and lower the vehicle to the floor.

6 Rear brake linings – inspection and renewal

1   Due to the fact that the rear brake drums are combined with the hubs, which makes removal of the drums more complicated than is the case with detachable drums, inspection of the shoe linings can be carried out at the specified intervals by prising out the small inspection plug from the brake backplate and observing the linings through the hole using a mirror.

2   A minimum thickness of friction material must always be observed on the shoes; if it is worn down to this level, renew the shoes.

3   Do not attempt to re-line shoes yourself, but always obtain factory re-lined shoes.

4   Renew the shoes in an axle set (four shoes), even if only one is worn to the minimum.

5   Chock the front wheels. Slacken the roadwheel bolts, raise the rear of the vehicle and support it securely. Remove the roadwheels.

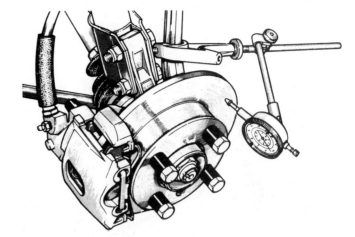

Fig. 8.5 Checking the brake disc run-out using a dial gauge (Sec 5)

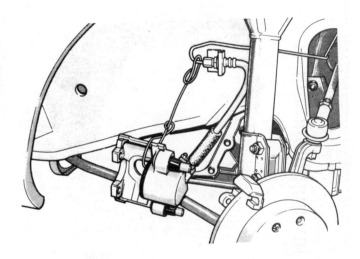

Fig. 8.6 Remove and support the caliper unit (Sec 5)

6   Release the handbrake fully.

7   Tap off the hub dust cap, remove the split pin, nut lock, nut and thrust washer (photos).

8   Pull the hub/drum towards you and then push it back enough to be able to take the outer bearing from the spindle.

6.7A Remove the dust cap ...

6.7B ... the split pin and nut lock, ...

6.7C ... the nut and thrust washer

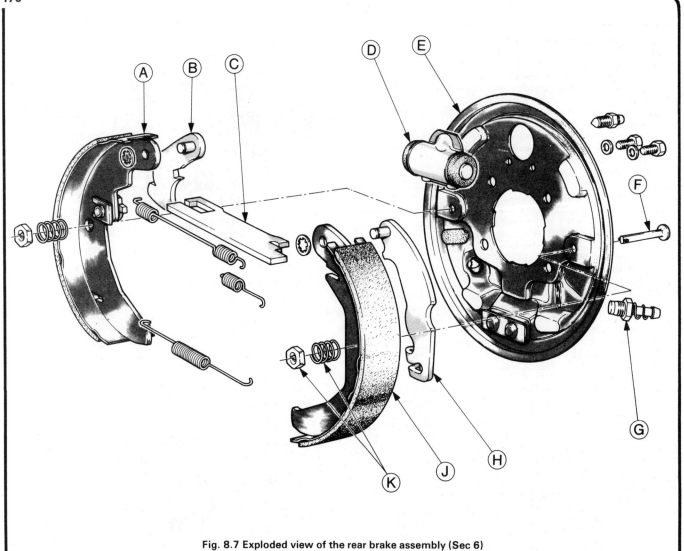

Fig. 8.7 Exploded view of the rear brake assembly (Sec 6)

A	Leading shoe	D	Wheel cylinder
B	Adjuster ratchet	E	Carrier (back) plate
C	Adjustment strut	F	Hold-down pin

G	Adjustment plunger	J	Trailing shoe
H	Handbrake lever	K	Hold-down spring and cup

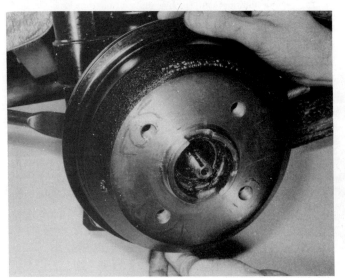

6.9 Withdrawing the brake drum

6.10 Brake hold-down spring and retainer removal

9   Remove the hub/drum and brush out any dust **taking care not to inhale it** (photo).

10   Remove the shoe hold-down spring from the leading shoe (photo). Do this by gripping the dished washer with a pair of pliers, depressing it and turning it through 90°. Remove the washer, spring and the hold-down post.

11   Note the locations of the leading and trailing shoes and also the upper and lower return springs. Unhook the brake shoes from the lower anchor plate and detach the lower return spring.

12   Detach the brake shoes from the wheel cylinder, manoeuvre them away from the backplate and disengage the handbrake cable from the relay arm.

13   The brake pull-off springs and adjuster strut can then be disconnected at the top end of the brake shoes. Again note orientation for refitting.

14   To detach the large ratchet and handbrake lever remove the circlips.

15   Prior to reassembly, wipe the carrier (back) plate clean and apply a light coating of brake grease (Thermopaul 1) to the brake shoe contact points indicated in Fig. 8.9.

16   Refit the large ratchet to the leading brake shoe and the handbrake relay lever to the trailing brake shoe.

17   Relocate the pull-off springs into position between the top end of the leading and trailing shoe (as noted during removal).

18   Apply a small amount of Thermopaul 1 brake grease to the large ratchet and handbrake relay lever contact surfaces, then reconnect the handbrake cable to the relay lever on the trailing shoe. **Do not** get any brake grease onto the brake linings.

19   Refit the brake shoes into position, prising open the leading edges to fit on the wheel cylinder at the top. Support in this position, relocate the lower brake pull-off spring then prise open the shoes at the bottom (trailing edges) and engage on the lower anchor plate (photos).

20   Centralise the shoes, by tapping them with the hand if necessary, then relocate the shoe hold-down pin, spring and dished washer. Depress and twist the washers through 90° to secure (photo).

21   Before refitting the brake drum, check that the shoes are centralised, and release the automatic adjuster to fully contract the shoes.

22   Lubricate the inboard bearing and oil seal lips in the brake drum/hub and fit the drum/hub onto the stub axle; taking care not to damage the oil seal lips.

23   Fit the outboard bearing and thrust washer (lubricated with suitable wheel bearing grease) and screw the retaining nut into position.

24   Tightening the nut also sets the wheel bearing adjustment and it is therefore important that the correct procedure is followed. Refer to Section 7 in Chapter 10 for details.

25   With the wheel bearing adjustment completed and the nut retainer and split pin in position, refit the dust cap.

26   Depress the brake pedal hard several times to actuate the self-adjusting mechanism and to bring the shoes up close to the drum.

27   Refit the roadwheel and lower the vehicle to the floor.

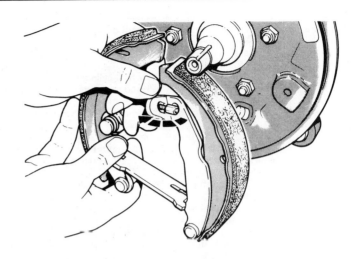

Fig. 8.8 Disconnecting the handbrake cable from the relay arm (Sec 6)

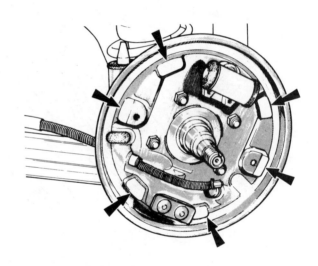

Fig. 8.9 Lightly lubricate the brake shoe contact points (arrowed) with brake grease Thermopaul 1 (Sec 6)

6.19A Brake shoe assembly at the top

6.19B Brake shoe assembly at the bottom

6.20 Rear brake shoes fully assembled

7   Rear wheel cylinder – removal, overhaul and refitting

1   Remove the brake drum, as described in paragraphs 5 to 9 inclusive in the previous Section.
2   Disconnect the fluid pipeline from the wheel cylinder and cap the end of the pipe to prevent loss of fluid. A bleed screw rubber dust cap is useful for this.
3   Unscrew the two bolts which hold the wheel cylinder to the brake backplate (Fig. 8.10).
4   To avoid removing the brake shoes when withdrawing the wheel cylinder, prise the shoes away from the cylinder (at the top) so that the automatic adjuster holds them clear of it. The cylinder can then be withdrawn.
5   Clean away external dirt and then pull off the dust-excluding covers from the cylinder unit.
6   The pistons will probably shake out. If they do not, apply air pressure (from a tyre pump) at the fluid inlet hole to eject them.
7   Examine the surfaces of the pistons and the cylinder bores for scoring or metal-to-metal rubbing areas. If evident, renew the complete cylinder assembly.
8   Where the components are in good condition, discard the rubber seals and dust excluders and obtain a repair kit.
9   Any cleaning should be done using hydraulic fluid or methylated spirit – nothing else.

Fig. 8.10 Rear wheel cylinder retaining bolts (arrowed) (Sec 7)

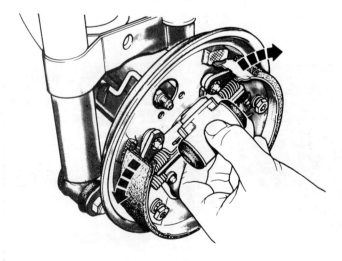

Fig. 8.11 Rear wheel cylinder removal (with brake shoes expanded in direction of arrows) (Sec 7)

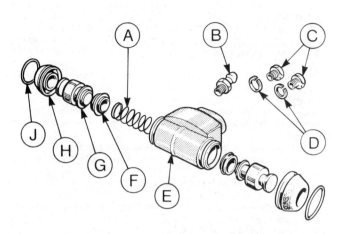

Fig. 8.12 Wheel cylinder components (Sec 7)

A Spring	F Piston seal
B Bleed nipple	G Piston
C Retaining bolts	H Dust cover
D Lockwasher	J Gaiter springs
E Piston housing	

10   Reassemble by dipping the first piston in clean hydraulic fluid and inserting it into the cylinder. Fit a dust excluder to it.
11   From the opposite end of the cylinder body, insert a new seal, spring, a second new seal, the second piston and the remaining dust excluder. Use only the fingers to manipulate the seals into position and make quite sure that the lips of the seals are the correct way round.
12   Refit the cylinder to the backplate and secure with the two bolts and lockwashers.
13   Remove the plug and reconnect the hydraulic fluid pipe, taking care not to cross-thread the connection. Do not overtighten the union, but tighten it sufficiently to seal it. For the torque setting refer to the Specifications.
14   Relocate the brake shoes against the cylinder pistons by releasing the automatic adjuster.
15   Refit the brake drum and hub unit, as described in paragraphs 22 to 25 inclusive in the previous Section, but prior to lowering the vehicle bleed the hydraulic circuit, as described in Section 12.

8   Brake drum – inspection and renewal

1   Whenever a brake drum is removed (see Section 6), brush out dust from it, **taking care not to inhale it** as it contains asbestos and is injurious to health.
2   Examine the internal friction surface of the drum. If deeply scored, or so worn that the drum has become pocketed to the width of the shoes, then the drums must be renewed.
3   Regrinding is not recommended as the internal diameter will no longer be compatible with the shoe lining contact diameter.
4   If renewing the brake drum it is also advisable to renew the hub bearings and inner oil seal rather than transferring the old. The seal will need renewal in any case.

9   Master cylinder – removal, overhaul and refitting

1   Syphon out as much fluid as possible from the master cylinder reservoir using an old battery hydrometer or a poultry baster. Do not drip the fluid onto the paintwork or it will act as an effective paint stripper.
2   Disconnect the pipelines from the master cylinder by unscrewing the unions (photo).
3   Disconnect the leads from the level warning switch in the reservoir cap. Remove the cap.
4   On models not fitted with a brake servo unit, unclip and remove the trim panel beneath the facia on the driver's side to give access to

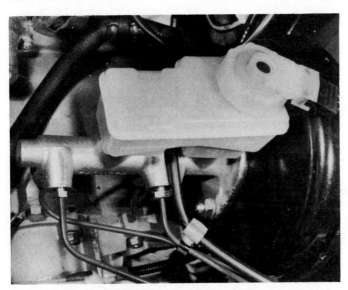

9.2 Master cylinder and hydraulic pipe connections

the brake pedal. Extract the brake pedal-to-pushrod clevis pin retaining clip and withdraw the pin.

5   Unbolt and remove the master cylinder. On non-servo models remove from the bulkhead whilst, on servo equipped models, the master cylinder is removed from the servo unit.

6   Clean away external dirt and then detach the fluid reservoir by tilting it sideways and gently pulling. Remove the two rubber seals.

7   Secure the master cylinder carefully in a vice fitted with jaw protectors.

8   Pull the dust excluder back from around the pushrod and using circlip pliers, extract the circlip which is now exposed.

9   Remove the pushrod, dust excluder and washer.

10   Withdraw the primary piston assembly, which will already have been partially ejected.

11   Using a small diameter rod, insert it into the end of the cylinder

and push the secondary piston in so that the locking pin can be extracted (Fig. 8.13).

12   Tap the end of the master cylinder on a block of wood and eject the secondary piston assembly.

13   Examine the pistons and cylinder bore surfaces for scoring or signs of metal-to-metal rubbing. If evident, renew the cylinder complete.

14   The primary piston unit cannot be dismantled and must be renewed as a unit.

15   Prise free and remove the secondary piston seals, noting their orientation. Once removed the seals must be discarded and a repair kit obtained for their renewal.

16   Cleaning of components should be done in brake hydraulic fluid or methylated spirit only – nothing else.

17   Using the new seals from the repair kit, assemble the secondary piston, making sure that the seal lips are the correct way round, as noted during dismantling.

18   Dip the piston assemblies in clean hydraulic fluid and enter them into the cylinder bore.

19   Fit the pushrod complete with new dust excluder and secure with a new circlip.

20   Engage the dust excluder with the master cylinder.

21   Depress the pushrod and locate the secondary piston lockpin.

22   Locate the two rubber seals and push the fluid reservoir into position.

23   It is recommended that a small quantity of fluid is now poured into the reservoir and the pushrod operated several times to prime the unit.

24   Refit the master cylinder by reversing the removal operations.

25   Do not overtighten the hydraulic line unions and take care that they are clean and not cross-threaded when reconnecting. Refer to the specifications for the torque wrench setting.

26   Bleed the complete hydraulic system on completion of the work (see Section 12).

10   Brake pressure control valve – removal and refitting

1   The brake pressure control valve assembly is located towards the rear of the vehicle and mounted to the chassis on the right-hand side. The assembly consists of a pair of control valve cylinders mounted to a common bracket. One valve controls the pressure to the right-hand rear brake, the other to the left-hand rear brake (photo).

2   The valves are removed as a pair. First raise and support the vehicle at the rear using safety stands. Chock the front wheels.

3   Clean the valves and connections externally, then unscrew the

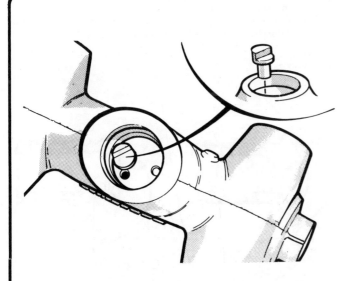

Fig. 8.13 Master cylinder secondary piston stop pin (Sec 9)

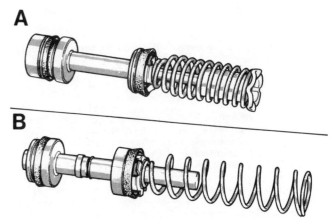

Fig. 8.14 Master cylinder primary (A) and secondary (B) piston assemblies (Sec 9)

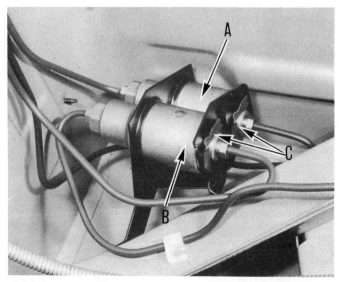

10.1 Brake pressure control valve

A *Right-hand rear brake circuit valve*
B *Left-hand rear brake circuit valve*
C *Retaining clips*

11.2 Flexible-to-rigid brake pipe connection showing spring anchor clip (arrowed)

clip from the support bracket (photo) and then, using two close-fitting spanners, disconnect the rigid line from the flexible hose.
3   Once disconnected from the rigid pipe, the flexible hose may be unscrewed from the caliper or wheel cylinder.
4   When reconnecting pipeline or hose fittings, remember that all union threads are to metric sizes. No copper washers are used at unions and the seal is made at the swaged end of the pipe, so do not try to wind a union in if it is tight yet still stands proud of the surface into which it is screwed.
5   A flexible hose must never be installed twisted, but a slight 'set' is permissible to give it clearance from an adjacent component. Do this by turning the hose slightly before inserting the bracket spring clip.
6   Rigid pipelines can be made to pattern by factors supplying brake components.
7   If you are making up a brake pipe yourself, observe the following essential requirements.
8   Before flaring the ends of the pipe, trim back the protective plastic coating by a distance of 5.0 mm (0.2 in).
9   Flare the end of the pipe as shown (Fig. 8.17).
10 The minimum pipe bend radius is 12.0 mm (0.5 in), but bends of less than 20.0 mm (0.8 in) should be avoided if possible.

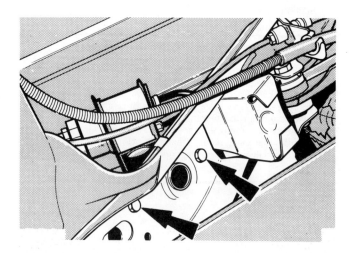

Fig. 8.15 Brake pressure control valve securing bolts (arrowed)
(Sec 10)

hydraulic line unions from the valves. Plug the disconnected lines to prevent excessive fluid leakage and the ingress of dirt.
4   Unscrew and remove the valve mounting bracket bolts and withdraw the valve assembly (Fig. 8.15).
5   Each valve is secured to the bracket by means of a clip which can be prised free to release the valve from the bracket.
6   Refitting is the reversal of the removal procedure. Check that the hydraulic line connections are clean before reconnecting, and take care not to cross-thread the unions.
7   Before lowering the vehicle at the rear bleed the hydraulic system, as described in Section 12.

---

11 Flexible and rigid hydraulic pipes – removal and refitting

1   Inspection has already been covered in Section 2 of this Chapter.
2   Always disconnect a flexible hose by prising out the spring anchor

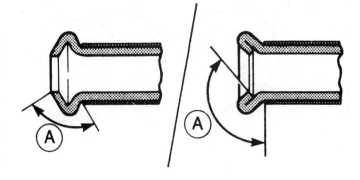

Fig. 8.16 Brake pipe flare (Sec 11)

A *Protective coating removed before flaring*

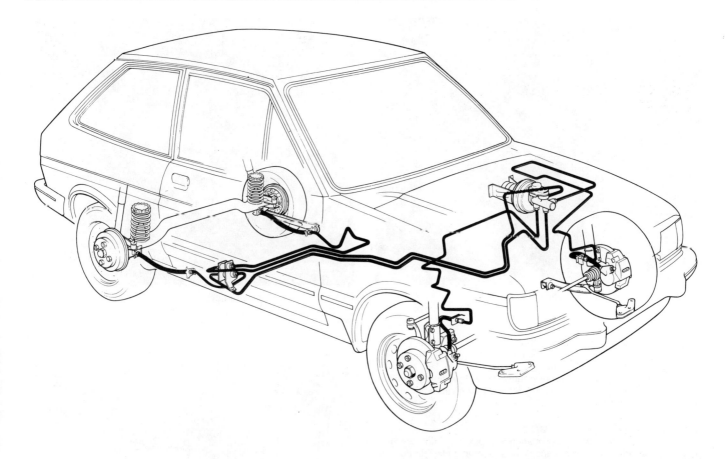

Fig. 8.17 Brake line circuits of the Fiesta (Sec 11)

12 Hydraulic system – bleeding

1   This is not a routine operation, but will be required after any component in the system has been removed and refitted or any part of the hydraulic system has been 'broken'. When an operation has only affected one circuit of the hydraulic system, then bleeding will normally only be required to that circuit (front and rear diagonally opposite). If the master cylinder or the pressure regulating valve have been disconnected and reconnected, then the complete system must be bled.

2   One of three methods can be used to bleed the system.

Bleeding – two-man method

3   Gather together a clean jar and a length of rubber or plastic bleed tubing which will fit the bleed screw tightly. The help of an assistant will be required.

4   Take great care not to spill onto the paintwork as it will act as a paint stripper. If any is spilled, wash it off at once with cold water.

5   Clean around the bleed screw on the front right-hand caliper and attach the bleed tube to the screw (photo).

6   Check that the master cylinder reservoir is topped up and then destroy the vacuum in the brake servo (where fitted) by giving several applications of the brake foot pedal.

7   Immerse the open end of the bleed tube in the jar, which should contain 50 to 76 mm (2 to 3 in) of hydraulic fluid. The jar should be positioned about 300 mm (12.0 in) above the bleed nipple to prevent any possibility of air entering the system down the threads of the bleed screw when it is slackened.

8   Open the bleed screw half a turn and have your assistant depress the brake pedal slowly to the floor and then quickly remove his foot to allow the pedal to return unimpeded. Tighten the bleed screw at the end of each downstroke to prevent expelled air and fluid being drawn back into the system.

12.5 Bleed tube attached to bleed screw on front brake

9   Observe the submerged end of the tube in the jar. When air bubbles cease to appear, fully tighten the bleed screw when the pedal is being held down by your assistant.

10 Top up the fluid reservoir. It must be kept topped up throughout the bleeding operations. If the connecting holes in the master cylinder are exposed at any time due to low fluid level, then air will be drawn into the system and work will have to start all over again.

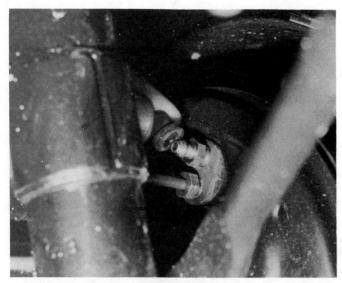

12.11 Rear brake bleed screw and protective cap

13.1 Vacuum servo pipe removal

11   Repeat the operations on the left-hand rear brake (photo), the left-hand front and the right-hand rear brake in that order (assuming that the whole system is being bled).

12   On completion, remove the bleed tube. Discard the fluid which has been bled from the system unless it is required for bleed jar purposes, **never** use it for filling the system.

Bleeding – with one-way valve

13   There are a number of one-man brake bleeding kits currently available from motor accessory shops. It is recommended that one of these kits should be used whenever possible as they greatly simplify the bleeding operation and also reduce the risk of expelled air or fluid being drawn back into the system.

14   Connect the outlet tube of the bleeder device to the bleed screw and then open the screw half a turn. Depress the brake pedal to the floor and slowly release it. The one-way valve will prevent expelled air from returning to the system at the completion of each stroke. Repeat this operation until clean hydraulic fluid, free from air bubbles, can be seen coming through the tube. Tighten the bleed screw and remove the tube.

15   Repeat the procedure on the remaining bleed nipples in the order described in paragraph 11. Remember to keep the master cylinder reservoir full.

Bleeding – with pressure bleeding kit

16   These are available from motor accessory shops and are usually operated by air pressure from the spare tyre.

17   By connecting a pressurised container to the master cylinder fluid reservoir, bleeding is then carried out by simply opening each bleed screw in turn and allowing the fluid to run out, rather like turning on a tap, until no air bubbles are visible in the fluid being expelled.

18   Using this system, the large reserve of fluid provides a safeguard against air being drawn into the master cylinder during the bleeding operations.

19   This method is particularly effective when bleeding 'difficult' systems or when bleeding the entire system of routine fluid renewal.

All systems

20   On completion of bleeding, top up the fluid level to the mark. Check the feel of the brake pedal, which should be firm and free from any 'sponginess' which would indicate air still being present in the system.

13   Vacuum servo unit – removal and refitting

1   Using a suitable screwdriver as a lever, prise free the vacuum servo pipe connector from the servo unit (photo).

Fig. 8.18 Clevis pin removal using long-nosed pliers (Sec 13)

2   Remove the master cylinder, as described in Section 9.

3   Unscrew and remove the four servo unit-to-mounting bracket retaining nuts.

4   Extract the spring clip from the connecting rod clevis pin using a pair of long-nosed pliers. Withdraw the clevis pin and remove the servo unit from the mounting bracket.

5   The servo unit cannot be repaired and if defective must therefore be renewed.

6   Refitting is a reversal of the removal procedure. Refer to Section 9 when refitting the master cylinder and Section 12 to bleed the hydraulic system.

7   On completion, check the operation of the brake stop-light switch and, if necessary, readjust it (see Section 17).

14   Handbrake – adjustment

1   Adjustment of the handbrake is normally automatic by means of the self-adjusting mechanism working on the rear brake shoes.

2   However, due to cable stretch, occasional inspection of the handbrake adjusters is recommended. Adjustment must be carried out if the movement of the control lever becomes excessive.

3   Chock the front wheels then fully release the handbrake.
4   Raise and support the vehicle at the rear with safety stands.
5   On adjustment check that the plunger protrudes from each rear brake backplate (photo), their respective length of movement indicating the handbrake adjustment condition. Before checking their movement (stroke) length, firmly apply the footbrake to ensure that the automatic adjuster mechanism is fully actuated.
6   Now check the plunger stroke movement. If the total movement of both sides added together is between 0.5 and 3.0 mm (0.02 and 0.118 in) then adjustment is satisfactory. This should give three to six clicks (notches) of handbrake application movement. If there is no measurable plunger movement or if the total measurement exceeds that specified adjust as follows.
7   Loosen the handbrake cable locknut, then rotate the adjuster sleeve (photo) so that the plungers can just rotate and the total movement of both plungers is as specified above.
8   Hand tighten the locknut against the sleeve so that two engagement clicks are felt, then further tighten another two clicks using a suitable wrench.

15   Handbrake cables – renewal

1   Chock the front wheels, then fully release the handbrake.
2   Raise and support the vehicle at the rear with safety stands.

Primary cable

3   Extract the spring clip and clevis pin and disconnect the primary cable from the equaliser.
4   Working inside the vehicle, disconnect the cable from the handbrake control lever, again by removal of clip and pin. Drift out the cable guide to the rear and withdraw the cable through the floorpan.
5   Refitting is a reversal of removal. Adjust the handbrake, if necessary, as described in Section 14.

Secondary cable

6   Remove the rear roadwheel each side then refer to Section 6 and remove the brake drums. Disengage the handbrake secondary cable from the rear brake assembly and pass through the brake backplate, having released the retaining clip (Fig. 8.19).
7   Extract the circlip and remove the clevis pin from the cable equaliser unit.
8   Disengage and remove the secondary cable from the body bracket clips and unhook it from the body supports. The cable can then be removed from under the vehicle (photo).

14.5 Handbrake cable assembly

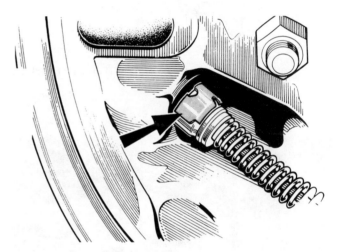

Fig. 8.19 Handbrake cable-to-brake backplate securing clip (Sec 15)

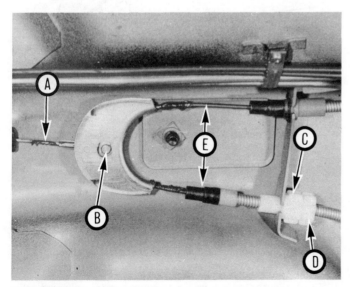

14.7 Handbrake cable assembly

A	Primary cable	D	Locknut
B	Equaliser	E	Secondary cable
C	Adjuster sleeve		

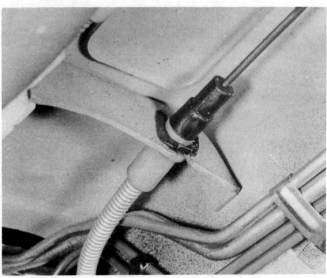

15.8 Secondary cable location bracket

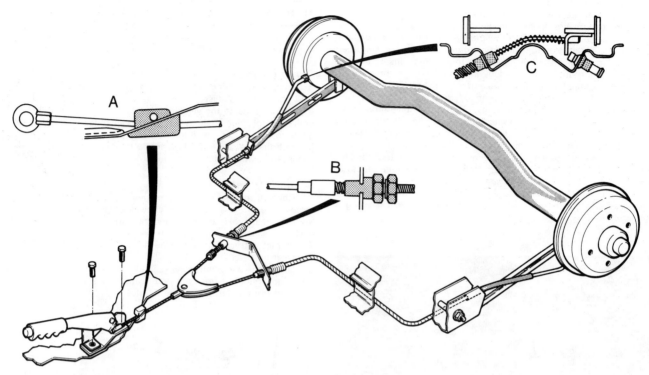

Fig. 8.20 Handbrake system layout (Sec 15)

A   Cable guide   B   Adjuster   C   Carrier (back) plate plunger

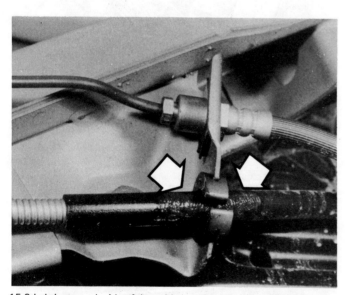

15.9 Lubricate each side of the cable location clip (arrowed)

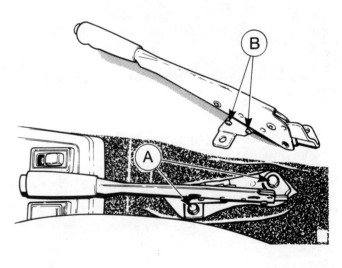

Fig. 8.21 Handbrake lever mounting bolts (A) and warning light switch screws (B) (Sec 16)

9   Refitting is a reversal of removal. Grease the cable groove in the equaliser and also each side of the outer cable location clip (photo). Adjust the handbrake on completion, as described in Section 14.

---

16 Handbrake lever – removal and refitting

1   Chock the front wheels, raise and support the vehicle at the rear using safety stands. Release the handbrake.
2   Working underneath the vehicle, extract the lever-to-equaliser

cable retaining clip, remove the pin and separate the cable from the equaliser.
3   Remove the front seats. It may also be necessary to remove the carpet.
4   Detach the handbrake warning switch.
5   Disconnect the cable from the handbrake lever by extracting the clip and pin.
6   Unscrew the lever securing bolts and remove the lever.
7   Refit in the reverse order of removal. On completion, check the handbrake adjustment, as given in Section 14.

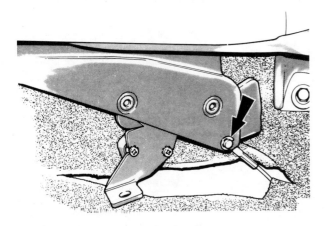

Fig. 8.22 Primary cable-to-handbrake lever clevis pin and clip (arrowed) (Sec 16)

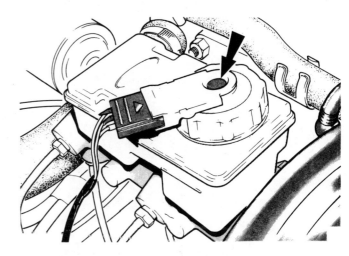

Fig. 8.23 Brake warning light check plunger (arrowed) (Sec 17)

17 Brake warning lamps – description and renewal

1   As already mentioned, all models are fitted with a low fluid level warning switch in the master cylinder reservoir cap and a brake pedal stop-lamp switch.

2   Also fitted is a handbrake ON warning lamp switch.

3   Warning indicator lamps are mounted on the instrument panel. Their renewal is covered in Chapter 11.

4   Access to the handbrake switch is obtained after removal of the front seats and floor carpets. The switch is secured to the lever by means of two retaining screws.

5   Whenever the switch is fully removed and refitted, check the operation of the switch and warning lamp with the ignition on prior to refitting the floor carpet and seats.

6   The low fluid level warning lamp switch operation can be checked by depressing the plunger in the top of the switch (Fig. 8.23).

7   The stop-lamp switch is activated by brake pedal movement. To remove the switch, unclip and remove the facia underpanel, disconnect the multi-plug connector to the switch then turn the switch anti-clockwise to remove it.

8   To refit the switch, fit it into its lockring aperture, pressing inwards so that the switch barrel touches the pedal which must be against its stop. Twist the switch clockwise to lock it in this position then reattach the wiring connector.

9   On completion check the switch for satisfactory operation.

Fig. 8.24 Brake stop-light switch removal (Sec 17)

18 Fault diagnosis – braking system

Symptom	Reason(s)
Pedal travels to floorboards before brakes operate	Brake fluid too low Caliper leaking Master cylinder leaking (bubbles in master cylinder fluid) Brake flexible hose leaking Brake line fractured Brake system unions loose Rear automatic adjusters seized
Brake pedal feels springy	New linings not yet bedded in Brake discs or drums badly worn or cracked Master cylinder securing nuts loose
Brake pedal feels spongy and soggy	Caliper or wheel cylinder leaking Master cylinder leaking (bubbles in master cylinder reservoir) Brake pipeline or flexible hose leaking Unions in brake system loose Air in hydraulic system
Excessive effort required to brake car	Pad or shoe linings badly worn New pads or shoes recently fitted – not yet bedded in Vacuum servo unit defective

Chapter 9 Steering

Contents

Fault diagnosis – steering 10	Steering gear – overhaul 8
General description 1	Steering gear – removal and refitting 7
Maintenance and precautions – steering 2	Steering gear bellows – renewal 3
Steering angles and wheel alignment 9	Steering wheel – removal and refitting 5
Steering column – removal, overhaul and refitting 6	Tie-rod end balljoint – renewal 4

Specifications

General
Type .... Rack and pinion with universally-jointed shaft and deformable column
Lubricant type .... To Ford specification SAM-1C-9106-A

Steering angles
See Specifications, Chapter 10

Torque wrench settings

	Nm	lbf ft
Steering gear unit to bulkhead	40 to 50	30 to 37
Steering shaft to pinion coupling	45 to 56	33 to 41
Steering wheel to steering shaft nut	27 to 34	20 to 25
Steering column tube mounting nuts	20 to 25	15 to 18
Tie-rod end locknut	57 to 68	42 to 50
Tie-rod inner balljoint	68 to 90	50 to 66
Pinion cover nut	60 to 70	44 to 52
Slipper plug	4 to 5	3 to 4

1 General description

The steering is of rack and pinion type, with a safety steering column which incorporates a jointed lower shaft and a convoluted column tube.

The pinion of the steering gear is supported in a needle roller bearing at its lower end and in a ball-bearing at its upper end. Pinion bearing preload adjustment has been eliminated.

The steering tie-rods are attached to the steering rack by means of balljoints working in nylon seats. The balljoints are precisely preloaded, set and locked in position during production.

The tie-rod outer balljoints are of screw-on type with a locking nut.

Rack-to-pinion contact is maintained by a spring-loaded slipper working against a cover plate which is located on the housing using selective shims.

The tie-rods are adjustable for lengths in order to vary the front wheel alignment. Other steering angles are set in production and cannot be adjusted.

Integral lock stops are built into the steering gear and these are also non-adjustable.

The steering gear is lubricated with a semi-fluid grease but in case of difficulty in supply, use Hypoy 90 oil.

The steering column lock unit is integral with the column and cannot be replaced separately, but the ignition switch unit can.

2 Maintenance and precautions – steering

1 Regularly check the condition of the steering gear bellows and the tie-rod balljoint dust excluders (photo). If split, they must be renewed immediately and in the case of the steering gear, the lubricant cleared out and fresh injected (see Section 3).

2 With an assistant turning the steering wheel from side-to-side,

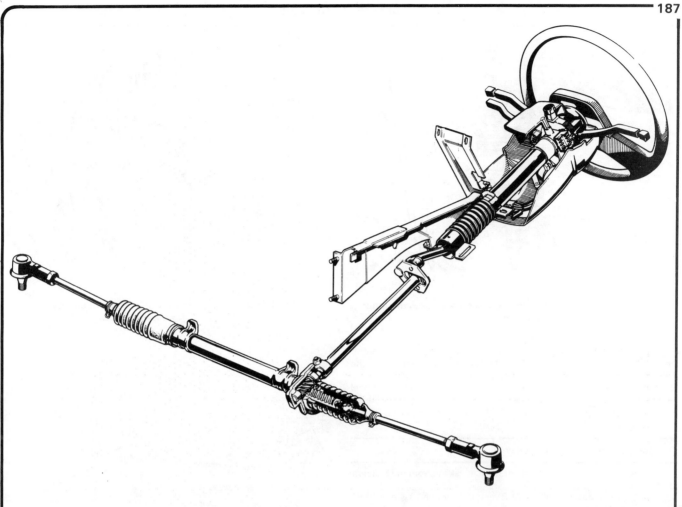

Fig. 9.1 Steering wheel, column and rack assembly (Sec 1)

2.1 Check steering rack bellows

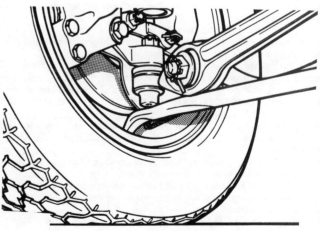

Fig. 9.2 Apply leverage to check for excessive balljoint wear (Sec 2)

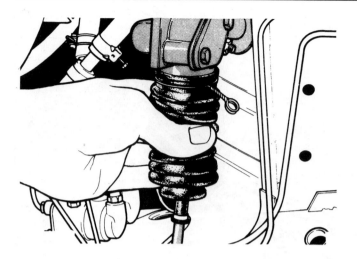

Fig. 9.3 Feel through the gaiter for excessive wear in the inner
tie-rod joints (Sec 2)

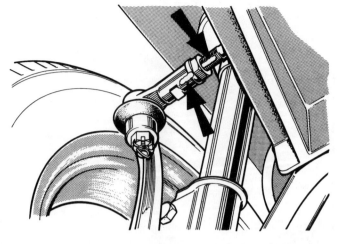

Fig. 9.4 Mark relative positions of balljoint and tie rod
(arrowed) (Sec 3)

check for lost motion at the tie-rod end balljoints. If evident, renew the
balljoints (see Section 4) as no repair or lubrication is possible.
3   When the front wheels are raised, avoid turning the steering wheel
rapidly from lock-to-lock. This could cause hydraulic pressure build-up,
with consequent damage to the bellows.

3   Steering gear bellows – renewal

1   At the first indication of a split or grease leakage from the bellows,
renew them.
2   The tie-rod diameter will be 11.8 mm (0.46 in) or 13.3 mm (0.52
in). It is important to identify which type is fitted in order that the
correct bellows replacement kit is obtained.
3   Raise the front of the vehicle and support it securely; remove the
front roadwheels. Turn the wheels slowly to full lock to gain access to
the tie-rod balljoint.
4   Prior to undoing the tie-rod end locknut, make a relative alignment
mark across the faces of the tie-rod and balljoint to ensure correct
alignment on refitting. Release the tie-rod end locknut, but only
unscrew it one quarter of a turn.
5   Extract the split pin and remove the nut from the balljoint taper
pin.
6   Using a suitable balljoint extractor, separate the balljoint taper pin
from the eye of the steering arm.
7   Unscrew the balljoint from the end of the tie-rod.
8   Release the clips from both ends of the damaged bellows and slide
them from the rack and the tie-rod.
9   Turn the steering wheel gently to expel as much lubricant as
possible from the rack housing. It is recommended that the bellows on
the opposite side be released by detaching their inboard clip, turning
the bellows back and clearing the lubricant as it is also ejected at this
end of the rack housing.
10   Smear the narrow neck of the new bellows with the specified
grease and slide them over the tie-rod into position on the rack
housing.
11   If new bellows are being fitted to the pinion end of the rack, leave
both ends of the bellows unclamped at this stage.
12   If the bellows are being fitted to the rack support bush end of the
rack housing, clamp only the inner end of the bellows and leave the
outer end unfastened.
13   Screw on the tie-rod end until the locknut requires only $\frac{1}{4}$ turn to
lock it.
14   Connect the tie-rod end balljoint to the steering arm, tighten the
nut to the specified torque and insert a new split pin.
15   Lubricate the support bush end of the rack by applying 50 cc (0.08
pint) of the specified lubricant into the bellows at that end. Check that
the bellows are correctly engaged in the groove at the tie-rod end, then
secure using a new clip.

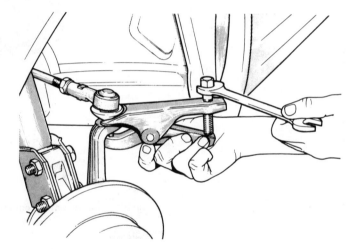

Fig. 9.5 Detaching the balljoint with a separator (Sec 3)

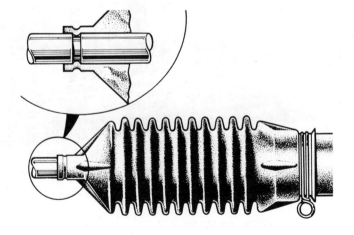

Fig. 9.6 Bellows must engage in rod groove (inset) (Sec 3)

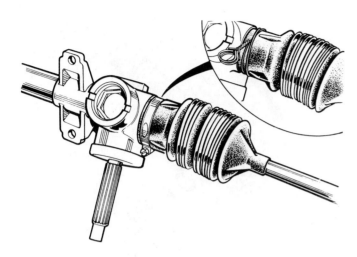

Fig. 9.7 Discard original wire type bellows retaining clip (inset) and use new worm drive type (Sec 3)

16 Repeat this procedure with the pinion end of the rack but apply 70 cc (0.12 pint) of lubricant.

17 Tighten the tie-rod end locknut against the tie-rod end and check that the alignment marks correspond. Refit the roadwheels and lower the vehicle.

18 If the position of the tie-rod locknut was not altered from its original setting, the front wheel alignment (toe) will not have altered, but it is recommended that the alignment be checked at the earliest opportunity, as described in Section 9.

4 Tie-rod end balljoint – renewal

1 If, as the result of inspection, the tie-rod end balljoints are found to be worn, remove them as described in the preceding Section.

2 When the balljoint nuts are unscrewed, it is sometimes found that the balljoint taper pin turns in the eye of the steering arm to prevent the nut from unscrewing. Should this happen, apply pressure to the top of the balljoint using a length of wood as a lever to seat the taper pin while the nut is unscrewed. When this condition is met, a balljoint extractor is unlikely to be required to free the taper pin from the steering arm.

3 With the tie-rod end removed, wire brush the threads of the tie-rod and apply grease to them.

4 Screw on the new tie-rod to take up a position similar to the original. Due to manufacturing differences, the fitting of a new component will almost certainly mean that the front wheel alignment will require some adjustment. Check this, as described in Section 9.

5 Connect the balljoint to the steering arm as described in Section 3.

5 Steering wheel – removal and refitting

1 According to model, either pull off the steering wheel trim or prise out the insert which carries the Ford motif at the centre of the steering wheel (photo). Insert the ignition key and turn it to position I.

2 Hold the steering wheel from turning and have the front road-wheels in the straight-ahead attitude, while the steering wheel retaining nut is unscrewed using a socket with extension (photo).

3 Scribe an alignment mark between the steering wheel and shaft end face to ensure correct realignment when refitting.

4 Remove the steering wheel from the shaft. No effort should be required to remove the steering wheel as it is located on a hexagonal section shaft which does not cause the binding associated with splined shafts.

5 Note the steering shaft direction indicator cam which has its peg uppermost.

6 Refitting is a reversal of removal. Check that the roadwheels are

5.1 Removing the steering wheel trim

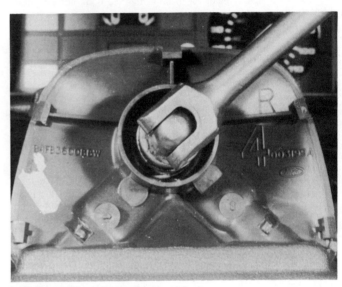

5.2 Undoing the steering wheel retaining nut

still in the straight-ahead position and locate the steering wheel so that the alignment index marks made on the steering wheel and shaft end face correspond. Refit and tighten the steering wheel retaining nut to the specified torque setting. Refit the steering wheel trim.

6 Steering column – removal, overhaul and refitting

1 Disconnect the battery earth lead then remove the steering wheel, as described in Section 5. Also remove the indicator cam from the steering shaft.

2 Unscrew and recover the steering column shroud retaining screws, then detach and remove the upper and lower column shrouds.

3 Extract the retaining clip from the bonnet release pivot pin, remove the lever and disconnect the cable.

4 Undo the four retaining screws and remove the column multi-function switches. Detach the ignition switch wiring connector.

5 Unclip and withdraw the facia lever insulating panel on the driver's side.

6 Unscrew and remove the upper and lower column mounting clamp retaining nuts and washers, then slide free and withdraw the column tube and tolerance ring.

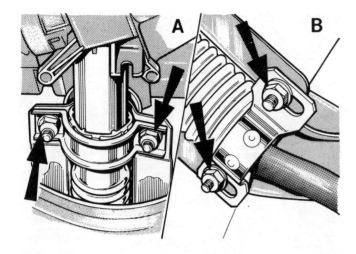

Fig. 9.8 Steering column upper (A) and lower (B) mountings (Sec 6)

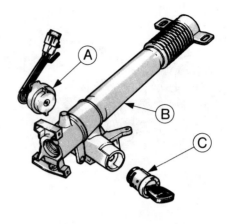

Fig. 9.9 Steering column tube (B), ignition switch (A) and ignition key barrel (C) (Sec 6)

7   Use a suitable screwdriver or implement to hook out the upper thrust bearing.

8   To remove the steering column shafts, unscrew and remove the lower shaft-to-pinion coupling clamp bolt (photo) then withdraw the upper and lower shafts as a unit. If any difficulty is experienced in separating the lower shaft from the pinion gear, prise the coupling open slightly with a screwdriver.

9   The upper and lower shafts can be separated and the bushes renewed if necessary.

10 Refit the shafts reversing the removal procedure and check that the bulkhead seal is not disturbed or distorted when the shaft is refitted.

11 Reconnect the lower shaft to the steering gear pinion shaft and loosely engage the clamp for the moment.

12 The steering column tube assembly can now be fitted.

13 With the upper thrust bearing located in the column, fit the column tube over the shaft, align the mounting clamp holes with the fixing studs then engage and fit the washers and retaining nuts, but do not fully tighten them yet. Semi-tighten the nuts so that the column tube is supported as far up as possible.

14 Locate the upper column shroud and then adjust the column so that the shroud and instrument panel (facia) are not in contact and tighten the column retaining nuts to the specified torque wrench

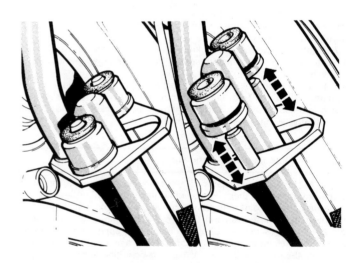

Fig. 9.10 Steering column upper-to-lower shaft coupling (Sec 6)

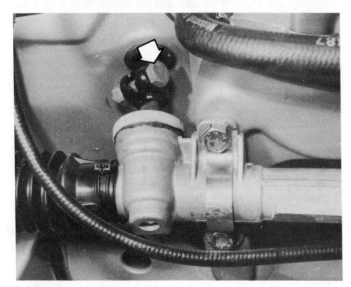

6.8 Pinion coupling clamp bolt (arrowed)

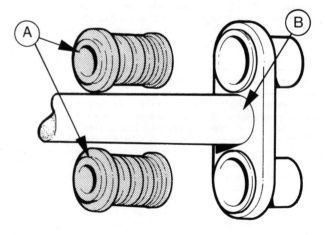

Fig. 9.11 Steering column lower shaft coupling (B) and bushes (A) (Sec 6)

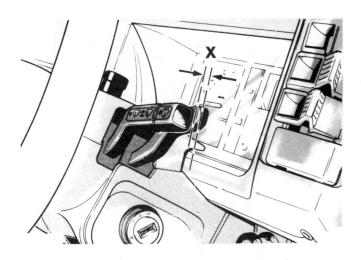

Fig. 9.12 Set column to give small clearance at (X) between the
shrouds and facia panel (Sec 6)

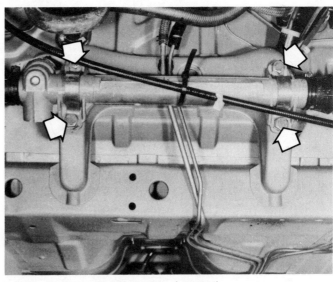

7.6 Steering gear unit securing bolts (arrowed)

setting. When tightened, check that the upper and lower steering shaft
coupling pins and bushes are still fully engaged.

15 The upper shroud is now removed again to allow the ignition
switch multi-plug to be reconnected and the steering column switches
to be relocated and secured with the four screws.

16 Secure the wiring looms of the switches to the column with a
plastic strap clip.

17 Locate and secure the bonnet release catch and cable.

18 Locate and secure the upper and lower column shrouds.

19 Relocate the bearing tolerance ring then refit the direction
indicator arm.

20 Refit the steering wheel, as described in Section 5.

21 Recheck that the upper and lower steering shaft coupling pegs
and bushes are still fully engaged, then tighten the lower shaft-to-
pinion clamp bolt to the specified torque wrench setting.

22 Refit the facia lower insulating panel.

23 To complete, check that the steering action is satisfactory,
reconnect the battery earth lead and check that the column multi-
function switches, ignition switch and steering lock are operational.

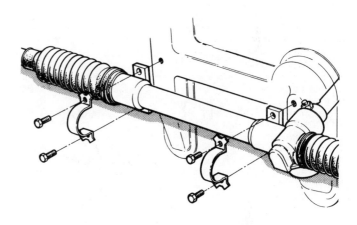

Fig. 9.13 Steering gear mounting components (Sec 7)

---

7 Steering gear – removal and refitting

1 Set the front roadwheels in the straight-ahead position.

2 Raise the front of the vehicle and fit safety stands.

3 Working under the bonnet, remove the pinch-bolt from the
coupling at the base of the steering column shaft.

4 Extract the split pins from the tie-rod balljoint taper pin nuts,
unscrew the nuts and remove them.

5 Separate the balljoints from the steering arms using a suitable
tool.

6 Flatten the locktabs on the steering gear securing bolts and
unscrew and remove the bolts (photo). Withdraw the steering gear
downwards to separate the coupling from the steering shaft and then
take it out from under the front wing.

7 Refitting is a reversal of removal. If a new rack and pinion
assembly is being installed, the tie-rod ends will have to be removed
from the original unit and screw onto the new tie-rods to
approximately the same setting. If a note was not made of the position
of the original tie-rod ends on their rods, inspection of the threads will
probably indicate their original location. In any event it is important
that the new tie-rod ends are screwed on an equal amount at this
stage.

8 Make sure that the steering gear is centred. Do this by turning the
pinion shaft to full lock in one direction and then count the number of
turns required to rotate it to the opposite lock. Now turn the splined
pinion shaft through half the number of turns just counted.

9 Check that the roadwheels and the steering wheel are in the

straight-ahead attitude, offer up the steering gear and connect the
shaft coupling without inserting the pinch-bolt.

10 Bolt up the gear housing and lock the bolts with their lockplate
tabs.

11 Reconnect the tie-rod ends to the steering arms. Use new split
pins.

12 Tighten the coupling pinch-bolt to the specified torque. Lower the
vehicle to the floor.

13 If the tie-rod ends were disturbed or if a new assembly was
installed, check and adjust the front wheel alignment, as described in
Section 9.

---

8 Steering gear – overhaul

1 Remove the steering gear unit, as described in the previous
Section, then clean it externally in paraffin and wipe dry. Before
dismantling it should be noted that when reassembling you will need
to use Ford special service tools 13-009-A (pinion nut and yoke
adjuster), 15-041 (torque gauge) or, in this instance, a suitable spring
balance will suffice, and some Loctite 542 or equivalent sealant.
Unless these items are available the steering gear overhaul should be
entrusted to your Ford dealer as it will not be possible to adjust the
rack and pinion engagement accurately.

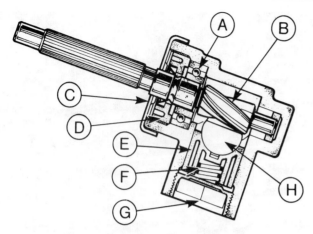

Fig. 9.14 Sectional view of the steering gear pinion and yoke assembly (Sec 8)

A	Bearing	E	Slipper
B	Pinion	F	Spring
C	Dust cover	G	Slipper plug
D	Pinion cover	H	Rack

2   Mount the steering gear in a vice then remove and discard the clips and slide the rubber bellows off the tie-rods.

3   Move the rack fully to the left and grip the tack in a soft-jawed vice.

4   If the original tie-rods are fitted use a pipe wrench to unscrew the balljoint from the rack and remove the tie-rod. If service replacement tie-rods are fitted use a spanner on the machined flats.

5   Remove the right-hand tie-rod in the same way. Each tie-rod must be refitted to the same end of the rack so keep them in order of fitting.

6   Unscrew and remove the slipper plug and remove the spring and slipper. Unscrew the slipper plug using the hexagonal end of service tool 13-009-A.

7   Now engage the segmented end of the service tool into the slots in the head of the pinion retaining nut and unscrew it. Remove the nut and the seal. Withdraw the pinion and bearing using a twisting action.

8   The rack can now be withdrawn from the steering gear housing.

9   Clean all the components in paraffin and wipe dry. Examine them for wear and damage and renew them as necessary. If necessary the rack support bush in the housing can be renewed.

10 Lightly coat the rack with the specified semi-fluid grease and insert it into the housing.

11 Centralise the steering rack within the tube then coat the pinion and bearing with grease and locate it in the housing, meshing it with the rack. When in position the pinion flat must be at 90° relative to the slipper plug on the pinion end side of the tube.

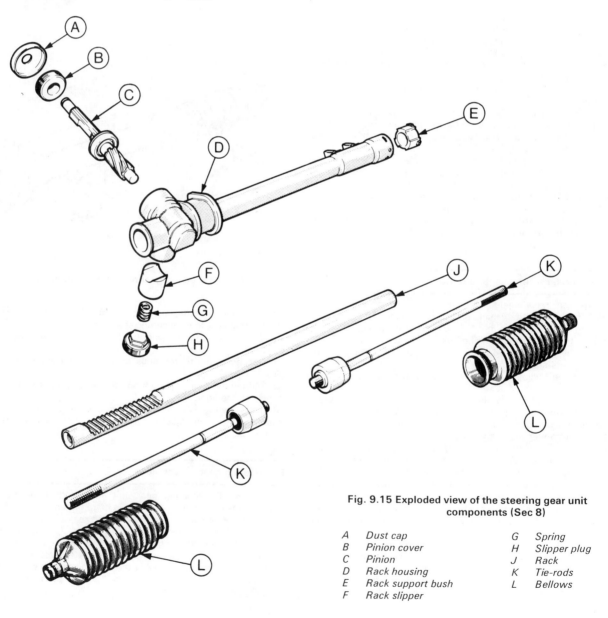

Fig. 9.15 Exploded view of the steering gear unit components (Sec 8)

A	Dust cap	G	Spring
B	Pinion cover	H	Slipper plug
C	Pinion	J	Rack
D	Rack housing	K	Tie-rods
E	Rack support bush	L	Bellows
F	Rack slipper		

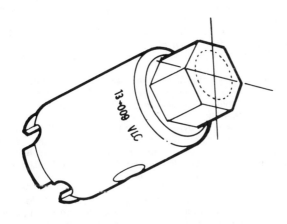

Fig. 9.16 Ford special steering gear service tool 13-009-A (Sec 8)

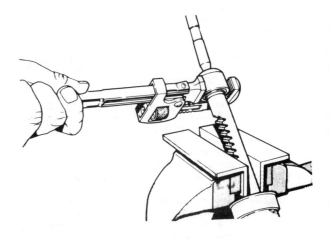

Fig. 9.17 Tie-rod removal/refitting method (Sec 8)

Failure to secure rack as shown can damage the pinion bearing

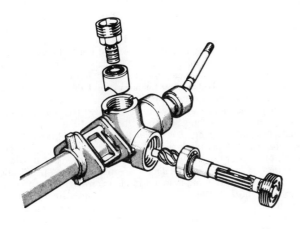

Fig. 9.18 The pinion, bearing and slipper assembly (Sec 8)

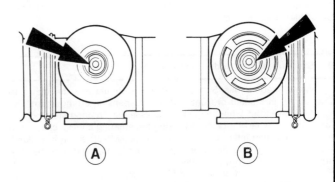

Fig. 9.19 Pinion alignment position (Sec 8)

A   *Left-hand-drive steering*   B   *Right-hand-drive steering*

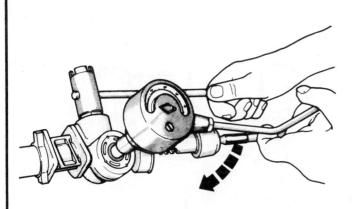

Fig. 9.20 Pinion turning torque check method using Ford special tools (Sec 8)

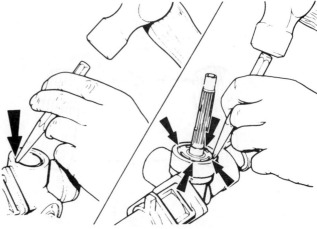

Fig. 9.21 Peen to lock set positions of the pinion cover and the slipper plug (Sec 8)

12 Before fitting the pinion nut, smear its threads with sealant and tighten it to the specified torque wrench setting using the special service tool (13-009-A). Lock the nut by peening the housing in four places.

13 With the rack still centralised, refit the slipper spring and plug. The plug threads should be smeared with a suitable sealant before fitting (Loctite 542 or similar). Tighten the plug using the special service tool to the specified torque wrench setting, then loosen it off 60° to 70°.

14 Using a piece of string and a spring balance check that the turning torque of the pinion is between 0.3 and 1.3 Nm (0.22 and 1.0 lbf ft). To do this accurately turn the pinion anti-clockwise half a turn from its central position and measure the torque while turning the pinion clockwise through one complete turn.

15 If necessary tighten or loosen the slipper plug until the torque is correct. Then lock by peening the housing in three positions around the periphery of the plug.

16 Refit the tie-rod inner balljoint units to the steering rack, reversing the method used for removal. If re-using the original tie-rod units they must be fitted to their original sides and tightened so that their original staking marks align with the steering rack grooves. When tightening ensure that the rack (not the tube) is secured in a soft-jawed vice. If new tie-rods are being fitted they must be tightened to the specified torque wrench setting using an open ended torque wrench adaptor then staked to the steering rack groove.

17 Refit the steering gear bellows, as described in Section 3. Lubricate at each end as described in that Section before fastening the bellows with screw-type clamps.

18 Refill the pinion dust cover with grease (to Ford specification SM1C-1021-A) and refit the cover.

9   Steering angles and wheel alignment

1   When reading this Section, reference should also be made to Chapter 10 in respect of front and rear suspension arrangement.

2   Accurate front wheel alignment is essential to good steering and for even tyre wear. Before considering the steering angles, check that the tyres are correctly inflated, that the roadwheels are not buckled, the hub bearings are not worn or incorrectly adjusted and that the steering linkage is in good order.

3   Wheel alignment consists of four factors:

Camber is the angle at which the roadwheels are set from the vertical when viewed from the front or rear of the vehicle. Positive camber is the angle (in degrees) that the wheels are tilted outwards at the top, from the vertical.

Castor is the angle between the steering axis and a vertical line when viewed from each side of the vehicle. Positive castor is indicated when the steering axis is inclined towards the rear of the vehicle at its upper end.

Steering axis inclination is the angle, when viewed from the front or rear of the vehicle, between the vertical and an imaginary line drawn between the upper and lower suspension swivel balljoints or upper and lower strut mountings.

Toe is the amount by which the distance between the front inside edges of the roadwheel differs from that between the rear inside edges. If the distance at the front is less than that at the rear, the wheels are said to toe-in. If the distance at the front inside edges is greater than that at the rear, the wheels toe-out.

4   Due to the need for precision gauges to measure the small angles of the steering and suspension settings, it is preferable to leave this work to your dealer. Camber and castor angles are set in production and are not adjustable. If these angles are ever checked and found to be outside specification then either the suspension components are damaged or distorted, or wear has occurred in the bushes at the attachment point.

5   If you wish to check front wheel alignment yourself, first make sure that the lengths of both tie-rods are equal when the steering is in the straight-ahead position. This can be measured reasonably accurately by counting the number of exposed threads on the tie-rod adjacent to the balljoint assembly.

6   Adjust if necessary by releasing the locknut from the balljoint assembly and the clamp at the small end of the bellows.

7   Obtain a tracking gauge. These are available in various forms from accessory stores, or one can be fabricated from a length of steel tubing, suitably cranked to clear the sump and bellhousing, and having a setscrew and locknut at one end.

8   With the gauge, measure the distance between the two inner rims of the roadwheels (at hub height) at the rear of the wheel. Push the vehicle forward to rotate the wheel through 180° (half a turn) and measure the distance between the wheel inner rims, again at hub height, at the front of the wheel. This last measurement should differ from the first one by the specified toe-in/toe-out (see Specifications).

9   Where the toe setting is found to be incorrect, release the tie-rod balljoint locknuts and turn the tie-rods by an equal amount. Only turn them through a quarter turn at a time before rechecking the alignment. Do not grip the threaded part of the tie-rod during adjustment and make sure that the bellows outboard clip is released, otherwise the

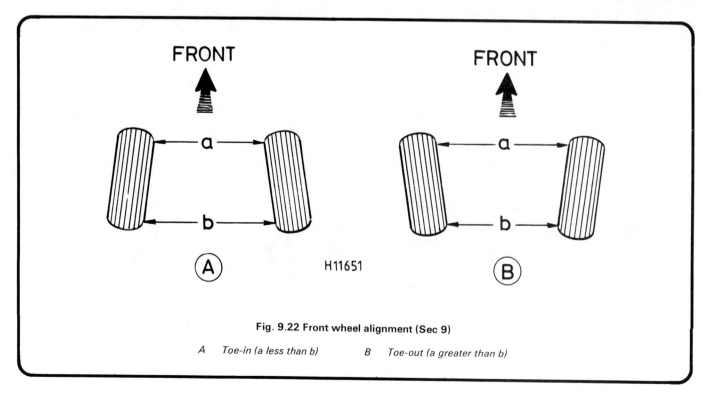

H11651

Fig. 9.22 Front wheel alignment (Sec 9)

A   Toe-in (a less than b)   B   Toe-out (a greater than b)

Fig. 9.23 Steering wheel position showing anti-clockwise (A) and clockwise (B) errors (Sec 9)

check that the steering wheel position is centralised, with the front roadwheels in the straight-ahead position.

11 If the steering wheel angular position is incorrect, but the tracking alignment of the front roadwheels is correct, proceed as follows:

12 Where the steering wheel misalignment is less than 30° then the wheel can be left in position.

13 Where the steering wheel is misaligned by more than 60°, turn the steering onto full lock then move it back to centralise it in the centre point of the lock-to-lock travel. You will now need to remove the steering wheel (Section 5) and refit it in the correct alignment position.

14 To correct further misalignment between the position of the steering wheel and the roadwheels when in the straight-ahead position, you will need to raise and support the front of the vehicle on safety stands.

15 Mark the relative positions of the tie-rods to joints, loosen the locknut and the outer steering bellows clip, then rotate each tie-rod an equivalent amount in the same direction to correct the steering wheel misalignment. Note that 30° of tie-rod rotation equals 1° of steering wheel angular correction. Rotate the rods clockwise (viewed from the left-hand side of the car) to correct a clockwise misalignment of the steering wheel. Rotate the tie-rods anti-clockwise to correct an anti-clockwise misalignment (also viewed from the left-hand side of the vehicle).

16 After the steering wheel and tie-rod adjustment is complete, recheck the wheel alignment (paragraphs 5 to 9 inclusive) and retighten the locknuts without altering the positional settings of the tie-rods. Hold the balljoint assembly at the mid-point of its arc of travel (flats are provided on it for a spanner) while the locknuts are tightened.

17 Finally, tighten the bellows clamps.

18 Rear wheel alignment is set in production and is not adjustable, but when dismantling any part, it is essential that all washers are refitted in their original positions as they control the wheel setting for the life of the vehicle (see Chapter 10).

bellows will twist as the tie-rod is rotated. When each tie-rod is viewed from the rack housing, turning the rods clockwise will increase the toe-out. Always turn the tie-rods in the same direction when viewed from the centre of the vehicle, otherwise they will become unequal in length. This would cause the steering wheel spoke alignment to alter and also cause problems on turning with tyre scrubbing.

10 After adjustment of the tie-rods check that the exposed thread portion of each is equal and does not exceed 28 mm (1.10 in). Also

10 Fault diagnosis – steering

Symptom	Reason(s)
Steering feels vague, vehicle wanders	Uneven tyre pressures Worn tie-rod balljoints Incorrect pinion adjustment
Stiff and heavy steering	Tyres under-inflated Dry suspension strut swivels Tie-rod end balljoints dry or corroded Incorrect toe setting Other steering angles incorrect Pinion adjusted too tightly Steering column misaligned

Chapter 10 Suspension

Contents

Fault diagnosis – suspension 16
Front hub bearings – checking, removal and renewal 3
Front suspension lower arm – removal, bush replacement and
refitting 4
Front suspension strut – removal, overhaul and refitting 6
Front tie-bar – removal and refitting 5
General description 1
Panhard rod – removal, bush renewal and refitting 10
Rear axle and suspension unit – removal and refitting 13

Rear axle unit – removal and refitting 14
Rear coil spring – removal and refitting 12
Rear hub bearings – adjustment 7
Rear hub bearings – removal and refitting 8
Rear shock absorber – removal, testing and refitting 9
Rear anti-roll bar – removal, bush renewal and refitting 11
Roadwheels and tyres – general 15
Routine maintenance – suspension 2

Specifications

General

Front suspension .... Independent, MacPherson strut. Double-acting shock absorbers incorporated in the struts

Rear suspension .... Independent with coil spring and double-acting shock absorbers. Anti-roll bar on certain models

	Standard models	XR2
Track:		
Front	1367 mm (53.9 in)	1385 mm (54.6 in)
Rear	1321 mm (52.0 in)	1339 mm (52.8 in)
Wheelbase	2288 mm (90.1 in)	2288 mm (90.1 in)
Wheel bearing grease	To Ford specification SAM 1C 9111A	
Tie-bar bracket grease	To Ford specification SLM 1C 9104A	

Suspension angles

	Nominal	Tolerance
Castor (non-adjustable)		
1.0, 1.1 and 1.3 litre (standard)	0° 30′	−0° 30′ to 1° 45′
1.0 and 1.1 litre (heavy duty)	0° 30′	−0° 30′ to 1° 45′
1.3 litre (heavy duty)	0° 15′	−0° 45′ to 1° 30′
1.1 and 1.3 litre (Sport)	0° 45′	−0° 15′ to 2° 0′
1.6 litre (XR2)	0° 40′	−0° 20′ to 1° 55′
Maximum allowable variation (side to side)	1° 0′	
Camber (non-adjustable):	**Nominal**	**Tolerance**
1.0 and 1.1 litre (standard)	2° 1′	1° 0′ to 3° 0′
1.3 litre (standard)	1° 45′	0° 45′ to 2° 45′
1.0 and 1.1 litre (heavy duty)	1° 45′	0° 45′ to 2° 45′
1.3 litre (heavy duty)	1° 30′	0° 30′ to 2° 30′
1.1 litre (Sport)	1° 45′	0° 45′ to 2° 45′
1.3 litre (Sport)	1° 30′	0° 30′ to 2° 30′
1.6 litre (XR2)	0° 36′	0° 24′ to 1° 36′
Maximum allowable variation (side to side)	1° 15′	

Toe-out (service tolerance):
    Standard models .... −3 mm toe-out ± 3 mm or −0° 30′ toe-out ± 0° 30′
    XR2 model .... 2 mm toe-out ± 3 mm or 0° 20′ toe-out ± 0° 30′
Toe-out setting (if outside tolerance):
    Standard models .... −3 mm toe-out ± 1 mm or −0° 30′ toe-out ± 0° 10′
    XR2 model .... 2 mm toe-out ± 1 mm or 0° 20′ toe-out ± 0° 10′

Roadwheels and tyres

Wheels:
    Type .... Pressed steel
    Size:
        Standard 13x4.50J
        Sport and Ghia 13x5J
        XR2 .... 13x6J
Tyres:
    Type .... Radial
    Sizes:
        XR2 .... 185/60 HR 13
        Other models .... 135 SR 13, 155/70 SR 13 or 165/65 SR 13

Tyre pressures (cold) bar (lbf/in²):	Front	Rear
135 SR 13:		
Normal loading/usage (up to three people)	1.8 (26)	1.8 (26)
Fully laden (normal usage)	2.7 (38)	2.9 (41)
155/70 SR 13:		
Normal loading/usage (up to three people)	1.6 (23)	1.8 (26)
Fully laden (normal usage)	2.1 (30)	2.3 (33)
165/65 SR 13:		
Normal loading/usage (up to three people)	1.6 (23)	1.8 (26)
Fully laden (normal usage)	2.1 (30)	2.3 (33)
185/60 HR 13:		
Normal loading/usage (up to three people)	1.8 (26)	1.8 (26)
Fully laden (normal usage)	2.0 (28)	2.0 (28)

Increase the above pressures by 0.1 bar (1.4 lbf/in²) for every 10 kph (6 mph) above 160 kph (100 mph) for sustained high speed use

Torque wrench settings

	Nm	lbf ft
Front suspension		
Hub retaining nut	230	170
Lower arm inboard pivot bolt	45	33
Lower arm balljoint pinch-bolt	30	22
Balljoint lower arm/tie-bar	85	63
Strut to spindle carrier	93	69
Tie-bar to mounting bracket	50	37
Tie-bar mounting bracket to body	50	37
Top mounting locknut	50	37
Top mounting thrust bearing nut (plain)	50	37
Rear suspension		
Lower arm-to-body bolts	50	37
Lower arm-to-axle bolts	50	37
Shock absorber bottom mounting bolts	50	37
Shock absorber top mounting nuts	30	22
Panhard rod-to-body bolts	50	37
Panhard rod-to-axle bolts	50	37
Brake backplate bolts	23	17
Anti-roll bar-to-body nuts	23	17
Anti-roll bar-to-body screws	23	17
Wheels		
Roadwheel bolts	100	74

1 General description

The front suspension is of independent type with MacPherson struts. The strut assembly on each side is controlled transversely by a fabricated lower (track control) arm whilst the fore and aft control is by means of a tie-bar connected between the lower arm and a mounting

bracket on the chassis. The right-hand tie-bar on the XR2 model differs from that fitted to other models in the range.

The rear suspension is of five-point link type, and consists of the axle beam, coil springs, double-acting telescopic shock absorbers, a Panhard rod and trailing arms. Certain models are also fitted with an anti-roll bar.

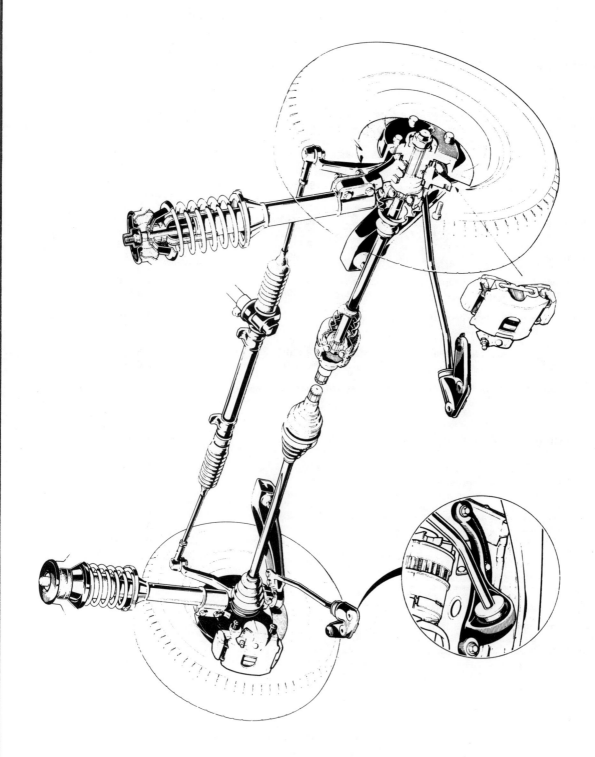

Fig. 10.1 The front suspension and driveshaft assembly (Sec 1)

Inset shows tie-bar bracket used on the XR2 model

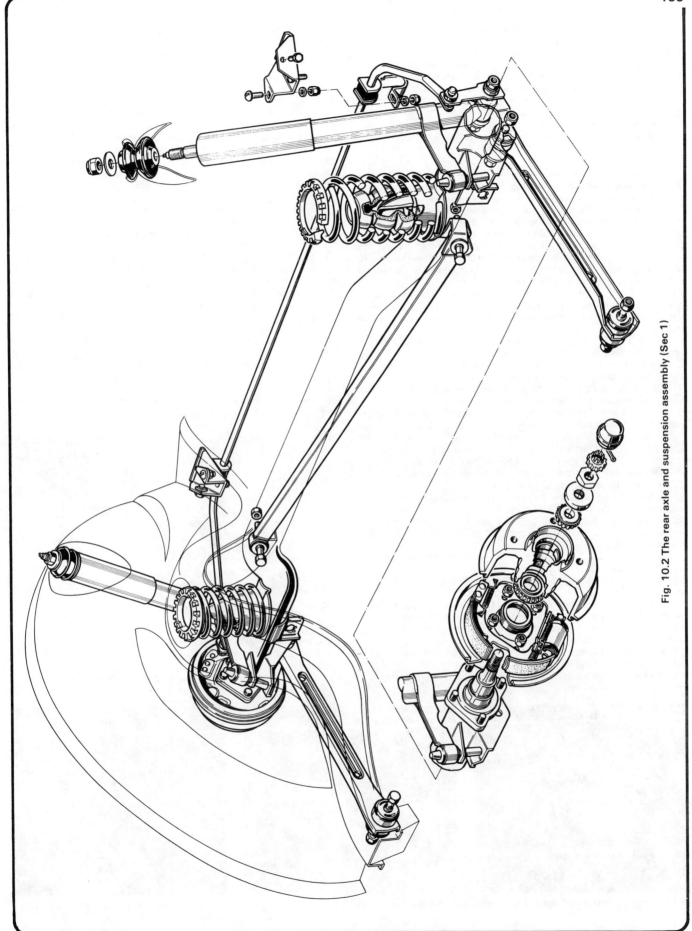

Fig. 10.2 The rear axle and suspension assembly (Sec 1)

2   Routine maintenance – suspension

This calls for a regular inspection of all suspension flexible bushes for wear, and periodically checking the torque wrench settings of all bolts and nuts with the weight of the vehicle on its roadwheels.

A periodic check should be made to ensure that the shock absorbers are securely located and show no signs of fluid leakage. If fluid leakage is evident the shock absorber must be renewed.

The roadwheels and tyres must be maintained as described in Section 15.

3   Front hub bearings – checking, removal and renewal

1   All models are fitted with non-adjustable front hub bearings, the bearing play being set when the hub nut is tightened to its specified setting during initial assembly or overhaul.
2   To check the bearings for excessive wear, raise and support the vehicle at the front end so that the roadwheels are clear of the ground.
3   Grip the roadwheel tyre at the top and bottom and use a rocking motion to check for play of the bearings.
4   A small amount of endfloat may be detected when checking for play (even after fitting new bearings) but when the wheel is spun there should be no sign of roughness, binding or vibration caused by the bearings.
5   If the hub bearings are suspect or obviously worn beyond an acceptable level they must be renewed.
6   Before removing the roadwheel(s) the vehicle must be suitably supported on safety stands at the front.
7   Get an assistant to apply the footbrake then undo the roadwheel bolts and remove the wheel.
8   Refit two of the roadwheel bolts as a means of anchorage for the disc when the hub nut is unscrewed.
9   Have an assistant apply the footbrake and then unscrew the staked hub nut and remove it, together with the plain washer. This nut is very tight so, if you are unsure of the raised car's stability, refit the roadwheel(s) and undo the hub nut with the car on the ground.
10   Remove the wheel and/or wheel bolts.
11   Unbolt the brake caliper and tie it up to the suspension strut to avoid strain on the flexible hose (photo).
12   Withdraw the hub/disc. If it is tight, use a two-legged puller.
13   Extract the split pin and unscrew the castellated nut from the tie-bar end balljoint.
14   Using a suitable balljoint splitter, separate the balljoint from the steering arm (photo).
15   Unscrew and remove the special Torx pinch-bolt which holds the lower arm balljoint to the stub axle carrier (photo).
16   Support the driveshaft on a block of wood and remove the bolt which holds the stub axle carrier to the base of the suspension strut.
17   Using a suitable lever, separate the carrier from the strut by prising open the clamp jaws.
18   Support the driveshaft at the outboard CV joint and pull the stub axle carrier clear of the driveshaft.
19   Remove the stub axle carrier and grip it in a vice fitted with jaw protectors.

20   Using pliers, pull out the dust shield from the groove in the stub axle carrier.
21   Prise out the inner and outer oil seals.
22   Lift out the bearings.
23   With a suitable drift, drive out the bearing tracks.
24   Clean away all the old grease from the stub axle carrier.
25   Drive the new bearing tracks squarely into their seats using a piece of suitable diameter tubing or press tool.
26   Liberally pack grease into the bearings, making sure to work plenty into the spaces between the rollers, using the specified grease.
27   Install the bearing to one side of the carrier, then fill the lips of the new oil seal with grease and tap it squarely into position.
28   Fit the bearing and its seal to the opposite side in a similar way.
29   Fit the dust shield by tapping it into position using a block of wood.
30   Smear the driveshaft splines with grease, then install the carrier over the end of the driveshaft.
31   Connect the carrier to the suspension strut and tighten the bolt to the specified torque.
32   Reconnect the suspension lower arm balljoint to the carrier and secure by passing the pinch-bolt through the groove in the balljoint stud.
33   Reconnect the tie-bar to the steering arm, tighten the castellated nut and secure with a new split pin.
34   Install the hub/disc and push it on to the driveshaft as far as it will go using hand pressure.
35   In the absence of the special hub installer tool (14-022), draw the hub/disc onto the driveshaft by using a two or three-legged puller with legs engaged behind the carrier. On no account try to knock the hub/disc into position using hammer blows or the CV joint will be damaged.
36   Grease the threads at the end of the driveshaft, fit the plain washer and screw on a new nut, finger tight.

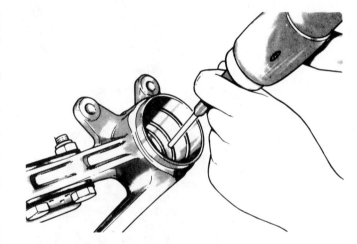

Fig. 10.3 Bearing track removal from stub axle carrier (Sec 3)

3.11 Brake caliper retaining bolts (arrowed)

3.14 Separate the balljoint

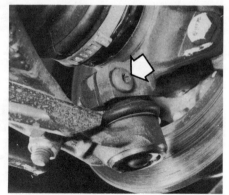

3.15 Lower arm balljoint and stub axle carrier Torx bolt (arrowed)

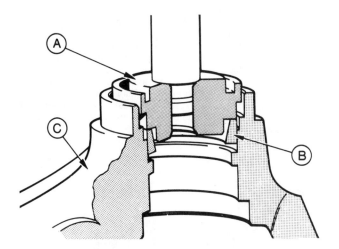

Fig. 10.4 Bearing track installation (Sec 3)

A   Press tool   C   Stub axle carrier
B   Bearing track

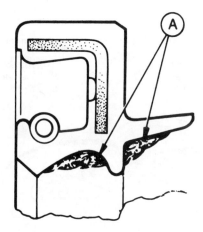

Fig. 10.5 Apply grease to the points indicated (A) (Sec 3)

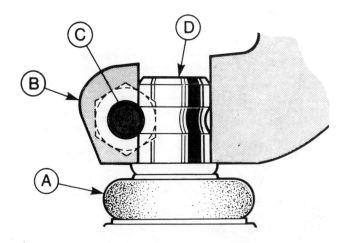

Fig. 10.6 Balljoint pinch-bolt location (Sec 3)

A   Balljoint   C   Pinch-bolt
B   Carrier   D   Balljoint stud

37 Fit the brake caliper, tightening the mounting bolts to the specified torque (Chapter 8).

38 Screw in two wheel bolts and have an assistant apply the footbrake.

39 Tighten the hub nut to the specified torque. This is a high torque and if a suitably calibrated torque wrench is not available, use a socket with a knuckle bar 18 in (457.2 mm) in length. Applying maximum leverage to the knuckle bar should tighten the nut to very close to its specified torque (photo). For safety it is probably better to leave the final tightening of the hub nut until the car is on its wheels.

40 Stake the nut into the driveshaft groove, if applicable (photo).

41 Remove the temporary roadwheel bolts.

42 Fit the roadwheel and lower the vehicle to the floor. Fully tighten the roadwheel bolts and hub nut (if applicable). If necessary stake the hub nut.

3.39 Tighten the front hub nut to the specified torque ...

3.40 ... and stake the nut to secure

4   Front suspension lower arm – removal, bush replacement and refitting

1   Raise the front of the vehicle and support it securely on safety stands.

2   Unbolt and remove the pivot bolt from the inboard end of the suspension arm.

4.4 Tie-bar-to-lower suspension arm retaining nuts (arrowed)

3   At the outboard end of the suspension arm, disengage the arm
from the hub carrier by unscrewing and removing the pinch-bolt.
4   Unscrew the tie-bar-to-lower arm attachment nuts and withdraw
the lower arm (photo).
5   Renewal of the pivot bush at the inboard end of the suspension
arm is possible using a nut and bolt, or a vice, and suitable distance
pieces. Apply some brake hydraulic fluid to facilitate installation of the
new bush. If the balljoint is worn or corroded, renew the suspension
arm complete.
6   Refitting the arm is a reversal of removal. Tighten all nuts and
bolts to the specified torque when the weight of the vehicle is again on
the roadwheels.

5   Front tie-bar – removal and refitting

1   Jack up the front of the vehicle and support securely on axle
stands.
2   Unscrew and remove the nut which holds the tie-bar to the large
pressed steel mounting bracket. Take off the dished washer and the
rubber insulator (photo).

5.2 Tie-bar and mounting bracket
Note that the XR2 differs slightly from that fitted to other models

3   Unscrew and remove the tie-bar-to-lower arm retaining nuts then
push the tie-bar upwards and clear of the arm.
4   Remove the tie-bar, together with the remaining bush and washer.
5   Where necessary, the bush in the pressed-steel mounting bracket
can be renewed if the old bush is drawn out using a bolt, nut and
suitable distance pieces.
6   Lubricate the bush-to-bracket contact faces before inserting the
replacements with the specified lubricant (see Specifications).
7   Refitting the tie-bar is a reversal of removal. Finally tighten all nuts
and bolts to the specified torque only when the weight of the vehicle
is again on its roadwheels.

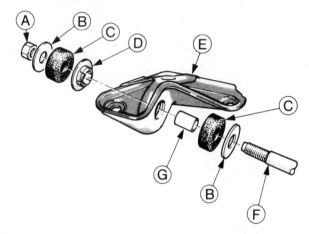

Fig. 10.7 Tie-bar mounting bracket and bush components (Sec 5)

A	Retaining nut	E	Bracket
B	Washer	F	Tie-bar
C	Bush	G	Bush sleeve
D	Bearing		

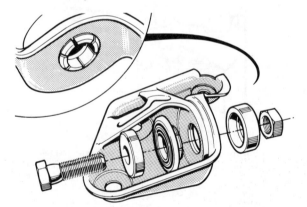

**Fig. 10.8 Tie-bar bush renewal, using draw bolt and cupped
washers (Sec 5)**

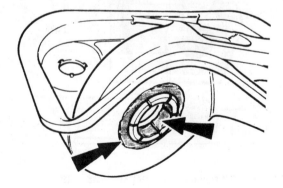

**Fig. 10.9 Lubricate tie-bar bush internally and externally when
fitting (Sec 5)**

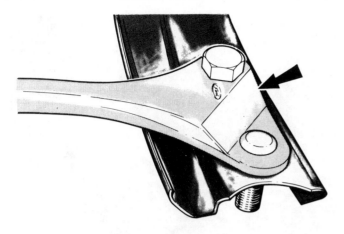

Fig. 10.10 Shouldered face of tie-bar must face top when fitted
(Sec 5)

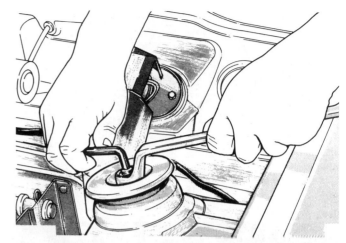

Fig. 10.11 Strut top mounting nut removal (Sec 6)

Note Allen key to prevent rod from turning

6 Front suspension strut – removal, overhaul and refitting

1   Slacken the roadwheel bolts, raise the front of the vehicle and support it securely on stands, then remove the roadwheel.
2   Position a jack beneath the stub axle carrier unit and raise it to support the stub axle carrier, driveshaft and CV joints in their normal positions to ensure that they are not damaged.
3   Undo the retaining nuts and withdraw the two bolts securing the suspension strut to the stub axle carrier (photo).
4   Detach the brake hose and location grommet from the strut bracket.
5   Working at the top end of the strut, detach the cover and then unscrew the strut retaining nut.
6   Withdraw the complete strut assembly from under the front wing.
7   Clean away external dirt and mud.
8   If the strut has been removed due to oil leakage or to lack of damping, then it should be renewed with a new or factory reconditioned unit. Dismantling of the original strut is not recommended and internal components are not generally available.
9   Before the strut is exchanged, the coil spring will have to be removed. To do this, a spring compressor or compressors will be needed. These are generally available from tool hire centres or they can be purchased at most motor accessory shops.

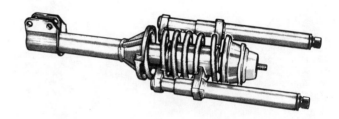

Fig. 10.12 Typical spring compressor in position (Sec 6)

10 Engage the compressors over at least three coils of the spring and compress the spring sufficiently to release spring tension from the top mounting.
11 Once the spring is compressed, unscrew and remove the nut from the end of the piston rod which retains the top mounting. As there will be a tendency for the piston rod to turn while the nut is unscrewed, provision is made at the end of the rod to insert a 6 mm Allen key to hold the rod still.
12 Remove the top mounting and lift off the spring and compressor.
13 The compressor need not be released if the spring is to be fitted immediately to a new strut. If the compressor is to be released from the spring, make sure that you do it slowly and progressively.
14 The top mounting can be dismantled by sliding off the thrust bearing and withdrawing the spring upper seat, gaiter spring and, where fitted, insulator. Also, if fitted, slide the bump stop from the piston rod.
15 Renew any worn or damaged components. If the front strut and/or coil spring is to be renewed then it is advisable also to renew the equivalent assembly on the other side.
16 Fit the spring to the strut, making sure that the ends of the coils locate correctly in the shaped parts of the spring seats.
17 Fit the top mounting components, being very careful to maintain the correct order of assembly of the individual components.
18 Gently release and remove the spring compressor.
19 With the spring compressor removed, check that the ends of the spring are fully located in the shaped sections of the spring seatings, then refit the strut unit reversing the removal procedure.
20 The suspension strut-to-stub axle carrier fitting position is critical and, during manufacture, this is set using a jig and normal production bolts fitted. When reassembling the stub axle carrier and strut two new

6.3 Suspension strut-to-stub axle carrier retaining bolts

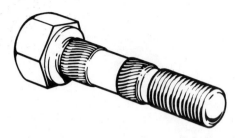

Fig. 10.13 Special service bolts for attaching strut to carrier (Sec 6)

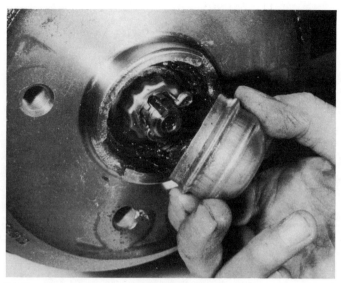

7.3 Rear hub dust cap removal

6.21 Suspension strut top mounting nut and plastic cover

Fig. 10.14 Rear wheel bearing adjustment (Sec 7)

Ford special service bolts must be used to ensure the correct carrier-to-strut fitting position is restored. These bolts can be identified by their knurled shank, see Fig. 10.13.

21 Lower the vehicle so that it is free-standing before tightening the top mounting nuts to its specified wrench setting, then refit the plastic cover (photo).

7 Rear hub bearings – adjustment

1   Raise and support the rear of the vehicle on safety stands. Release the handbrake.

2   This adjustment will normally only be required if, when the top and bottom of the roadwheel are gripped and 'rocked', excessive movement can be detected in the bearings. Slight movement is essential.

3   Remove the roadwheels. Using a hammer and cold chisel, tap off the dust cap from the end of the hub (photo).

4   Extract the split pin and take off the nut retainer.

5   Tighten the hub nut to a torque of between 20 and 25 Nm (15 and 18 lbf ft), at the same time rotating the roadwheel in an anti-clockwise direction.

6   Unscrew the nut one half a turn and then tighten it only finger tight.

7   Fit the nut retainer so that two of its slots line up with the split pin hole. Insert a new split pin, bending the end **around** the nut, **not** over the end of the stub axle.

8   Tap the dust cap into position.

9   Recheck the play as described in paragraph 2. A fractional amount of wheel movement **must** be present.

10 Repeat the operations on the opposite hub, refit the roadwheels and lower the vehicle to the floor.

8 Rear hub bearings – removal and refitting

1   Remove the brake drum, as described in Chapter 8 (Section 6).

2   With the drum removed the bearings and inner hub can be cleaned and inspected, but avoid getting grease onto the braking surface of the drum.

3   Use a suitable tool and hook out the grease retainer from the inner hub.

4   Extract the inner bearing cone.

5   Using a suitable punch, drive out the bearing outer tracks, taking care not to burr the bearing seats.

6   If new bearings are being fitted to both hubs do not mix up the bearing components, but keep them in their individual packs until required.

7   Drive the new bearing tracks squarely into their hub recesses.

8   Pack both bearings with a lithium-based grease, working plenty into the rollers. Be generous, but there is no need to fill the cavity between the inner and outer bearings.

9   Locate the inboard bearing and then grease the lips of a new oil seal (grease retainer) and tap it into position.

10 Fit the brake drum/hub onto the stub axle, taking care not to catch the oil seal (grease retainer) lips.

11 Fit the outboard bearing and the thrust washer and screw the retaining nut into position. Adjust the bearing endfloat as described in the previous Section and lower the vehicle to complete.

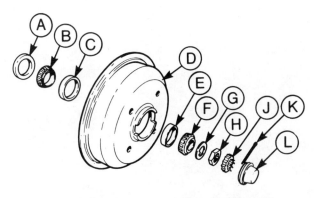

Fig. 10.15 Rear hub/drum components (Sec 8)

A	Grease retainer	F	Tapered roller bearing
B	Tapered roller bearing		(outer)
	(inner)	G	Thrust washer
C	Bearing track	H	Nut
D	Hub/drum	J	Nut lock
E	Bearing track	K	Split pin
		L	Grease cap

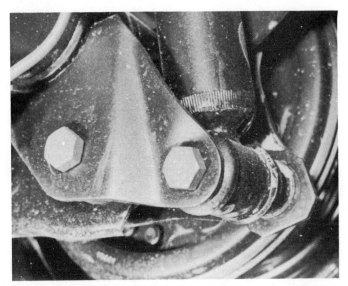

9.5 Rear suspension shock absorber lower mounting

9 Rear shock absorber – removal, testing and refitting

1   Slacken the rear roadwheel bolts, raise and support the rear of the vehicle using safety stands. Remove the roadwheel.

2   Position a jack beneath the rear axle for support.

3   Raise the tailgate and, from within the vehicle at the rear, prise free the plastic cap covering the top end of the rear shock absorber on the side concerned.

4   Unscrew and remove the shock absorber upper mounting locknut, washer and insulator (photo).

5   Unscrew and remove the shock absorber lower mounting locknut (photo). Withdraw the bolt then lever the shock absorber unit upwards to disengage it from its location peg and remove it.

6   To test the shock absorber, grip its lower mounting in a vice so that the unit is vertical.

7   Fully extend and extract the shock absorber ten or twelve times. Any lack of resistance in either direction will indicate the need for renewal, as will evidence of leakage of fluid.

8   Refitting is a reversal of removal, but if a new unit is being installed, prime it first in a similar way to that described for testing.

9   To ease the fitting of the shock absorber lower arm onto the location peg, lubricate the bush and peg with a solution of soapy water. Locate a suitable section of tubing or a socket on the top face

9.9 Rear suspension shock absorber lower arm location over peg

9.4 Rear suspension shock absorber top mounting

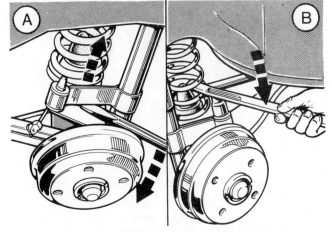

Fig. 10.16 Lever rear shock absorber clear of locating peg to remove it from the peg (A) or position on the peg (B) when refitting (Sec 9)

of the shock absorber location arm bushing and lever it down into position on the peg, as shown in Fig. 10.16 (photo).

10 Locate the lower mounting bolt and loosely fit the locknut.

11 Extend the shock absorber and locate it at the top end fitting the insulator, washer and nut.

12 Lower the vehicle and when free-standing tighten the upper and lower mounting nuts to the specified torque wrench settings.

10 Panhard rod – removal, bush renewal and refitting

1   Raise the vehicle at the rear and support on safety stands.

2   Undo and remove the Panhard rod-to-body retaining bolt.

3   Unscrew and remove the locknut and bolt retaining the Panhard rod to the axle and remove the rod.

4   Renewal of the Panhard rod bushes can be accomplished by using sockets or distance pieces and applying pressure in the jaws of a vice. Lubricate the new bushes with paraffin to ease fitting.

5   Refit the Panhard rod by reversing the removal procedure. Tighten the retaining nuts to their specified torque wrench settings when the vehicle is lowered and free-standing.

11.3 Rear anti-roll bar to body mounting

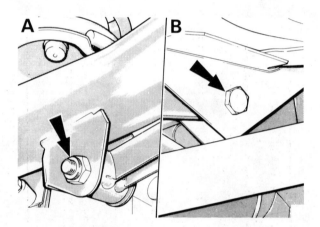

Fig. 10.17 Panhard rod mounting to axle (A) and body (B) (Sec 10)

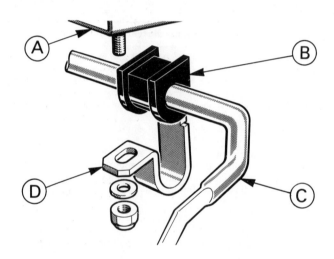

Fig. 10.19 Rear anti-roll bar (C), body mounting (A), bush (B), retaining clamp with nut and washer (D) (Sec 11)

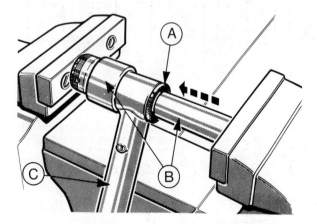

Fig. 10.18 Panhard rod bush removal method (Sec 10)

A   Bush   C   Panhard rod
B   Sockets

11 Rear anti-roll bar – removal, bush renewal and refitting

1   Loosen the roadwheel bolts on each side at the rear, raise the rear of the vehicle, support on safety stands and remove the rear wheels.

2   Unscrew and remove the shock absorber lower mounting bolt nuts, but do not withdraw the bolt.

3   Unscrew and remove the anti-roll bar-to-body mounting bracket nuts. Withdraw the mounting bush clamps (photo).

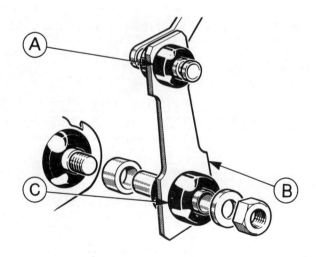

Fig. 10.20 Rear anti-roll bar connecting link (B) with upper (A) and lower (C) bush assemblies (Sec 11)

4 The anti-roll bar and connecting link assembly can now be disengaged from the lower shock absorber mounting and the bar removed.

5 To remove the body mounting bushes prise them open by levering within the split on their rear face.

6 To detach the connecting links from the anti-roll bar press free the upper bush. This bush can be renewed if worn or defective, but the lower bush cannot and it will therefore be necessary to renew the complete link if this is defective.

7 If the anti-roll bar is damaged or distorted it must be renewed.

8 Refitting is a reversal of the removal procedure. When refitting the connecting link to the anti-roll bar ensure that the longer tube end faces towards the centre of the vehicle.

9 Do not fully tighten the anti-roll bar location and mounting nuts until the vehicle is lowered and free-standing.

Fig. 10.21 Rear coil spring and insulator ring (arrowed) (Sec 12)

12 Rear coil spring — removal and refitting

1 Slacken the roadwheel bolts, raise the rear of the vehicle and support it securely with safety stands.

2 Locate a jack under the rear axle and raise it to support (not lift) the axle.

3 Remove the retaining nut and disconnect the shock absorber at its upper mounting, as described in Section 9.

4 Unscrew and remove the lower arm through-bolt from the axle.

5 Slowly lower the jack under the axle to release the spring tension and allow its removal. Remove the insulator ring.

6 If required, the bump stop rubber can be prised free from its location hole in the axle. When refitting the bump stop, press it down firmly into its location hole and turn it so that its lower section is felt to snap into position (photo).

7 Refitting is a reversal of the removal procedure. Do not tighten the lower arm and shock absorber retaining nuts until after the vehicle is lowered and is free-standing.

12.6 Rear suspension coil spring and bump stop rubber

13 Rear axle and suspension unit — removal and refitting

1 Raise the rear of the vehicle and support on safety stands.

2 Release the handbrake then disconnect the handbrake cable from the equalizer and the outer cable from the body location clips. Refer to Chapter 8 for further details.

3 Detach the flexible brake liner from the lower arm connections on each side. Clean the hydraulic line connections before disconnecting and, to prevent excessive fluid loss, plug the pipe ends once they are detached.

4 Undo the Panhard rod-to-axle pivot bolt and retaining nut and withdraw the bolt.

5 Unbolt and detach the exhaust downpipe at the flange connection.

6 Unbolt and remove the Panhard rod from the body.

7 Remove the rear anti-roll bar, as described in Section 11 (where fitted).

8 Locate a jack beneath the rear axle and raise it to support the axle (trolley type, if possible).

9 Disconnect the shock absorber at its top body mounting (Section 9).

10 Undo and remove the lower arm-to-body through-bolts (photo).

11 The axle and suspension unit can now be lowered and withdrawn from the underside of the vehicle, but take care not to snag the brake hydraulic pipes.

12 Refitting is a reversal of the removal procedure, but note the following:

    (a) Do not fully tighten the chassis and suspension fastening until after the vehicle is lowered and is free-standing. The respective torque wrench settings are given in the Specifications at the start of this Chapter

    (b) Reconnect the handbrake cable and adjust it, as described in Chapter 8. When the brake lines are reconnected top up the hydraulic fluid level and bleed the hydraulic circuit, as given in that Chapter also

13.10 Rear suspension lower arm-to-body pivot bolt and nut

14 Rear axle unit – removal and refitting

1   Proceed as described in the previous Section, paragraphs 1 to 8 inclusive.
2   Referring to Section 9, disconnect the shock absorber on each side at its lower end.
3   The axle tube and coil spring assemblies can now be lowered and withdrawn from the underside of the vehicle. Take care not to snag the brake hydraulic lines when removing.
4   Refitting is a direct reversal of the removal procedure.
5   Reconnect the shock absorbers at their lower mountings, as described in Section 9.
6   Note that the special remarks made in paragraph 12 of the previous Section also apply when refitting the axle unit.

15 Roadwheels and tyres – general

1   All models are fitted with pressed-steel type wheels which are secured to the hubs by bolts.
2   The wheel trims differ according to model, but all trim types are of press-fit design and must be removed for access to the wheel bolts.

3   Periodically clean away the mud deposited on the inside rims of the roadwheels and touch up any rusty areas.
4   Avoid changing the wheel rims through careless kerbing.
5   Whenever changing a roadwheel, always locate the jack as recommended in the introductory Section of this manual.
6   The tyres fitted during manufacture are steel radial type and this type should be used when replacements become necessary.
7   The tyre pressures should be checked weekly and at the same time the tread wear examined. Remove any flints or stones which may have become embedded in the tyres and also examine the tyres for damage and splits. Renew the tyres if the tread depth is approaching the legal minimum. The wheels should be rebalanced halfway through the life of the tyres to compensate for loss of rubber and also whenever the roadwheels have been repositioned.
8   Wheel balancing must be entrusted to your Ford dealer or a competent tyre specialist. If they have to fit balance weights to the wheels ensure that they fit the correct Ford type.
9   If it is desired to move the position of the roadwheels to minimise tyre wear, only move them front to rear or rear to front of the same side of the vehicle – never from side to side with radial tyres.
10 If snow chains are to be fitted at any time it is likely that you will need to reduce the size of the tyres fitted to allow for the additional clearance requirements. Check this with your Ford dealer before fitting.

16 Fault diagnosis – suspension

Symptom	Reason(s)
Steering feels vague, car wanders and floats at speed	Tyre pressures uneven Shock absorbers worn Broken or weak coil springs Suspension geometry incorrect Suspension pick-up points out of alignment
Stiff and heavy steering	Suspension geometry incorrect Dry or corroded suspension balljoints Low tyre pressures
Wheel wobble and vibration	Roadwheel bolts loose Wheels/tyres out of balance Worn hub bearings Weak front coil spring Weak front struts

Chapter 11 Electrical system

Contents

Aerial – removal and refitting 52
Alternator – description, maintenance and precautions 7
Alternator – in-vehicle testing 8
Alternator – removal and refitting 9
Alternator (Bosch) – overhaul 11
Alternator brushes and regulator – renewal 10
Alternator (Lucas) – overhaul 12
Alternator (Motorola) – overhaul 13
Auxiliary driving lamps – bulb renewal 31
Auxiliary driving lamps – removal, refitting and adjustment 32
Battery – charging 5
Battery – electrolyte replenishment 4
Battery – maintenance 2
Battery – removal and refitting 3
Bulbs (exterior) – renewal 28
Bulbs (interior) – renewal 27
Cigar lighter – removal and refitting 25
Clock (facia-mounted) – removal and refitting 23
Clock (roof-mounted) – removal and refitting 24
Drivebelt – removal, refitting and tensioning 6
Exterior lamp units – removal and refitting 29
Fault diagnosis – electrical system 54
Fuses, relays and circuit breakers – general 21
General description 1
Headlamps – alignment 30
Heater blower motor – removal and refitting 46
Horn(s) – removal and refitting 36
In-car entertainment equipment 47

Instrument cluster – dismantling and assembly 34
Instrument cluster unit – removal and refitting 33
Loudspeaker – removal and refitting 50
Manual choke knob illuminating bulb – renewal 26
Radio – removal and refitting 48
Radio/cassette player – removal and refitting 49
Radio equipment (non-standard) – interference-free
installation 53
Rear window washer nozzle and pipe – removal and refitting 45
Rear window washer pump – removal and refitting 43
Rear window wiper motor – removal and refitting 41
Speaker fader joystick – removal and refitting 51
Speedometer cable – removal and refitting 35
Starter motor – description 14
Starter motor – in-vehicle testing 15
Starter motor – removal and refitting 16
Starter motor (Bosch long frame type and Cajavec) – overhaul ... 17
Starter motor (Bosch short frame type) – overhaul 18
Starter motor (Lucas) – overhaul 19
Starter motor (Nippondenso) – overhaul 20
Switches – removal and refitting 22
Windscreen washer nozzle and pipe – removal and refitting 44
Windscreen washer pump – removal and refitting 42
Windscreen wiper blades and arms – removal and refitting 37
Windscreen wiper linkage – removal and refitting 40
Windscreen wiper motor – removal and refitting 39
Wiper blade rubber – renewal 38
Wiring diagrams .... see end of manual

Specifications

System type .... 12V negative earth, belt-driven alternator, pre-engaged starter motor

Battery
Type .... 12V, lead-acid
Charge condition:
    12.5V or above .... Satisfactory
    Below 12.5V .... Recharge

Alternator

	Bosch	Lucas (type B)	Lucas (type D)	Motorola
Make				
Rated output (13.5V at 6000 rpm)	45A (K1-45A) or 55A (K1-55A)	45A (A133/45) or 55A (A133/55)	45A or 55A	45A (45A (SD-45)
Maximum continuous speed	15 000 rpm	15 000 rpm	15 000 rpm	15 000 rpm
Minimum brush length	5 mm (0.197 in)	5 mm (0.197 in)	5 mm (0.197 in)	4 mm (0.158 in)
Regulator voltage at 4000 rpm (3 to 7A load)	13.7 to 14.6 volts	13.7 to 14.6 volts	13.7 to 14.6 volts	13.7 to 14.6 volts
Stator winding resistance (ohms/phase)	0.09 to 0.099 (K1-45A) or 0.07 to 0.077 (K1-55A)	0.285 to 0.305* (A133/45) or 0.088 to 0.108† (A133/45) 0.203 (A133/55)	0.229 to 0.254	0.23 to 0.33 (SD-45)
Rotor winding resistance at 20°C (ohms)	3.40 to 3.74 (K1-45A and K1-55A)	3.04 to 3.36 (A133/45 and A133/55)	3.04 to 3.36 (A127/45 and A127/55)	3.8 to 4.2 (SD-45)

* Lucas Delta-type winding
† Lucas Star-type winding

Drivebelt tension:
    Using a belt tension gauge:
        Lucas type D .... New belt: 400 to 500N (90 to 113 lbf)
             Used belt: 300 to 400N (68 to 90 lbf)
        All other types .... New belt: 350 to 450N (79 to 101 lbf)
             Used belt: 250 to 350N (56 to 79 lbf)
    Using finger pressure:
        Lucas type D .... 4 mm (0.16 in) deflection on longest run
        All other types .... 10 mm (0.4 in) deflection on longest run
A used belt is one which has been in operation for at least 10 minutes

Starter motor

Type .... Pre-engaged

Make	Bosch*	Bosch†	Lucas	Femsa	Nippondenso	Cajavec
	1.7 kW or 0.8 kW	085 kW or 0.95 kW	8M90 or 9M90	MOK-12/1	0.6 kW or 0.9 kW	0.85 kW

* *Bosch short frame type*
† *Bosch long frame type*
Number of brushes .... 4, except Nippondenso 0.6 kW and Femsa MOK-12/1 which have 2
Minimum brush length:
    Bosch, Cajavec and Lucas .... 8.0 mm (0.32 in)
    Nippondenso .... 10.0 mm (0.39 in)
    Femsa .... 12.0 mm (0.47 in)
Minimum commutator diameter:
    Bosch and Cajavec .... 32.8 mm (1.29 in)
    Nippondenso .... 28.0 mm (1.10 in)
    Femsa .... 30.0 mm (1.18 in)
Armature endfloat:
    Bosch, Cajavec and Femsa .... 0.3 mm (0.01 in)
    Nippondenso .... 0.6 mm (0.02 in)
    Lucas .... 0.25 mm (0.01 in)

Bulbs

Headlamp:
    Halogen 55/60W
    Tungsten 40/45W
Parking lamp 5W
Stop/tail lamp 21/5W
Reversing lamp 21W
Rear number plate lamp 10W
Rear foglamp 21W
Direction indicator lamps (front and rear) 21W
Instrument warning lamps .... 1.3 or 2.6W
Panel illumination lamps .... 1.3 or 2.6W
Glovebox lamp 4W
Interior lamps 10W
Cigar lighter illumination lamp 1.4W

Fuses

Circuits	Fuse number	Fuse rating (amp)
Hazard flasher, horn, remote luggage compartment release	1	30
Interior light, clock, windscreen washer	2	15
Wiper motor (front/rear), rear window washer and reversing lamp	4	20
Heater blower motor	5	20
Cooling fan (engine)	6	20
Heated rear window	7	30
Direction indicators, brake lights, fuel gauge	8	10
Sidelamps (left), number plate lights, instrument panel lamps, cigar lighter, heater control switch, glovebox lamp	9	10
Sidelamps (right), illumination for switches	10	10
Dipped beam (left) and rear foglamp	11	10
Dipped beam (right)	12	10
Main beam (left)	13	10
Main beam (right)	14	10
Additional in-tune or relay fuse circuits	(a) Radio	
	(b) Remote tailgate release switch	
	(c) Auxiliary driving lights	

Relays (on fusebox)

I .... Ignition switch
II .... Heated rear window and heated door mirror (with automatic cut-out)
III .... Remote tailgate release
IV .... Intermittent wiper motor
V .... Headlamp washers (if fitted)
VI .... Direction indicators

1 General description

The electrical system is of 12V, negative earth type. The major components include an alternator, a pre-engaged starter and a lead-acid battery.

The electricity equipment varies according to the particular model. The system is fully fused, with circuit breakers and any necessary relays incorporated in the fusebox and under the facia panel.

2 Battery – maintenance

1 Every 12 000 miles (20 000 km) disconnect the leads from the battery and clean the terminals and lead ends. After refitting the leads smear the exposed metal with petroleum jelly (photo).

2 The battery fitted as standard equipment is probably of the low maintenance type and only requires checking at 4 year (or 60 000 mile/100 000 km) intervals. However if a non-standard battery is fitted the following checks should be made on a monthly basis.

3 Check that the plate separators inside the battery are covered with electrolyte. To do this remove the battery covers and inspect through the top of the battery. On batteries with a translucent case it may be possible to carry out the check without removing the covers. If necessary top up the cells with distilled or de-ionized water as described in Section 4.

4 At the same time wipe clean the top of the battery with a dry cloth to prevent the accumulation of dust and dampness which may cause the battery to become partially discharged over a period.

5 Also check the battery clamp and platform for corrosion. If evident remove the battery and clean the deposits away. Then treat the affected metal with a proprietary anti-rust liquid and paint with the original colour.

6 Whenever the battery is removed it is worthwhile checking it for cracks and leakage. Cracks can be caused by topping-up the cells with distilled water in winter *after* instead of *before* a run. This gives the water no chance to mix with the electrolyte, so the former freezes and splits the battery case. If the case is fractured, it may be possible to repair it with a proprietary compound, but this depends on the material used for the case. If electrolyte has been lost from a cell refer to

Section 4 for details of adding a fresh solution.

7 If topping-up the battery becomes excessive and the case is not fractured, the battery is being over-charged and the voltage regulator may be faulty.

8 If the car covers a small annual mileage it is worthwhile checking the specific gravity of the electrolyte every three months to determine the state of charge of the battery. Use a hydrometer to make the check and compare the results with the following table:

	Ambient temperature above 25°C (77°F)	Ambient temperature below 25°C (77°F)
Fully charged	1.210 to 1.230	1.270 to 1.290
70% charged	1.170 to 1.190	1.230 to 1.250
Fully charged	1.050 to 1.070	1.110 to 1.130

Note that the specific gravity readings assume an electrolyte temperature of 15°C (60°F); for every 10°C (18°F) below 15°C (60°F) subtract 0.007. For every 10°C (18°F) above 15°C (60°F) add 0.007.

9 If the battery condition is suspect, first check the specific gravity of electrolyte in each cell. A variation of 0.040 or more between any cells indicates loss of electrolyte or deterioration of the internal plates.

10 In cases where a sealed-for-life maintenance-free battery is fitted, topping-up and testing of the electrolyte in each cell is not possible.. The condition of the battery type can therefore only be tested using a battery condition indicator or a voltmeter, as with a standard or low maintenance type battery.

11 If testing the battery using a voltmeter, connect it across the battery and compare the result with those given in the Specifications under 'charge condition'. The test is only accurate if the battery has not been subject to any kind of charge for the previous six hours. If this is not the case switch on the headlights for 30 seconds then wait four to five minutes before testing the battery after switching off the headlights. All other electrical components must be switched off, so check that the doors and boot lid are fully shut when making the test.

12 If the voltage reading is less than the 12.2 volts then the battery is discharged, whilst a reading of 12.2 to 12.5 volts indicates a partially discharged condition.

13 If the battery is to be charged, remove it from the vehicle and charge it as described in Section 5.

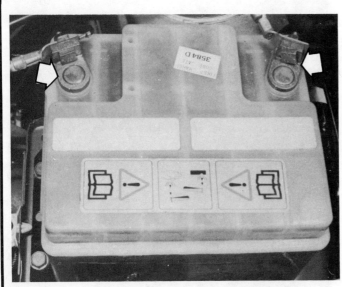

2.1 Battery lead terminals must be secure and clean (arrowed)

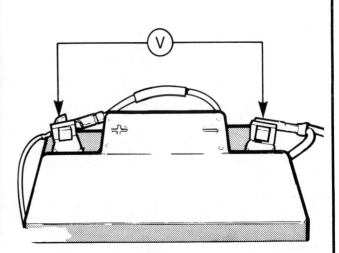

Fig. 11.1 Battery test method using voltmeter (Sec 2)

3 Battery – removal and refitting

1   Open the bonnet and support it on its stay.
2   The battery is mounted on the left-hand side in the engine compartment.
3   Disconnect the negative (earth) lead, followed by the positive lead.
4   Unbolt and remove the clamps from the nibs at the base of the battery casing (photo).
5   Lift the battery from its location, taking care not to spill electrolyte on the paintwork.
6   Refitting is a reversal of removal.

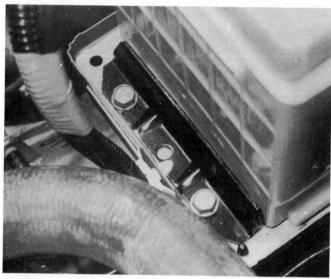

3.4 Battery retaining clamp

4 Battery – electrolyte replenishment

1   If the battery is in a fully charged state and one or more of the cells maintains a specific gravity reading which is 0.040 or more lower than the others, then it is likely that electrolyte has been lost from the cell at some time.
2   Top up the cell with a solution of 1 part sulphuric acid to 2.5 parts of distilled water. If the cell is already topped up draw some electrolyte out of it with a pipette.
3   It is preferable to obtain ready mixed electrolyte; however, if the solution is to be mixed note that **the water must never be added to the sulphuric acid otherwise it will explode.** Always pour the acid slowly onto the water in a glass or plastic container.

5 Battery – charging

1   In winter time when heavy demand is placed upon the battery, such as when starting from cold and much electrical equipment is continually in use, it is a good idea to have the battery occasionally fully charged from an external source.

Conventional and low maintenance batteries
2   Charge the battery at a rate of 3.5 to 4 amps and continue to charge the battery at this rate until no further rise in specific gravity is noted over a four hour period.
3   Alternatively, a trickle charger charging at a rate of 1.5 amps can be safely used overnight.
4   Specially rapid 'boost' charges which are claimed to restore the power of the battery in 1 to 2 hours are not recommended as they can cause serious damage to the battery plates through overheating.
5   While charging the battery note that the temperature of the electrolyte should never exceed 37.8°C (100°F).

Maintenance-free batteries
6   This battery type takes considerably longer to fully recharge than the conventional type, the time taken being dependent on the extent of discharge, but it can take anything up to three days.
7   A constant voltage type charger is required and this set, when connected, to 13.9 to 14.9 volts with a charger current below 25 amps. Using this method the battery should be useable within three hours, giving a voltage reading of 12.5 volts, but this is for a partially discharged battery and, as mentioned, full charging can take considerably longer.
8   If the battery is to be charged from a fully discharged state (condition reading less than 12.2 volts) have it recharged by your Ford dealer or local automotive electrician as the charge rate is higher and constant supervision during charging is necessary.

6 Drivebelt – removal, refitting and tensioning

1   A conventional vee drivebelt is used to drive the alternator, power being transmitted from a pulley on the front end of the crankshaft.
2   To remove a belt, slacken the alternator mounting bolts and the bolts on the adjuster link, push the alternator in towards the engine and slip the belt from the pulleys (photos).

6.2A Alternator mounting bolts

6.2B Alternator adjusting strap bolt (arrowed)

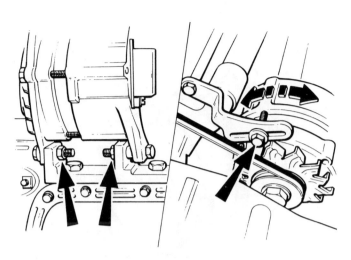

Fig. 11.2 Alternator securing bolts and adjustment strap bolt
(Sec 6)

6.4A Check drivebelt tension is correct ...

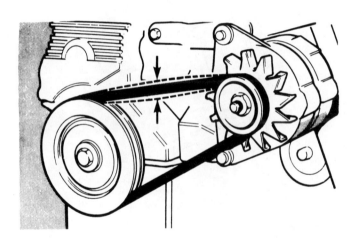

Fig. 11.3 Alternator drivebelt deflection (Sec 6)

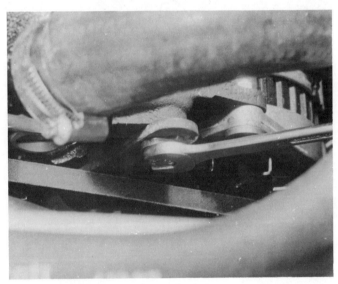

6.4B ... then tighten strap and mounting bolts

3   Fit the belt by slipping it over the pulley rims while the alternator is still loose on its mountings. Never be tempted to remove or fit a belt by prising it over a pulley without releasing the alternator. The pulley, and possibly the alternator, will be distorted or damaged.

4   To retension the belt, pull the alternator away from the engine until the belt is fairly taut and nip up the adjuster strap bolt. Check that the total deflection of the belt is as specified when tested on the longest belt run. A little trial and error may be required to obtain the correct tension. If the belt is too slack, it will slip and soon become glazed or burnt and the alternator will not perform correctly, with consequent low battery charge. If the belt is too tight, the bearings in the alternator will soon be damaged (photos).

5   Do not lever against the body of the alternator to tension the belt, or damage may occur.

7   Alternator – description, maintenance and precautions

1   One of three different makes of alternator may be fitted, dependent upon model and engine capacity. The maximum output of the alternator varies similarly.

2   The alternator is belt-driven from the crankshaft pulley, it is fan cooled and incorporates a voltage regulator.

3   The alternator provides a charge to the battery at very low engine revolutions and basically consists of a stator in which a rotor rotates. The rotor shaft is supported in ball-bearings, and slip rings are used to conduct current to and from the field coils through carbon brushes.

4   The alternator generates ac (alternating current) which is rectified by an internal diode system to dc (direct current) which is the type of current needed for battery storage.

5   Maintenance consists of occasionally checking the security of the electrical connections and wiping away external dirt.

6   At regular intervals check the tension of the drivebelt and also its condition. Renewal and tensioning of the drivebelt is described in the previous Section.

7   Never connect the battery leads to the wrong terminals, or disconnect a battery lead as a means of stopping the engine, as damage to the alternator may result.

8   If electric welding is being carried out on the vehicle, always disconnect the battery and alternator.

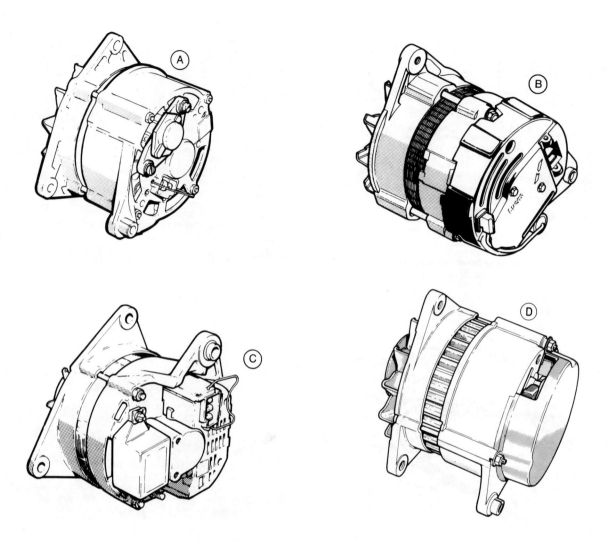

Fig. 11.4 Alternator types (Sec 7)

| A | Bosch | B | Lucas (type B) | C | Motorola | D | Lucas (type D) |

8   Alternator – in-vehicle testing

1   The following in-vehicle alternator tests can be made irrespective of which type of alternator is fitted provided a 10 to 20 volt voltmeter, an ammeter (70 amp +) and a load rheostat are available. Alternatively a proprietary multimeter can be used.
2   Prior to undertaking any of the following tests, first check that the drivebelt tension is correct and that the battery is well charged.

Wiring continuity check

3   Detach the battery earth lead, then disconnect the wiring multi-plug connector from the alternator.
4   Reconnect the earth lead, switch the ignition on and connect a voltmeter to a good earth point. Now check the voltage reading on each of the multi-plug terminals. A zero reading indicates an open circuit in the wiring whilst a battery voltage reading proves the wiring to be in good condition (Fig. 11.5).

Alternator output check

5   Connect up the voltmeter, ammeter and rheostat, as shown in Fig. 11.6.
6   Switch the headlights on, also the heater blower motor and heated rear window (where fitted). Start the engine and keep it running at

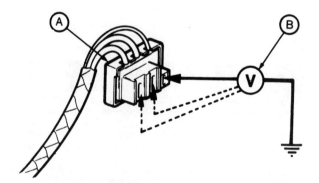

Fig. 11.5 Check charging circuit continuity (Sec 8)

3000 rpm whilst varying the resistance to increase the current loading. The rated output shouldd be achieved without the voltage dropping below 13 volts.
7   Complete the check by disconnecting the test instruments and switching off the ignition, headlights, blower motor and heated rear window.

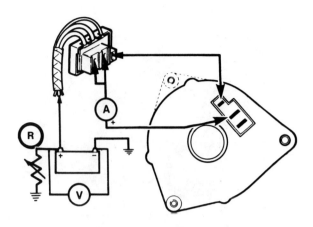

Fig. 11.6 Check alternator output (Sec 8)

A   Ammeter
V   Voltmeter

R   Rheostat (30 amps rating
     resistor)

Positive side voltage check

8   Connect up the voltmeter, as shown in Fig. 11.7, switch on the headlamps then start the engine and note the voltage drop. Now run the engine at 3000 rpm. If the voltage shown is above 0.5 volt it is indicative of a high resistance in the positive side of the charge circuit, and this will need to be located and rectified. Switch the ignition and headlights off to complete.

Negative side voltage check

9   Proceed as described in paragraph 8, but refer to Fig. 11.8 when connecting the voltmeter. A voltmeter reading in excess of 0.25 volts is indicative of a high resistance fault in the negative side wiring.

Regulator control voltage check

10   Referring to Fig. 11.9, connect up the voltmeter and ammeter as shown then start the engine and check the voltage reading.
11   Increase the engine speed to 3000 rpm and note the ammeter reading. This should fall to between 3 and 5 amps at which point check the voltmeter which should read between 13.7 and 14.5 volts. Any readings given which are not within these limits indicate a fault in the voltage control regulator and this must be renewed.
12   Switch the ignition off and detach the test equipment. Disconnect the battery earth lead and reconnect the alternator multi-plug. Reconnect the battery earth lead to complete.

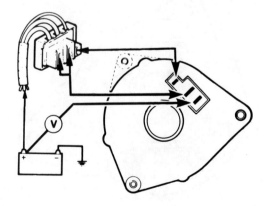

Fig. 11.7 Charge circuit voltage drop check – positive side (Sec 8)

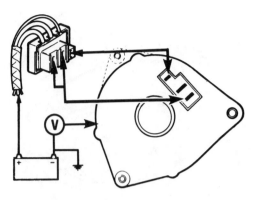

Fig. 11.8 Charge circuit voltage drop check – negative side (Sec 8)

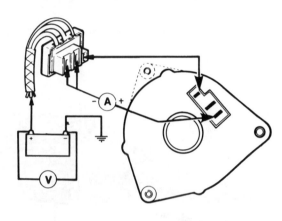

Fig. 11.9 Regulator control voltage check (Sec 8)

9   Alternator – removal and refitting

1   The operations are similar for all makes of alternator.
2   Disconnect the battery and disconnect the multi-plug or leads from the rear of the alternator. Remove the head shield (where fitted).
3   Release the mounting and adjuster link bolts, push the alternator in towards the engine and slip the drivebelt from the pulley.
4   Unscrew and remove the mounting bolts and adjuster link bolt and withdraw the alternator from the engine.
5   Refit by reversing the removal operations, and adjust the drivebelt tension, as described in Section 6.

10   Alternator brushes and regulator – renewal

1   With the alternator removed from the engine, clean the external surfaces free from dirt.

Bosch

2   Remove the regulator screws from the rear cover and withdraw the regulator. Check the brush length; if less than the specified minimum, renew them.
3   Unsolder the brush wiring connectors and remove the brushes and the springs.
4   Refit by reversing the removal operations.

Lucas type B

5   Remove the alternator rear cover.
6   Extract the brush box retaining screws and withdraw the brush assemblies from the brush box.

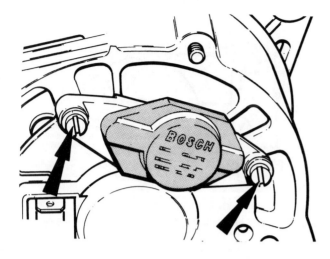

Fig. 11.10 Regulator unit securing screws (Bosch) (Sec 10)

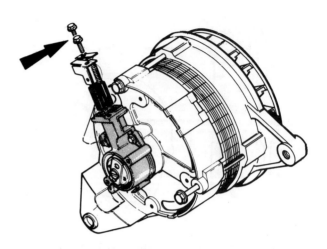

Fig. 11.12 Brush box retaining screws (Lucas type B) (Sec 10)

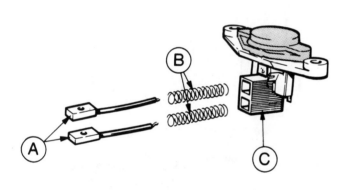

Fig. 11.11 Brush box components (Bosch) (Sec 10)

A   Brushes   C   Brush box
B   Springs

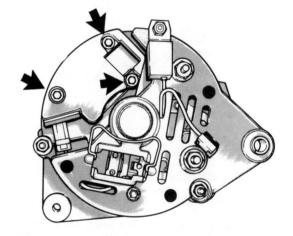

Fig. 11.13 Brush box retaining screws (Lucas type D) (Sec 10)

7   If the length of the brushes is less than the specified minimum, renew them. Refit by reversing the removal operations.
8   To remove the regulator, disconnect the wires from the unit and unscrew the retaining screw.
9   Refit by reversing the removal operations, but check that the small plastic spacer and the connecting link are correctly located.

Lucas type D
10   Proceed as described in paragraphs 5 and 6.
11   If the brushes are worn beyond the minimum length specified, disconnect the field connector and renew the brush box/regulator complete as the brushes are not individually replaceable.
12   Refit in the reverse order to removal.

Motorola
13   Extract the two regulator securing screws, disconnect the two regulator leads and withdraw the unit.
14   Extract the brush box retaining screws and pull and tilt the brush box from its location, taking care not to damage the brushes during the process.
15   If necessary, unsolder the brush connections.
16   Fit the new brushes by reversing the removal operations.

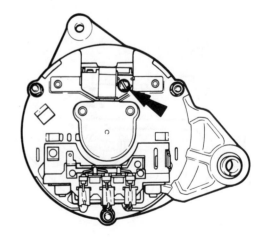

Fig. 11.14 Brush box retaining screw (Motorola) (Sec 10)

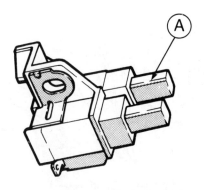

Fig. 11.15 Brush box and brushes (A) – Motorola (Sec 10)

11 Alternator (Bosch) – overhaul

1 With the alternator removed from the vehicle, unscrew the pulley retaining nut. To prevent the pulley rotating, place an old drivebelt in the pulley grooves and grip both runs of the belt in a vice as close to the pulley as possible.

2 Take off the washer, pulley, fan, spacer and the Woodruff key.

3 Remove the brush box.

4 Remove the tie-bolts and separate the drive end housing and rotor from the slip ring end housing.

5 Press out the rotor from the drive end housing.

6 Remove the drive end bearing and its retainer.

7 Remove the slip ring end bearing from the rotor shaft.

8 Extract the rectifier diode pack retaining screws and lift out the stator and the rectifier pack.

9 Unsolder the stator-to-diode pack connections, using a pair of pliers as a heat sink to prevent the heat spreading to the diodes.

10 With the alternator dismantled, check the positive diodes by connecting a 12V supply through a 5W test bulb wired to form a circuit through one of the diodes. Connect to the positive section of the diode pack with the negative terminal attached to the upper side of one of the diode. Connect the positive terminal to the lower surface of the diodes. The test lamp should illuminate if the diode is in good condition.

11 Repeat the operations on the remaining two positive diodes.

12 Reverse the test circuit terminals so that the positive one goes to the upper side of the diode and the negative one to the lower surface. If the test bulb lights up, the diode is defective.

13 To check the field diodes, connect the test lamp (as shown in Fig. 11.18) with the negative terminal coupled to the brush box terminal and the positive one to the diode. The bulb will light up if the diode is in good condition.

14 Repeat the test on the remaining two diodes.

15 Now reverse the terminals and repeat the test. If the bulb lights up then the diode is defective.

16 Now check the negative diodes by connecting the test lamp circuit to the negative section of the diode pack so that the positive terminal is attached to the top surface of one of the diodes and the negative terminal to the under surface. If the test lamp lights up then the diode is in good condition (Fig. 11.19).

17 Repeat the test operations of the remaining two diodes.

18 Reverse the test circuit terminals and repeat. If the bulb lights up then that particular diode is defective.

19 To check the rotor and stator insulation, a 110V ac power supply and test lamp will be required and as this is unlikely to be available, the testing of these items will probably have to be left to your dealer.

20 Where the suitable voltage supply is available, make the test circuit between one slip ring contact and one of the rotor poles. If the test lamp lights up then the insulation is defective.

21 Test the stator in a similar way by connecting between one stator cable and the lamination pack. If the bulb lights up, the insulation is defective.

22 An ohmmeter can be used to determine rotor and stator winding continuity. Connect as shown (Figs 11.20, 11.21 and 11.22) and refer to the Specifications for resistance values.

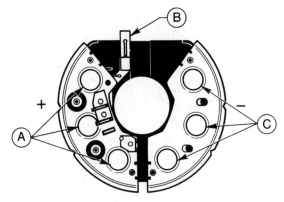

Fig. 11.16 Diode locations (Bosch) (Sec 11)

A Positive diodes C Negative diodes
B Brush box terminal

Fig. 11.17 Test circuit for positive diodes – A (Bosch) (Sec 11)

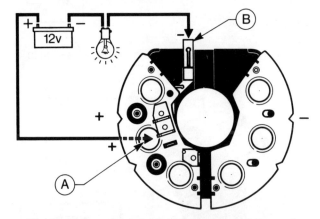

Fig. 11.18 Test circuit for field diodes (Bosch) (Sec 11)

A Positive diode B Brush box terminal

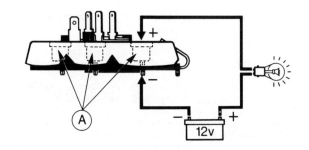

Fig. 11.19 Test circuit for negative diodes – A (Bosch) (Sec 11)

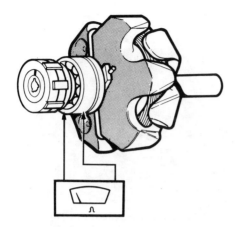

Fig. 11.20 Checking rotor winding for continuity (Bosch) (Sec 11)

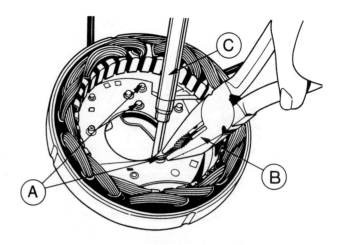

Fig. 11.23 Solder the stator-to-diode pack connections (Bosch)
(Sec 11)

A   Stator connections   C   Soldering iron
B   Pliers

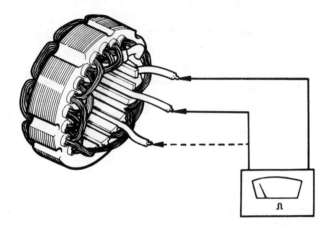

Fig. 11.21 Checking stator winding for continuity (Bosch) (Sec 11)

12 Alternator (Lucas) – overhaul

1   With the alternator removed from the vehicle and cleaned, remove the pulley and fan as described in the preceding Section, paragraph 1.
2   Remove the rear cover.
3   Remove the regulator.
4   Remove the brush box.
5   Unsolder the stator connections from the rectifier pack, using a pair of pliers as a heat sink as described in the preceding Section.
6   Extract the three bolts and remove the pack.
7   Checking the diodes should be carried out in a similar way to that described in the preceding Section, but note the different design of the diode pack.
8   Remove the through-bolts and separate the drive end bearing housing with rotor from the slip ring end housing and withdraw the stator.
9   Unsolder the leads from the slip rings and remove the slip rings from the shaft.
10   Press or drive out the rotor from the drive end housing.
11   To remove the drive end bearing from its housing, undo the screws securing the retaining plate, withdraw the plate then, supporting the bearing housing on a piece of wood for protection, drive or press out the bearing.
12   To remove the slip ring end bearing, cut a slot in a suitable size washer so that it can be inserted under the bearing as shown in Fig. 11.29. Press or drift the shaft down through the bearing.
13   Check the rotor and stator for winding continuity and insulation as described in the preceding Section, paragraphs 19 to 22.
14   Commence reassembly by fitting the drive end bearing shim pack, the bearing and the thrust washer. If the original bearing is being used again, work some high melting-point grease into it.
15   Relocate the retainer plate and refit the securing screws.
16   Make sure that the rotor wires are correctly located in their grooves in the rotor shaft and install the slip ring end bearing to the shaft. If the original bearing is being used, work some high melting-point grease into it. Refit the slip rings and resolder their leads.
17   Fit the rotor assembly to the slip ring end housing.
18   Locate the stator in the slip ring end housing and reconnect the slip ring and drive end housings. Pull the housings evenly together by tightening the through-bolts.
19   Fit the rectifier diode pack and resolder the stator-to-rectifier diode pack wiring. Use 60/40 electricians' solder if available.
20   Refit the brush box unit.
21   Refit the regulator, the rear cover and the pulley/fan assembly to complete.

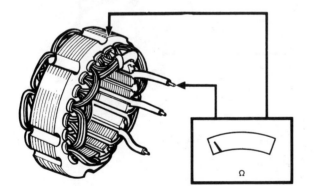

Fig. 11.22 Checking stator winding for good insulation (Bosch)
(Sec 11)

23   Commence reassembly by resoldering the stator-to-diode pack connections, again using a pair of pliers as a heat sink to reduce heat spread.
24   Install the stator and diode pack into the slip ring end housing.
25   Press the slip ring end housing onto the rotor shaft.
26   Refit the drive end bearing and secure with its retainer plate.
27   Fit the rotor into the drive end housing and assemble the rotor and drive end housing to the slip ring end housing.
28   Refit the brush box and the fan/pulley assembly. Make sure that the pulley spacer has its concave face against the fan as it acts as a vibration damper.

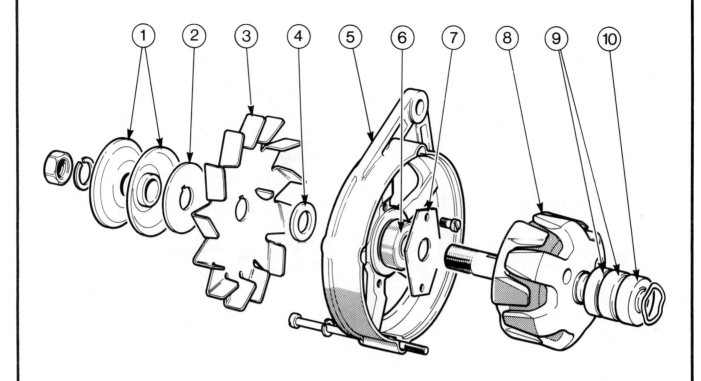

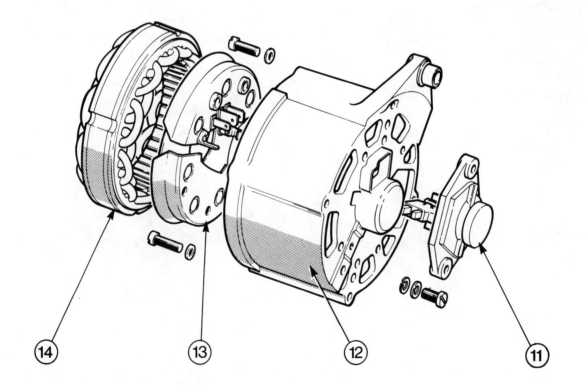

Fig. 11.24 Exploded view of the Bosch alternator (Sec 11)

1 Pulley	5 Drive end housing	8 Rotor	12 Slip ring end housing
2 Spacer	6 Drive end bearing	9 Slip rings	13 Rectifier (diode) pack
3 Fan	7 Drive end bearing retaining	10 Slip ring end bearing	14 Stator
4 Spacer	plate	11 Brush box and regulator	

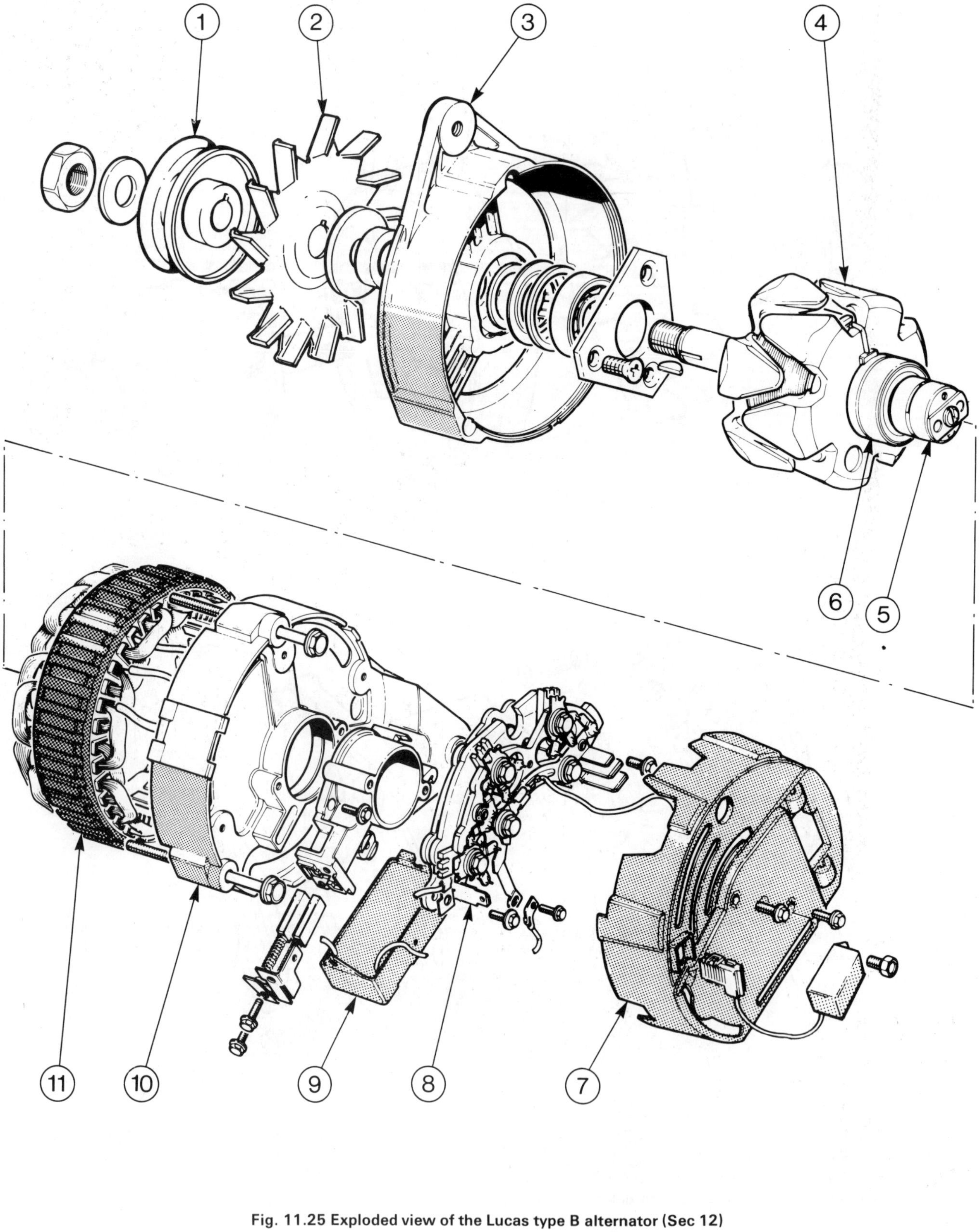

Fig. 11.25 Exploded view of the Lucas type B alternator (Sec 12)

1 Pulley	4 Rotor	7 End cover	10 Slip ring end bearing
2 Fan	5 Slip ring	8 Rectifier pack	11 Stator
3 Drive end housing	6 End bearing	9 Regulator	

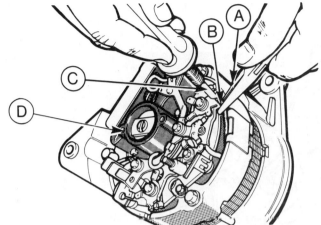

Fig. 11.26 Unsoldering stator/diode connections (Lucas type B) (Sec 12)

A   Pliers
B   Stator connection
C   Soldering iron
D   Brush box

Fig. 11.27 Diode pack (Lucas type B) (Sec 12)

A   Field diodes
B   Positive diodes
C   Negative diodes
D   Field terminal
E   Positive terminal

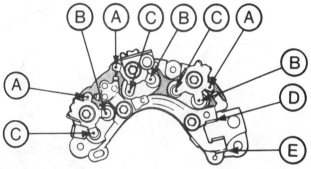

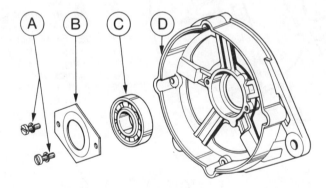

Fig. 11.28 Drive end bearing (C), retaining plate (B), screws (A) and end housing (D) (Lucas type B) (Sec 12)

Fig. 11.29 End bearing removal from rotor (Lucas type B) (Sec 12)

A   Bearing
B   Press tool
C   Rotor shaft
D   Slotted plate washer

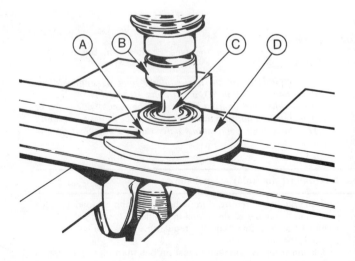

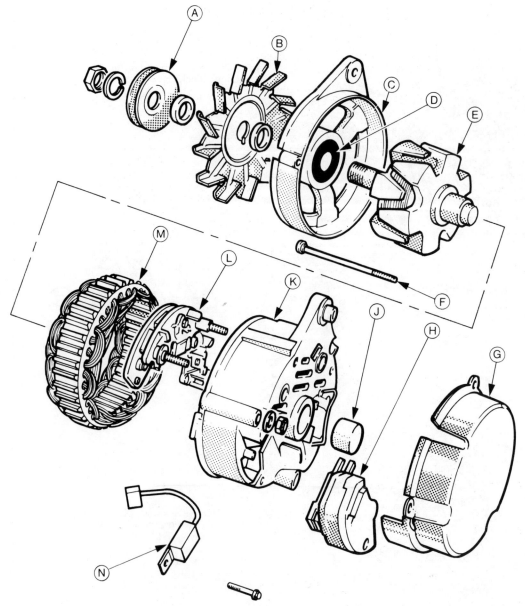

Fig. 11.30 Exploded view of the Lucas type D alternator (Sec 12)

A	Pulley
B	Fan
C	Drive end housing
D	Drive end bearing
E	Rotor
F	Through-bolt
G	End cover
H	Regulator/brushbox
J	Slip ring end bearing
K	Slip ring end housing
L	Rectifier pack
M	Stator
N	Suppressor

Lucas type D

22 Proceed as described for the type B alternator, but note the following differences:

   (a) *The combined brush box/regulator unit is removed as described in Section 10, paragraphs 10 and 11*

   (b) *If the drive end bearing is found to be excessively worn or defective, the housing and bearing must be renewed as a unit*

   (c) *The diode pack connections differ and are as shown in Fig. 11.31*

---

13 Alternator (Motorola) – overhaul

1   With the alternator removed from the engine and cleaned, remove the pulley/fan assembly as described in Section 11, paragraph 1.

2   Remove the rear cover and the regulator.

3   Remove the brush box.

4   Check the rotor by connecting test probes from an ohmmeter to each slip ring. The resistance must be within the limits given in the Specifications.

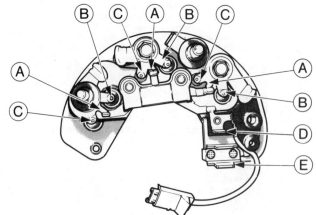

Fig. 11.31 Diode pack (Lucas type D) (Sec 12)

A	Field diodes	D	Field terminal
B	Positive diodes	E	Positive terminal
C	Negative diodes		

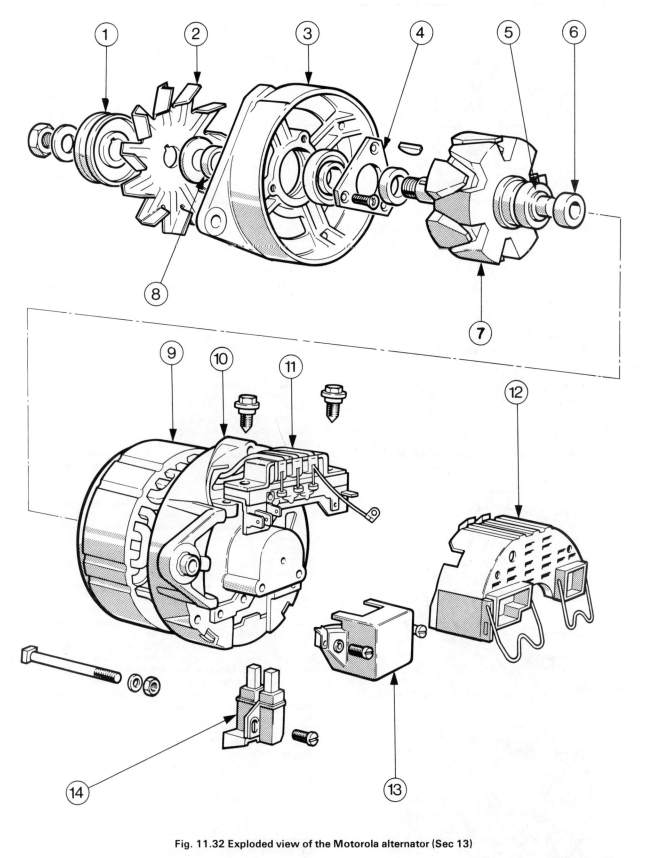

Fig. 11.32 Exploded view of the Motorola alternator (Sec 13)

1	Pulley	4	Drive end bearing retaining plate	7	Rotor
2	Fan			8	Spacer
3	Drive end housing	5	Slip ring	9	Stator
		6	Slip ring end bearing	10	Slip ring end housing

11	Diode bridge
12	End cover
13	Regulator
14	Brush box

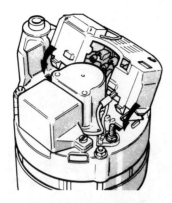

Fig. 11.33 Unclip and remove the rear cover (Motorola) (Sec 13)

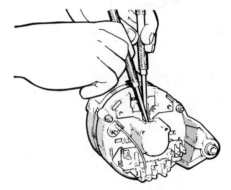

Fig. 11.34 Checking the rotor (Motorola) (Sec 13)

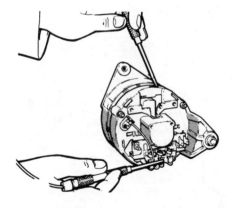

Fig. 11.35 Checking the stator (Motorola) (Sec 13)

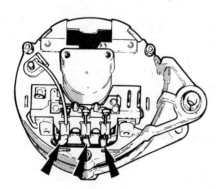

Fig. 11.36 Diode bridge connections – arrowed (Motorola) (Sec 13)

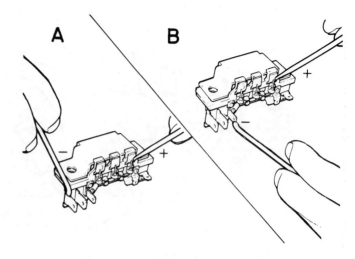

Fig. 11.37 Checking the positive (A) and field (B) diodes (Motorola) (Sec 13)

5   Connect an ohmmeter between a slip ring and the alternator housing. No reading should be indicated.
6   Check the stator insulation by connecting the ohmmeter between the alternator housing and each stator phase winding in turn. No reading should be indicated.
7   Unsolder the stator-to-diode bridge connections and remove the bridge.
8   Test the diode bridge using a 5W test lamp and 12V supply. Connect the indicator lamp, between each positive diode phase terminal and the B^3 terminal (Fig. 11.37). The lamp should light up if the diode is in good condition.
9   Reverse the test lead probes and the lamp should not light up unless the diode is faulty.
10   To check the negative diodes, connect the test lamps between each phase terminal and earth. If the diode is in good condition, the bulb should light up. Now reverse the test probes when the bulb should not light up unless the diode is faulty.
11   Remove the through-bolts separate the drive end and slip ring end housings and withdraw the stator.
12   Pull off the rear bearing using a two-legged extractor.
13   Unsolder the wires from the slip rings.
14   Extract the three screws which hold the bearing plate at the drive end and press out the bearing assembly.
15   Commence reassembly by installing the drive end bearing and the bearing plate and screws. If the original bearing is being used, work some high melting-point grease into it.
16   Locate the inner slip ring on the rotor shaft, making sure that the lead holes are correctly aligned. Press the slip ring into position and solder the lead, using 60/40 electricians' solder if available.
17   Install the outer slip ring in a similar way.
18   Fit the rotor and drive end bearing to the drive end housing. If the original bearing is being used, work some high melting-point grease into it.
19   Locate the stator in the slip ring end housing and connect it to the drive end housing. Pull the assemblies evenly together using the through-bolts.
20   Fit the diode bridge and resolder the stator/diode wiring connections.
21   Fit the brush box, the regulator and the rear cover.
22   Fit the Woodruff key and the fan/pulley assembly.

14 Starter motor – description

The starter motor is of pre-engaged type and incorporates an integral solenoid.
One of five different marks may be fitted: Lucas, Bosch, Nippondenso, Femsa or Cajavec, the last mentioned type being similar to the Bosch long frame starter motor.

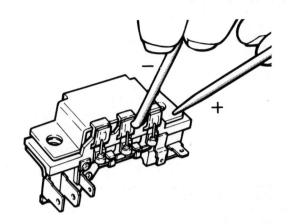

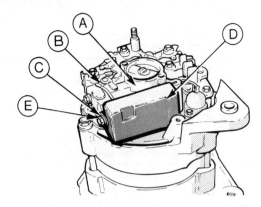

Fig. 11.39 Regulator and associate components (Motorola) (Sec 13)

Fig. 11.38 Checking the negative diodes (Motorola) (Sec 13)

A   Brush box
B   Field link
C   Plastic spacer

D   Regulator
E   Retaining screw

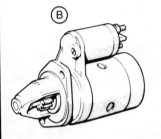

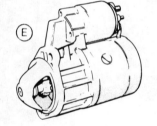

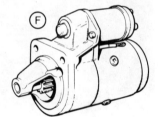

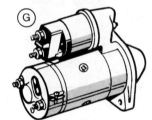

Fig. 11.40 The starter motor types fitted (Sec 14)

B   Bosch long frame
C   Cajavec
D   Nippondenso
E   Bosch short frame
F   Lucas
G   Femsa

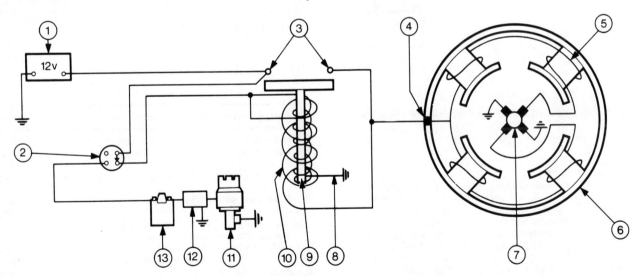

Fig. 11.41 Starter motor and associated starter wiring circuit (Sec 14)

1   Battery
2   Ignition switch
3   Solenoid main contacts
4   Starter main terminal

5   Field winding
6   Starter motor
7   Armature

8   Hold-on winding
9   Solenoid armature
10 Closing winding

11 Distributor
12 Ignition switching module
13 Ignition coil

15 Starter motor – in-vehicle testing

1   Check that the battery is fully charged.
2   First test the solenoid. To do this, disconnect the battery negative lead and both leads from the solenoid. Check the continuity of the solenoid windings by connecting a test lamp (12V with 2 to 3W bulb) between the starter feed terminal and the solenoid body. The lamp should light up.
3   Now make the test circuit as shown in Fig. 11.43 using a higher wattage (18 to 21W) bulb. Energise the solenoid by applying 12V between the spade terminal and the starter feed terminal. The solenoid should be heard to operate and the test bulb should light up, indicating that the solenoid contacts have closed.

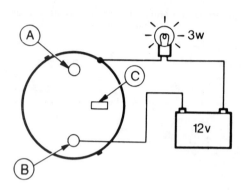

Fig. 11.42 Checking the solenoid winding (Sec 15)

A   *Battery terminal*   C   *Spade terminal*
B   *Feed terminal*

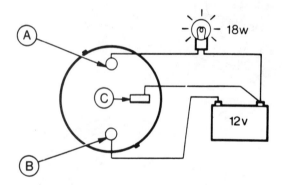

Fig. 11.43 Checking the solenoid for continuity (Sec 15)

A   *Battery terminal*   C   *Spade terminal*
B   *Feed terminal*

4   Connect a voltmeter directly between the battery terminals. Disconnect the positive LT lead from the ignition coil and operate the starter. The voltmeter should indicate not less than 10.5V.
5   Now connect the voltmeter between the starter main terminal and the body of the starter motor. Operate the starter, with the coil LT lead still disconnected. The reading on the voltmeter should be no more than 1.0V lower than that indicated during the test described in paragraph 4. If it is, check the battery-to-starter motor wiring.
6   Connect the voltmeter between the battery positive terminal and the starter motor main feed terminal. Operate the starter (with the LT coil positive lead disconnected) for two or three seconds and observe the meter readings. A reading of 12V should stop to less than 1.0V. If the reading is higher, a high resistance is indicated (refer to paragraph 7). If the reading is lower, refer to paragraph 8.
7   Connect the voltmeter between the two main stud terminals of the starter solenoid. With the positive LT lead disconnected from the coil,

operate the starter for two or three seconds and note the meter readings. Battery voltage (12V) should be indicated first, followed by a voltage drop of less than 0.5V. If outside this tolerance, a faulty switch or connections may be the cause, or loose or corroded terminals in the circuit.
8   Connect a voltmeter between the battery negative terminal and the starter motor main casing. With the positive LT lead disconnected from the coil, operate the starter for two or three seconds. If the earth line is satisfactory, the reading should be less than 0.5V. If it is 0.6V or more then there is a high resistance in the earth return side of the circuit. This may be due to a loose or corroded connection either at the battery or at the engine block.

16 Starter motor – removal and refitting

1   Disconnect the battery.
2   Working from under the vehicle, disconnect the main starter motor cable and the two wires from the starter solenoid.
3   Unbolt the starter motor and withdraw it from its location (photo).
4   Refit the starter motor by reversing the removal procedure.

16.3 Starter motor

17 Starter motor (Bosch long frame type and Cajavec) – overhaul

1   With the starter motor removed from the vehicle and cleaned, grip the starter motor in the jaws of a vice which have been fitted with soft metal protectors.
2   Disconnect the field winding connector link from the solenoid stud.
3   Extract the solenoid fixing screws and withdraw the solenoid yoke from the drive end housing and the solenoid armature. Unhook the solenoid armature from the actuating lever.
4   Extract the two screws or nuts and washers and remove the commutator end cap and rubber seal.
5   Wipe away any grease and withdraw the C-clip and shims.
6   Remove the tie-nuts and remove the commutator end housing.
7   Remove the brushes by prising the brush springs clear and sliding the brushes from their holders. Remove the brushplate.
8   Separate the drive end housing and armature from the yoke by tapping apart with a plastic-faced hammer.
9   Remove the tie-bolts to release the drive pinion clutch stop bracket.
10 Withdraw the armature assembly and unhook the actuating arm from the drive pinion flange.

11 To remove the drive pinion from the armature shaft, drive the thrust collar down the shaft with a piece of tubing to expose the clip. Remove the clip from its groove and slide the collar and drive pinion off the shaft.

12 Examine the components and renew as necessary.

13 If the brushes have worn to less than the specified minimum, renew them as a set. To renew the brushes, cut their leads at their midpoint and make a good soldered joint when connecting the new brushes.

14 The commutator face should be clean and free from burnt spots. Where necessary burnish with fine glass paper (**not** emery) and wipe with a fuel-moistened cloth. If the commutator is in really bad shape it can be skimmed on a lathe provided its diameter is not reduced below the specified minimum. If recutting the insulation slots, take care not to cut into the commutator metal.

15 The field winding can be checked for continuity only if a 110V ac power source is available, probably a job for your dealer. Where facilities are to hand, connect the test lamp between each field winding brush in turn and a clean, unpainted area of the yoke. The test lamp should not light up.

16 Renew the end housing bushes, which are of self-lubricating type and should have been soaked in clean engine oil for at least 20 minutes before installation.

17 Commence reassembly by sliding the drive pinion and stop collar onto the armature shaft. Fit the C-clip into the shaft groove and then use a two-legged puller to draw the stop collar over the clip.

18 Align the clutch retaining bracket and secure it with the two tie-bolts.

19 Fit the rubber insert into the drive end housing.

20 Guide the yoke over the armature and tap home onto the drive end housing.

21 Fit the brush plate, the brushes and their springs. Where the brush plate is located over studs, slide the plate engagement slots over the stubs to correctly position the brush plate. Where the brush plate is secured by screws align the plate location slots with the field winding loops (Figs. 11.51 and 11.52).

22 Guide the commutator end housing into position, at the same time sliding the rubber insulator into the cut-out in the commutator housing. Secure the commutator end housing with the stud nuts and washers or screws, as applicable.

23 Slide the armature into position in its bearings so that the shaft has the maximum projection at the commutator bearing end.

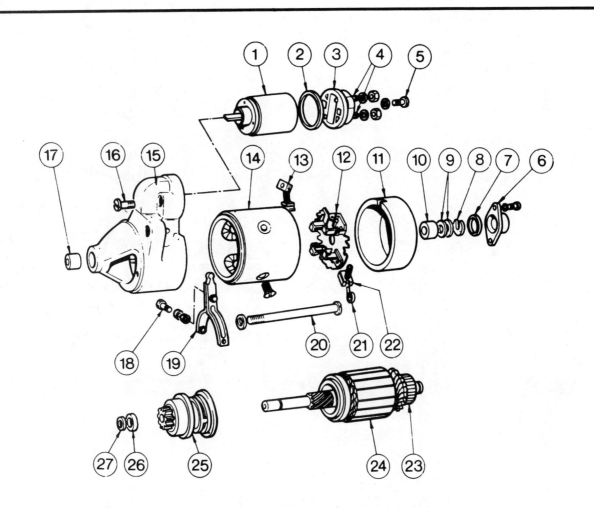

Fig. 11.44 Exploded view of the Bosch long frame starter motor
(Sec 17)

1	Solenoid body	8	C-clip
2	Gasket	9	Shim
3	Contact switch assembly	10	Bearing
4	Main terminals	11	Commutator end housing
5	Retaining screws	12	Brush box
6	End cover	13	Link connector
7	Seal	14	Main casing (yoke)

15	Drive end housing	22	Brush
16	Solenoid fixing screw	23	Commutator
17	Bearing	24	Armature
18	Pivot screw	25	Drive pinion/roller clutch
19	Actuating lever	26	Bearing
20	Tie-bolt	27	Thrustwasher
21	Brush spring		

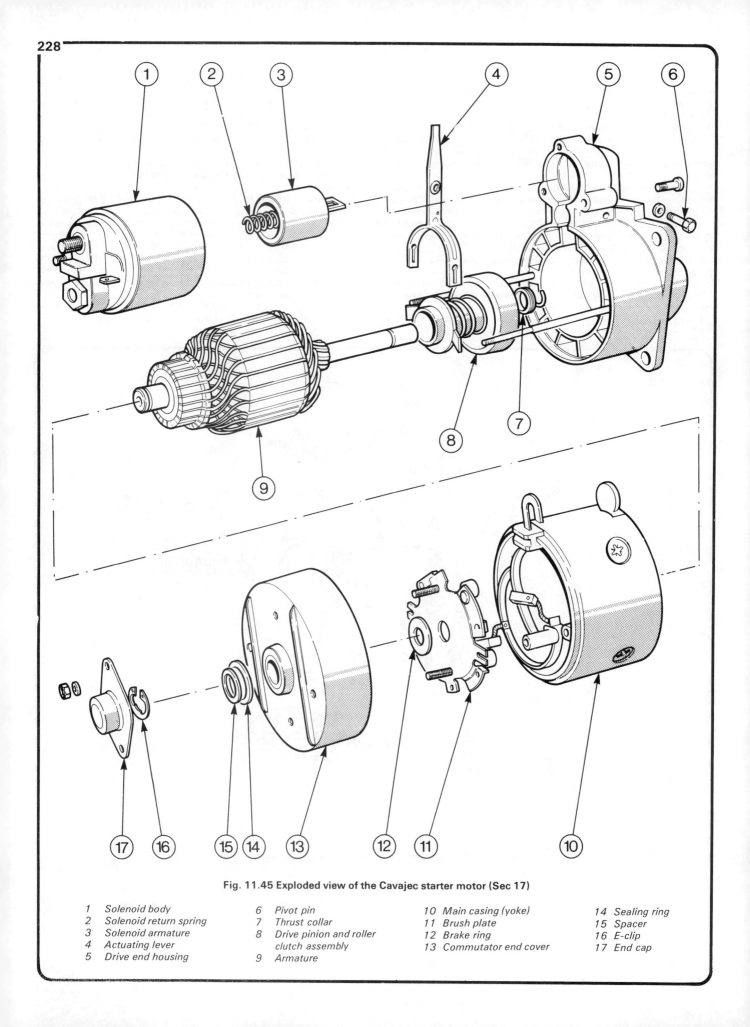

Fig. 11.45 Exploded view of the Cavajec starter motor (Sec 17)

1	Solenoid body	6	Pivot pin	10	Main casing (yoke)	14 Sealing ring
2	Solenoid return spring	7	Thrust collar	11	Brush plate	15 Spacer
3	Solenoid armature	8	Drive pinion and roller	12	Brake ring	16 E-clip
4	Actuating lever		clutch assembly	13	Commutator end cover	17 End cap
5	Drive end housing	9	Armature			

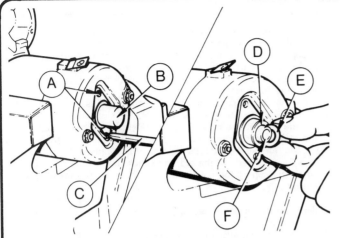

Fig. 11.46 End housing components removal – Bosch long frame type and Cajavec (Sec 17)

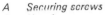

A   Securing screws   D   Shims
B   Housing cap   E   C-clip
C   Screwdriver   F   Armature shaft

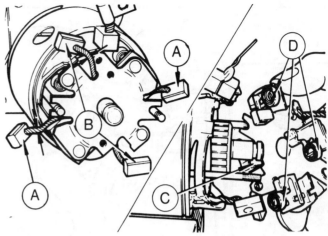

Fig. 11.47 Brush plate removal – Bosch long frame type and Cajavec (Sec 17)

A   Field brushes   C   Brush plate
B   Terminal brushes   D   Brush retaining springs

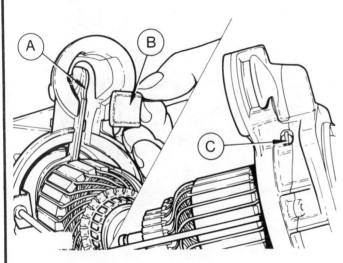

Fig. 11.48 Remove the actuating arm (A), pad (B) and pivot pin (C) – Bosch long frame type and Cajavec (Sec 17)

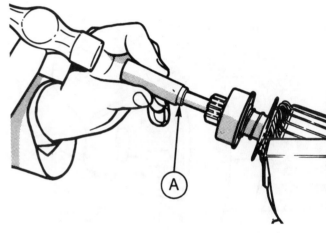

Fig. 11.49 Driving down the armature thrust collar (A) – Bosch long frame type and Cajavec (Sec 17)

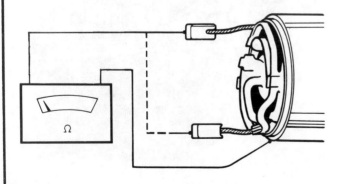

Fig. 11.50 Checking the field winding insulation (Sec 17)

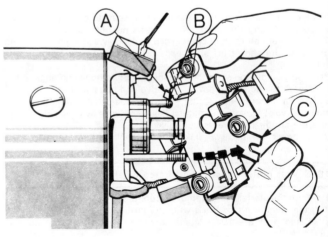

Fig. 11.51 Brush plate assembly fitted onto studs (Sec 17)

A   Alignment lug   C   Alignment lug
B   Fixing studs

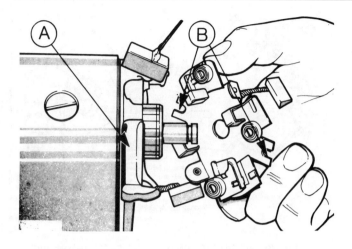

Fig. 11.52 Brush plate assembly fitted with screws (Sec 17)

A   *Field winding loops*   B   *Location slots*

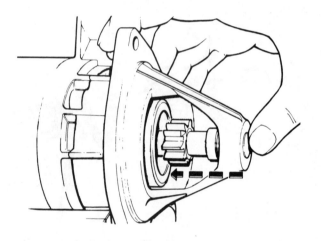

Fig. 11.53 Checking the endfloat of the armature (Bosch) (Sec 17)

24 Fit sufficient shims onto the armature shaft to eliminate endfloat when the C-clip is installed, which should now be done.
25 Fit the armature shaft bearing cap seal, apply a little lithium-based grease to the end of the shaft and refit the bearing cap with its two screws.
26 Apply some grease to the solenoid armature hook and engage the hook with the actuating arm in the drive end housing. Check that the solenoid armature return spring is correctly located and then guide the solenoid yoke over the armature. Align the yoke with the drive end housing and fit the three securing screws.
27 Connect the field wire link to the solenoid terminal stud.

18 Starter motor (Bosch short frame type) – overhaul

1   With the starter motor removed from the vehicle and cleaned, grip it in the jaws of a vice fitted with soft protectors.
2   Disconnect the field winding connector cable from the solenoid stud.
3   Undo the three screws and withdraw the solenoid.
4   Undo the two screws and remove the commutator end housing cap. Prise free the C-clip and withdraw the washer.
5   Undo the two nuts and remove the end housing.
6   The brushes, springs and brush holder boxes are now removed by pressing the boxes in towards the commutator and unclipping them

from the brush plate. Release the brushes from their boxes before removing the brush plate to prevent damaging the brushes.
7   Separate the drive end housing and armature from the yoke by tapping them apart with a plastic hammer.
8   Remove the drive pinion assembly, as described in paragraph 11 in the previous Section.
9   Clean and inspect the internal components as described in paragraphs 12 to 16 of the previous Section.
10 If the brushes are to be renewed, release each brush lead from its stand-off connection on the brush plate. Cut the leads at their midway point and remove the old brushes. Solder the leads of the new brushes to the severed leads of the old and check that each soldered joint is secure. The clip of the new brush unit must be positioned over the stand-off connector and soldered in position.
11 Commence reassembly by refitting the drive pinion and thrust collar onto the armature shaft, as described in paragraph 17 of the previous Section.
12 Refit the yoke over the armature and fit to the drive end housing by carefully tapping home using a soft-faced hammer. Check that the rubber block is positioned correctly.
13 Relocate the brush plate into position over the armature and fit the brush boxes, springs and brushes. Check that the clips are securely located.

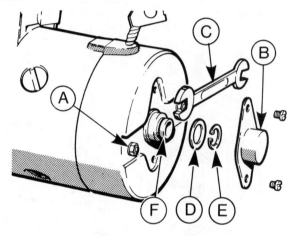

Fig. 11.54 Commutator end housing components – Bosch short frame type (Sec 18)

A   *Securing screws*   D   *Shims*
B   *Housing cap*   E   *C-clip*
C   *Spanner*   F   *Armature shaft*

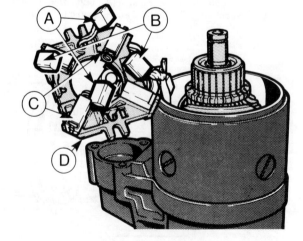

Fig. 11.55 Brush plate removal – Bosch short frame type (Sec 18)

A   *Field brushes*   C   *Brush plate*
B   *Terminal brushes*   D   *Brush holders*

Fig. 11.56 Brush lead clip (2) and stand-off connector (1) –
Bosch short frame type (Sec 18)

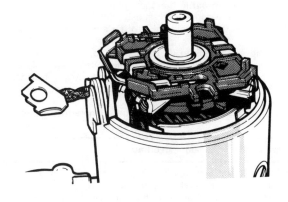

Fig. 11.57 Brush plate position – Bosch short frame type
(Sec 18)

Fig. 11.58 Bosch short frame
starter motor components
(Sec 18)

1　Solenoid
2　Solenoid spring
3　Solenoid yoke
4　Actuating lever
5　Rubber block
6　Drive end housing
7　Solenoid bolts
8　C-clip
9　Thrust collar
10　Armature
11　Main casing (yoke)
12　Pole shoe
13　Brush plate
14　Commutator end housing
15　Sealing ring
16　Spacer
17　C-clip
18　End cover
19　Securing bolt
20　Tie-bolt

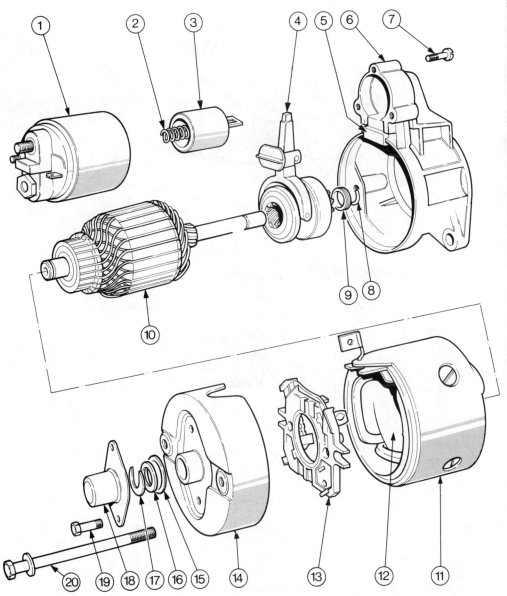

14 Refit the commutator end housing and engage the rubber insulator into the cut-out in the commutator housing. Insert the two screws to retain the housing and brush plate.

15 Align and fit the solenoid yoke to the armature and secure with screws.

16 Refit the armature into its bearing and adjust as necessary, as described in the previous Section in paragraphs 23 and 24.

17 Smear the end of the armature with a little lithium-based grease then refit the bearing cap and secure with the two screws and washers.

18 Attach the field winding cable to the solenoid to complete.

19 Starter motor (Lucas) – overhaul

1 With the starter removed from the vehicle and cleaned, grip it in a vice fitted with soft metal jaw protectors.

2 Remove the plastic cap from the commutator endplate.

3 Using a very small cold chisel, remove the star clip from the end of the armature shaft. Do this by distorting the prongs of the clip until it can be removed.

4 Disconnect the main feed link from the solenoid terminal.

5 Unscrew the two mounting nuts and withdraw the solenoid from the drive end housing, at the same time unhooking the solenoid armature from the actuating lever.

6 Extract the two drive end housing fixing screws. Guide the housing and the armature clear of the yoke.

7 Withdraw the armature from the drive end housing and the actuating lever assembly will come out with it, complete with plastic pivot block and rubber pad.

8 Use a piece of tubing to drive the stop collar down the armature shaft to expose the C-clip. Remove the C-clip and take off the stop collar and drive pinion.

9 To separate the actuating lever from the drive pinion, extract the C-clip and remove the spacer. Separate the two halves of the plastic drive collar and withdraw the actuating lever.

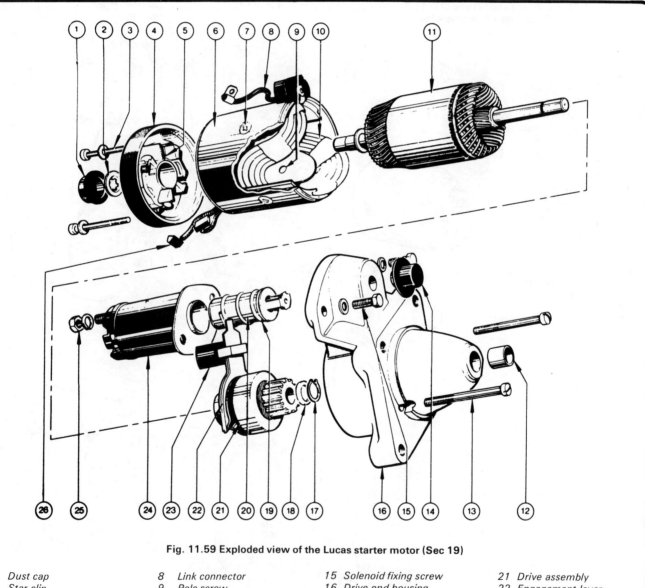

Fig. 11.59 Exploded view of the Lucas starter motor (Sec 19)

1 Dust cap	8 Link connector	15 Solenoid fixing screw	21 Drive assembly
2 Star clip	9 Pole screw	16 Drive end housing	22 Engagement lever
3 Endplate bolt	10 Field coils	17 C-clip	23 Pivot
4 Endplate	11 Armature	18 Spacer	24 Solenoid body
5 Brush housing	12 Bearing	19 Return spring	25 Terminal nut and washer
6 Main casing (yoke)	13 Housing screws	20 Solenoid armature	26 Brushes
7 Pole screw	14 Dust cover		

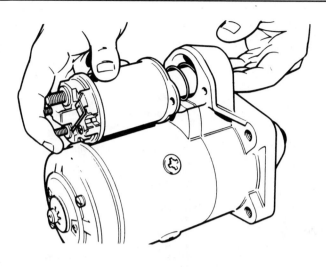

Fig. 11.60 Removing the solenoid – Lucas (Sec 19)

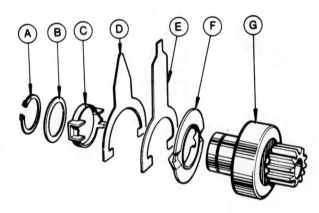

Fig. 11.61 Drive pinion/clutch assembly – Lucas (Sec 19)

A	C-clip	E	Actuating lever
B	Spacer	F	Drive collar
C	Drive collar	G	Drive pinion
D	Actuating lever		

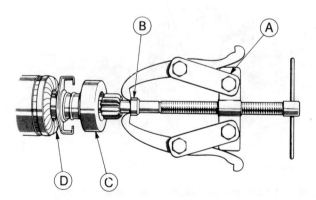

Fig. 11.62 Drive pinion thrust collar fitting method – Lucas (Sec 19)

A	Two-legged puller	C	Drive pinion assembly
B	Thrust collar	D	Armature

10 Remove the commutator endplate screws and tap the plate free of the yoke.

11 Lift the plate far enough to give access to the two field winding brushes. Disconnect two of the brushes from the brush box to permit complete removal of the commutator endplate.

12 The brush box and commutator endplate are only supplied as a complete assembly and should be renewed together if necessary.

13 Examine all the components for wear. If the brushes have worn to less than the specified minimum length, renew them as a set.

14 Two of the brushes come complete with the commutator endplate terminal, but the field winding brushes will have to be cut and new ones soldered. Cut the original leads 6.0 mm (0.25 in) from the field winding conductor.

15 New brush springs are only supplied complete with a new brush box.

16 Recondition the commutator where necessary, as described in Section 17, paragraph 14.

17 Check the field winding for continuity, as described in Section 17, paragraph 15.

18 Renewal of the field winding is not usually within the scope of the home mechanic unless a pressure driver is available to release the pole piece retaining screws.

19 The endplate bearing bushes should be renewed, as described in Section 17, paragraph 16.

20 Commence reassembly by locating two field winding brushes in their brush box channels. Align the commutator endplate and secure it with four screws.

21 Fit the actuating lever to the drive pinion, the two halves of the drive collar and the spacer. Secure with the C-clip.

22 Slide the drive pinion and thrust collar onto the armature shaft. Fit the C-clip and use a two-legged puller to draw the stop collar over the clip.

23 Hook the plastic pivot block over the actuating arm, position the rubber pad and insert into the solenoid mounting housing.

24 Guide the armature into the drive end housing.

25 Guide the armature and drive end housing through the yoke and align the armature shaft with the endplate bush. Secure the yoke and housing with two fixing screws.

26 Fit a new star clip to the end of the armature shaft, making sure that it is firmly fixed to eliminate shaft endfloat. Fit the plastic cap.

27 Locate the solenoid armature onto the actuating arm, guide the solenoid valve over the armature and secure with studs and nuts.

28 Refit the connecting link between the solenoid and the main feed terminal.

20 Starter motor (Nippondenso) – overhaul

1 With the starter motor removed from the engine and cleaned, secure it in a vice with jaws protected with soft metal.

2 Disconnect the field winding connector from the solenoid terminal.

3 Remove the solenoid retaining nuts.

4 Withdraw the solenoid and unhook the armature hook from the actuating lever.

5 Remove the bearing cap (two screws).

6 Slide the C-washer from its groove in the armature shaft and take off the coil spring.

7 Unbolt and remove the rear housing cover.

8 Withdraw the two field brushes and remove the brush gear mounting plate.

9 Withdraw the armature and drive end housing from the main housing.

10 Withdraw the armature and the actuating lever from the drive end housing. Remove the actuating lever.

11 Use a piece of tubing to tap the stop collar down the armature shaft to expose the C-clip. Remove the clip and pull off the stop collar and drive pinion.

12 Inspect all components for wear. If the brushes have worn down to less than the specified minimum, renew them as a set. To do this, the original brush leads will have to be cut at the midpoint of their length and the new ones joined by soldering.

13 Recondition the commutator, as described in Section 17, paragraph 14.

14 Check the field winding for continuity, as described in Section 17, paragraph 15.

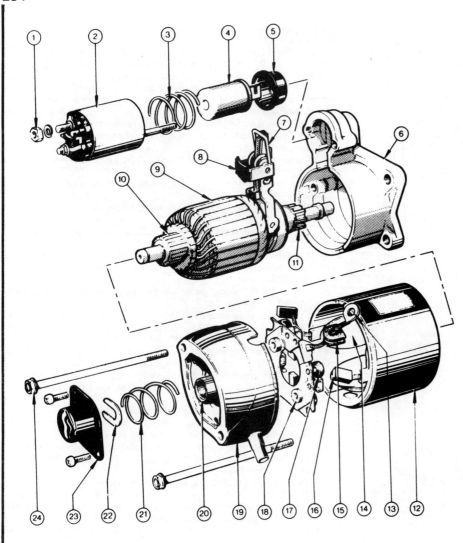

Fig. 11.63 Exploded view of the Nippondenso starter motor (Sec 20)

1 Solenoid terminal nut
2 Solenoid body
3 Return spring
4 Solenoid armature
5 Seal
6 Drive end housing
7 Actuating lever
8 Pivot
9 Armature
10 Commutator
11 Drive pinion/roller clutch
12 Main casing
13 Link connector
14 Pole shoe
15 Seal
16 Brush
17 Brush spring
18 Brush plate
19 Commutator end housing
20 Bush
21 Spring
22 C-clip
23 End cover
24 Tie-bolt

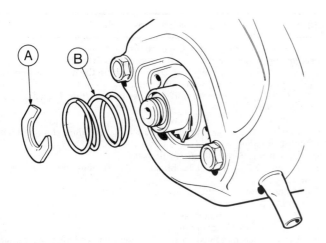

Fig. 11.64 Remove the C-washer (A) and coil spring (B) – Nippondenso (Sec 20)

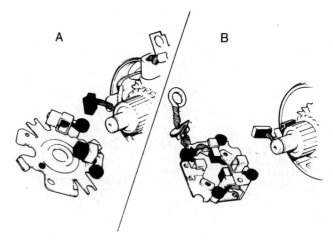

Fig. 11.65 Brush unit identification – Nippondenso (Sec 20)

A 0.6 kW   B 0.9 kW

15 The endplate bearing brushes should be renewed where necessary, as described in Section 17, paragraph 16.

16 Commence reassembly by sliding the drive pinion and stop collar onto the armature shaft. Fit the C-clip and using a two-legged puller, draw the stop collar over the clip.

17 Align the actuating lever in the drive end housing. Guide the armature into position, at the same time locating the actuating lever onto the drive pinion flange.

18 Tap the yoke into engagement with the drive end housing.

19 Locate the brush plate, aligning the cut-outs in the plate with the loops in the field winding. The brush assembly will be positively located when the fixing screws are screwed in.

20 Position the brushes in their brush box locations and retain with their springs.

21 Guide the commutator end housing into position and secure with the fixing nuts.

22 To the commutator end of the armature shaft, fit the coil spring and the C-clip.

23 Smear the end of the shaft with lithium-based grease and then fit the cap (two screws).

24 Connect the solenoid armature hook onto the actuating lever in the drive end housing. Align the solenoid yoke and fit the two fixing bolts.

21.6 Fuse unit removed from facia for access to relays

21 Fuses, relays and circuit breakers – general

1 These are combined in one unit under the facia panel (photo).

2 The fuses are numbered to identify the circuit which they protect and the circuits are represented by symbols on the plastic cover of the box.

3 When an accessory or other electrical component or system fails, always check the fuse first. The fuses are coloured red (10A), blue (15A), yellow (20/25A) or green (30A). Never replace a fuse with one of higher rating or bypass it with tinfoil, and, if the new fuse blows immediately, check the reason before renewing again. The most common cause of a fuse blowing is faulty insulation creating a short-circuit.

4 Spare fuses are carried in the fusebox lid.

5 An in-line fuse is used on models fitted with a radio (without cassette) and this is of 2 or 2.5 amp rating. On models with a radio/cassette, the fuse will be integral in, or at the rear of, the unit case; the fuse being of 2.5, 3.15 or 6.3 amp rating, depending on car model. Earlier electronic ignition models with a radio/cassette will also have a line fuse of 0.5 amp rating.

6 Relays are of the plug-in type (photo). The circuits they serve are listed in the Specifications.

22 Switches – removal and refitting

Disconnect the battery before removing any switches

Steering column combination switches

1 Both the indicator and light switch can be removed in the same manner. First undo the recessed retaining screws and carefully remove the upper and lower steering column shrouds. Guide the lower shroud over the bonnet release lever when removing it.

2 Undo the two screws of the switch concerned and withdraw the switch from the column. Disconnect the wiring at the multi-plug (photos).

3 Refit in the reverse order of removal, but check the switch for satisfactory operation before refitting the column shrouds.

Courtesy light switch

4 Open the door on the side concerned, unscrew the switch retaining screw and withdraw the switch and wiring so that the wire connector is accessible. Disconnect the wiring at the connector to fully withdraw the switch.

5 Refit in the reverse order of removal locating the switch in the rubber shroud in the pillar aperture.

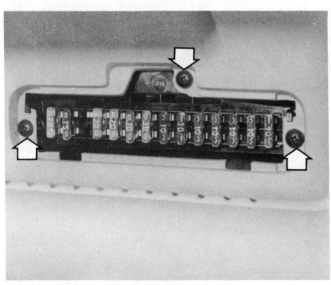

21.1 Fuse unit (cover removed). Note three unit retaining screws (arrowed)

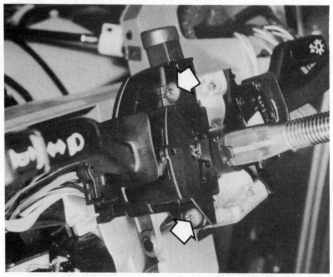

22.2A Steering column multi-function switch retaining screws (arrowed)

22.2B Windscreen wash/wipe switch retaining screws (arrowed)

Heater motor rocker switch (low series)
6   This switch can simply be prised free from the dash panel using a suitable flat-bladed screwdriver (Fig. 11.66). Locate a piece of cardboard or similar between the panel and the screwdriver as a protector pad when levering.
7   Withdraw the switch and disconnect the wiring multi-plug.
8   Refit in the reverse order to removal.

Heater motor switch (high series)
9   Pull free the three heater control knobs, undo the four screws then remove the bulb holders and the heater facia.
10 Reach behind the switch, depress the two retaining tabs and withdraw the switch and wiring. Disconnect the wiring at the multi-plug.
11 Refit in the reverse order to removal.

Facia panel 'tab' switches
12 Insert a small thin-edged screwdriver between the edge of the switch (on the left-hand side) and the panel and carefully prise it free (photo). To avoid possible damage to the facia position a piece of cardboard or similar as a pad between the screwdriver and panel.
13 Withdraw the switch and disconnect the multi-plug (photo).
14 Refit in the reverse order of removal.

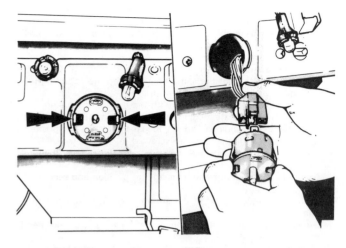

Fig. 11.67 High series heater motor switch removal (Sec 22)

22.12 Prise at point shown ...

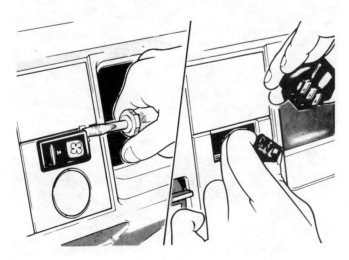

Fig. 11.66 Low series heater motor rocker switch removal
(Sec 22)

22.13 ... to release and withdraw the tab switch

Handbrake warning light switch

15 Remove the handbrake lever, as described in Chapter 8, undo the two switch retaining screws, disconnect the wiring multi-plug and remove the switch.

16 Refit in the reverse order of removal. Check the switch for satisfactory operation on completion.

Stop-light switch

17 Refer to Chapter 8, Section 17.

Econolights switch

18 These are located in the engine compartment and are mounted on the bulkhead. To remove a switch, detach the vacuum line, disconnect the wiring connector and undo the switch retaining screws. (Fig. 11.68).

19 Refit in the reverse order to removal. Restart the engine on completion and check the instrument lights for correct operations.

Reversing light switch

20 This is accessible from the engine compartment. Disconnect the switch wiring connector then unscrew and remove the switch from its location on the side of the gearbox.

Luggage compartment switch (lid release)

21 This is a rocker type switch and is fitted to the central floor console. It can be removed in the same manner as that described for the heater motor switch in paragraph 6.

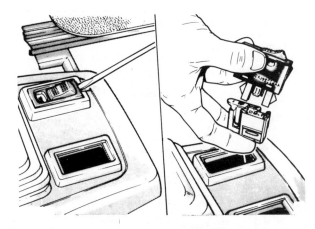

Fig. 11.70 Luggage compartment lid release switch removal (Sec 22)

23 Clock (facia-mounted) – removal and refitting

1 Detach the battery earth lead.

2 Use a suitable thin-bladed screwdriver as a lever and prise free the clock from the facia. Position a small piece of cardboard between the facia and the screwdriver blade to avoid the possibility of damage to the facia.

3 Withdraw the clock and disconnect the wiring multi-plug (photo).

4 Refit in the reverse order to removal.

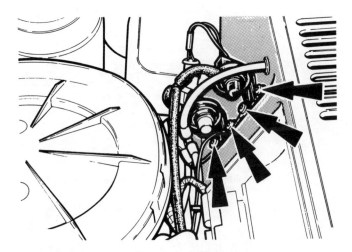

Fig. 11.68 Econolight switch location and securing screws (arrowed) (Sec 22)

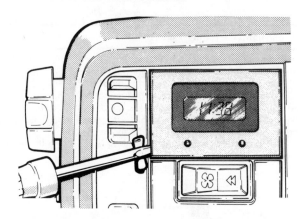

Fig. 11.71 Facia-mounted clock removal (Sec 23)

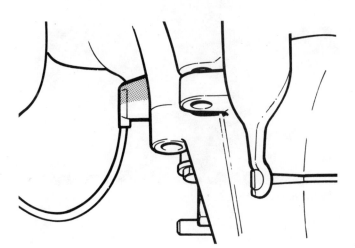

Fig. 11.69 Reversing light switch location on transmission (Sec 22)

23.3 Facia-mounted clock removal

24 Clock (roof-mounted) – removal and refitting

1   Disconnect the battery earth lead.
2   Undo the two screws securing the clock unit to the header panel, withdraw the clock/courtesy lamp unit and disconnect the wiring multi-plug.
3   Refitting is a reversal of the removal procedure.

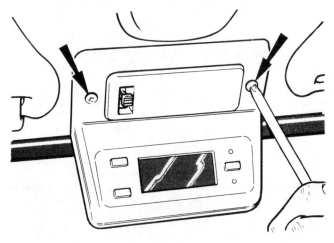

Fig. 11.72 Roof-mounted clock retaining screws (arrowed)
(Sec 24)

25 Cigar lighter – removal and refitting

1   Disconnect the battery earth lead.
2   Carefully withdraw the cigar lighter element.
3   Pull out the body and ring from the bezel.
4   Detach the wiring multi-plug and illumination bulb.
5   To renew the lighter elements, depress the knob so that the coil locknut is accessible. Grip the shaft with some thin nose pliers, unscrew the locknut (Fig. 11.73) and remove the coil.
6   Fit the new coil and refit the cigar lighter by reversing the removal procedure.

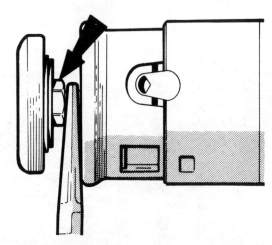

Fig. 11.73 Cigar lighter coil retaining nut (arrowed) (Sec 25)

26 Manual choke knob illuminating bulb – renewal

1   Extract the choke knob retaining clip and withdraw the knob and sleeve.
2   Press the bulb fully home into its holder (against spring tension)

then simultaneously use a thin-bladed screwdriver and push the bulb base holder downwards to remove the bulb.
3   To refit the bulb, press it into its holder and push the base holder upwards to secure. Slide the sleeve into position, refit the knob and locate its retaining clip.

27 Bulbs (interior) – renewal

1   *It is always advisable to disconnect the battery earth lead when renewing the bulbs.*

Interior lamp
2   Check that the switch is off then carefully prise the lamp unit from the header panel by levering at the opposite end to the switch (Fig. 11.74). When levering, push the plastic retaining clip inwards and lever the light unit away.
3   The bulb is now accessible for inspection and replacement, if necessary. If required, completely remove the unit by disconnecting the wire at the multi-plug (photo).

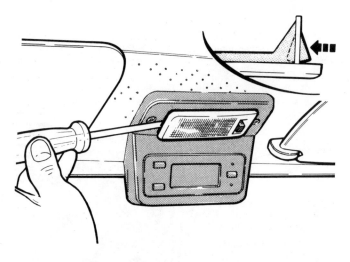

Fig. 11.74 Interior lamp removal – high series (Sec 27)

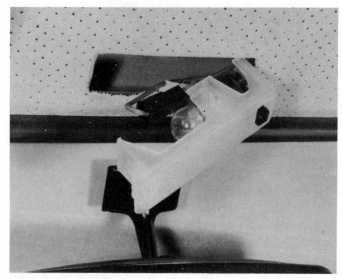

27.3 Interior light unit removal

Glovebox lamp
4   With the glovebox lid opened, press the lamp holder out of the latch unit. The bulb can now be removed from its holder for inspection and replacement.

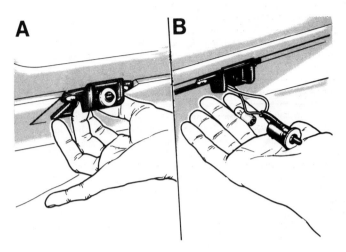
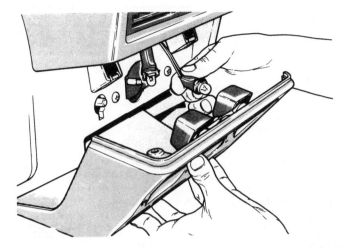

Fig. 11.75 Press out glovebox lamp holder (A) and remove bulb (B) (Sec 27)

Fig. 11.77 Heater control bulb removal – high series (Sec 27)

Heater control illumination bulbs (high series)

5   Pull free the three control knobs then undo the four heater panel retaining screws and remove the facia panel (Fig. 11.76).
6   Untwist the bulb holders from the facia panel and pull free the bulbs.

Heater control illumination bulbs (low series)

7   Referring to Section 33, remove the instrument panel surround.
8   Untwist the bulb holder and withdraw it, then pull the bulb from the holder for inspection/replacement (photo).

Hazard warning bulb

9   Pull the switch cover upwards and remove it to expose the bulb, then pull the bulb free from its holder (photo).

Luggage compartment lamp

10   Using a thin-bladed screwdriver, prise free the lamp from the trim panel.
11   The festoon bulb can then be unclipped from its holder for inspection/replacement.

All lamps

12   Refitting is the reversal of removal for all lamp assemblies. Check their operation is satisfactory on completion.

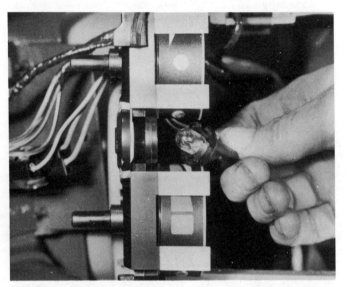

27.8 Heater control illumination bulb replacement

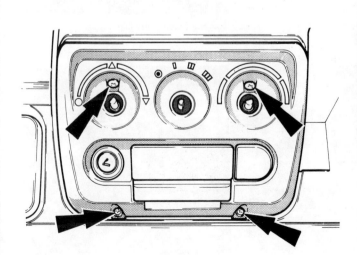

Fig. 11.76 Heater panel retaining screws (arrowed) – high series (Sec 27)

27.9 Hazard warning switch bulb replacement

28 Bulbs (exterior) – renewal

1   *It is advisable to disconnect the battery earth lead when renewing the bulbs.*

Headlamp

2   Open the bonnet and, working from the engine compartment side, disconnect the wiring multi-plug from the rear of the headlamp concerned (photo).
3   Remove the rubber gaiter and rotate the bulb securing clip or extract the spring clip according to type (photo).
4   Withdraw the bulb (photo).
5   Fit the bulb, avoiding handling it with the fingers. If you have touched it, wipe the bulb with a pad moistened in methylated spirit.

Front parking lamp (sidelamp)

6   The operations are similar to those just described for the headlamp bulb. Twist the parking lamp bulb holder from the headlamp unit (photo).

Front indicator lamp

7   Working inside the engine compartment, twist the bulb holder from the rear of the lamp (photo).
8   Remove the bulb from the holder.

Rear lamps

9   Remove the spare wheel cover from the luggage compartment, then carefully detach and withdraw the rear side trim panel on the side concerned for access to the lamp unit.
10   Push the bulb holder unit retaining clip upwards to release and remove the unit (photo). The bulb(s) can now be untwisted and removed from the holder, as required.

Rear number plate lamp

11   Using a suitable thin-bladed screwdriver, prise free the light unit from the bumper and withdraw the unit (photo).
12   Prise open the retaining clips on each side and withdraw the lens from the unit body (photo). The bulb can then be removed from the holder unit by pressing and untwisting it.

Rear foglamp

13   With the tailgate opened, remove the lockable compartment lid (if fitted) and the load compartment box. Detach the wiring multi-plug.
14   Undo the plastic retainer knobs, then withdraw the foglamp unit from under the rear bumper (photos).
15   Depress the securing tangs and separate the reflector from the unit for access to the bulb which can be removed by pressing and untwisting from its holder (photo).

All lamps

16   Refitting of the bulb and associated components is a reversal of the removal procedure in all cases. Check the bulb for satisfactory operation on completion.

29 Exterior lamp units – removal and refitting

1   *Disconnect the battery earth lead before removing any of the lamp units.*

Headlamp

2   Raise the bonnet then disconnect the wiring multi-plug at the rear of the headlamp unit.
3   Undo the retaining bolt at the top of the unit (photo).
4   Unclip the vertical adjustment screw unit from the top of the lamp and withdraw the lamp, lifting it from the lower location lugs.

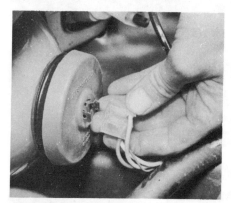

28.2 Detach lead connector from rear of headlight ...

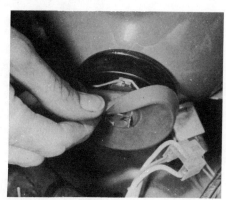

28.3A ... prise free the gaiter ...

28.3B ... release the clips ...

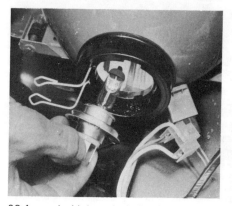

28.4 ... and withdraw the bulb with holder

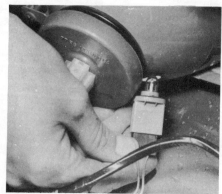

28.6 Sidelamp removal

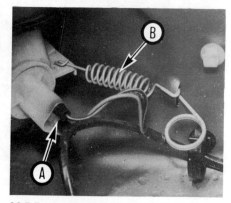

28.7 Front indicator bulb holder (A). Note indicator unit retaining spring (B)

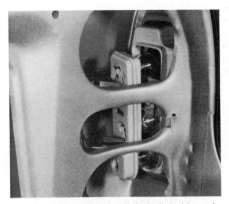

28.10 Rear combination light bulb holder unit removal

28.11 Prise free the number plate lamp unit ...

28.12 ... and separate the lens and body for access to the bulb

28.14A Foglamp unit retaining knobs

28.14B Remove the foglight ...

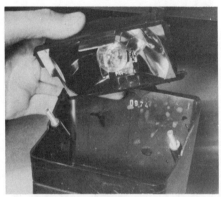

28.15 ... and separate lens from body for access to the bulb

29.3 Headlight unit retaining bolt removal

29.4 Detach headlight unit adjuster at the top

29.7 Front indicator lamp unit removal

5 Refitting is a reversal of the removal procedure, but on completion check the operation of the light unit and adjust it, as described in Section 30.

Front indicator lamp
6 Working from the engine compartment side, disengage the lamp unit retaining spring by pulling to the rear.
7 Untwist the bulb holder and remove the lamp unit (photo).
8 Refit reversing the removal procedure and check operation on completion.

Rear lamp unit
9 Proceed as described in paragraphs 9 and 10 of the previous Section and remove the bulb holder.

10 Undo the three retaining nuts from the inside and withdraw the unit.
11 Refit in reverse order to removal and check operation of all lights on completion.

30 Headlamps – alignment

1 The headlights are adjustable individually for both horizontal and vertical alignment from within the engine compartment.
2 Adjustments should not normally be necessary and, if their beam alignment is suspect, they should be checked by a Ford garage with optical alignment equipment.
3 A temporary adjustment can be made by turning the vertical

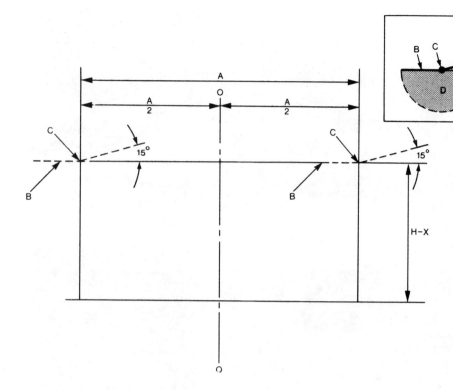

Fig. 11.78 Headlamp beam alignment diagram
(Sec 30)

*Left-hand drive shown. Transpose 15° beam
inclination angle to the left for right-hand drive.*

A   Distance between headlamp centres
B   Light/dark boundary
C   Dipped beam centre
D   Dipped beam pattern
H   Height from ground to centre of headlamps
X   10 to 12 cm, preferably with full tank
OO   Vehicle centre line

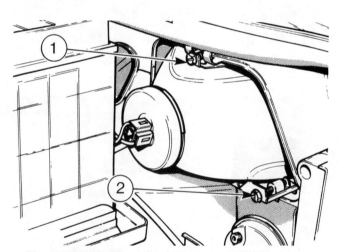

Fig. 11.79 Headlamp vertical (1) and horizontal (2) adjuster
screws (Sec 30)

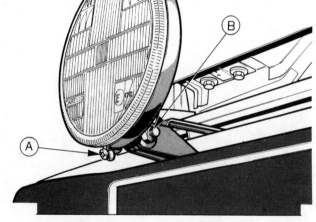

Fig. 11.80 Auxiliary lamp lens securing screw (A) and unit
securing nut (Sec 31)

and/or horizontal adjuster screws at the rear of each headlight unit.
When making an alignment check, the car tyre pressure must be
correct and the car standing unladen on level ground.
4   To assist in making an alignment check/adjustment the accompanying diagram shows the provisional headlamp beam alignment with
the vehicle parked a distance of 10 m (33 feet) from a wall or aiming
board (see Figs. 11.78 and 11.79). The headlamps are 'dipped'.

31 Auxiliary driving lamps – bulb renewal

1   Undo and remove the lens retaining screw from the lower edge of
the light unit (Fig. 11.80).
2   Prise free the lens from the light bowl, starting at the lower edge.
When free, detach the wiring connectors, release the bulb retaining
clip and withdraw the bulb from the holder in the reflector. Avoid
touching the bulb with the fingers (see headlight bulb handling
precautions, Section 28).
3   Refit in the reverse order to removal.

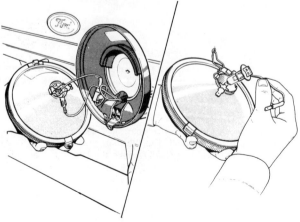

Fig. 11.81 Bulb replacement – auxiliary lamp (Sec 31)

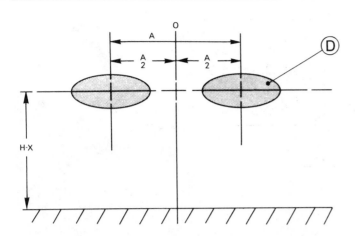

Fig. 11.82 Auxiliary lamp beam alignment chart (Sec 32)

Fig. 11.83 Instrument panel surround securing screw locations (arrowed) – high series (Sec 33)

A   Lamp centre distance   O   Centre line of vehicle
H   Lamp centre line to ground   X   18 cm (7.1 in)
     distance

32 Auxiliary driving lamps – removal, refitting and adjustment

1   Disconnect the battery earth lead.
2   Detach the lamp wire from its main loom connector.
3   Unscrew and remove the mounting bolt nut, withdraw the bolt and remove the light unit.
4   Refit in the reverse order to removal and check alignment before fully tightening the mounting bolt and nut.
5   As with the headlamps, the auxiliary driving lamps should be adjusted using optical beam setting equipment and this task is best entrusted to your Ford dealer. However, to assist when making initial adjustments, reference should be made to the accompanying diagram which shows a beam setting pattern with the vehicle parked on level ground at a distance of 10 m (33 feet) from a wall or aiming board. The wall should be marked accordingly to enable the beams to be set as required (Fig. 11.82).

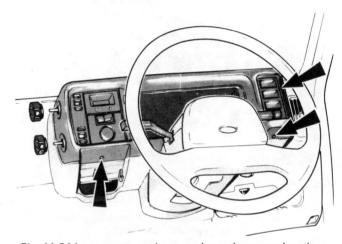

Fig. 11.84 Instrument panel surround securing screw locations (arrowed) – low series (Sec 33)

33 Instrument cluster unit – removal and refitting

1   Disconnect the battery earth lead.
2   Remove the steering column upper shroud wheel is secured by a single screw.
3   On low series models, pull free the heater control knobs (photo).
4   Undo and remove the panel surround retaining screws (photo), referring to Fig. 11.83 or 11.84 for their locations (as applicable). Carefully withdraw the surround. On low series models pivot the surround from the right, reach to the rear of the clock, depress the retaining tabs and withdraw the clock, then move the surround to the left to clear the heater controls and withdraw it.

5   Undo the retaining screw at each corner and carefully withdraw the cluster panel enough to disconnect the multi-plug connections. To disconnect the speedometer cable compress the grooved section of the cable lock catch and pull the cable free. It will probably be necessary for an assistant to push the speedometer cable through the bulkhead from the engine compartment side to provide sufficient clearance for it to be accessible for detachment (photo).
6   Withdraw the instrument cluster unit.
7   Refitting is a reversal of the removal procedure. Take care not to damage the printed circuit and its connections on the rear face of the unit. Check operation of instruments on completion.

33.3 Remove the heater control knobs (low series) ...

33.4 ... undo the unit retaining screws ...

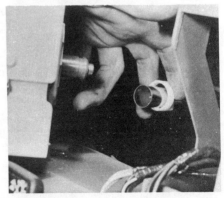

33.5 ... and disconnect the speedometer cable

34 Instrument cluster – dismantling and assembly

With the instrument cluster removed, its various components can be removed individually or collectively as required. When handling the instrument cluster and its components care must be taken not to knock or damage them in any way.

Printed circuit

1   Referring to paragraphs 9 and 10, remove the tachometer unit and the fuel/temperature gauge.
2   Undo the four screws and remove the lens.
3   Using a suitable implement, press the printed circuit retaining tabs at the front of the cluster (Fig. 11.85) and pull free the retainer at the rear.
4   The printed circuit can now be detached from its connections at the rear of the cluster and removed, but take care not to damage it if it is to be re-used.

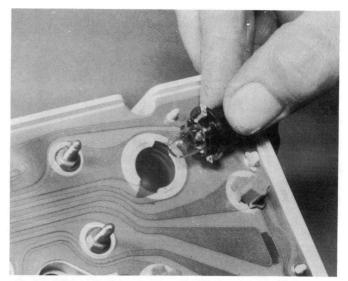

34.5 Bulb and holder removed from instrument cluster panel

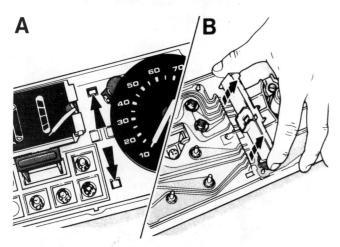

Fig. 11.85 Press tabs arrowed (A) and withdraw printed circuit retainer (B) (Sec 34)

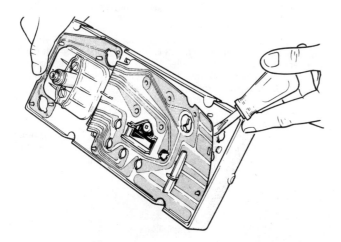

Fig. 11.86 Remove printed circuit with care (Sec 34)

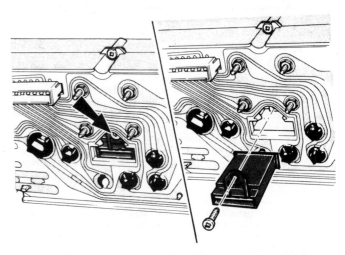

Fig. 11.87 Undo screw (arrowed) and withdraw the econolight unit (Sec 34)

Instrument warning and illumination bulbs

5   Grip the bulb holder and twist it to disengage it from the rear of the cluster unit (photo). The bulb can be removed from the holder by pulling it free.

Econolight warning light

6   Undo the retaining screw and withdraw the econolight unit from the rear face of the cluster. If defective this unit must be renewed as a complete assembly.

Speedometer head

7   Undo the four retaining screws and remove the cluster lens.
8   Undo the two speedometer head retaining screws from the rear face of the unit and then carefully withdraw the head unit from the front.

Tachometer

9   This is removed in a similar manner to that of the speedometer head except that it is secured by three nuts and washers.

Fuel/temperature gauge

10   This is removed in a similar manner to that described for the speedometer head except that it is secured by four nuts and washers.

Cluster assembly

11   Refitting of all instrument cluster components is a reversal of the removal procedure. When refitting the lens to the front face, position it on the cluster body with the two engagement pegs protruding through on each top corner; the lugs on the lower edge of the body must correspondingly engage in the cut-outs in the cluster body.

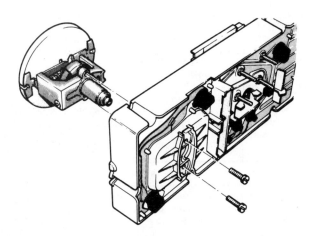

Fig. 11.88 Speedometer unit removal – low series (Sec 34)

36.2 Horn support bracket and lead connection (arrowed)

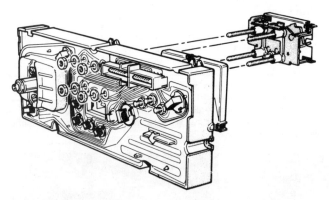

Fig. 11.89 Fuel/temperature gauge unit removal – high series
(Sec 34)

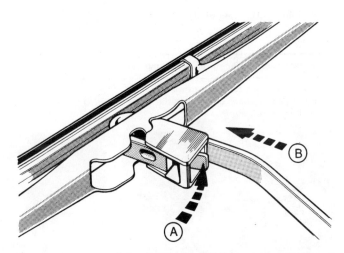

Fig. 11.90 Press clip (A) and slide arm (B) through blade holder to
release (Sec 37)

35 Speedometer cable – removal and refitting

1   Disconnect the battery and remove the instrument cluster, as
described in Section 33.
2   Disconnect the cable from the transmission and release it from its
clips and grommets.
3   Withdraw the cable through the bulkhead.
4   Refitting is a reversal of removal. The inner and outer cables are
supplied as a complete assembly.

36 Horn(s) – removal and refitting

1   The horn(s) are located in the left-hand front corner of the engine
compartment. Before removing, disconnect the battery.
2   Disconnect the lead from the horn (photo).
3   Unscrew the single bolt and remove the horn and bracket.
4   Refitting is a reversal of removal.

37 Windscreen wiper blades and arms – removal and refitting

1   Pull the wiper arm away from the glass until the glass locks.
2   Depress the small clip on the blade and slide the blade out of the
hooked part of the arm (Fig. 11.90).
3   Before removing the wiper arms it is worthwhile marking their
parked position on the glass with a strip of masking tape as an aid to
refitting. Raise the plastic nut cover (photo).

37.3 Wiper arm retaining nut

4   Unscrew the nut which holds the arm to the pivot shaft and pull the arm from the shaft splines.
5   Refit by reversing the removal operations.

38 Wiper blade rubber – renewal

1   Remove the wiper blade, as described in the preceding Section.
2   Using the thumb, draw back the rubber insert until the spring clip can be removed (Fig. 11.91).
3   Slide the rubber insert from the blade.
4   Refit by reversing the removal operations.

Fig. 11.91 Wiper blade rubber retaining clip (Sec 38)

39 Windscreen wiper motor – removal and refitting

1   Disconnect the battery earth lead.
2   Pull free the plastic cover from the wiper motor which is mounted on the bulkhead (photos).

3   Detach the wiring multi-plug from the wiper motor.
4   Undo the three retaining bolts and withdraw the wiper motor and mounting plate.
5   The wiper motor can now be disconnected from the arm and connecting link. Take care not to bend the link arm or damage the bush and ball.
6   Unscrew and remove the three securing bolts and detach the wiper motor from the mounting plate.
7   Refit in the reverse order of removal. Lubricate the bush and ball with grease prior to assembling and, when fitting the mounting plate to the bulkhead, check that the foam seal strip is in position between the mating surfaces.

40 Windscreen wiper linkage – removal and refitting

1   Remove the windscreen wiper motor, as described in the previous Section, and the wiper arms and blades, as described in Section 37.
2   Undo the six bolts which secure the bonnet lock mounting plate to the bulkhead (photo), disconnect the actuating cable to the lock and remove the mounting plate/lock unit (photo).
3   Unclip and remove the heater blower motor from its recess then disconnect the motor wiring at the multi-plug connectors (photo).
4   Unscrew and remove the wiper spindle arm nuts and washers, then withdraw the linkage assembly through the aperture in the bulkhead.
5   Refit in the reverse order to removal. Lubricate the linkage joints with grease. Check the operation of the wiper motor, the blower motor and the bonnet release lock on completion.

41 Rear window wiper motor – removal and refitting

1   Disconnect the battery earth lead.
2   Remove the rear window wiper arm and blade in the manner described in Section 37.

39.2A Remove plastic cover ...

39.2B ... for access to wiper motor unit (windscreen)

40.2A Undo the retaining bolts ...

40.2B ... and withdraw the mounting plate/lock unit

40.3 Heater blower motor location. Note retaining clip positions (arrowed)

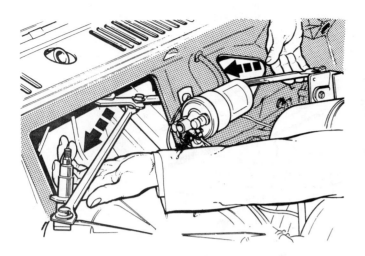

Fig. 11.92 Wiper motor linkage withdrawal (Sec 40)

41.5 Rear window wiper motor location and retaining bolts (arrowed)

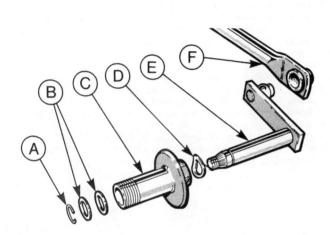

Fig. 11.93 Wiper pivot shaft components (front) (Sec 40)

A	Circlip	D	Wave washer
B	Shim washers	E	Pivot shaft
C	Bearing and housing	F	Link arm

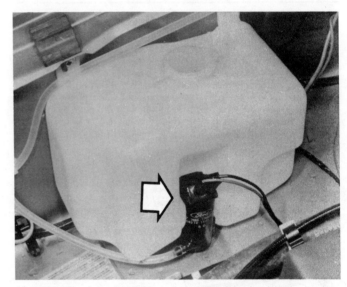

42.1 Windscreen washer fluid container and pump (arrowed)

3   Undo the nut retaining the wiper arm pivot shaft.
4   Open and raise the tailgate and carefully detach the inner trim panel by prising free the securing clips.
5   Undo the two wiper motor bracket-to-tailgate retaining bolts (photo).
6   Detach the earth lead which is retained by a screw to the tailgate. Disconnect the wiring multi-plug then withdraw the wiper motor and operating linkage from the tailgate cavity.
7   Refit in the reverse order of removal and check operation prior to refitting the tailgate trim panel.

42 Windscreen washer pump – removal and refitting

1   Drain the washer fluid container (photo).
2   Disconnect the lead and washer pipe from the pump unit.
3   Ease the washer pump away from the fluid container and remove it.

4   Refitting is a reversal of removal; check that the pump sealing grommet is a good fit.
5   Check for leaks and that pump operation is satisfactory on completion.

43 Rear window washer pump – removal and refitting

1   Lift out the spare wheel cover from the luggage compartment.
2   Unhook the rubber securing band retaining the reservoir in position.
3   Drain the contents of the reservoir, disconnect the wiring connector to the pump unit at the top and the washer pipe at the bottom.
4   Carefully ease the washer pump away from the reservoir.
5   Refit in the reverse order to removal. Check that the pump seal grommet is a good fit.
6   Check for leaks and that pump operation is satisfactory on completion.

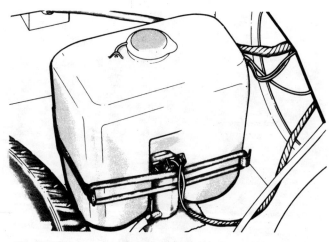

Fig. 11.94 Rear housing window washer pump and reservoir (Sec 43)

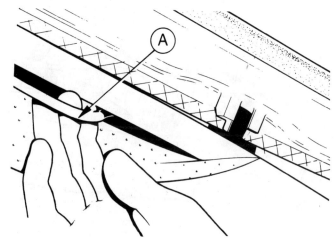

Fig. 11.96 Rear window washer nozzle hose (A) (Sec 45)

44 Windscreen washer nozzle and pipe – removal and refitting

1   To remove the nozzle(s), push the nozzle to the rear whilst pulling it up on its front edge. When the nozzle is clear of its location hole detach the fluid feed pipe.
2   If the pipe is to be removed, disconnect it at the pump end and pull it clear through the plenum chamber.
3   Refit in the reverse order to removal. Ensure that the feed pipe is located in rubber grommets where it passes through body panels.
4   On completion check for satisfactory operation of the washers and, if necessary, adjust the nozzles for jet spray direction by inserting a pin into the nozzle and moving it in the required direction.

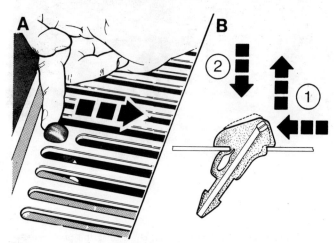

Fig. 11.95 Windscreen washer nozzle removal (A) and fitting (B) (Sec 44)

45 Rear window washer nozzle and pipe – removal and refitting

1   Open the tailgate, then carefully prise down the headlining at its rear edge for access to the underside of the nozzle. The weatherstrip will have to be prised free to allow the headlining to be detached, so take care not to damage it.
2   Pull free the feed pipe from the washer nozzle, undo the retaining nut, withdraw the shakeproof washer and seal then remove the nozzle.
3   To remove the hose, detach it from the reservoir pump and pull it through the body channels. To ease refitting of the hose, attach a length of cord to the end of the hose before removal. The cord can be left in position and tied to the new hose to ease refitting.
4   Refit in the reverse order to removal.

46 Heater blower motor – removal and refitting

1   Disconnect the battery earth lead.
2   Undo and remove the six screws securing the bonnet lock mounting plate and then position the plate (and bonnet lock) to one side.
3   Reach through the plate aperture and detach the lead connector from the fan motor, also detach the earth lead.
4   Bend back the two retaining clips and disengage the fan unit.
5   Rotate and remove the fan; pulling it out through the aperture in the cowl panel.
6   Disconnect the fan cover then, using a suitable screwdriver (Fig. 11.97), lift the motor securing clamp and remove the motor.
7   Refitting is a reversal of the removal procedure.

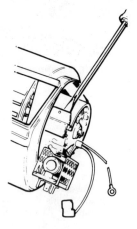

Fig. 11.97 Heater fan motor retaining clamp (Sec 46)

47 In-car entertainment equipment

1   The following Sections (48 to 52) cover radio/cassette player equipment fitted during production which is of Ford manufacture.
2   Where equipment is to be installed at a later date and is not necessarily of Ford make, refer to Section 53.
3   When fitted during production, the radio will be located in the lower centre console (low series variants) or in the instrument panel directly above the central air vents (high series variants).

4   Production fitted speakers will be mounted in the passenger door (mono system) or one in each door and one in each rear quarter trim panel (stereo system). On all models and for all systems the aerial is mounted in the front wing panel on the driver's side. Note that only manual aerials are fitted in production.

48 Radio – removal and refitting

1   Disconnect the battery.
2   Remove the radio control knobs and withdraw the tuning knob spacer and the tone control lever.
3   Unscrew and remove the facia plate retaining nuts and washers, then withdraw the facia plate (photo).
4   The radio retaining tangs can now be pulled inwards (towards the centre of the radio) and the radio withdrawn from its aperture. You may need to make a suitable hook-ended rod (welding rod is ideal) to pull the tangs inwards to release the radio (Figs. 11.98 and 11.99).
5   With the radio withdrawn, disconnect the power lead, the speaker plug, earth lead, the aerial cable and feed.
6   From the rear of the radio remove the plastic support bracket and locating plate, then remove the radio from the front bracket.
7   Refitting is the reversal of the removal procedure.

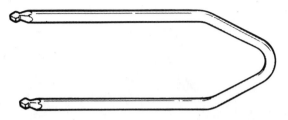

Fig. 11.99 Radio/cassette extractor tool (Secs 48 and 49)

49 Radio/cassette player – removal and refitting

1   Disconnect the battery earth lead.
2   To withdraw the radio/cassette unit from its aperture you will need to fabricate the U-shaped extractor tools from wire rod of suitable gauge to insert into the withdrawal slots on each side of the unit (in the front face) – Fig. 11.99.
3   Insert the withdrawal tools as shown (see Figs. 11.100 and 11.101) then, pushing each outwards simultaneously, pull them evenly to withdraw the radio/cassette unit. It is important that an equal pressure is applied to each tool as the unit is withdrawn.

48.3 Radio facia plate retaining nut (arrowed) with control knob removed

Fig. 11.100 Insert removal tool into radio/cassette (Sec 49)

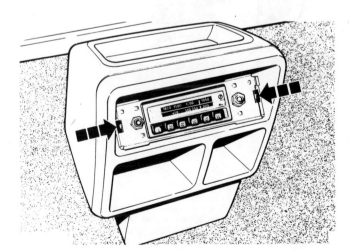

Fig. 11.98 Press securing tangs inwards to remove radio (Sec 48)

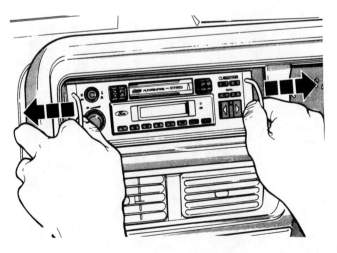

Fig. 11.101 Radio cassette withdrawal (Sec 49)

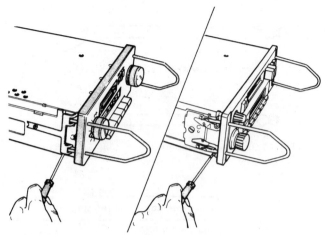

Fig. 11.102 Releasing the removal tool (Sec 49)

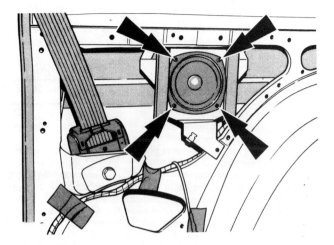

Fig. 11.104 Rear quarter panel speaker unit location and securing
screws (arrowed) (Sec 50)

4   Once withdrawn from its aperture disconnect the aerial cable, the
power lead, the aerial feed, the speaker plugs, the earth lead and the
light and memory feed (where applicable).
5   Push the retaining clips inwards to remove the removal tool from
each side (Fig. 11.102).
6   Refit in the reverse order of removal. The withdrawal tools do not
have to be used, simply push the unit into its aperture until the
securing clips engage in their slots.

50 Loudspeaker – removal and refitting

Door-mounted
1   Remove the door trim panel, as described in Chapter 12.
2   Unscrew the four retaining screws, withdraw the speaker unit and
disconnect the wiring.
3   Refit in the reverse order to removal.

Rear quarter panel-mounted
4   Remove the rear seat cushion and the seat backrest.
5   Detach and remove the rear quarter lower trim panel. To avoid
disconnecting the seat belt anchor, slide the panel up the belt and
position out of the way to provide access to the speaker.
6   Undo the four retaining screws, remove the speaker and detach
the leads.
7   Refit in reverse order to removal.

51 Speaker fader joystick – removal and refitting

1   Disconnect the battery earth lead.

High series variant
2   Unscrew and remove the single bezel retaining screw, lower the
bezel and slide it away and detach from the upper bracket.
3   Rotate the joystick retaining clip anti-clockwise, remove the clip
and withdraw the joystick from the bracket. Detach the wiring multi-
plug.
4   Refit in the reverse order to removal.

Fig. 11.105 Speaker joystick removal (high series) (Sec 51)

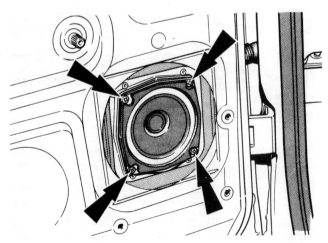

Fig. 11.103 Door-mounted speaker unit and securing screws
(arrowed) (Sec 50)

Low series variant
5   Use a flat-bladed screwdriver to prise free the bezel and pivot the
bezel upwards at the lower edge to disengage it from the bracket at
the top edge.
6   Rotate the joystick retaining clip anti-clockwise, remove the clip
and withdraw the joystick from its mounting bracket. Detach the
wiring multi-plug.
7   Refit in the reverse order to removal.

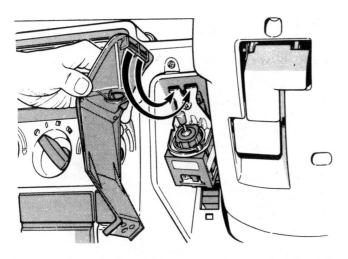

Fig. 11.106 Speaker joystick bezel removal (low series) (Sec 51)

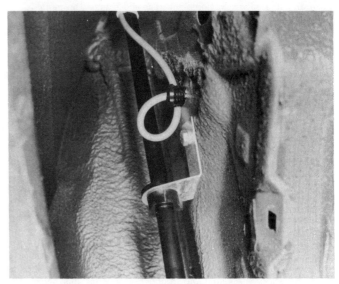

52.4 Wing-mounted aerial viewed from wing underside

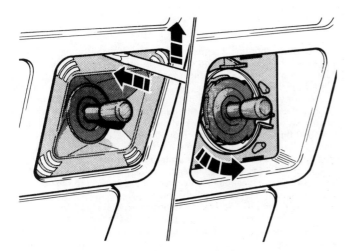

Fig. 11.107 Speaker joystick removal (low series) (Sec 51)

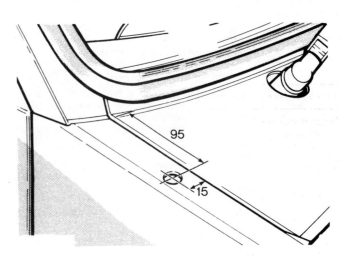

Fig. 11.108 Aerial location hole position in wing panel (Sec 52)

Dimensions shown in mm

52 Aerial – removal and refitting

1 Unclip and remove the lower insulating panel from the dash panel on the driver's side.

2 Reach up behind the radio and disconnect the aerial lead.

3 Detach and remove the dirt guard on the trailing edge under the front wing on the driver's side. To ease access, raise and support the front of the vehicle and remove the front roadwheels on that side.

4 Undo and remove the aerial mounting bracket bolt from the inner wing (photo).

5 Carefully pull the aerial lead down through the body panel, removing the grommet if necessary.

6 At the top end of the aerial, remove the collar securing nut, bezel and seal washer and withdraw the aerial.

7 Refitting is a reversal of the removal procedure. If a new wing panel has been fitted you will need to drill a 22 mm (0.87 in) aerial location hole in its top edge working to the dimensions shown in Fig. 11.108.

8 When refitting the aerial to an existing wing panel, clean any dirt away from the aerial location hole (de-rust if necessary) and, when the aerial is fitted, apply a suitable paint to protect any bare metal areas. Ensure that the grommet is secure when the lead is disconnected.

53 Radio equipment (non-standard) – interference-free installation

Aerials – selection and fitting

The choice of aerials is now very wide. It should be realised that the quality has a profound effect on radio performance, and a poor, inefficient aerial can make suppression difficult.

A wing-mounted aerial is regarded as probably the most efficient for signal collection, but a roof aerial is usually better for suppression purposes because it is away from most interference faults. Stick-on wire aerials are available for attachment to the inside of the windscreen, but are not always free from the interference field of the engine and some accessories.

Motorised automatic aerials rise when the equipment is switched on and retract at switch-off. They require more fitting space and supply leads, and can be a source of trouble.

There is no merit in choosing a very long aerial as, for example, the type about three metres in length which hooks or clips on to the rear of the car, since part of this aerial will inevitably be located in an interference field. For VHF/FM radios the best length of aerial is about one metre. Active aerials have a transistor amplifier mounted at the base and this serves to boost the received signal. The aerial rod is sometimes rather shorter than normal passive types.

A large loss of signal can occur in the aerial feeder cable, especially over the Very High Frequency (VHF) bands. The design of feeder cable is invariably in the co-axial form, ie a centre conductor surrounded by a flexible copper braid forming the outer (earth) conductor. Between the inner and outer conductors is an insulator material which can be in solid or stranded form. Apart from insulation, its purpose is to maintain the correct spacing and concentricity. Loss of signal occurs in this insulator, the loss usually being greater in a poor quality cable. The quality of cable used is reflected in the price of the aerial with the attached feeder cable.

The capacitance of the feeder should be within the range 65 to 75 picofarads (pF) approximately (95 to 100 pF for Japanese and American equipment), otherwise the adjustment of the car radio aerial trimmer may not be possible. An extension cable is necessary for a long run between aerial and receiver. If this adds capacitance in excess of the above limits, a connector containing a series capacitor will be required, or an extension which is labelled as 'capacity-compensated'.

Fitting the aerial will normally involve making a 22 mm (0.87 in) diameter hole in the bodywork, but read the instructions that come with the aerial kit. Once the hole position has been selected (see Fig. 11.108 for wing mounting position) use a centre punch to guide the drill. Use sticky masking tape around the area for this helps with marking out and drill location, and gives protection to the paintwork should the drill slip. Three methods of making the hole are in use:

(a) Use a hole saw in the electric drill. This is, in effect, a circular hacksaw blade wrapped around a former with a centre pilot drill.

(b) Use a tank cutter which also has cutting teeth, but is made to shear the metal by tightening with an Allen key.

(c) The hard way of drilling out the circle is using a small drill, say $\frac{1}{8}$ in (3 mm), so that the holes overlap. The centre metal drops out and the hole is finished with round and half-round files.

Whichever method is used, the burr is removed from the body metal and paint removed from the underside. The aerial is fitted tightly ensuring that the earth fixing, usually a serrated washer, ring or clamp, is making a solid connection. *This earth connection is important in reducing interference.* Cover any bare metal with primer paint and topcoat, and follow by underseal if desired.

Aerial feeder cable routing should avoid the engine compartment and areas where stress might occur, eg under the carpet where feet will be located. Roof aerials require that the headlining be pulled back and that a path is available down the door pillar. It is wise to check with the vehicle dealer whether roof aerial fitting is recommended.

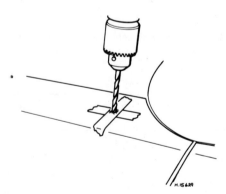

Fig. 11.109 Drilling the bodywork for aerial mounting (Sec 53)

Loudspeakers

Speakers should be matched to the output stage of the equipment, particularly as regards the recommended impedance. Power transistors used for driving speakers are sensitive to the loading placed on them.

Before choosing a mounting position for speakers, check whether the vehicle manufacturer has provided a location for them. Generally door-mounted speakers give good stereophonic reproduction.

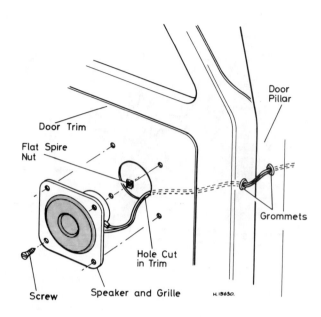

Fig. 11.110 Door-mounted speaker installation (Sec 53)

For door mounting, first remove the trim, which is often held on by 'poppers' or press studs, and then select a suitable gap in the inside door assembly. Check that the speaker would not obstruct glass or winder mechanism by winding the window up and down. A template is often provided for marking out the trim panel hole, and then the four fixing holes must be drilled through. Mark out with chalk and cut cleanly with a sharp knife or keyhole saw. Speaker leads are then threaded through the door and door pillar, if necessary drilling 10 mm diameter holes. Fit grommets in the holes and connect to the radio or tape unit correctly. Do not omit a waterproofing cover, usually supplied with door speakers. If the speaker has to be fixed into the metal of the door itself, use self-tapping screws, and if the fixing is to the door trim use self-tapping screws and flat spire nuts.

For rear-mounted speakers the best position is in the rear quarter panel. The speaker unit fitting is similar to that described for the door-mounted speaker. For trim panel removal and mounting position refer to Section 50.

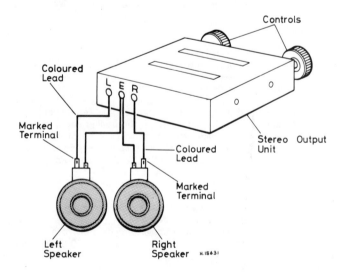

Fig. 11.111 Speaker connections must be correctly made (Sec 53)

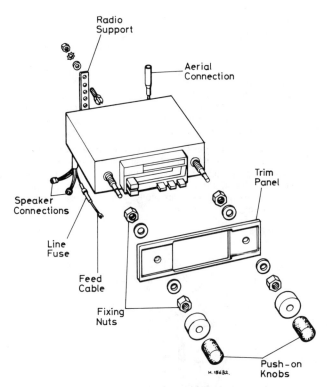

Fig. 11.112 Mounting component details for radio/cassette (Sec 53)

Unit installation

It is recommended that a standard sized receiver is purchased and fitted into the location provided in the facia panel or centre console.

A further mounting method is a three-sided cover in the form of a cradle which is obtainable from car radio dealers and this gives a professional appearance to the installation; in this case choose a position where the controls can be reached by a driver with his seat belt on.

Installation of the radio/audio unit is basically the same in all cases, and consists of offering it into the aperture after removal of the knobs (not push buttons) and the trim plate. In some cases a special mounting plate is required to which the unit is attached. It is worthwhile supporting the rear end in cases where sag or strain may occur, and it is usually possible to use a length of perforated metal strip attached between the unit and a good support point nearby. In general it is recommended that tape equipment should be installed at or nearly horizontal.

Connections to the aerial socket are simply by the standard plug terminating the aerial downlead or its extension cable. Speakers for a stereo system must be matched and correctly connected, as outlines previously.

Note: *While all work is carried out on the power side, it is wise to disconnect the battery earth lead. Beofre connection is made to the vehicle electrical system, check that the polarity of the unit is correct. Radio/audio units often have a reversible plug to convert the set to either + or − earth. Incorrect connection may cause serious damage.* With the Fiesta ensure that the unit is set for negative (−) earth.

The power lead is often permanently connected inside the unit and terminates with one half of an in-line fuse carrier. The other half is fitted with a suitable fuse (3 or 5 amperes) and a wire which should go to a power in the electrical system. This may be the accessory terminal on the ignition switch, giving the advantage of power feed with ignition or with the ignition key at the 'accessory' position. Power to the unit stops when the ignition key is removed. Alternatively, the lead may be taken to a live point at the fusebox with the consequence of having to remember to switch off at the unit before leaving the vehicle.

Before switching on for initial test, be sure that the speaker connections have been made, for running without load can damage the output transistors. Switch on next and tune through the bands to

ensure that all sections are working, and check the tape unit if applicable. The aerial trimmer should be adjusted to give the strongest reception on a weak signal in the medium wave band, at say 200 metres.

Interference

In general, when electric current changes abruptly, unwanted electrical noise is produced. The motor vehicle is filled with electrical devices which change electric current rapidly, the most obvious being the contact breaker.

When the spark plugs operate, the sudden pulse of spark current causes the associated wiring to radiate. Since early radio transmitters used sparks as a basis of operation, it is not surprising that the car radio will pick up ignition spark noise unless steps are taken to reduce it to acceptable levels.

Interference reaches the car radio in two ways:

(a) by conduction through the wiring
(b) by radiation to the receiving aerial

Initial checks presuppose that the bonnet is down and fastened, the radio unit has a good earth connection (not through the aerial downlead outer), no fluorescent tubes are working near the car, the aerial trimmer has been adjusted, and the vehicle is in a position to receive radio signals, ie not in a metal-clad building.

Switch on the radio and tune it to the middle of the medium wave (MW) band off-station with the volume (gain) control set fairly high. Switch on the ignition (but do not start the engine) and wait to see if irregular clicks or hash noise occurs. Tapping the facia panel may also produce the effects. If so, this will be due to the voltage stabiliser, which is an on-off thermal switch to control instrument voltage. It is located usually on the back of the instrument panel, often attached to the speedometer. Correction is by attachment of a capacitor and, if still troublesome, chokes in the supply wires.

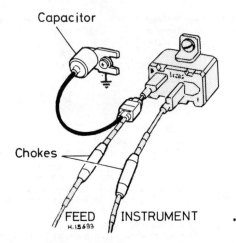

Fig. 11.113 Voltage stabilizer interference suppression (Sec 53)

Switch on the engine and listen for interference on the MW band. Depending on the type of interference, the indications are as follows.

A harsh crackle that drops out abruptly at low engine speed or when the headlights are switched on is probably due to a voltage regulator.

A whine varying with engine speed is due to the alternator. Try temporarily taking off the drivebelt − if the noise goes this is confirmation.

Regular ticking or crackle that varies in rate with the engine speed is due to the ignition system. With this trouble in particular and others in general, check to see if the noise is entering the receiver from the wiring or by radiation. To do this, pull out the aerial plug, (preferably shorting out the input socket or connecting a 62 pF capacitor across it). If the noise disappears it is coming in through the aerial and is *radiation noise*. If the noise persists it is reaching the receiver through the wiring and is said to be *line-borne*.

Interference from wipers, washers, heater blowers, turn-indicators, stop lamp, etc is usually taken to the receiver by wiring, and simple treatment using capacitors and possibly chokes will solve the problem. Switch on each one in turn (wet the screen first for running wipers!) and listen for possible interference with the aerial plug in place and again when removed.

Note that if most of the vehicle accessories are found to be creating interference all together, the probability is that poor aerial earthing is to blame.

Component terminal markings

Throughout the following sub-sections reference will be found to various terminal markings. These will vary depending on the manufacturer of the relevant component. If terminal markings differ from those mentioned, reference should be made to the following table, where the most commonly encountered variations are listed.

Alternator	Alternator terminal (thick lead)	Exciting winding terminal
DIN/Bosch	B+	DF
Delco Remy	+	EXC
Ducellier	+	EXC
Ford (US)	+	DF
Lucas	+	F
Marelli	+B	F

Ignition coil	Ignition switch terminal	Contact breaker terminal
DIN/Bosch	15	1
Delco Remy	+	–
Ducellier	BAT	RUP
Ford (US)	B/+	CB/–
Lucas	SW/+	–
Marelli	BAT/+B	D

Voltage regulator	Voltage input terminal	Exciting winding terminal
DIN/Bosch	B+/D+	DF
Delco Remy	BAT/+	EXC
Ducellier	BOB/BAT	EXC
Ford (US)	BAT	DF
Lucas	+/A	F
Marelli		F

Suppression methods – ignition

Suppressed HT cables are supplied as original equipment by manufacturers and will meet regulations as far as interference to neighbouring equipment is concerned. It is illegal to remove such suppression unless an alternative is provided, and this may take the form of resistive spark plug caps in conjunction with plain copper HT cable. For VHF purposes, these and 'in-line' resistors may not be effective, and resistive HT cable is preferred. Check that suppressed cables are actually fitted by observing cable. Identify lettering, or measuring with an ohmmeter – the value of each plug lead should be 5000 to 10 000 ohms.

A 1 microfarad capacitor connected from the LT supply side of the ignition coil to a good nearby earth point will complete basic ignition interference treatment. *NEVER fit a capacitor to the coil terminal to the contact breaker – the result would be burnt out points in a short time.*

If ignition noise persists despite the treatment above, the following sequence should be followed:

(a) Check the earthing of the ignition coil; remove paint from fixing clamp.

(b) If this does not work, lift the bonnet. Should there be no change in interference level, this may indicate that the bonnet is not electrically connected to the car body. Use a proprietary braided strap across a bonnet hinge ensuring a first class electrical connection. If, however, lifting the bonnet increases the interference, then fit resistive HT cables of a high ohms-per-metre value.

(c) If all these measures fail, it is probable that re-radiation from metallic components is taking place. Using a braided strap between metallic points, go round the vehicle systematically – try the following: engine to body, exhaust system to body,

front suspension to engine and to body, steering column to body, gear lever to engine and to body. Bowden cable to body, metal parcel shelf to body. When an offending component is located it should be bonded with the strap permanently.

(d) As a next step, the fitting of distributor suppressors to each lead at the distributor end may help.

(e) Beyond this point is involved the possible screening of the distributor and fitting resistive spark plugs, but such advanced treatment is not usually required for vehicles with entertainment equipment.

Electronic ignition systems have built-in suppression components, but this does not relieve the need for using suppressed HT leads. In some cases it is permitted to connect a capacitor on the low tension supply side of the ignition coil, but not in every case. Makers' instructions should be followed carefully, otherwise damage to the ignition semiconductors may result.

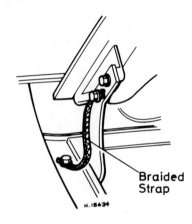

Fig. 11.114 Braided earth strap between bonnet and body (Sec 53)

Suppression methods – generators

Alternators should be fitted with a 3 microfarad capacitor from the B+ main output terminal (thick cable) to earth. Additional suppression may be obtained by the use of a filter in the supply line to the radio receiver.

It is most important that:

(a) *Capacitors are never connected to the field terminals of the alternator.*

(b) *Alternators must not be run without connection to the battery.*

Suppression methods – voltage regulators

All Fiesta variants are fitted with an alternator having a built-in voltage regulator.

Integral electronic voltage regulators do not normally generate much interference, but when encountered this is in combination with alternator noise. A 1 microfarad or 2 microfarad capacitor from the warning lamp (IND) terminal to earth for Lucas ACR alternators and Femsa, Delco and Bosch equivalents should cure the problem.

Suppression methods – other equipment

Wiper motors – Connect the wiper body to earth with a bonding strap. For all motors use a 7 ampere choke assembly inserted in the leads to the motor.

Heater motors – Fit 7 ampere line chokes in both leads, assisted if necessary by a 1 microfarad capacitor to earth from both leads.

Electronic tachometer – The tachometer is a possible source of ignition noise – check by disconnecting at the ignition coil CB terminal. It usually feeds from ignition coil LT pulses at the contact breaker terminal. A 3 ampere line choke should be fitted in the tachometer lead at the coil CB terminal.

Horn – A capacitor and choke combination is effective if the horn is directly connected to the 12 volt supply. The use of a relay is an

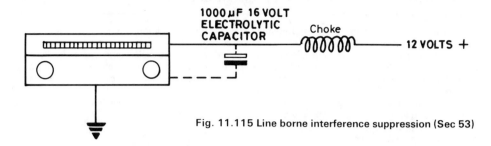

Fig. 11.115 Line borne interference suppression (Sec 53)

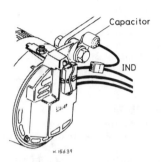

Fig. 11.116 Suppression of interference from electronic voltage regulator when integral with alternator (Sec 53)

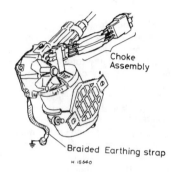

Fig. 11.117 Wiper motor suppression (Sec 53)

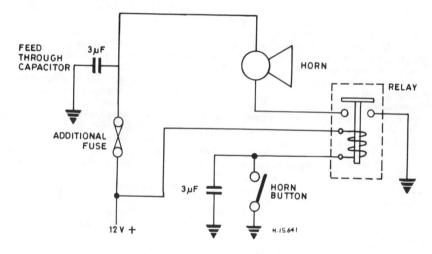

Fig. 11.118 Use of relay to reduce horn interference (Sec 53)

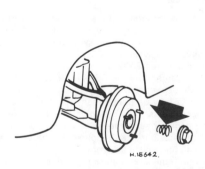

Fig. 11.119 Use of spring contacts at wheels (Sec 53)

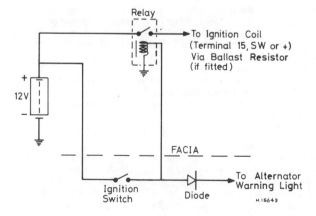

Fig. 11.120 Use of ignition coil relay to suppress case breakthrough (Sec 53)

alternative remedy, as this will reduce the length of the interference-carrying leads.

Electrostatic noise – Characteristics are erratic crackling at the receiver, with disappearance of symptoms in wet weather. Often shocks may be given when touching bodywork. Part of the problem is the build-up of static electricity in non-driven wheels and the acquisition of charge on the body shell. It is possible to fit spring-loaded contacts at the wheels to give good conduction between the rotary wheel parts and the vehicle frame. Changing a tyre sometimes helps – because of tyres' varying resistances. In difficult cases a trailing flex which touches the ground will cure the problem. If this is not acceptable it is worth trying conductive paint on the tyre walls.

Radio/cassette breakthrough

Magnetic radiator from dashboard wiring may be sufficiently intense to break through the metal case of the radio/cassette player. Often this is due to a particular cable routed too close and shows up as ignition interference on AM and cassette play and/or alternator whine on cassette play.

The first point to check is that the clips and/or screws are fixing all parts of the radio/cassette case together properly. Assuming good earthing of the case, see if it is possible to re-route the offending cable – the chances of this are not good, however, in most cars.

Next release the radio/cassette player and locate it in different positions with temporary leads. If a point of low interference is found, then if possible fix the equipment in that area. This also confirms that local radiation is causing the trouble. If re-location is not feasible, fit the radio/cassette player back in the original position.

Alternator interference on cassette play is now caused by radiation from the main charging cable which goes from the battery to the output terminal of the alternator, usually via the + terminal of the starter motor relay. In some vehicles this cable is routed under the dashboard, so the solution is to provide a direct cable route. Detach the original cable from the alternator output terminal and make up a new cable of a least 6 mm² cross-sectional area to go from alternator to battery with the shortest possible route. *Remember – do not run the engine with the alternator disconnected from the battery.*

Ignition breakthrough on AM and/or cassette play can be a difficult problem. It is worth wrapping earthed foil round the offending cable run near the equipment, or making up a deflector plate well screwed down to a good earth. Another possibility is the use of a suitable relay to switch on the ignition coil. The relay should be mounted close to the ignition coil; with this arrangement the ignition coil primary circuit is not taken into the dashboard area and does not flow through the ignition switch. A suitable diode should be used since it is possible that at ignition switch-off the output from the warning lamp alternator terminal could hold the relay on.

Connectors for suppression components

Capacitors are usually supplied with tags on the end of the lead, while the capacitor body has a flange with a slot or hole to fit under a nut or screw with washer.

Connections to feed wires are best achieved by self-stripping connectors. These connectors employ a blade which, when squeezed down by pliers, cuts through cable insulation and makes connection to the copper conductors beneath.

Chokes sometimes come with bullet snap-in connectors fitted to the wires, and also with just bare copper wire. With connectors, suitable female cable connectors may be purchased from an auto-accessory shop together with any extra connections required for the cable ends after being cut for the choke insertion. For chokes with bare wires, similar connectors may be employed together with insulation sleeving as required.

VHF/FM broadcasts

Reception of VHF/FM in an automobile is more prone to problems than the medium and long wavebands. Medium/long wave transmitters are capable of covering considerable distances, but VHF transmitters are restricted to line of sight, meaning ranges of 10 to 50 miles, depending upon the terrain, the effects of buildings and the transmitter power.

Because of the limited range it is necessary to retune on a long journey, and it may be better for those habitually travelling long distances or living in areas of poor provision of transmitters to use an AM radio working on medium/long wavebands.

When conditions are poor, interference can arise, and some of the suppression devices described previously fall off in performance at very high frequencies unless specifically designed for the VHF band. Available suppression devices include reactive HT cable, resistive distributor caps, screened plug caps, screened leads and resistive spark plugs.

For VHF/FM receiver installation the following points should be particularly noted:

(a) Earthing of the receiver chassis and the aerial mounting is important. Use a separate earthing wire at the radio, and scrape paint away at the aerial mounting.

(b) If possible, use a good quality roof aerial to obtain maximum height and distance from interference generating devices on the vehicle.

(c) Use of a high quality aerial download is important, since losses in cheap cable can be significant.

(d) The polarisation of FM transmissions may be horizontal, vertical, circular or slanted. Because of this the optimum mounting angle is at 45° to the vehicle roof.

Citizens' Band radio (CB)

In the UK, CB transmitter/receivers work within the 27 MHz and 934 MHz bands, using the FM mode. At present interest is concentrated on 27 MHz where the design and manufacture of equipment is less difficult. Maximum transmitted power is 4 watts, and 40 channels spaced 10 kHz apart within the range 27.60125 to 27.99125 MHz are available.

Aerials are the key to effective transmission and reception. Regulations limit the aerial length to 1.65 metres including the loading coil and any associated circuitry, so tuning the aerial is necessary to obtain optimum results. The choice of a CB aerial is dependent on whether it is to be permanently installed or removable, and the performance will hinge on correct tuning and the location point on the vehicle. Common practice is to clip the aerial to the roof gutter or to employ wing mounting where the aerial can be rapidly unscrewed. An alternative is to use the boot rim to render the aerial theftproof, but a popular solution is to use the 'magmount' – a type of mounting having a strong magnetic base clamping to the vehicle at any point, usually the roof.

Aerial location determines the signal distribution for both transmission and reception, but it is wise to choose a point away from the engine compartment to minimise interference from vehicle electrical equipment.

The aerial is subject to considerable wind and acceleration forces. Cheaper units will whip backwards and forwards and in so doing will alter the relationship with the metal surface of the vehicle with which it forms a ground plane aerial system. The radiation pattern will change correspondingly, giving rise to break-up of both incoming and outgoing signals.

Interference problems on the vehicle carrying CB equipment fall into two categories:

(a) Interference to nearby TV and radio receivers when transmitting.

(b) Interference to CB set reception due to electrical equipment on the vehicle.

Problems of break-through to TV and radio are not frequent, but can be difficult to solve. Mostly trouble is not detected or reported because the vehicle is moving and the symptoms rapidly disappear at the TV/radio receiver, but when the CB set is used as a base station any trouble with nearby receivers will soon result in a complaint.

It must not be assumed by the CB operator that his equipment is faultless, for much depends upon the design. Harmonics (that is, multiples) of 27 MHz may be transmitted unknowingly and these can fall into other user's bands. Where trouble of this nature occurs, low pass filters in the aerial or supply leads can help, and should be fitted in base station aerials as a matter of course. In stubborn cases it may be necessary to call for assistance from the licensing authority, or, if possible, to have the equipment checked by the manufacturers.

Interference received on the CB set from the vehicle equipment is, fortunately, not usually a severe problem. The precautions outlined previously for radio/cassette units apply, but there are some extra points worth noting.

It is common practice to use a slide-mount on CB equipment enabling the set to be easily removed for use as a base station, for example. Care must be taken that the slide mount fittings are properly earthed and that first class connection occurs between the set and slide-mount.

Vehicle manufacturers in the UK are required to provide suppression of electrical equipment to cover 40 to 250 MHz to protect TV and VHF radio bands. Such suppression appears to be adequately effective at 27 MHz, but suppression of individual items such as alternators, clocks, stabilisers, flashers, wiper motors, etc, may still be necessary. The suppression capacitors and chokes available from auto-electrical suppliers for entertainment receivers will usually give the required results with CB equipment.

Other vehicle radio transmitters

Besides CB radio already mentioned, a considerable increase in the use of transceivers (ie combined transmitter and receiver units) has taken place in the last decade. Previously this type of equipment was fitted mainly to military, fire, ambulance and police vehicles, but a large business radio and radio telephone usage has developed.

Generally the suppression techniques described previously will suffice, with only a few difficult cases arising. Suppression is carried out to satisfy the 'receive mode', but care must be taken to use heavy duty chokes in the equipment supply cables since the loading on 'transmit' is relatively high.

54 Fault diagnosis – electrical system

Symptom	Reason(s)
Starter fails to turn engine	Battery discharged Battery defective internally Leads loose, or terminals corroded Loose connections at starter motor Engine earth strap loose, broken or missing Starter motor faulty or solenoid not functioning Starter motor brushes worn Commutator dirty or worn Starter motor armature faulty Field coils earthed
Starter turns engine very slowly	Battery in discharged condition Starter brushes badly worn, sticking or brush wires loose Loose wires in starter motor circuit
Starter spins but does not turn engine	Pinion or flywheel gear teeth broken or worn Battery discharged
Starter motor noisy or excessively rough engagement	Pinion or flywheel gear teeth broken or worn Starter motor retaining bolts loose
Battery will not hold charge for more than a few days	Battery defective, internally Electrolyte level too low or electrolyte too weak due to leakage Plate separators no longer fully effective Battery plates severely sulphated Alternator drivebelt slipping Battery terminal connections loose or corroded Alternator not charging Short-circuit causing continual battery drain Integral regulator unit not working correctly
Ignition light fails to go out, battery runs flat in a few days	Alternator drivebelt loose and slipping or broken Alternator brushes worn, sticking, broken or dirty Alternator brush springs weak or broken Internal fault in alternator

Failure of individual electrical equipment to function correctly is dealt with under the headings listed below

Horn

Horn operates all the time	Horn push either earthed or stuck down Horn cable to horn push earthed
Horns fails to operate	Blown fuse Cable or cable connection loose, broken or disconnected Horn has an internal fault
Horn emits intermittent or unsatisfactory noise	Cable connections loose Horn incorrectly adjusted

Lights

Lights do not come on	If engine not running, battery discharged Wire connections loose, disconnected or broken Light switch shorting or otherwise faulty Light bulb filament burnt out or bulbs broken
Lights give very poor illumination	Lamp glasses dirty Lamps badly out of adjustment

Symptom	Reason(s)
Lights work erratically – flashing on and off, especially over bumps	Battery terminals or earth connection loose Lights not earthing properly Contacts in light switch faulty

Wipers

Symptom	Reason(s)
Wiper motor fails to work	Blown fuse Wire connections loose, disconnected or broken Brushes badly worn Armature worn or faulty Field coils faulty
Wiper motor works very slowly and takes excessive current	Commutator dirty, greasy or burnt Armature bearings dirty or unaligned Armature badly worn or faulty
Wiper motor works slowly, takes little current	Brushes badly worn Commutator dirty, greasy or burnt Armature badly worn or faulty
Wiper motor works, but blades remain static	Wiper motor gearbox or linkages badly worn

Chapter 12 Bodywork and fittings

Contents

Body adhesive emblems – removal and refitting	40
Body side mouldings – removal and refitting	41
Bonnet – removal and refitting	5
Bonnet lock – removal and refitting	7
Bonnet release cable – removal and refitting	6
Bumpers – removal and refitting	29
Door – removal and refitting	21
Door exterior handle – removal and refitting	20
Door latch unit – removal and refitting	17
Door lock – removal and refitting	16
Door mirror and glass – removal and refitting	14
Door quarter window (fixed) – removal and refitting	22
Door quarter window (opening) – removal and refitting	23
Door remote control handle – removal and refitting	18
Door striker plate – removal, refitting and adjustment	19
Door trim panel – removal and refitting	15
Door window – removal and refitting	24
Door window regulator – removal and refitting	25
Facia crash padding and vents – removal and refitting	33
Front and rear wheel arch spoilers – removal and refitting	32
Front quarter bumpers – removal and refitting	30
General description	1
Interior mirror – removal and refitting	26
Maintenance – bodywork and underframe	2
Maintenance – upholstery and carpets	3
Minor body damage – repair	4
Radiator grille – removal and refitting	8
Rear wheel and cover – removal and refitting	39
Seat belts – maintenance, removal and refitting	37
Seats – removal and refitting	38
Sill panel moulding – removal and refitting	43
Spoiler (front) – removal and refitting	31
Sunroof handle bracket – removal and refitting	35
Sunroof hinge retainer – removal and refitting	36
Sunroof panel – removal and refitting	34
Tailgate – removal and refitting	9
Tailgate and fixed rear quarter window – removal and refitting ...	28
Tailgate aperture mouldings – removal and refitting	42
Tailgate latch – removal and refitting	11
Tailgate lock barrel – removal and refitting	10
Tailgate striker – removal and refitting	12
Tailgate strut (damper unit) – removal and refitting	13
Windscreen – removal and refitting	27

Specifications

For details of sizes and weights refer to the introductory sections at start of this manual

Torque wrench settings

	Nm	lbf ft
All seat belt anchor bolts	29 to 41	21 to 30
Front belt stalk-to-seat frame screws	25 to 30	18 to 22
Bumper retaining nuts	11 to 13	8 to 10

1 General description

The body is of a monocoque all-steel, welded construction with impact absorbing front and rear sections.

The vehicle has two side doors and a full-length lifting tailgate for easy access to the rear compartment. The side doors are fitted with antiburst locks and incorporate a key-operated lock; window frames are adjustable for position. The tailgate hinges are bolted to the underside of the roof panel and welded to the tailgate. Gas-filled dampers support the tailgate in the open position; when closed it is fastened by a key-operated lock.

Wrap-around polycarbonate bumpers are fitted front and rear, and further body protection is given by side mouldings which are also manufactured in this material.

Rust and corrosion protection is applied to all new vehicles and includes zinc phosphate dipping and wax injection of the box sections and door interiors.

All body panels are welded, including the front wings, so it is recommended that major body damage repairs are left to your dealer.

All vehicles have individual reclining front bucket seats, which tip forward for rear seat access after operating a safety catch. The rear seat back on all models tips forward for increased luggage carrying capacity.

2 Maintenance – bodywork and underframe

The general condition of a vehicle's bodywork is the one thing that significantly affects its value. Maintenance is easy but needs to be regular. Neglect, particularly after minor damage, can lead quickly to further deterioration and costly repair bills. It is important also to keep watch on those parts of the vehicle not immediately visible, for instance the underside, inside all the wheel arches and the lower part of the engine compartment.

The basic maintenance routine for the bodywork is washing – preferably with a lot of water, from a hose. This will remove all the loose solids which may have stuck to the vehicle. It is important to flush these off in such a way as to prevent grit from scratching the finish. The wheel arches and underframe need washing in the same way to remove any accumulated mud which will retain moisture and tend to encourage rust. Paradoxically enough, the best time to clean the underframe and wheel arches is in wet weather when the mud is thoroughly wet and soft. In very wet weather the underframe is usually cleaned of large accumulations automatically and this is a good time for inspection.

Periodically, except on vehicles with a wax-based underbody protective coat, it is a good idea to have the whole of the underframe of the vehicle steam cleaned, engine compartment included, so that a thorough inspection can be carried out to see what minor repairs and renovations are necessary. Steam cleaning is available at many garages and is necessary for removal of the accumulation of oily grime which sometimes is allowed to become thick in certain areas. If steam cleaning facilities are not available, there are one or two excellent grease solvents available which can be brush applied. The dirt can then be simply hosed off. Note that these methods should not be used on vehicles with wax-based underbody protective coating or the coating will be removed. Such vehicles should be inspected annually, preferably just prior to winter, when the underbody should be washed down and any damage to the wax coating repaired. Ideally, a completely fresh coat should be applied. It would also be worth considering the use of such wax-based protection for injection into door panels, sills, box sections etc, as an additional safeguard against rust damage.

After washing paintwork, wipe off with a chamois leather to give an unspotted clear finish. A coat of clear protective wax polish will give added protection against chemical pollutants in the air. If the paintwork sheen has dulled or oxidised, use a cleaner/polisher combination to restore the brilliance of the shine. This requires a little effort, but such dulling is usually caused because regular washing has been neglected. Care needs to be taken with metallic paintwork, as special non-abrasive cleaner/polisher is required to avoid damage to the finish. Always check that the door and ventilator opening drain holes and pipes are completely clear so that water can be drained out (photo). Bright work should be treated in the same way as paintwork. Windscreens and windows can be kept clear of the smeary film which often appears by the use of a proprietary glass cleaner. Never use any form of wax or other body or chromium polish on glass.

2.4 Keep drain holes clear

3 Maintenance – upholstery and carpets

Mats and carpets should be brushed or vacuum cleaned regularly to keep them free of grit. If they are badly stained remove them from the vehicle for scrubbing or sponging and make quite sure they are dry before refitting. Seats and interior trim panels can be kept clean by wiping with a damp cloth. If they do become stained (which can be more apparent on light coloured upholstery) use a little liquid detergent and a soft nail brush to scour the grime out of the grain of the material. Do not forget to keep the headlining clean in the same way as the upholstery. When using liquid cleaners inside the vehicle do not over-wet the surfaces being cleaned. Excessive damp could get into the seams and padded interior causing stains, offensive odours or even rot. If the inside of the vehicle gets wet accidentally it is worthwhile taking some trouble to dry it out properly, particularly where carpets are involved. *Do not leave oil or electric heaters inside the vehicle for this purpose.*

4 Minor body damage – repair

The photographic sequences on pages 262 and 263 illustrate the operations detailed in the following sub-sections.

Repair of minor scratches in bodywork

If the scratch is very superficial, and does not penetrate to the metal of the bodywork, repair is very simple. Lightly rub the area of the scratch with a paintwork renovator, or a very fine cutting paste, to remove loose paint from the scratch and to clear the surrounding bodywork of wax polish. Rinse the area with clean water.

Apply touch-up paint to the scratch using a fine paint brush; continue to apply fine layers of paint until the surface of the paint in the scratch is level with the surrounding paintwork. Allow the new paint at least two weeks to harden: then blend it into the surrounding paintwork by rubbing the scratch area with a paintwork renovator or a very fine cutting paste. Finally, apply wax polish.

Where the scratch has penetrated right through to the metal of the bodywork, causing the metal to rust, a different repair technique is required. Remove any loose rust from the bottom of the scratch with a penknife, then apply rust inhibiting paint to prevent the formation of rust in the future. Using a rubber or nylon applicator fill the scratch with bodystopper paste. If required, this paste can be mixed with cellulose thinners to provide a very thin paste which is ideal for filling narrow scratches. Before the stopper-paste in the scratch hardens, wrap a piece of smooth cotton rag around the top of a finger. Dip the finger in cellulose thinners and then quickly sweep it across the surface of the stopper-paste in the scratch; this will ensure that the surface of the stopper-paste is slightly hollowed. The scratch can now be painted over as described earlier in this Section.

Repair of dents in bodywork

When deep denting of the vehicle's bodywork has taken place, the first task is to pull the dent out, until the affected bodywork almost attains its original shape. There is little point in trying to restore the original shape completely, as the metal in the damaged area will have stretched on impact and cannot be reshaped fully to its original contour. It is better to bring the level of the dent up to a point which is about $\frac{1}{8}$ in (3 mm) below the level of the surrounding bodywork. In cases where the dent is very shallow anyway, it is not worth trying to pull it out at all. If the underside of the dent is accessible, it can be hammered out gently from behind, using a mallet with a wooden or plastic head. Whilst doing this, hold a suitable block of wood firmly against the outside of the panel to absorb the impact from the hammer blows and thus prevent a large area of the bodywork from being 'belled-out'.

Should the dent be in a section of the bodywork which has a double skin or some other factor making it inaccessible from behind, a different technique is called for. Drill several small holes through the metal inside the area – particularly in the deeper section. Then screw long self-tapping screws into the holes just sufficiently for them to gain a good purchase in the metal. Now the dent can be pulled out by pulling on the protruding heads of the screws with a pair of pliers.

The next stage of the repair is the removal of the paint from the damaged area, and from an inch or so of the surrounding 'sound' bodywork. This is accomplished most easily by using a wire brush or abrasive pad on a power drill, although it can be done just as effectively by hand using sheets of abrasive paper. To complete the preparation for filling, score the surface of the bare metal with a screwdriver or the tang of a file, or alternatively, drill small holes in the affected area. This will provide a really good 'key' for the filler paste.

To complete the repair see the Section on filling and re-spraying.

Repair of rust holes or gashes in bodywork

Remove all paint from the affected area and from an inch or so of the surrounding 'sound' bodywork, using an abrasive pad or a wire brush on a power drill. If these are not available a few sheets of abrasive paper will do the job just as effectively. With the paint removed you will be able to gauge the severity of the corrosion and therefore decide whether to renew the whole panel (if this is possible) or to repair the affected area. New body panels are not as expensive as most people think and it is often quicker and more satisfactory to fit a new panel than to attempt to repair large areas of corrosion.

Remove all fittings from the affected area except those which will act as a guide to the original shape of the damaged bodywork (eg headlamp shells etc). Then, using tin snips or a hacksaw blade, remove all loose metal and any other metal badly affected by corrosion. Hammer the edges of the hole inwards in order to create a slight depression for the filler paste.

Wire brush the affected area to remove the powdery rust from the surface of the remaining metal. Paint the affected area with rust inhibiting paint; if the back of the rusted area is accessible treat this also.

Before filling can take place it will be necessary to block the hole in some way. This can be achieved by the use of aluminium or plastic mesh, or aluminium tape.

Aluminium or plastic mesh is probably the best material to use for a large hole. Cut a piece to the approximate size and shape of the hole to be filled, then position it in the hole so that its edges are below the level of the surrounding bodywork. It can be retained in position by several blobs of filler paste around its periphery.

Aluminium tape should be used for small or very narrow holes. Pull a piece off the roll and trim it to the approximate size and shape required, then pull off the backing paper (if used) and stick the tape over the hole; it can be overlapped if the thickness of one piece is insufficient. Burnish down the edges of the tape with the handle of a screwdriver or similar, to ensure that the tape is securely attached to the metal underneath.

Bodywork repairs – filling and re-spraying

Before using this Section, see the Sections on dent, deep scratch, rust holes and gash repairs.

Many types of bodyfiller are available, but generally speaking those proprietary kits which contain a tin of filler paste and a tube of resin hardener are best for this type of repair. A wide, flexible plastic or nylon applicator will be found invaluable for imparting a smooth and well contoured finish to the surface of the filler.

Mix up a little filler on a clean piece of card or board – measure the hardener carefully (follow the maker's instructions on the pack) otherwise the filler will set too rapidly or too slowly.

Using the applicator apply the filler paste to the prepared area; draw the applicator across the surface of the filler to achieve the correct contour and to level the filler surface. As soon as a contour that approximates to the correct one is achieved, stop working the paste – if you carry on too long the paste will become sticky and begin to 'pick up' on the applicator. Continue to add thin layers of filler paste at twenty-minute intervals until the level of the filler is just proud of the surrounding bodywork.

Once the filler has hardened, excess can be removed using a metal plane or file. From then on, progressively finer grades of abrasive paper should be used, starting with a 40 grade production paper and finishing with 400 grade wet-and-dry paper. Always wrap the abrasive paper around a flat rubber, cork, or wooden block – otherwise the surface of the filler will not be completely flat. During the smoothing of the filler surface the wet-and-dry paper should be periodically rinsed in water. This will ensure that a very smooth finish is imparted to the filler at the final stage.

At this stage the 'dent' should be surrounded by a ring of bare metal, which in turn should be encircled by the finely 'feathered' edge of the good paintwork. Rinse the repair area with clean water, until all of the dust produced by the rubbing-down operation has gone.

Spray the whole repair area with a light coat of primer – this will show up any imperfections in the surface of the filler. Repair these imperfections with fresh paste or bodystopper, and once more smooth the surface with abrasive paper. If bodystopper is used, it can be mixed with cellulose thinners to form a really thin paste which is ideal for filling small holes. Repeat this spray and repair procedure until you are satisfied that the surface of the filler, and the feathered edge of the paintwork are perfect. Clean the repair area with clean water and allow to dry fully.

The repair area is now ready for final spraying. Paint spraying must be carried out in a warm, dry, windless and dust free atmosphere. This condition can be created artificially if you have access to a large indoor working area, but if you are forced to work in the open, you will have to pick your day very carefully. If you are working indoors, dousing the floor in the work area with water will help to settle the dust which would otherwise be in the atmosphere. If the repair area is confined to one body panel, mask off the surrounding panels; this will help to minimise the effects of a slight mis-match in paint colours. Bodywork fittings (eg chrome strips, door handles etc) will also need to be

masked off. Use genuine masking tape and several thicknesses of newspaper for the masking operations.

Before commencing to spray, agitate the aerosol can thoroughly, then spray a test area (an old tin, or similar) until the technique is mastered. Cover the repair area with a thick coat of primer; the thickness should be built up using several thin layers of paint rather than one thick one. Using 400 grade wet-and-dry paper, rub down the surface of the primer until it is really smooth. While doing this, the work area should be thoroughly doused with water, and the wet-and-dry paper periodically rinsed in water. Allow to dry before spraying on more paint.

Spray on the top coat, again building up the thickness by using several thin layers of paint. Start spraying in the centre of the repair area and then, using a circular motion, work outwards until the whole repair area and about 2 inches of the surrounding original paintwork is covered. Remove all masking material 10 to 15 minutes after spraying on the final coat of paint.

Allow the new paint at least two weeks to harden, then, using a paintwork renovator or a very fine cutting paste, blend the edges of the paint into the existing paintwork. Finally, apply wax polish.

Major damage

Where damage or corrosion has affected any welded or structural part of the vehicle, repair should be left to your dealer or a body builder having the necessary alignment jigs which are essential for safe and satisfactory repair of this range of Fiestas.

---

5 Bonnet – removal and refitting

1 Open the bonnet and support it by using a prop or have an assistant hold it.
2 Undo and remove the bolt which secures the stay at one end.
3 Grip each end of the radiator grille and pull it upwards to detach it from its lower support (Figure 12.2) then withdraw it and disconnect it from the three top fasteners.
4 Mark an outline around the hinge plates to aid realignment of the bonnet when refitting it, then undo the four hinge bolts and lift the bonnet clear.
5 Refit by reversing the removal operations. If a new bonnet is being installed, position it so that an equal gap is provided at each side when it is being closed.
6 The bonnet should close smoothly and positively without excessive pressure. If it does not, carry out the following adjustment.
7 Loosen the bolts retaining the bonnet lock unit on the bulkhead plenum chamber cover, then locate the bonnet so that the clearance between it and the cowl panel is as shown in Fig. 12.3. Align the bonnet so that the gap between it and the wing panels is even and set at the clearance shown.
8 Lower or raise the lock unit so that the bonnet is level with the cowl panel and wings. Tighten the securing bolts and recheck bonnet alignment and release unit for satisfactory operation.

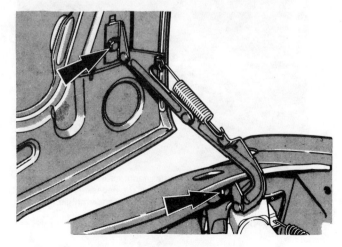

Fig. 12.1 Bonnet stay retaining bolts (arrowed) (Sec 5)

This sequence of photographs deals with the repair of the dent and paintwork damage shown in this photo. The procedure will be similar for the repair of a hole. It should be noted that the procedures given here are simplified — more explicit instructions will be found in the text

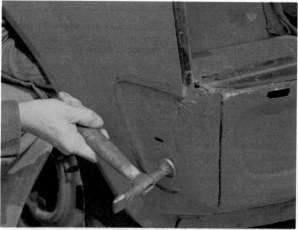

In the case of a dent the first job — after removing surrounding trim — is to hammer out the dent where access is possible. This will minimise filling. Here, the large dent having been hammered out, the damaged area is being made slightly concave

Now all paint must be removed from the damaged area, by rubbing with coarse abrasive paper. Alternatively, a wire brush or abrasive pad can be used in a power drill. Where the repair area meets good paintwork, the edge of the paintwork should be 'feathered', using a finer grade of abrasive paper

In the case of a hole caused by rusting, all damaged sheet-metal should be cut away before proceeding to this stage. Here, the damaged area is being treated with rust remover and inhibitor before being filled

Mix the body filler according to its manufacturer's instructions. In the case of corrosion damage, it will be necessary to block off any large holes before filling — this can be done with aluminium or plastic mesh, or aluminium tape. Make sure the area is absolutely clean before ...

... applying the filler. Filler should be applied with a flexible applicator, as shown, for best results; the wooden spatula being used for confined areas. Apply thin layers of filler at 20-minute intervals, until the surface of the filler is slightly proud of the surrounding bodywork

Initial shaping can be done with a Surform plane or Dreadnought file. Then, using progressively finer grades of wet-and-dry paper, wrapped around a sanding block, and copious amounts of clean water, rub down the filler until really smooth and flat. Again, feather the edges of adjoining paintwork

The whole repair area can now be sprayed or brush-painted with primer. If spraying, ensure adjoining areas are protected from over-spray. Note that at least one inch of the surrounding sound paintwork should be coated with primer. Primer has a 'thick' consistency, so will find small imperfections

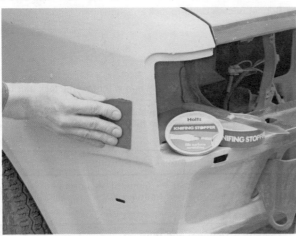

Again, using plenty of water, rub down the primer with a fine grade wet-and-dry paper (400 grade is probably best) until it is really smooth and well blended into the surrounding paintwork. Any remaining imperfections can now be filled by carefully applied knifing stopper paste

When the stopper has hardened, rub down the repair area again before applying the final coat of primer. Before rubbing down this last coat of primer, ensure the repair area is blemish-free — use more stopper if necessary. To ensure that the surface of the primer is really smooth use some finishing compound

The top coat can now be applied. When working out of doors, pick a dry, warm and wind-free day. Ensure surrounding areas are protected from over-spray. Agitate the aerosol thoroughly, then spray the centre of the repair area, working outwards with a circular motion. Apply the paint as several thin coats

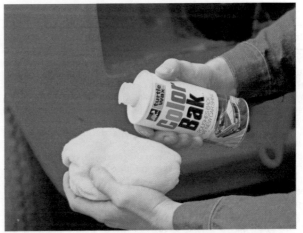

After a period of about two weeks, which the paint needs to harden fully, the surface of the repaired area can be 'cut' with a mild cutting compound prior to wax polishing. When carrying out bodywork repairs, remember that the quality of the finished job is proportional to the time and effort expended

Fig. 12.2 Radiator grille removal: pull up (A), pull out (B) and then swing the grille downwards (Sec 5)

6.3 Bonnet release cable-to-lock attachment

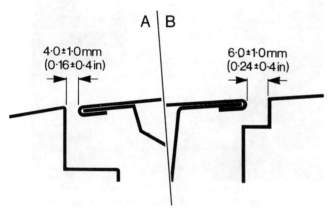

Fig. 12.3 Bonnet surround clearance to wing (A) and to the cowl panel (B) (Sec 5)

3   Undo the two retaining bolts and withdraw the lock unit from the plenum chamber cover plate.
4   Refit by reversing the removal procedure. If necessary adjust the position of the lock unit prior to fully tightening the retaining bolts.

8   Radiator grille – removal and refitting

The radiator grille can be removed as described in Section 5, paragraph 3 of this Chapter. Refitting is the reversal of removal.

9   Tailgate – removal and refitting

1   Open the tailgate fully and disconnect the leads from the heated rear window and the wiper (where fitted).
2   From the top edge of the tailgate aperture, remove the weatherstrip and then peel back the headlining.
3   With an assistant supporting the tailgate, unbolt and remove the struts. The strut balljoint is released by prising out the small plastic peg.

6   Bonnet release cable – removal and refitting

1   Working inside the vehicle, extract the three screws and remove the steering column shroud. Open the bonnet. Releasing the bonnet when the cable is broken is not easy: support the car securely on safety stands or ramps (a pit would make the job less hard). Reach up between the bulkhead and remove the bolts securing the lock unit to the plenum chamber cover plate. The bonnet should be free to lift.
2   Draw the cable sideways and disengage the inner cable nipple from the release lever.
3   On the engine compartment side of the bulkhead, detach the cable grommet from the location bracket on the bonnet lock unit, and disconnect the cable from the lock (photo).
4   Withdraw the cable through the bulkhead and into the car interior for removal.
5   Refitting is a reversal of the removal procedure. On completion check the operation of the release mechanism before shutting the bonnet and again afterwards.

7   Bonnet lock – removal and refitting

1   Open and support the bonnet.
2   Detach the cable grommet from the location bracket on the lock unit and disconnect the cable from the lock.

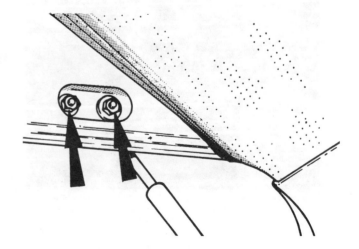

Fig. 12.4 Tailgate hinge retaining nuts (arrowed) (Sec 9)

4   Make an outline marking around the hinge mounting positions to provide an alignment guide when refitting the tailgate.
5   Unscrew the hinge nuts, remove them with the washers and lift the tailgate from the vehicle.
6   The tailgate lock and (if fitted) the wiper motor are accessible for removal once the trim panel has been released from its securing clips.
7   Refitting is a reversal of removal, but do not fully tighten the hinge screws until the tailgate has been adjusted to give an equal gap all round (Fig. 12.5).

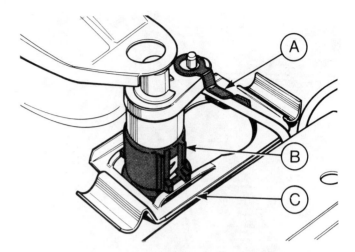

Fig. 12.6 Tailgate lock barrel clip (A), cylinder (B) and retainer (C) (Sec 10)

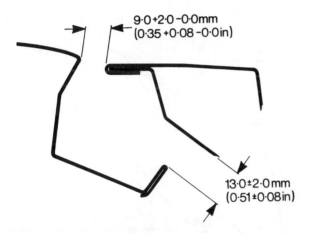

Fig. 12.5 Tailgate-to-roof alignment clearance and to weatherstrip flange (Sec 9)

10 Tailgate lock barrel – removal and refitting

1   Open and support the tailgate.
2   Unclip and detach the tailgate trim panel.
3   Unclip and detach the rod from the plastic lever (Fig. 12.6).
4   Slide the lock retainer along so that its exposed large aperture aligns with the lock barrel, then remove the retainer and extract the lock unit and pad from the tailgate.
5   Refitting is a reversal of the removal procedure.

11 Tailgate latch – removal and refitting

1   Proceed as described in paragraphs 1 to 3 in the previous Section.
2   Undo the three screws and remove the latch unit, together with the lever and rod (Fig. 12.7).
3   Refit reversing the removal procedure. Check that the latch is fitted so that the rod and lever are in alignment with the end of the lock barrel.

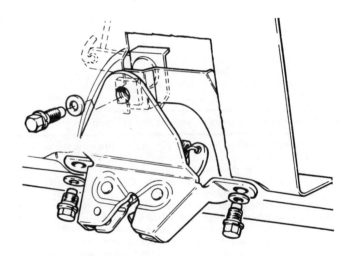

Fig. 12.7 Tailgate latch and securing bolts (Sec 11)

12 Tailgate striker – removal and refitting

1   Open and support the tailgate.
2   Make an outline marking around the striker to provide an alignment guide when refitting it.
3   Undo the two retaining bolts and remove them, together with the washers, then withdraw the striker.
4   Refit in the reverse order to removal. Check that the striker is correctly aligned with the previously made outline marking before fully tightening the retaining bolts.

13 Tailgate strut (damper unit) – removal and refitting

1   Open the tailgate and support it with a prop or get an assistant to support it.
2   Using a screwdriver (as shown in Fig. 12.8), prise free and release

Fig. 12.8 Tailgate damper strut detachment (Sec 13)

13.2 Tailgate strut damper joint with retaining peg (arrowed)

Fig. 12.9 Door mirror glass retainer removal (Sec 14)

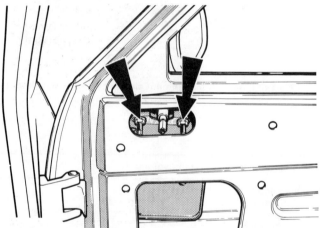

Fig. 12.10 Door mirror attachment nuts (arrowed) (Sec 14)

the strut retaining peg (photo) at each end and remove the strut by pulling it free from the joints.

3   Refit in the reverse order to removal.

14 Door mirror and glass – removal and refitting

1   To renew the glass, prise free the retainer from the mirror body using a coin or similar suitable lever and remove the glass.

2   Locate the new glass into position and press the new retainer evenly aound its perimeter onto the body. Check that the retainer is fully engaged on completion.

3   To remove the mirror unit complete, prise free the plastic cover from the adjustment knob using a suitable screwdriver.

4   Remove the knob and door trim panel, as described in Section 15.

5   Support the mirror body and unscrew and remove the two securing nuts through the aperture in the door inner panel. Remove the mirror and gasket.

6   Refit in the reverse order of removal ensuring that the mirror-to-body gasket is correctly aligned before tightening the securing nuts.

15 Door trim panel – removal and refitting

1   Carefully prise free the cover pads from the window winder handle, the door mirror adjuster and the trim panel (one at the forward edge and one at the lower edge in the centre) – photos.

2   With the pads removed, unscrew and remove the retaining screws (photos).

3   Undo and remove the door control handle bezel retaining screw and withdraw the bezel (photo).

4   Remove the door pull/armrest which is secured by two screws.

5   Carefully prise free and remove the panel from the door (photo).

6   Withdraw the insulating washer from the window winder handle shaft then carefully peel back the plastic insulating screen from the door for access to the components within the door cavity.

7   Refit the panel in the reverse order of removal.

15.1A Remove cover pad from the window regulator handle ...

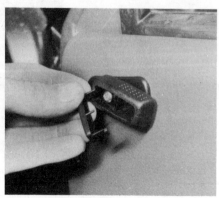

15.1B ... the door mirror adjuster ...

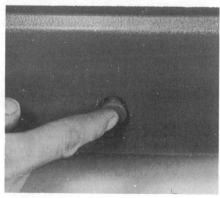

15.1C ... and the trim panel

15.2A Remove retaining screws ...

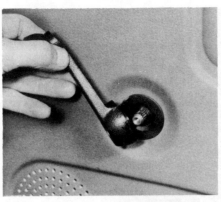

15.2B ... and withdraw the regulator handle

15.2C Remove the trim panel retaining screws

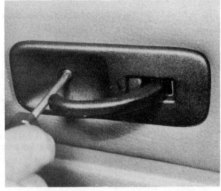

15.3 Remove door control handle bezel screw

15.5 Prise free the door panel and locating clips

16 Door lock – removal and refitting

1 Remove the door trim panel and insulation screen, as described in the previous Section.
2 Detach the lock rod from the latch then pull the retainer from the door cylinder.
3 Withdraw the lock cylinder, together with the lock rod, from the door.
4 Refitting is a reversal of the removal procedure. When inserting the lock cylinder, ensure that the cylinder lever points towards the front of the car and check that the lock barrel is correctly aligned before fitting the retainer.

17 Door latch unit – removal and refitting

1 Remove the door trim panel and insulation screen, as described in Section 15.
2 Unclip and detach the remote control rod, the exterior handle rod and the lock cylinder rods from the latch levers (Fig. 12.12).

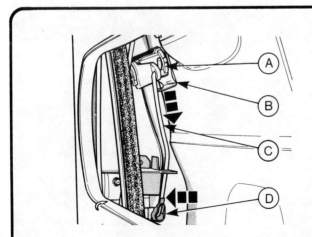

Fig. 12.11 Door lock barrel (A), retainer (B), lock rod (C) and clip (D) (Sec 16)

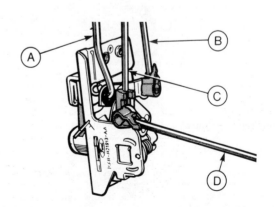

Fig. 12.12 Door latch and rod attachments (Sec 17)

A Private lock rod and bush C Exterior handle rod
B Lock rod (exterior) D Remote control rod

17.3 Door latch

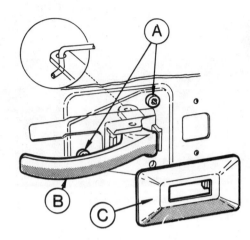

Fig. 12.14 Door remote control handle (B), retaining screw (A) and bezel (C) (Sec 18)

3   Undo the three screws and remove the latch unit, manoeuvring it free from the rear of the glass rim extension (photo).
4   Detach the private lock rod from the latch then the retaining clips and black bush from the levers (Fig. 12.13).
5   Refitting is a reversal of the removal procedure. To ease refitting of the black bush and sliding clip soak them in hot water prior to fitting. When fitting the latch unit into position it must be in its closed position. Check that all control rod securing clips are secure before refitting the door trim assembly.

19 Door striker plate – removal, refitting and adjustment

1   Loosen the striker locknut then unscrew and remove the striker, together with washer, from the door pillar (photo).
2   To refit the striker, locate the washer onto the threaded end of the striker so that the cone apex is adjacent to the nut face. Screw the striker into position, but do not fully tighten it yet.
3   Close and open the door and align the striker with the latch. When the door shuts in a satisfactory manner open it and retighten the locknut to set the striker in the required position.

20 Door exterior handle – removal and refitting

1   Refer to Section 15 and remove the door trim panel and insulation screen.
2   Detach the lock rod from the latch nut then unscrew and remove the handle retaining screws (photo). Remove the handle and lock rod from the door.
3   Refit in the reverse order of removal. When inserting the lock rod into the handle the rod latch end must face to the rear. Smear the end of the rod with Vaseline to ease assembly.

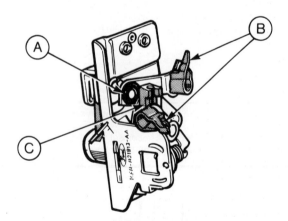

Fig. 12.13 Latch lever black bush (A), fixed clips (B) and sliding clip (C) (Sec 17)

18 Door remote control handle – removal and refitting

1   Remove the door trim panel and insulation screen as described in Section 15.
2   Unclip and detach the remote control rod from the latch then push free the anti-rattle retainer from the door.
3   Undo the two screws securing the remote control handle.
4   Fully raise the window, manoeuvre the handle and rod into the door cavity, disconnect the rod from the handle and extract the handle and rod.
5   Refitting is a reversal of the removal procedure. When refitting the handle to the inner door panel move it as far as possible to the rear before tightening the retaining screws.

19.1 Door striker

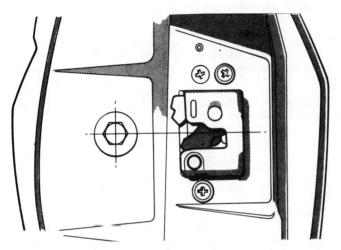

Fig. 12.15 Adjust striker position to align with the latch throat centre line (Sec 19)

Fig. 12.16 Inner door belt weatherstrip removal (Sec 22)

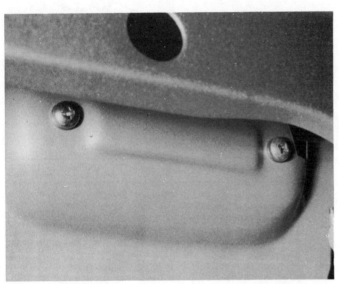

20.2 Door exterior handle retaining screws viewed from within the door

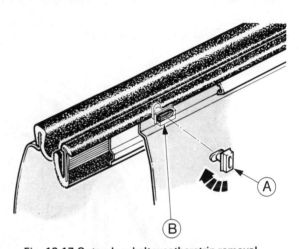

Fig. 12.17 Outer door belt weatherstrip removal (Sec 22)

A   Retaining clip   Note: remove bright external
B   Clip installed   moulding on L and GLS
                                    models

21 Door – removal and refitting

1   Open the door fully and support its lower edge on a jack or blocks covered with a pad of rag.
2   Detach and remove the plastic plugs from the door hinge pins.
3   Using a suitable length of rod or, if available, Ford special tool 41.002, drift out the hinge pins; knocking them downwards. Get an assistant to support and steady the door during this operation.
4   Lift the door clear of its hinge stubs and remove it.
5   Refit the door reversing the removal procedure. Lubricate the hinges and pins as they are fitted and ensure that the hinge pin holes are correctly aligned when drifting the new hinge pins into position.

22 Door quarter window (fixed) – removal and refitting

1   Lower the door window then remove the door trim panel and insulation screen, as described in Section 15.
2   Carefully prise free and remove the inner and outer door belt weatherstrips (Fig. 12.16 and 12.17).
3   Pull the window channel weatherstrip rubber down and undo screw B (Fig. 12.18) from the frame top corner.

Fig. 12.18 Quarter window channel (A), upper fixing (B), lower fixing (C) and adhesive pad (D) (Sec 22)

4 Undo the lower retaining screw, pull the channel rearwards to an angle of 45° and remove it.
5 Carefully prise free the triangular weatherstrip from its adhesive pad and retaining clips which untwist for removal.
6 Prise free the weatherstrip and glass from the door, then detach the weatherstrip from the glass (if required).
7 Refit in the reverse order of removal. Lubricate the weatherstrip with soapy water to ease its fitting to the glass. When refitting the glass and weatherstrip to the door insert as far forwards as possible. Clean off all soapy water from the weatherstrip prior to peeling off the backing paper from the adhesive pad and pressing it into position. If a new pad is not being fitted stick some double-sided adhesive tape to the old pad before fitting.

23 Door quarter window (opening) – removal and refitting

1 Proceed as described in paragraphs 1 and 2 in the previous Section.
2 Pull the window channel weatherstrip downwards and undo the retaining screw from the top end of the frame.
3 Detach the clips from the triangular portion of the weatherstrip and peel it away from the door frame to which it is retained by adhesive.
4 Prise free (taking care) the quarter window and channel, final removal of the channel being achieved by drilling out the two pop rivets (Fig. 12.19).

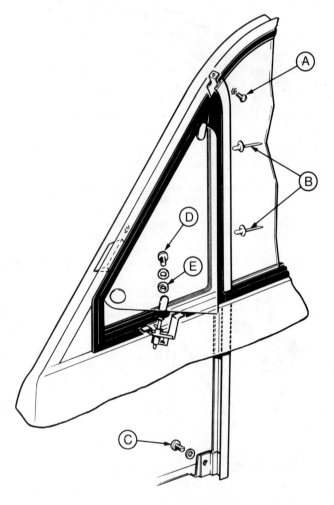

Fig. 12.19 Quarter window (opening) attachments (Sec 23)

A Upper screw   D Glass retaining screw
B Rivets   E Seal washer
C Lower screw

5 Refit in the reverse order of removal.
6 Ease refitting of the weatherstrip by applying soapy water to it. Avoid getting the soapy water onto the adhesive pad.
7 When fitting the window and channel check that the glass is located in the channel. Insert and, if required, push the weatherstrip vertical section upwards to get the window to fit correctly at the top corner.
8 When fitted, adjust the channel by loosening the upper and lower retaining screws so that the glass does not tilt in its frame, then retighten the screws.

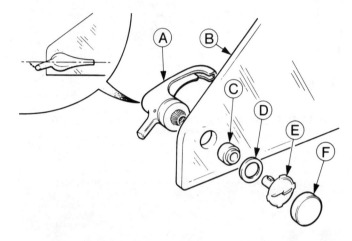

Fig. 12.20 Quarter window catch components (Sec 23)

A Handle   D Seal washer
B Glass   E End cap screw
C Bush   F End cap

24 Door window – removal and refitting

1 Refer to Section 21 or 22, as applicable, and remove the door quarter window.
2 Slide the door glass forward to detach the regulator arm from the glass bracket/slide.
3 Support the glass, holding it towards the innermost edge of the window opening, and withdraw it from the door.
4 Refit in the reverse order of removal. Tilt the glass down at the front end when inserting it into the door. Lubricate the regulator slide and check window operation prior to refitting the door trim panel.

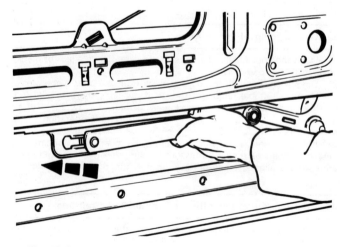

Fig. 12.21 Door window regulator arm detachment (Sec 24)

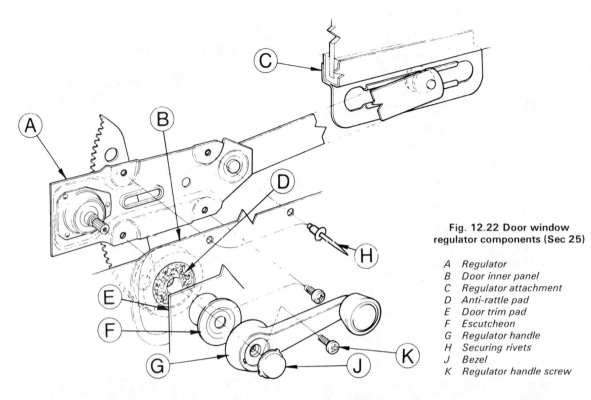

Fig. 12.22 Door window regulator components (Sec 25)

A   Regulator
B   Door inner panel
C   Regulator attachment
D   Anti-rattle pad
E   Door trim pad
F   Escutcheon
G   Regulator handle
H   Securing rivets
J   Bezel
K   Regulator handle screw

25 Door window regulator – removal and refitting

1   Remove the door trim panel and insulation screen, as described in Section 15.
2   Adjust the window position so that the regulator and bracket are accessible through the lower aperture in the door inner panel.
3   Use a suitable bit and drill through the four window regulator-to-inner panel securing rivets (Fig. 12.23).
4   Press the regulator into the door cavity, then slide the regulator arm to the rear and disengage it from the slide.
5   Push the window upwards into the closed position, support it with a prop and then carefully withdraw the window regulator from the door cavity.
6   Refit in the reverse order of removal, but note the following:
7   Locate the regulator into its approximate position with the winder

shaft resting on door panel aperture; then, with the window lowered to align its bracket with the aperture in the door inner panel, re-engage the regulator arm. Align the regulator unit rivet holes and using a pop-rivet gun, secure the regulator with four pop-rivets.
8   Check the window regulator operation prior to refitting the door trim panel and insulating screen.

26 Interior mirror – removal and refitting

1   The interior mirror in bonded to the windscreen glass. If it must be removed, use a length of thin nylon cord (Fig. 12.24) to break the adhesive bond between the stem of the mirror and the windscreen patch.
2   When refitting the mirror, the following preliminary work must first be carried out.

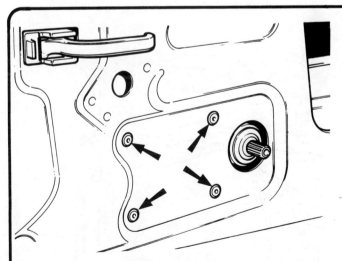

Fig. 12.23 Window regulator-to-door panel securing rivets (Sec 25)

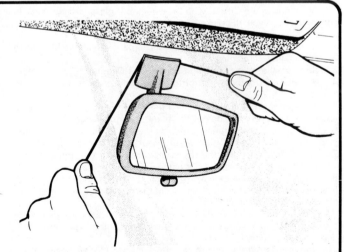

Fig. 12.24 Break adhesive bond of mirror to windscreen using cord (Sec 26)

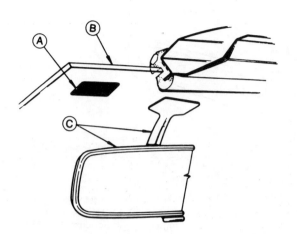

Fig. 12.25 Interior mirror mounting (Sec 26)

A   Adhesive black patch   C   Mirror and mounting stem
B   Windscreen

3   Remove existing adhesive from the windscreen glass using a
suitable solvent. Allow the solvent to evaporate. The location of the
mirror base is marked on the glass with a black patch, so that there
should not be any chance of an error when fitting.
4   If the original mirror is being refitted, clean away all the old
adhesive from the mirror mounting base, and apply a new adhesive
patch to it.
5   If a new windscreen is being installed, peel off the protective layer
from the black parch, which is pre-coated with adhesive.
6   Peel off the protective layer from the mirror adhesive patch and
locate the mirror precisely onto the black patch on the screen. Hold it
in position for at least two minutes.
7   For best results, the fitting of a bonded type mirror should be
carried out in an ambient temperature of 70°C (158°F). The careful
use of a blower heater on both the glass and mirror should achieve this
temperature level. Take necessary precautions to avoid burns.

27 Windscreen – removal and refitting

*The average DIY mechanic is advised to leave windscreen removal
and refitting to an expert. For the owner who insists on doing it
himself, the following paragraphs are given.*
1   All models are fitted with a laminated glass screen and in
consequence, even if cracked, it will probably be removed as one
piece.
2   Cover the bonnet in front of the windscreen with an old blanket to
protect against scratching.
3   Remove the wiper arms and blades (see Chapter 11).
4   Remove the rear view mirror from the windscreen as described in
Section 26.
5   Working inside the vehicle, push the lip of the screen weatherseal
under the top and the sides of the body aperture flange.
6   With an assistant standing outside the car to restrain the screen,
push the glass complete with weatherseal out of the bodyframe.
7   Where fitted, extract the bright moulding from the groove in the
weatherstrip and then pull the weatherstrip off the glass.
8   Unless the weatherstrip is in good condition, it should be renewed.
If using the old weatherstrip, check that its glass groove is free from
old sealant and glass chippings.
9   Check with a Ford dealer regarding the application of sealant to
the weatherstrip before fitting. Various weatherstrip types are used,
depending on model.
10 Commence refitting by fitting the weatherstrip to the glass. Locate
a length of nylon or terylene cord in the body flange groove of the
weatherstrip so that the ends of the cord emerge at the bottom centre
and cross over by a length of above 150 mm (6.0 in).
11 Offer the screen to the body and engage the lower lip of the
weatherstrip on its flange. With an assistant applying gentle, even

Fig. 12.26 Weatherstrip removal from aperture flange using a
lipping tool (Sec 27)

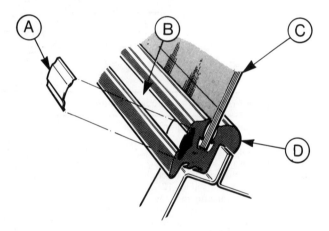

Fig. 12.27 Sectional view of weatherstrip (when fitted) (Sec 27)

A   Joint cover   C   Glass
B   Myler insert   D   Weatherstrip

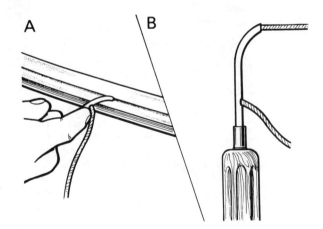

Fig. 12.28 Insert cord into weatherstrip as shown (A), using
special tool (B) if available (Sec 27)

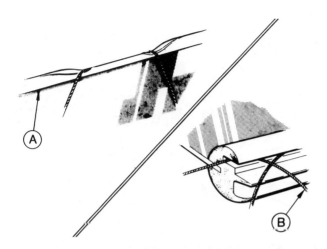

Fig. 12.29 Lip weatherstrip (A) over aperture flange with drawcord ends crossed over (B) (Sec 27)

pressure on the glass from the outside, pull the ends of the cord simultaneously at right-angles to the glass. This will pull the lip of the weatherstrip over the body flange. Continue until the cord is released from the centre top and the screen is fully fitted.

12 If a bright moulding was removed, refit it now. This can be one of the most difficult jobs to do without a special tool. The moulding should be pressed into its groove just after the groove lips have been prised open to receive it. Take care not to cut the weatherstrip if improvising with a made-up tool.

13 On completion, refit the rear view mirror, as described in Section 26.

28 Tailgate and fixed rear quarter window – removal and refitting

1 The operations are very similar to those described for windscreen renewal in the preceding Section.

2 Disconnect the leads from the heated rear window and the wiper motor (where fitted).

3 Both the tailgate and rear quarter windows are of toughened type, not laminated, so if it has shattered remove all the glass fragments with a vacuum cleaner.

29 Bumpers – removal and refitting

Front bumper – metal centre section type

1 From underneath each front wing, undo and remove the two bumper retaining nuts (photo).

2 Disengage the quarter bumper retainer each side then, from the front of the car, grip the bumper and pull it free.

3 Refit reversing the removal procedure. Check that the quarter bumper retainers are fully engaged each side and that the bumper is aligned correctly.

29.1 Bumper retaining bolts under wing panel

Front bumper – all moulded type

4 From underneath each front wing, undo and remove the bumper retaining nuts.

5 Open the bonnet and unscrew the bumper retaining nut beneath each headlamp unit (Fig. 12.31).

6 Disengage the quarter bumper retainer each side, then, from the front of the car, grip the bumper and pull it free.

7 Refit reversing the removal procedure. Check that the quarter bumper retainers are fully engaged each side and that the bumper is correctly aligned.

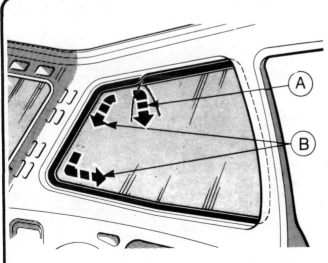

Fig. 12.30 Rear quarter window fitting (Sec 28)

A Pull cord at right angles to flange   B Start at the top

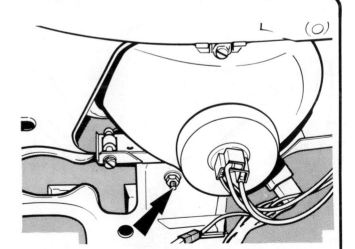

Fig. 12.31 Bumper retaining nut in engine compartment (Sec 29)

Rear bumper

8   Open the tailgate and lift out the floor cover and tool tray from the luggage compartment.

9   Detach the number plate wiring.

10 Undo the bumper retaining nuts from the rear face of the floor area on each side, then grip the bumper and withdraw it, simultaneously disengaging the quarter bumpers each side.

11 Refit in the reverse order to removal. Renew the rubber seal washers on the bumper retaining studs if they are perished or in poor condition. Ensure that the quarter bumper retainers fully engage when fitting.

30 Front quarter bumpers – removal and refitting

Quarter bumper – metal centre section type

1   Use a pair of suitable pliers and detach the quarter bumper retaining tangs, as shown in Fig. 12.32.

2   Once removed the quarter bumper must be renewed.

3   Refit by pushing the quarter bumper into position on the metal section.

Quarter bumper – all moulded type

4   Prise out and remove the moulding strip from the quarter bumper to expose the retainer heads.

5   Use a chisel and remove the rivet heads from the upper retainer, then press out the rivets.

6   Prise open and detach the bumper-to-quarter bumper retaining clips (Fig. 12.33), then remove the quarter bumper.

7   Clean the moulding recess out with methylated spirit to remove the adhesive.

8   Align and fit the quarter bumper to the main bumper and locate the securing clips and rivets.

9   Using a blowlamp, or similar, very carefully heat the new moulding so that it is warm to the touch then detach the backing paper from the moulding and locate the moulding into the quarter bumper channel recess, pressing it firmly into position.

31 Spoiler (front) – removal and refitting

1   Undo and remove the front spoiler retaining screws, two each side, from the positions indicated in Fig. 12.34.

2   The spoiler is further attached to the front panel by rivets, nine at the front and one at the top leading edge of the wheel arch spider each side. Use a suitable drill (4.5 mm diameter) and drill out the rivets.

3   The spoiler can now be withdrawn.

4   Refitting is a reversal of the removal procedure, but use the proper Ford rivets to secure the spoiler as they have a plastic body coating to protect against corrosion.

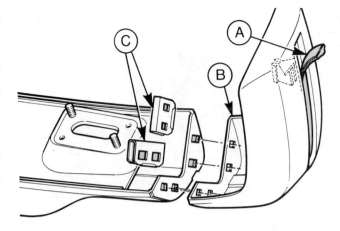

Fig. 12.33 Fully moulded quarter bumper attachments (Sec 30)

A   Moulding   C   Retaining clips
B   Quarter bumper

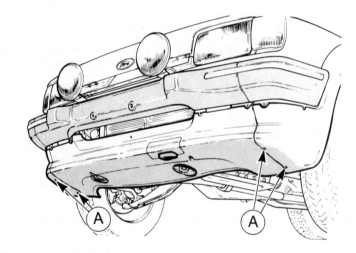

Fig. 12.34 Front spoiler attachment screw positions (A) (Sec 31)

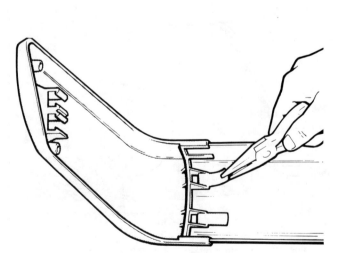

Fig. 12.32 Quarter bumper retaining tang removal (Sec 30)

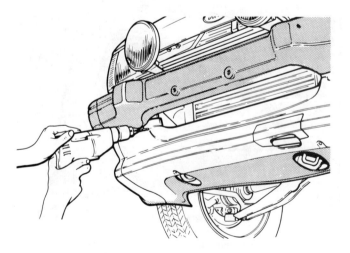

Fig. 12.35 Drill out the front spoiler retaining rivets (Sec 31)

32 Front and rear wheel arch spoilers – removal and refitting

Front wheel arch

1   Raise and support the vehicle at the front. Remove the roadwheel on the side concerned for improved access to the underside of the spoiler.

2   Referring to Fig. 12.36, undo and remove the five retaining nuts and two retaining screws from the positions indicated.

3   Use a 4.5 mm diameter drill and drill out the seven securing rivets from their locations indicated in Fig. 12.37.

4   Detach the spoiler retaining studs from the wheel arch, then grip the spoiler on its lower corner and pull it to disengage it from the push-fit fasteners.

5   To remove the plastic fasteners from the sill panel and wing edge, insert a self-tapping screw into them and pull them free.

6   Refitting is a reversal of the removal procedure.

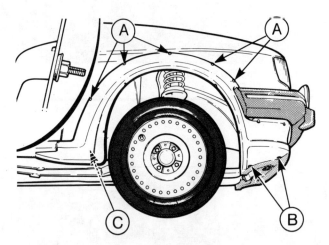

Fig. 12.36 Front wheel arch spoiler retaining nuts (A), joint screws (B) and rear lower corner (C) (Sec 32)

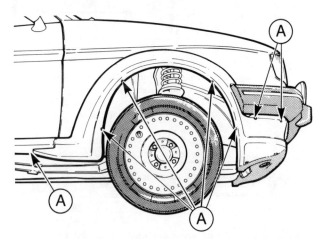

Fig. 12.37 Front wheel arch spoiler rivet positions (A) (Sec 32)

Rear wheel arch

7   Raise and support the rear of the vehicle on safety stands, remove the wheel on the side concerned for access to the spoiler underside.

8   Remove the rear bumper, as described in Section 29.

9   Undo and remove the two retaining screws from the wheel arch flange.

10 The spoiler is secured by five rivets (arrowed in Fig. 12.38). Carefully drill out the rivets using a 4.5 mm diameter drill.

11 Remove the two screws from the wheel arch and rear panel moulding joint.

12 Grip the moulding at the rear and pull it free from the wheel arch/rocker panel and push-fit fasteners. The moulding is additionally secured by means of adhesive tape to the bodywork, and the bond between the two must be broken carefully.

13 Remove the plastic fasteners from the wheel arch and rocker panel by inserting a self-tapping screw and pulling them free. Remove any adhesive tape remaining in position on the bodywork or moulding.

14 Clean the areas of contact for the adhesive tape with methylated spirits. Insert new plastic fasteners in place of those removed.

15 Carefully warm up the spoiler tape channel until it is warm to the touch. (Use a blow lamp, or similar, but take great care).

16 Apply primer and the new length of adhesive tape to the spider, then fit the spoiler front edge under the sill panel moulding, detach the protector film from the tape and locate the spoiler pressing firmly home into the push-in fasteners. Smooth the spider down and check that its top edge contacts the body along its full length.

17 Refitting is now a reversal of the removal procedure. Use Ford special rivets to secure the spoiler and leave tightening the retaining screws until after the rivets are fitted.

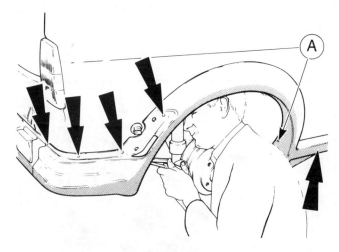

Fig. 12.38 Rear wheel arch spoiler flange screw (A) and rivet positions (Sec 32)

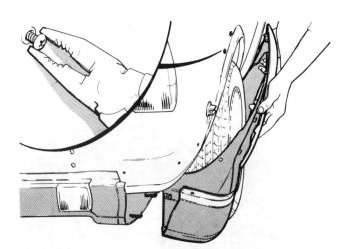

Fig. 12.39 Rear wheel arch removal (Sec 32)

Inset shows method of withdrawing the plastic fasteners

33 Facia crash padding and vents – removal and refitting

1   Disconnect the battery earth lead.

2   Remove the steering wheel, as described in Chapter 9.

3   Remove the steering column shrouds and combination switches, as described in Chapter 11.

4   Disconnect the bonnet release handle.

5　Referring to Chapter 11, disconnect and remove the following items:

- (a) *Facia trim and instrument cluster unit*
- (b) *Radio (where applicable)*
- (c) *Fuse/relay box*
- (d) *Indicator and facia switches*

6　Remove the heater control panel, as described in Chapter 2.

7　Detach and remove the carpet from underneath the dashboard.

8　Where applicable, remove the choke control cable housing which is secured by a single screw, then remove the choke knob and push the choke cable and switch forwards through the crash pad (photo).

9　Undo the heater control panel mounting screws. Push the bulb holders forwards to the underside of the crash pad.

10　Detach the screw covers from the top of the crash pad.

11　Detach the glovebox light wires and pull the wires through to the underside of the crash pad.

12　Undo and remove the six crash pad retaining screws and carefully withdraw the crash pad facia. The strengthening bar at the base can be removed as the facia crash pad is withdrawn.

13　The centre and side vents can be detached from the facia crash pad by undoing the retaining screws.

14　Refit in the reverse order of removal. Ensure that all electrical connections are correctly and securely made. On completion, check the operation of the various instruments and controls.

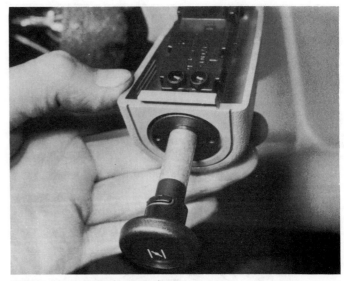

33.8 Choke control unit removal

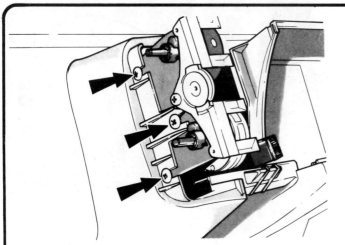

Fig. 12.40 Heater control panel retaining screws (Sec 33)

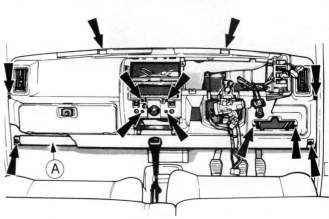

Fig. 12.42 Heater control panel and crash pad retaining screw positions (Sec 33)

Note position of strengthening bar (A)

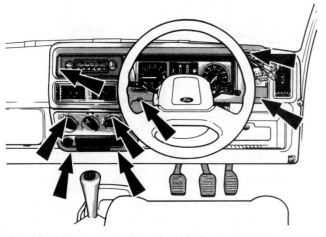

Fig. 12.41 Heater control panel and facia panel retaining screw positions (Sec 33)

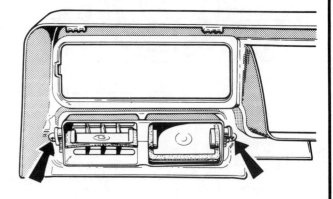

Fig. 12.43 Central vent retaining screws (Sec 33)

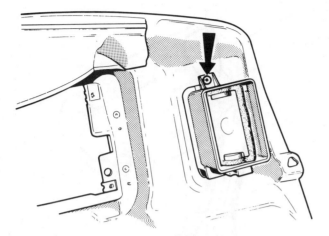

Fig. 12.44 Side vent retaining screw (Sec 33)

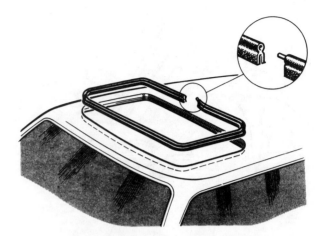

Fig. 12.45 Sunroof glass weatherstrip joint location (Sec 34)

34 Sunroof panel – removal and refitting

1   Compress the sunroof catch each side to disengage the handle pins from the bracket. Lift the roof panel, detach the stop clip and remove the panel.

2   If the sunroof panel is being renewed, undo the hinge plate retaining screws and remove it from the pedestal block. Remove the handle pivot retainers in a similar manner and withdraw the adjusting washer(s) from the handle screw block, then detach the block from the panel. Pull free the seal and pedestal block covers from the panel.

3   Refitting is a reversal of the removal procedure, but note the following:

4   When fitting a new seal to the roof tray flange, the seal ends must abut in the centre of the rear flange. Cut the seal to length as required.

5   When assembling the handle screw block to the panel, locate the shim, fit the block legs into their holes in the glass and then fit the washer onto each block leg.

6   If necessary, the hinge plates can be adjusted.

7   When the panel is fitted and closed, check the height of the roof tray and adjust, if required, by adding or subtracting washers under the handle so that the roof line is flush to the panel.

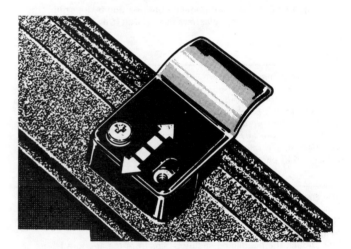

Fig. 12.46 Hinge plate adjustment direction (Sec 34)

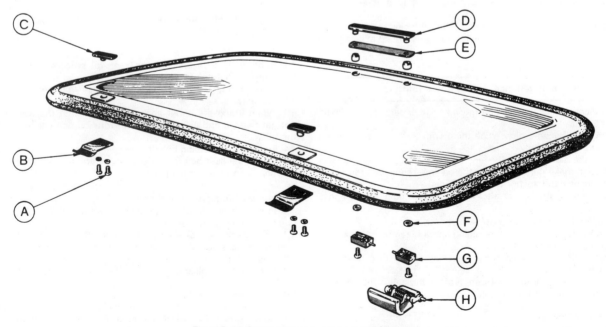

Fig. 12.47 Glass sunroof components (Sec 34)

A Screw	C Pedestal block	E Shim	G Pivot block
B Hinge plate	D Handle screw block	F Spacer	H Handle

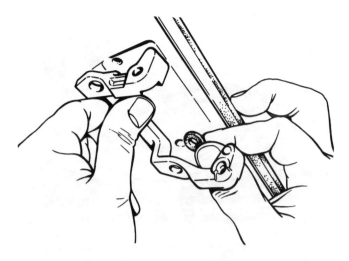

Fig. 12.48 Adjust roof panel height position by inserting (or removing) washers as required (Sec 34)

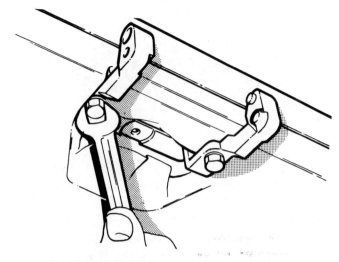

Fig. 12.49 Undo the bracket retaining bolts (Sec 35)

35 Sunroof handle bracket – removal and refitting

1   Remove the sunroof panel then undo and remove the handle cap securing screw. Lower and remove the handle cup.
2   Undo the two bracket retaining bolts and remove the bracket. Collect and note any adjustment washers.
3   Refit in the reverse order of removal and adjust, if necessary, as described in paragraph 7 in the previous Section.

36 Sunroof hinge retainer – removal and refitting

1   Remove the sunroof panel and then carefully prise free and remove the roof aperture weatherstrip.
2   Detach the headlining securing clips from the aperture flange and then pull down the headlining (with care) to expose the retainer and its securing screws.
3   Undo the retainer securing screws and withdraw it, together with its seal.
4   Refit in the reverse order of removal, but fit a new retainer seal. If necessary the panel height can be adjusted, as described in paragraph 7 of Section 34.

37 Seat belts – maintenance, removal and refitting

1   Periodically check the belts for fraying or other damage. If evident, renew the belt.
2   If the belts become dirty, wipe them with a damp cloth using a little liquid detergent only.
3   Check the tightness of the anchor bolts and, if they are ever disconnected, make quite sure that the original sequence of fitting of washers, bushes and anchor plate is retained.
4   **Never** modify the belt or alter its attachment point to the body.

Seat belt and stalk removal – front seats
5   Undo the lower anchor bar retaining bolt and remove the bar rear end from the mounting panel.
6   Remove the cover from the upper anchor and disconnect the upper anchor.
7   From the rear quarter panel trim, remove the belt webbing guide and let the belt retract onto its reel.
8   Detach and withdraw the quarter trim panel, as described in Section 50 in Chapter 11.
9   Undo the inertia reel unit retaining bolt and remove the reel unit.
10 The stalk and buckle unit can be detached by unscrewing the single retaining bolt, but note the locations of the washer, spacer and paper washer as they are removed.

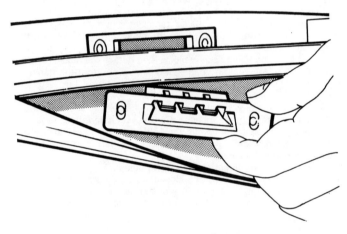

Fig. 12.50 Sunroof hinge retainer removal (Sec 36)

11 Refitting is a reversal of the removal procedure, but note the following special points:
12 When fitting the inertia reel unit check that the locating pegs engage fully.
13 When fitting the upper anchorage check that the webbing does not get twisted and also that the anti-rotation peg engages fully into the pillar.
14 Tighten the retaining bolts to the specified torque wrench settings.
15 Check the seat belt for satisfactory operation when the seats are readjusted to their normal positions.

Rear seat belt (where fitted)
16 Prise free and pivot up the inertia reel unit cover (if fitted) then undo and remove the retaining bolt.
17 Remove the rear seat cushion (Section 38), and push the buckles through the cushion slit as it is withdrawn.
18 Unscrew the six buckle and lower anchor retaining screws.
19 Remove the C pillar anchor point covers and disconnect the upper anchors.
20 Prise free the webbing guides from the package tray supports and remove the guides whilst letting the webbing wind into the reel.
21 Refitting is a reversal of the removal procedure. When fitting the reel unit to the quarter panel check that the location peg engages fully into its hole. Check that the webbing does not get twisted during refitting. Tighten retaining bolts to the specified torque wrench setting.
22 On completion check that the belt operation is satisfactory.

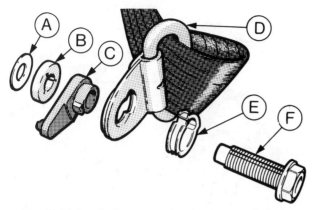

Fig. 12.51 Seat belt upper anchor components (Sec 37)

A Paper washer   D Anchor
B Spacer   E Bush
C Anti-rotation   F Bolt
   spacer

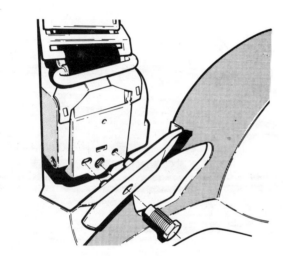

Fig. 12.52 Seat belt inertia reel retaining bolt (Sec 37)

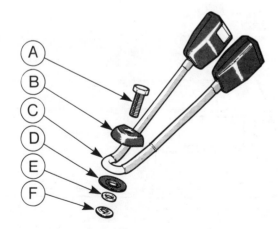

Fig. 12.53 Seat belt stalk and buckle components (Sec 37)

A Bolt   D Washer
B Cover   E Spacer
C Stalk and buckles F Paper washer

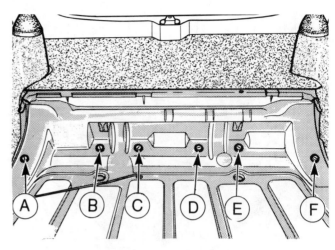

Fig. 12.54 Rear seat belt anchorage points (Sec 37)

A Inertia reel anchor   D Inertia reel buckles
   points   E Centre lap buckle
B Centre lap belt   F Inertia reel anchor point
C Inertia reel buckles

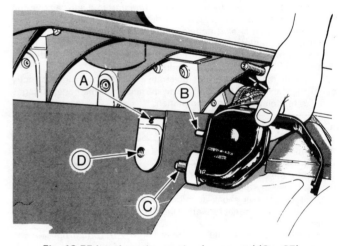

Fig. 12.55 Inertia reel mounting (rear seats) (Sec 37)

A Peg locating hole   C Mounting bolt
B Locating peg   D Mounting

38 Seats – removal and refitting

Front seat

1   Slide the seat as far forward as it will go.
2   Unscrew and remove the bolts which retain the rear of the seat slides to the floorpan.
3   Slide the seat as far to the rear as it will go and remove the bolts which secure the front ends of the slides to the floor.
4   Remove the seat from the vehicle interior.
5   If the seat slides must be detached from the seat, invert the seat and remove the two bolts from each side. Detach the cross-rod and clips.
6   Refitting is a reversal of removal. Tighten the front bolts before the rear ones to ensure that the seat is located evenly on the floorpan.

Rear seat cushion

7   Refer to Fig. 12.56 and undo the two retaining screws from the positions indicated.
8   Disengage the cushion from the retainer hooks at the rear then lift out the cushion.
9   Refit in the reverse order to removal.

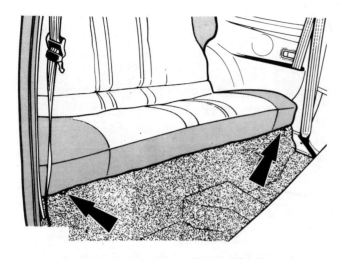

Fig. 12.56 Rear seat cushion securing screw positions (Sec 38)

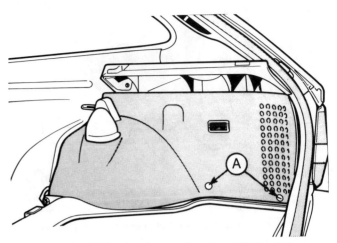

Fig. 12.57 Wheel arch cover fasteners (A) (Sec 39)

Rear seat backrest

10 Hinge the rear seat panel forwards then unscrew and remove the four rear panel retaining screws. Lift out the panel.

11 Where both rear seat panels and also the centre hinge are to be removed, first remove the panels then mark the outline of the hinge around its periphery to ensure correct realignment when refitting it. Undo the retaining bolts and withdraw the hinge.

12 Refit in the reverse order of removal. Align the hinge correctly before tightening the retaining screws. Check that the panel engages with its retaining catch on completion.

39 Rear wheel arch cover – removal and refitting

1 Open the tailgate and lift out the luggage compartment floor covers.

2 Detach the rear shock absorber upper mounting cover.

3 Pivot the seat panel forwards and then remove the seat striker and cover.

4 Detach the side panel fasteners (Fig. 12.57), then pull out the panel at the rear end and detach the interior lamp wiring.

5 Detach the panel cover at the top edge, beneath the parcel shelf support, move the cover rearwards and disconnect it from the quarter panel trim. Lift the panel out of the car.

6 Refit in the reverse order to removal. If necessary adjust the position of the rear seat striker on completion.

40 Body adhesive emblems – removal and refitting

1 The bonnet and tailgate Ford emblem are self-adhesive.

2 To remove them, it is recommended that a length of nylon cord is used to separate them from their mounting surfaces.

3 New emblems have adhesive already applied and a protective backing. Before sticking them into position, clean off all the old adhesive from the mounting surface of the vehicle with a suitable solvent.

4 The tailgate model letters are also self-adhesive, but their removal is best achieved by using suitable means to warm the emblem and general surrounding area for a couple of minutes. A room fan heater aimed at the emblems will ease their removal, but whatever method is used take care not to overheat the panel or the paint will blister.

5 Having heated the emblem it should be possible to peel it away from the panel.

6 Fit the new emblem by peeling off its backing paper; locate it exactly in position on the tailgate then press it firmly into position. The front application paper can then be peeled away.

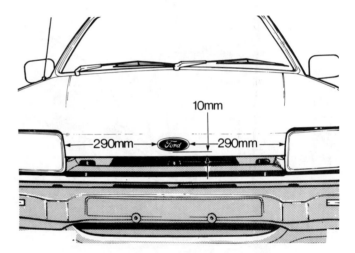

Fig. 12.58 Bonnet motif location (Sec 40)

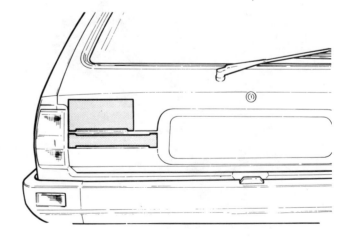

Fig. 12.59 Tailgate badge locations (Sec 40)

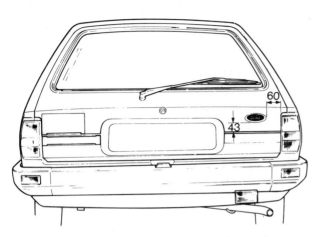

Fig. 12.60 Tailgate motif location (Sec 40)

41 Body side mouldings – removal and refitting

1   Using a thin-bladed screwdriver, prise away the moulding insert strip, carefully levering from the lower edge.

2   The moulding is secured by rivets and these can be drilled out using a 3 mm (0.12 in) drill. With the rivets drilled through, the moulding can be removed.

3   Refitting is a reversal of the removal procedure, but you will need a pop-rivet gun and supply of suitable rivets to secure the moulding. Check its alignment as the moulding is secured in position.

4   Where a new moulding is being fitted you will need to first drill the rivet holes in it. Use the old moulding as a suitable template to drill the holes in the new moulding.

42 Tailgate aperture mouldings – removal and refitting

1   Prise free or drill a hole in and hook out the upper moulding retaining screw caps then undo and remove the screws.

2   The upper moulding is now removed by carefully cutting through the adhesive tape which secures it in position along the front and rear edges. Use a soft-edge razor blade or similar to slice through the tape. Take care not to cut into the moulding or paintwork.

3   With the tailgate open, prise back the quarter trim to gain access to the lower moulding securing nut. Undo and remove the nut (Fig. 12.63).

4   Gripping the moulding at its top end, pull it away from the body panel so that the adhesive bond is broken, and remove the moulding.

5   Remove any adhesive tape still remaining on the body panel, wiping it off with a rag dipped in methylated spirits.

6   Before refitting, the mouldings will need to be heated so that they are warm to the touch and the contact surfaces coated in primer, followed by the adhesive tape.

7   Refitting is otherwise now a reversal of the removal procedure.

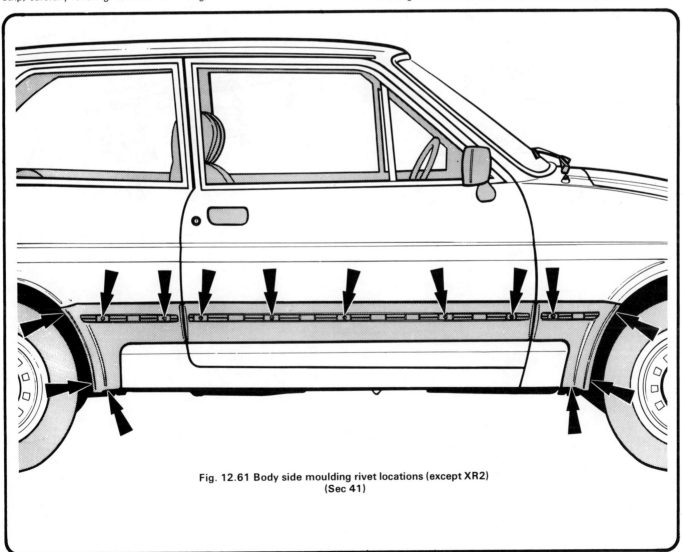

Fig. 12.61 Body side moulding rivet locations (except XR2)
(Sec 41)

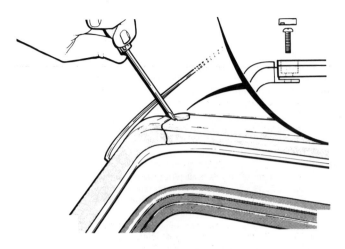

Fig. 12.62 Remove moulding screw cap for access to screw (Sec 42)

43 Sill panel moulding – removal and refitting

1   Raise and support the car at the front end.
2   Referring to Fig. 12.64, use a 4.5 mm (0.177 in) drill and drill out the moulding-to-sill rivets from the positions indicated.
3   Grip the moulding and pull it free from the car, pulling from its lower edge. The top edge is secured in position by press fit retainers and adhesive tape and should just pull free. If the top edge of the sill is reluctant to separate, carefully slit the adhesive tape along its length using a safe-edge razor or similar.
4   Clean the old adhesive from the sill panel using methylated spirits.
5   Before refitting the moulding it will need to be heated so that it is warm to the touch, the contact surfaces coated in primer and the adhesive tape applied.
6   Press the moulding into position along its top edge, ensuring that it is fully secured and correctly located in the retainers. Press and smooth the moulding down to ensure that it adheres to the sill along the full length.
7   Using a suitable pop-rivet gun, insert pop-rivets to secure the panel along its lower edge, but use only the special plastic capped type rivets supplied by Ford.
8   On completion lower the vehicle to the ground.

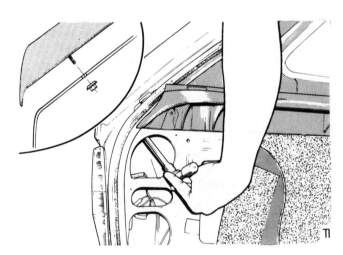

Fig. 12.63 Tailgate moulding lower retaining nut removal (Sec 42)

Fig. 12.64 Sill panel retaining rivet positions (Sec 43)

Conversion factors

Length (distance)
Inches (in)	X	25.4	= Millimetres (mm)	X 0.0394 = Inches (in)
Feet (ft)	X	0.305	= Metres (m)	X 3.281 = Feet (ft)
Miles	X	1.609	= Kilometres (km)	X 0.621 = Miles

Volume (capacity)
Cubic inches (cu in; in³)	X	16.387	= Cubic centimetres (cc; cm³)	X 0.061 = Cubic inches (cu in; in³)
Imperial pints (Imp pt)	X	0.568	= Litres (l)	X 1.76 = Imperial pints (Imp pt)
Imperial quarts (Imp qt)	X	1.137	= Litres (l)	X 0.88 = Imperial quarts (Imp qt)
Imperial quarts (Imp qt)	X	1.201	= US quarts (US qt)	X 0.833 = Imperial quarts (Imp qt)
US quarts (US qt)	X	0.946	= Litres (l)	X 1.057 = US quarts (US qt)
Imperial gallons (Imp gal)	X	4.546	= Litres (l)	X 0.22 = Imperial gallons (Imp gal)
Imperial gallons (Imp gal)	X	1.201	= US gallons (US gal)	X 0.833 = Imperial gallons (Imp gal)
US gallons (US gal)	X	3.785	= Litres (l)	X 0.264 = US gallons (US gal)

Mass (weight)
Ounces (oz)	X	28.35	= Grams (g)	X 0.035 = Ounces (oz)
Pounds (lb)	X	0.454	= Kilograms (kg)	X 2.205 = Pounds (lb)

Force
Ounces-force (ozf; oz)	X	0.278	= Newtons (N)	X 3.6 = Ounces-force (ozf; oz)
Pounds-force (lbf; lb)	X	4.448	= Newtons (N)	X 0.225 = Pounds-force (lbf; lb)
Newtons (N)	X	0.1	= Kilograms-force (kgf; kg)	X 9.81 = Newtons (N)

Pressure
Pounds-force per square inch (psi; lbf/in²; lb/in²)	X	0.070	= Kilograms-force per square centimetre (kgf/cm²; kg/cm²)	X 14.223 = Pounds-force per square inch (psi; lbf/in²; lb/in²)
Pounds-force per square inch (psi; lbf/in²; lb/in²)	X	0.068	= Atmospheres (atm)	X 14.696 = Pounds-force per square inch (psi; lbf/in²; lb/in²)
Pounds-force per square inch (psi; lbf/in²; lb/in²)	X	0.069	= Bars	X 14.5 = Pounds-force per square inch (psi; lbf/in²; lb/in²)
Pounds-force per square inch (psi; lbf/in²; lb/in²)	X	6.895	= Kilopascals (kPa)	X 0.145 = Pounds-force per square inch (psi; lbf/in²; lb/in²)
Kilopascals (kPa)	X	0.01	= Kilograms-force per square centimetre (kgf/cm²; kg/cm²)	X 98.1 = Kilopascals (kPa)

Torque (moment of force)
Pounds-force inches (lbf in; lb in)	X	1.152	= Kilograms-force centimetre (kgf cm; kg cm)	X 0.868 = Pounds-force inches (lbf in; lb in)
Pounds-force inches (lbf in; lb in)	X	0.113	= Newton metres (Nm)	X 8.85 = Pounds-force inches (lbf in; lb in)
Pounds-force inches (lbf in; lb in)	X	0.083	= Pounds-force feet (lbf ft; lb ft)	X 12 = Pounds-force inches (lbf in; lb in)
Pounds-force feet (lbf ft; lb ft)	X	0.138	= Kilograms-force metres (kgf m; kg m)	X 7.233 = Pounds-force feet (lbf ft; lb ft)
Pounds-force feet (lbf ft; lb ft)	X	1.356	= Newton metres (Nm)	X 0.738 = Pounds-force feet (lbf ft; lb ft)
Newton metres (Nm)	X	0.102	= Kilograms-force metres (kgf m; kg m)	X 9.804 = Newton metres (Nm)

Power
Horsepower (hp)	X	745.7	= Watts (W)	X 0.0013 = Horsepower (hp)

Velocity (speed)
Miles per hour (miles/hr; mph)	X	1.609	= Kilometres per hour (km/hr; kph)	X 0.621 = Miles per hour (miles/hr; mph)

Fuel consumption*
Miles per gallon, Imperial (mpg)	X	0.354	= Kilometres per litre (km/l)	X 2.825 = Miles per gallon, Imperial (mpg)
Miles per gallon, US (mpg)	X	0.425	= Kilometres per litre (km/l)	X 2.352 = Miles per gallon, US (mpg)

Temperature
Degrees Fahrenheit = (°C x 1.8) + 32   Degrees Celsius (Degrees Centigrade; °C) = (°F - 32) x 0.56

*It is common practice to convert from miles per gallon (mpg) to litres/100 kilometres (l/100km),
where mpg (Imperial) x l/100 km = 282 and mpg (US) x l/100 km = 235

Index

A

About this manual – 2
Accelerator cable
    removal, refitting and adjustment – 97
Accelerator pedal
    removal and refitting – 98
Acknowledgements – 2
Air cleaner
    description – 95
    element renewal – 96
    removal and refitting – 96
Alternator
    brushes and regulator renewal – 215
    description, maintenance and precautions – 213
    overhaul
        Bosch – 217
        Lucas – 218
        Motorola – 222
    removal and refitting – 215
    testing, in vehicle – 214
Antifreeze – 83

B

Battery
    charging – 212
    electrolyte replenishment – 212
    maintenance – 211
    removal and refitting – 212
Big-end bearings (ohv)
    examination and renovation – 46
Bleeding the brakes – 181
Bodywork and fittings – 259 *et seq*
Bodywork and fittings
    body adhesive emblems – 280
    body side mouldings – 281
    bonnet – 260, 261
    bumpers – 273, 274
    description – 259
    doors – 266 to 271
    facia crash padding and vents – 275
    fixed rear quarter window – 273
    interior mirror – 271
    maintenance
        bodywork and underframe – 259
        upholstery and carpets – 260
    radiator grille – 264
    rear wheel arch cover – 280
    repair, minor damage – 260
    seat belts – 278
    seats – 279
    sill panel moulding – 282
    spoiler, front – 274
    spoilers, front and rear wheel arch – 275
    sunroof – 277, 278
    tailgate – 264, 265, 273, 281
    torque wrench settings – 259
    windscreen – 272
Bodywork repair sequence (colour) – 262, 263
Bonnet
    lock removal and refitting – 261
    release cable removal and refitting – 261
    removal and refitting – 260
Braking system – 171 *et seq*
Braking system
    caliper piston assembly
        removal, overhaul and refitting – 174
    description – 172
    disc examination, removal and refitting – 175
    disc pads inspection and renewal – 173
    drum inspection and renewal – 178
    fault diagnosis – 185
    handbrake
        adjustment – 182
        cables renewal – 183
        lever removal and refitting – 184
    hydraulic system
        bleeding – 181
        pipes, flexible and rigid removal and refitting – 180
    maintenance, routine – 172
    master cylinder
        removal, overhaul and refitting – 178
    pressure control valve removal and refitting – 179
    rear brake
        linings inspection and renewal – 175
        wheel cylinder removal, overhaul and refitting – 178
    specifications – 171
    torque wrench settings – 171
    vacuum servo unit removal and refitting – 182
    warning lamps description and renewal – 185
Bulbs, lamp
    renewal
        auxiliary driving lamps – 242
        choke knob illumination – 238
        exterior lamps – 240
        interior lamps – 238
Bumpers
    removal and refitting – 273
Bumpers, front quarter
    removal and refitting – 274

C

Cam followers
examination and renovation
CVH engine – 72
ohv engine – 48
Camshaft (CVH engine)
removal and refitting – 60
Camshaft and bearings
examination and renovation
CVH engine – 72l
ohv engine – 48
Camshaft oil seal (CVH engine)
renewal – 59
Capacities, refill – 6
Carburettor (Ford IV)
adjustments – 100
description – 100
dismantling and reassembly – 102
removal and refitting – 102
Carburettor (Ford VV)
adjustments – 105
description – 103
dismantling and reassembly – 106
removal and refitting – 106
Carburettor (general)
dismantling and reassembly – 100
specifications – 93
Carburettor (Weber)
adjustments – 108
description – 107
dismantling, inspection and reassembly – 110
removal and refitting – 110
Choke cable
removal, refitting and adjustment – 99
Cigar lighter
removal and refitting – 238
Clock
removal and refitting
facia-mounted – 237
roof-mounted – 238
Clutch – 130 *et seq*
cable renewal – 13
description – 130
fault diagnosis – 135
inspection – 132
pedal removal and refitting – 134
refitting – 132
release bearing renewal – 132
removal – 130
specifications – 130
torque wrench settings – 130
Coil, ignition – 128
Condenser
renewal – 120
Contact breaker
gap adjustment – 118
points renewal – 118
Conversion factors – 283
Coolant pump
removal and refitting
CVH engine – 86
ohv engine – 86
Cooling, heating and ventilation system – 80 *et seq*
Cooling system
coolant mixtures – 83
coolant pump – 86
description – 81
draining, flushing and refilling – 83
drivebelt – 87
expansion tank – 87
fault diagnosis – 91
maintenance, routine – 82
radiator – 85
radiator fan – 84
specifications – 80

thermostat – 84
torque wrench settings – 81
Crankcase
examination and renovation
CVH engine – 48, 72
ohv engine – 48
Crankcase bearings (CVH engine)
examination and renovation – 72
Crankcase ventilation system
CVH engine – 67
ohv engine – 40
Crankshaft (ohv engine)
examination and renovation – 46
Crankshaft front oil seal
renewal
CVH engine – 63
ohv engine – 36
Cylinder bores (CVH engine)
examination and renovation – 72
Cylinder head (CVH engine)
decarbonising – 74
examination and renovation – 72
removal and refitting – 62
Cylinder head (ohv engine)
decarbonising – 49
examination and renovation – 48
removal and refitting – 34

D

Decarbonising
CVH engine – 74
ohv engine – 49
Dimensions, general – 6
Distributor (electronic ignition)
removal and refitting – 127
Distributor (mechanical ignition)
advance checking – 119
cap – 120
overhaul – 120
removal and refitting – 119
vacuum unit removal and refitting – 120
Door
exterior handle removal and refitting – 268
latch unit removal and refitting – 267
lock removal and refitting – 267
mirror and glass removal and refitting – 266
quarter window, fixed
removal and refitting – 269
quarter window, opening
removal and refitting – 270
remote control handle removal and refitting – 268
removal and refitting – 269
striker plate removal, refitting and adjusting – 268
trim panel removal and refitting – 266
window removal and refitting – 270
window regulator removal and refitting – 271
Drivebelt
removal, refitting and tensioning – 87, 212
Driveshafts – 163 *et seq*
Driveshafts
description and maintenance – 163
fault diagnosis – 170
inboard joint bellows renewal – 165
inboard oil seal renewal
1.0 and 1.1 litre – 164
1.3 and 1.6 litre – 165
intermediate driveshaft (1.3 and 1.6 litre)
removal and refitting – 167
outboard joint bellows renewal – 166
overhaul – 169
removal and refitting – 168
specifications – 163
torque wrench settings – 163

E

Electrical system – 20 *et seq*
Electrical system
  alternator – 213, 214, 215, 217, 218, 222
  auxiliary driving lamps – 242, 243
  battery – 211, 212
  bulbs – 238, 240
  cigar lighter – 238
  clock – 237, 238
  description – 211
  drivebelt – 212
  fault diagnosis – 23, 257
  fuses, relays and circuit breakers – 235
  headlamps – 241
  heater blower motor – 248
  horn(s) – 245
  in-car entertainment equipment – 248
  instrument cluster – 243, 244
  lamp units – 240
  radio – 249, 250, 251
  radio/cassette player – 249
  rear window washer – 247, 248
  rear window wiper – 246
  specifications – 209
  speedometer cable – 245
  starter motor – 224, 226, 230, 232, 233
  switches – 235
  windscreen washer – 247, 248
  windscreen wiper – 245, 246
  wiring diagrams – 289 to 310
Emblems, body adhesive
  removal and refitting – 280
Emission control system
  components
    maintenance and testing – 114
    removal and refitting – 115
  description – 112
Engine – 26 *et seq*
Engine (CVH)
  cam followers – 72
  camshaft and bearings – 60, 72
  camshaft oil seal – 58
  connecting rods – 64
  crankcase – 72
  crankcase ventilation system – 67
  crankshaft bearings – 72
  crankshaft front oil seal – 63
  cylinder bores – 72
  cylinder head – 62, 72, 74
  decarbonising – 74
  description – 56
  dismantling – 68
  examination and renovation – 72
  fault diagnosis – 79
  flywheel – 72
  lubrication system – 67
  maintenance, routine – 57
  mountings – 66
  oil filter – 66
  oil pump – 72
  oil seals and gaskets – 72
  operations possible with engine in vehicle – 58
  operations requiring engine removal – 58
  pistons – 64, 72, 74
  reassembly – 74
  reconnection to transmission – 78
  refitting with transmission – 79
  removal
    method – 68
    with transmission – 68
  rocker arms – 72
  specifications – 29
  sump – 63
  timing belt – 58, 72
  timing sprockets – 72
  torque wrench settings – 32

Engine (ohv)
  big-end bearings – 46
  cam followers – 48
  camshaft and bearings – 48
  connecting rods – 38
  crankcase – 48
  crankcase ventilation system – 40
  crankshaft – 46
  crankshaft front oil seal – 36
  cylinder head – 34, 48
  decarbonising – 49
  description – 32
  dismantling – 43
  examination and renovation – 46
  fault diagnosis – 24, 54
  flywheel – 47
  lubrication system – 38
  main bearings – 46
  maintenance, routine – 32
  mountings – 40, 66
  oil filter – 38
  oil pump – 38, 47
  oil seals and gaskets – 48
  operations possible with engine in vehicle – 32
  operations requiring engine removal – 33
  pistons – 38, 49
  reassembly – 50
  reconnection to transmission – 52
  refitting with transmission – 52
  removal
    method – 40
    with transmission – 40
  rocker gear – 36, 48
  specifications – 26
  sump – 36
  timing sprockets and chain – 47
  torque wrench settings – 29
  valves – 35
Exhaust system – 112
Expansion tank
  removal and refitting – 87

F

Facia crash padding and vents
  removal and refitting – 275
Fan, radiator
  removal and refitting – 84
Fault diagnosis
  braking system – 185
  clutch – 135
  cooling system – 91
  driveshafts – 170
  electrical system – 23, 257
  engine
    CVH – 24, 54, 79
    ohv – 24, 54
  fuel system – 115
  heating and ventilation system – 92
  ignition
    electronic – 129
    mechanical – 123
  introduction – 23
  steering – 195
  suspension – 208
  transmission – 162
Firing order
  CVH – 117
  ohv – 116
Flywheel
  examination and renovation
    CVH – 47, 72
    ohv – 47
Fuel, exhaust and emission control systems – 93 *et seq*
Fuel pump
  testing, removal and refitting – 96

Fuel system
    accelerator cable – 97
    accelerator pedal – 98
    air cleaner – 95, 96
    carburettor – 100 to 110
    choke cable – 99
    description – 94
    fault diagnosis – 115
    fuel pump – 96
    fuel tank – 96, 97
    maintenance, routine – 95
    specifications – 93
    torque wrench settings – 94
Fuel tank
    cleaning and repair – 97
    removal and refitting – 96
Fuses, relays and circuit breakers – 235

G

Gearbox *see* **Transmission**

H

Headlamps
    alignment – 241
Heater
    blower motor removal and refitting – 248
    controls
        adjustment – 89
        removal and refitting (Base and L) – 89
        removal and refitting (Ghia and XR2) – 89
    dismantling and reassembly – 91
Heating and ventilation system
    description – 87
    fault diagnosis – 92
Horn(s)
    removal and refitting – 245
Hub bearings
    front checking, removal and renewal – 200
    rear
        adjustment – 204
        removal and refitting – 204

I

Ignition amplifier module (electronic)
    description, removal and refitting – 127
Ignition lock cylinder
    removal and refitting – 128
Ignition system – 116 et seq
Ignition system (electronic)
    amplifier module – 127
    coil – 128
    description – 124
    distributor – 127
    fault diagnosis – 129
    ignition lock cylinder – 128
    maintenance, routine – 126
    spark plugs and HT leads – 120, 121, 128
    specifications – 117
    torque wrench settings – 117
Ignition system (mechanical)
    condenser – 120
    contact breaker – 118
    description – 117
    distributor – 119, 120
    fault diagnosis – 123
    maintenance, routine – 118
    spark plugs and HT leads – 120, 121
    specifications – 116
    timing – 119
    torque wrench settings – 117

In-car entertainment equipment – 244
Instrument cluster
    dismantling and reassembly – 244
    unit removal and refitting – 243

J

Jacking – 12

L

Lamp bulbs *see* **Bulbs, lamp**
Lamp units, exterior
    removal and refitting – 240
Lubricants and fluids, recommended – 14
Lubrication chart – 14
Lubrication system
    CVH engine – 67
    ohv engine – 38

M

Main bearings (ohv)
    examination and renovation – 46
Maintenance, routine
    bodywork and fittings
        bodywork and underframe – 259
        upholstery and carpets – 260
    braking system
        fluid level check – 172
        fluid renewal – 172
        general checks – 20, 21, 172
    cooling system
        coolant level check and top-up – 20, 82
        coolant mixture renewal – 22, 83
        coolant pump drivebelt (ohv) check – 82
        cooling fan check – 82
        hoses check – 82
    driveshafts – 163
    electrical system
        alternator – 213
        battery – 211
    emission control system – 95, 114
    engine
        crankcase emission control orifice cleaning – 32
        crankcase emission filter renewal – 32
        oil change – 20, 32
        oil filter renewal – 20, 32, 38
        oil level check – 20, 32
        valve clearances (ohv) check and adjust – 21, 32, 35
    exhaust system – 95
    fuel system
        air cleaner element renewal – 22, 95, 96
        engine idle speed check – 95
        general checks – 95
    ignition system (electronic)
        general check – 126
        spark plugs cleaning and adjustment – 20, 120, 128
        spark plugs renewal – 20, 120, 127
    ignition system (mechanical)
        contact breaker points renewal – 21, 118
        distributor (ohv) lubrication – 21
        general checks – 118
        spark plugs cleaning and adjustment – 20, 120
        spark plugs renewal – 20, 120
        timing/dwell angle (ohv) checking and adjusting – 118, 119
    safety – 15, 83
    schedules – 20, 21, 22
    steering – 186
    suspension – 200
    transmission oil level check and top-up – 21, 138

Manifolds – 112
Mirror
    removal and refitting
        door – 266
        interior – 271
Mountings, engine
    removal and refitting – 40, 66

O

Oil filter
    removal and refitting
        CVH engine – 66
        ohv engine – 38
Oil pump
    examination and renovation
        CVH engine – 72
        ohv engine – 47
    removal and refitting – 38

P

Piston/connecting rod
    removal and refitting
        CVH engine – 64
        ohv engine – 38
Pistons
    decarbonising
        CVH engine – 74
        ohv engine – 49
    examination and renovation – 72

R

Radiator
    removal, repair and refitting – 85
Radiator grille
    removal and refitting – 264
Radio
    aerial removal and refitting – 251
    loudspeaker removal and refitting – 250
    removal and refitting – 249
    speaker fader joystick removal and refitting – 250
Radio/cassette player
    removal and refitting – 249
Radio equipment (non-standard)
    interference-free installation – 251
Rear wheel arch cover
    removal and refitting – 280
Rear window washer
    nozzle and pipe removal and refitting – 248
    pump removal and refitting – 247
Rear window wiper
    motor removal and refitting – 246
Repair procedures, general – 11
Roadwheels see Wheels
Rocker arms (CVH engine)
    examination and renovation – 72
Rocker gear
    dismantling and reassembly – 36
    examination and renovation – 48
Routine maintenance see Maintenance, routine

S

Safety – 15
Seat belts
    maintenance, removal and refitting – 278
Seats
    removal and refitting – 279

Spare parts
    buying – 7
    to carry in car – 23
Spark plug conditions (colour chart) – 121
Spark plugs and HT leads – 120, 128
Speedometer cable
    removal and refitting – 245
Spoiler, front
    removal and refitting – 274
Spoilers, front and rear wheel arches
    removal and refitting – 275
Starter motor
    description – 224
    overhaul
        Bosch long frame type and Cajavec – 226
        Bosch short frame type – 230
        Lucas – 232
        Nippondenso – 233
    removal and refitting – 226
    testing, in-vehicle – 226
Steering – 186 et seq
Steering
    angles and wheel alignment – 194
    column removal, overhaul and refitting – 189
    description – 186
    fault diagnosis – 195
    gear
        overhaul – 191
        removal and refitting – 191
    gear bellows renewal – 188
    maintenance and precautions – 186
    specifications – 186
    tie-rod end balljoint renewal – 189
    torque wrench settings – 186
    wheel removal and refitting – 189
Sump
    removal and refitting
        CVH engine – 63
        ohv engine – 36
Sunroof
    handle bracket removal and refitting – 278
    hinge retainer removal and refitting – 278
    panel removal and refitting – 277
Suspension – 196 et seq
Suspension (front)
    hub bearings – 200
    lower arm
        removal, bush replacement and refitting – 201
    strut removal, overhaul and refitting – 203
    tie-bar removal and refitting – 202
Suspension (general)
    description – 197
    fault diagnosis – 208
    maintenance, routine – 200
    specifications – 196
    torque wrench settings – 197
Suspension (rear)
    anti-roll bar
        removal, bush renewal and refitting – 206
    coil spring removal and refitting – 207
    hub bearings – 204
    Panhard rod
        removal, bush renewal and refitting – 206
    rear axle and suspension unit
        removal and refitting – 207
    rear axle unit removal and refitting – 208
    shock absorber removal, testing and refitting – 205
Switches
    removal and refitting – 235

T

Tailgate
    aperture mouldings removal and refitting – 281
    glass removal and refitting – 273

latch removal and refitting – 265
lock barrel removal and refitting – 265
removal and refitting – 264
striker removal and refitting – 265
strut (damper unit) removal and refitting – 265
Thermostat
  removal, testing and refitting – 84
Timing belt (CVH)
  inspection, removal and refitting – 58
Timing, ignition (ohv engine)
  checking and adjustment – 119
Timing sprockets and belt (CVH engine)
  examination and renovation – 72
Timing sprockets and chain (ohv engine)
  examination and renovation – 47
Tools
  general – 9
  to carry in car – 23
Towing – 12
Transmission – 136 *et seq*
Transmission (five-speed gearbox)
  dismantling and overhaul of major assemblies – 157
  dismantling, general – 155
  gearchange mechanism
      removal, overhaul and refitting – 157
  reassembly – 160
Transmission (four-speed gearbox)
  dismantling – 145
  gearchange mechanism
      removal, overhaul and refitting – 138
  housing and selector mechanism – 157
  input shaft overhaul – 151
  mainshaft overhaul – 148
  reassembly – 153
  removal of major assemblies – 143
Transmission (general)
  description – 138
  differential unit overhaul – 151
  fault diagnosis – 162

gearchange mechanism adjustment – 138
maintenance, routine – 138
removal and refitting – 141
specifications – 136
speedometer driven gear removal and refitting – 155
torque wrench settings – 137
Tyres
  general – 208
  pressures – 197
  specifications – 197

V

Valves (ohv engine)
  clearances adjustment – 35
Vehicle identification numbers – 7

W

Weights, general – 6
Wheels
  general – 208
  specifications – 197
Windscreen
  removal and refitting – 272
Windscreen washer
  nozzle and pipe removal and refitting – 248
  pump removal and refitting – 247
Windscreen wiper
  blade rubber renewal – 246
  blades and arms removal and refitting – 245
  linkage removal and refitting – 246
  motor removal and refitting – 246
Wiring diagrams – 289 to 310
Working facilities – 10

GENERAL NOTES

THE WIRING DIAGRAM IS DIVIDED INTO VARIOUS
ELECTRICAL SYSTEMS. THE FUNCTION OF EACH
ELECTRICAL SYSTEM IS SHOWN FROM FUSE TO
ELECTRICAL CONSUMER GROUND. THE POWER
DISTRIBUTION TO THE FUSE IS SHOWN ON DIAG. 2.
PARTS OF THE ELECTRICAL SYSTEM WHICH HAVE
MORE THAN ONE FUNCTION MAY APPEAR MORE
THAN ONCE ON THE INDEX.

THE WIRING DIAGRAMS CONTAIN NO DATA
REGARDING WIRE SIZE AND INDEX OF THE CIRCUIT
NUMBERS.

THROUGH THE C-, S-, AND G-NUMBER SYSTEM THE
CONNECTIONS, SOLDERED JOINTS AND EARTH
POINTS ARE HOOKED TOGETHER.

ALL CONNECTORS ARE SHOWN ADDITIONALLY WITH
THEIR SYMBOL ON THE MATING FACE AND SHOW
THE EXACT POSITION OF WIRE-CRIMPINGS WITH
CIRCUIT-NO AND COLOUR.
(SEE FIGURE 1)
THE C-NUMBERS OF THE INSTRUMENT CLUSTER ARE
EXCEPTIONS.
THEY SHOW THE VARIATIONS FOR THE GHIA ONLY.
THE OTHER VARIATIONS ARE SHOWN ON THIS PAGE
WITH THE FOLLOWING C-NUMBERS,
C-905 C-906

SYMBOL – EXPLANATION:

S/P   2   POWER DISTRIBUTION FROM DIAG. 2

(2B 4)   SEE DIAG. LOCATION

(GB)   SHOWS SPECIFIC LEGAL
              REQUIREMENT OF THIS COUNTRY.

INDEX
WITH THE HELP OF THE INDEX IT IS EASIER TO FIND
THE DIFFERENT ELECTRICAL SYSTEMS AND
COMPONENTS.

THE INDEX CONTAINS:
1. SYSTEM LISTING AND DIAG. NO.
2. COLOUR CODE KEY
3. ALPHABETICAL LISTING OF COMPONENTS
   WITH PAGE NUMBERS, AND CO-ORDINATES.

FIGURE 1
1

SEPARATION BETWEEN CONNECTORS OR CONNECTOR AND COMPONENT

BASIC PART NUMBER OF THE WIRE

LOCATION IN CAR FOR CONNECTIONS

C-123   149584
           77-1 WS
14631   77-3 GE
77-1 WS
77-3 GE
DRV. SIDE B PILLAR

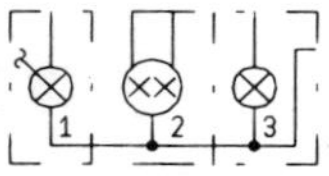

1 = FLASHER LAMP
2 = BRAKE – SIDE MARKER LAMP
3 = BACK UP LAMP

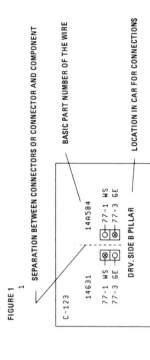

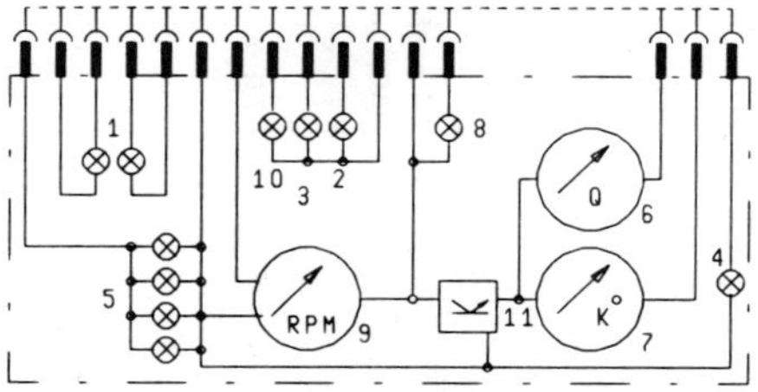

LH COMBINED REAR LAMP

INSTRUMENT CLUSTER GAUGE

1 = FLASHER CONTR. LAMP
2 = ALTERNATOR CONTR. LAMP
3 = BRAKE CONTR. LAMP
4 = MAIN BEAM CONTR. LAMP
5 = INSTR. ILLUMINATION
6 = FUEL INDICATOR
7 = COOL. WATER INDICATOR
8 = OIL PRESS LAMP
9 = TACHO
10 = BRAKE FLUID CONTR. LAMP
11 = VOLTAGE DIVIDER

Diagram 1 : explanatory notes for wiring diagrams

BOX LHD + RHD

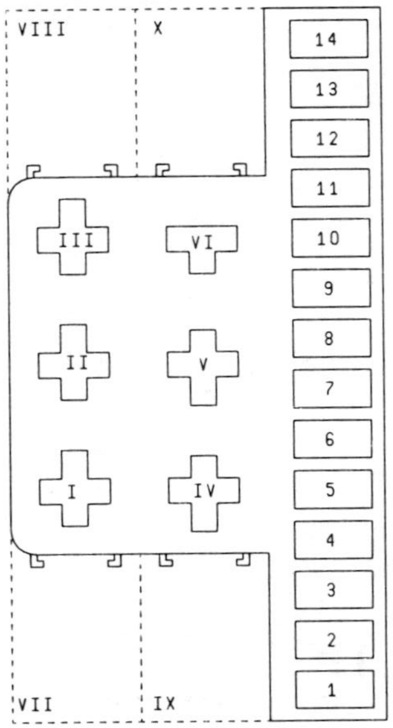

LOCATION RELAY IN BOX

I	IGNITION SWITCH
II	TIME DELAY HEATED REAR WINDOW
III	TAILGATE RELEASE
IV	WIPER INTERMITTENT FRONT
V	HEADL. WASH
VI	FLASHER
VII	
VIII	
IX	
X	

LOCATION RELAY BRACKET BEHIND BOX

XI	DAYTIME RUN. L. SWEDEN
XII	ADD. DAYTIME RUN. L. SWEDEN
XIII	HEATED SEAT **SWEDEN**
XIV	ADD. LONG RANGE LAMP

FUSE	FUSE CONNECTIONS
1	HAZARD WARNING, HORN, TAILGATE RELEASE
2	INTERIOR LIGHTING, WINDSH. WASHER, CLOCK
3	HEADLAMP WASH
4	WIPER, WIPER REAR, WASHER REAR, BACK UP LAMP
5	HEATER BLOWER
6	COOLING FAN MOTOR
7	HEATED REAR WINDOW
8	FLASHER, STOP LIGHT, ECONO LIGHT, CHOKE
9	LH SIDE L., INSTR. CLUST., SWITCH, GLOVE BOX ILLUMIN., LICENCE PL. LAMP
10	RH SIDE LIGHTS, SWITCH ILLUMINATION
11	LH LOW BEAM, REAR FOG LAMP (NOT FOR S + SF)
12	RH LOW BEAM
13	LH HIGH BEAM
14	RH HIGH BEAM

FUSE	FUSE CONNECTIONS	LOCATION FUSE
15	TAILGATE RELEASE	IN BOX SPACE VII
16	HEATED SEAT **SWEDEN**	AT RELAY XIV
17	REAR FOG LAMP (S)	AT RELAY XIII
18	REAR FOG LAMP (SF)	IN BOX SPACE IX
19	ADD. LONG RANGE LAMP	AT RELAY XV

Diagram 1: explanatory notes for wiring diagrams (continued)

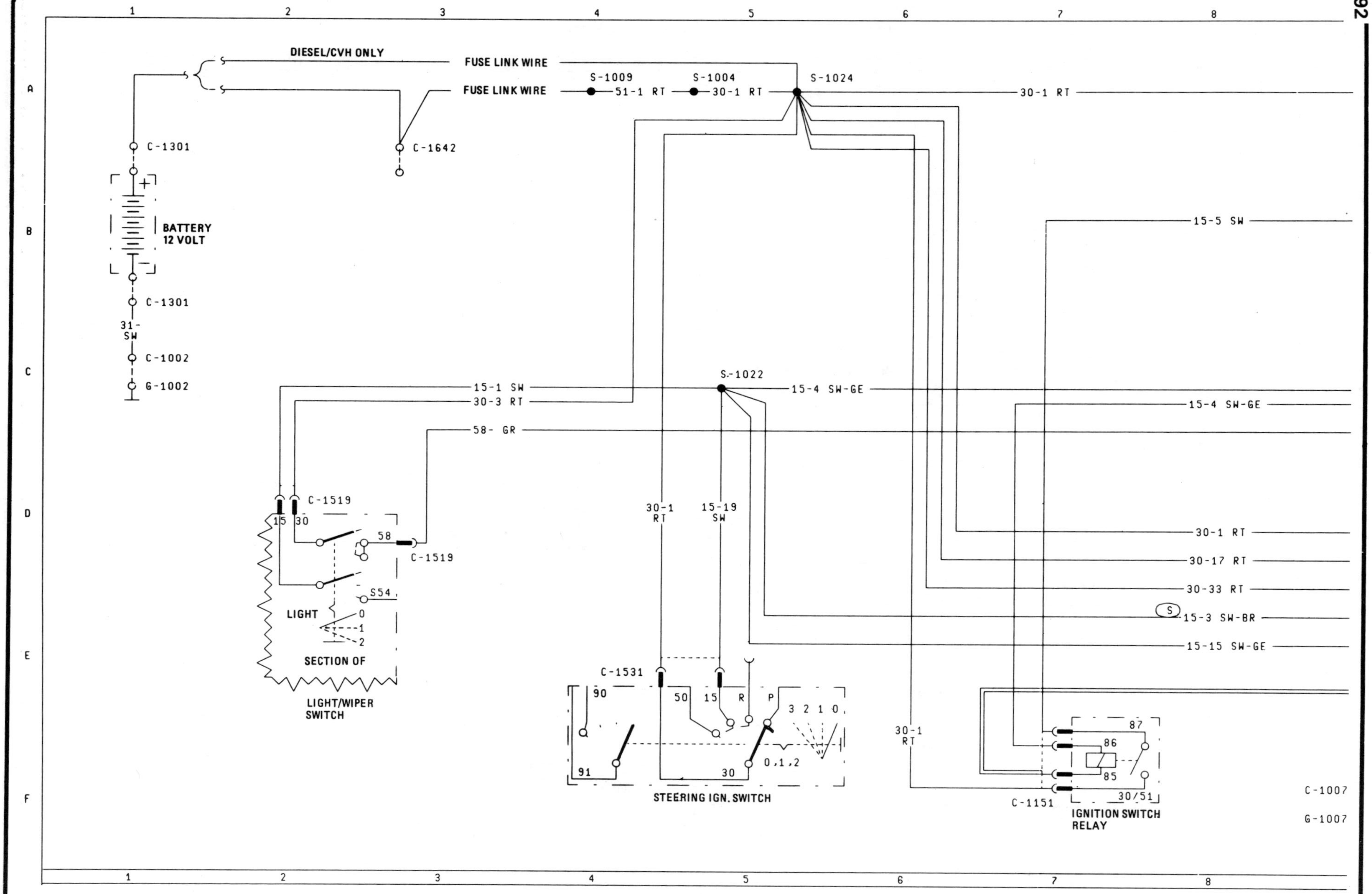

Diagram 2: feed system

15-5 SW

15-4 SW-GE

30-1 RT

30-17 RT

30-33 RT

15-3 SW-BR

15-15 SW-GE

C-1007
G-1007

IGNITION SWITCH RELAY

87
86
85
30/51

C-1151

30-1 RT

30-1 RT

S-1024

S-1022

15-4 SW-GE

15-19 SW

30-1 RT

STEERING IGN. SWITCH

3 2 1 0
0,1,2

P
R
15
50
30

C-1531

90
91

S-1009
S-1004
30-1 RT
51-1 RT

FUSE LINK WIRE
FUSE LINK WIRE

DIESEL/CVH ONLY

C-1642

15-1 SW
30-3 RT
58-GR

C-1519

58
S54

C-1519
30
15

LIGHT

0
1
2

SECTION OF
LIGHT/WIPER SWITCH

C-1301

BATTERY 12 VOLT

C-1301
31-SW
C-1002
G-1002

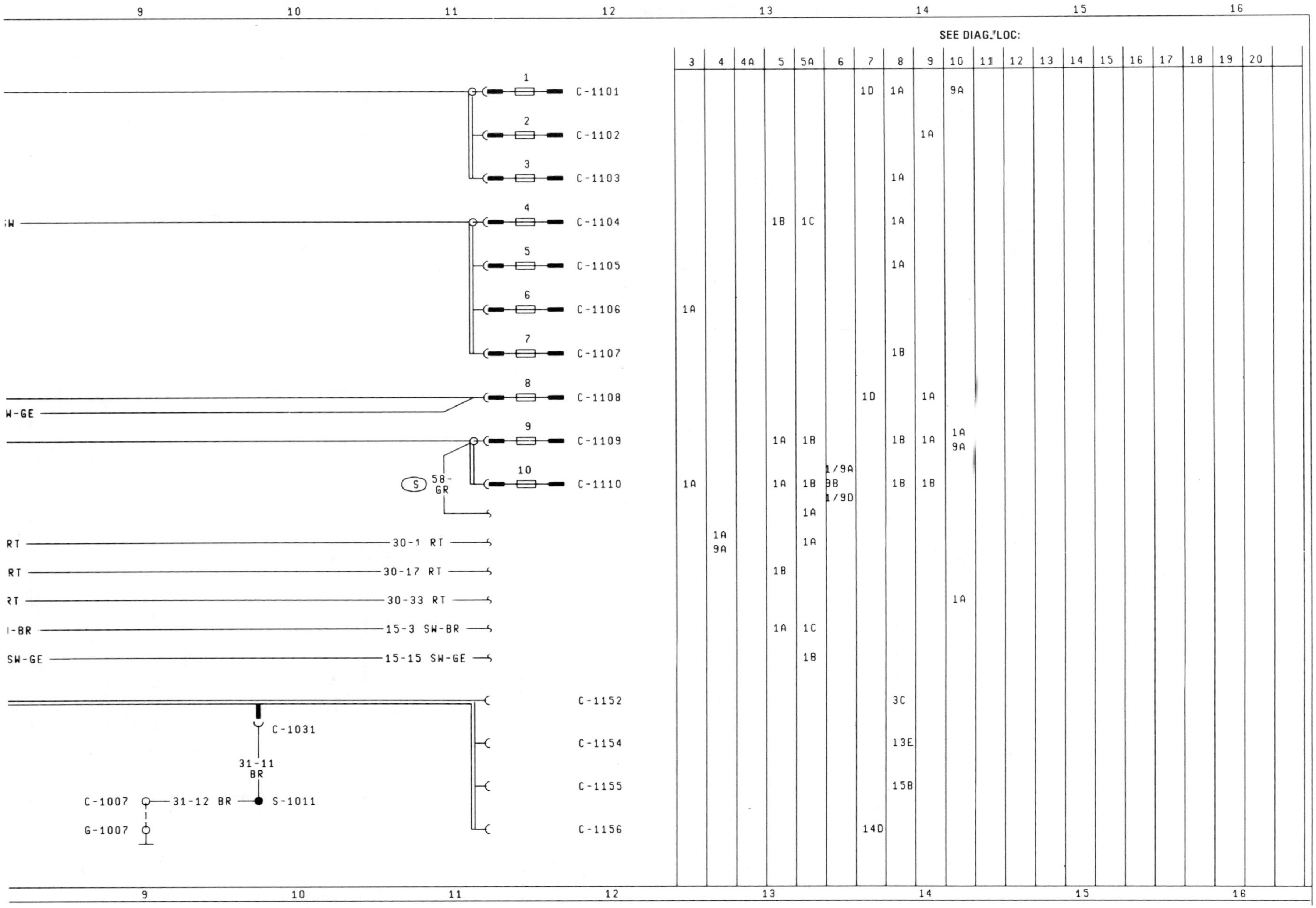

SEE DIAG.'LOC:

C-1101 1
C-1102 2
C-1103 3
C-1104 4
C-1105 5
C-1106 6
C-1107 7
C-1108 8
C-1109 9
C-1110 10

C-1152
C-1154
C-1155
C-1156

58-GR (S)

30-1 RT
30-17 RT
30-33 RT
15-3 SW-BR
15-15 SW-GE

RT
RT
RT
I-BR
SW-GE

SW-GE

C-1031
C-1007 — 31-12 BR — S-1011
31-11 BR
G-1007

Diagram 2: feed system (continued)

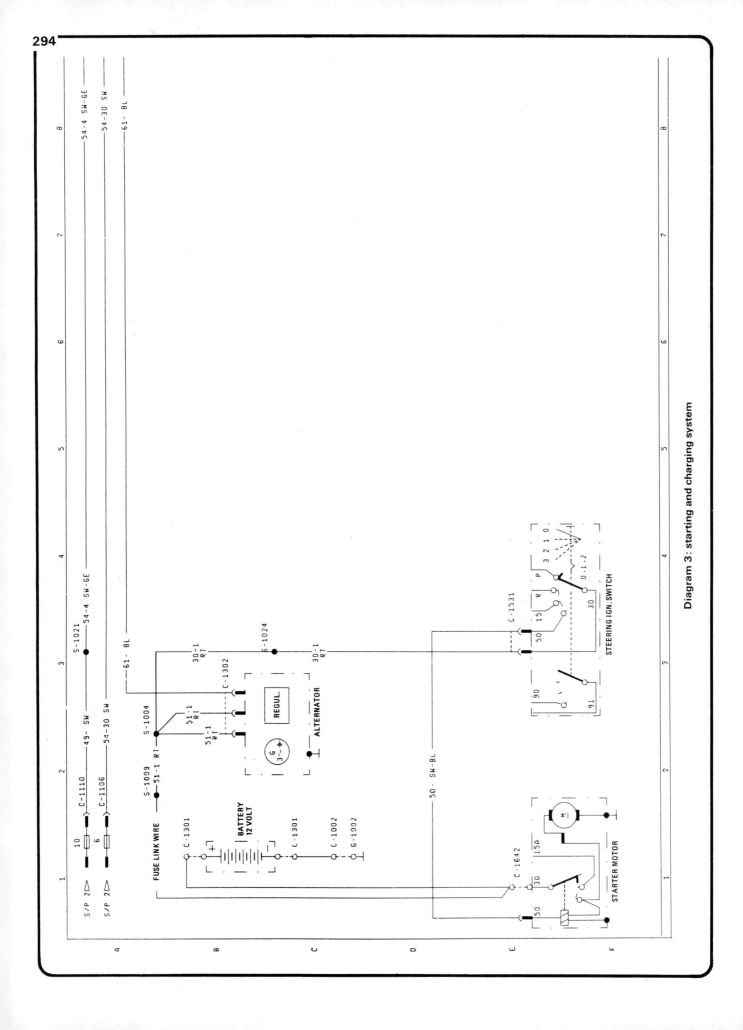

Diagram 3: starting and charging system

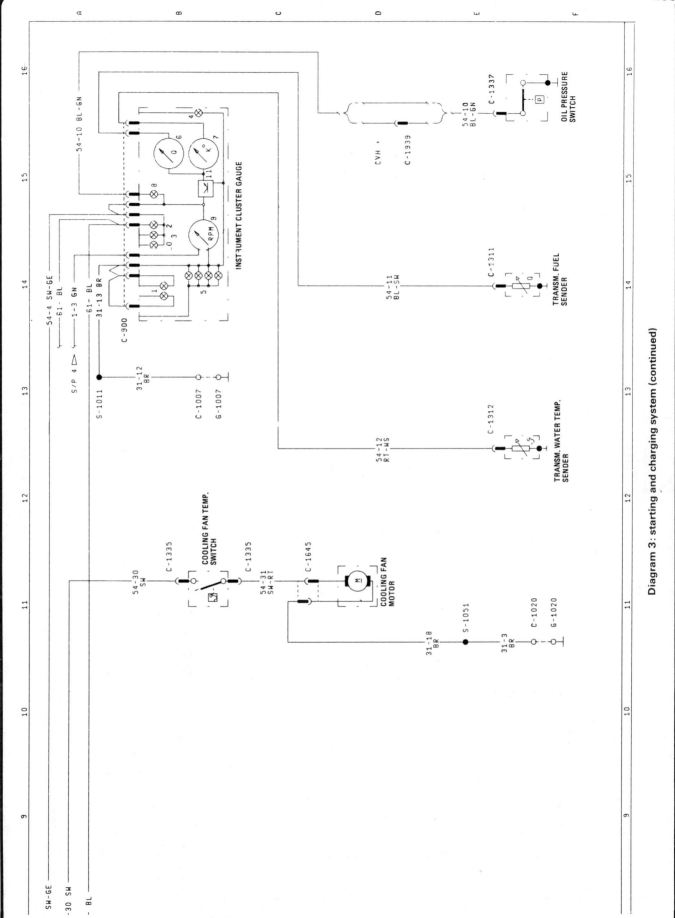

Diagram 3: starting and charging system (continued)

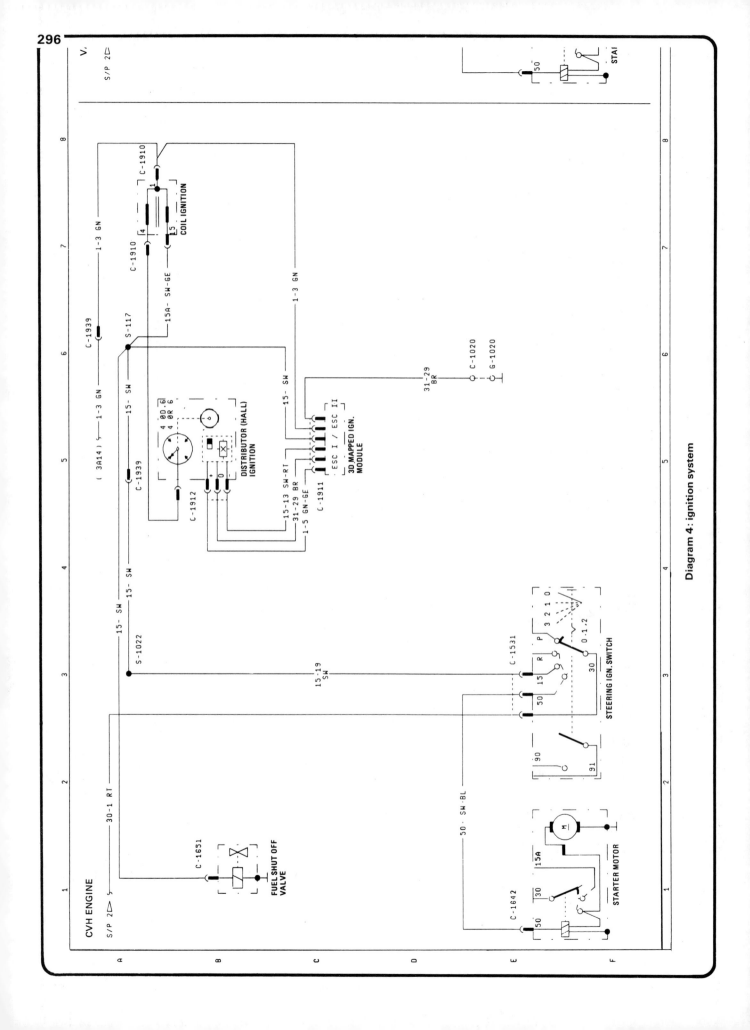

Diagram 4: ignition system

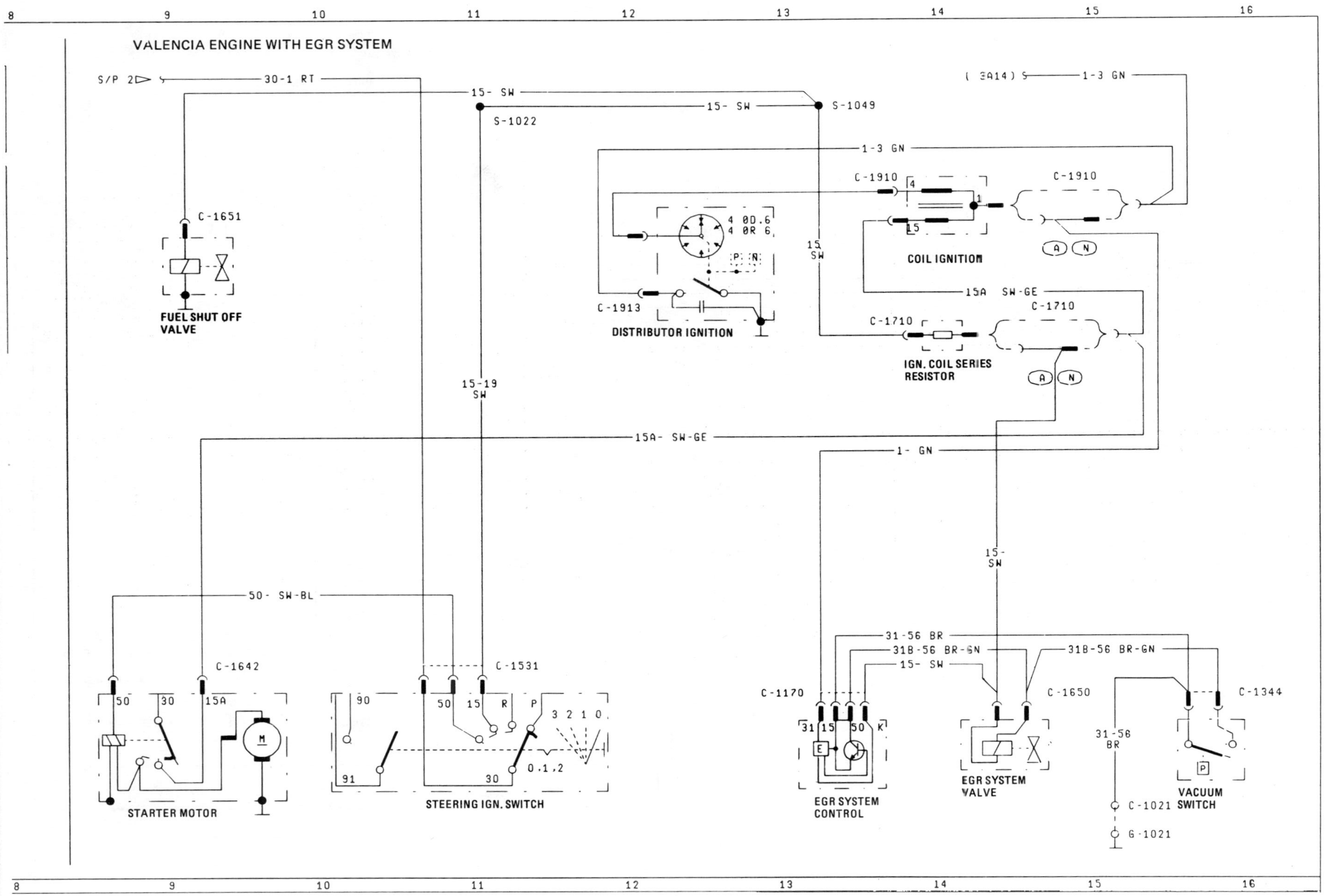

Diagram 4: ignition system (continued)

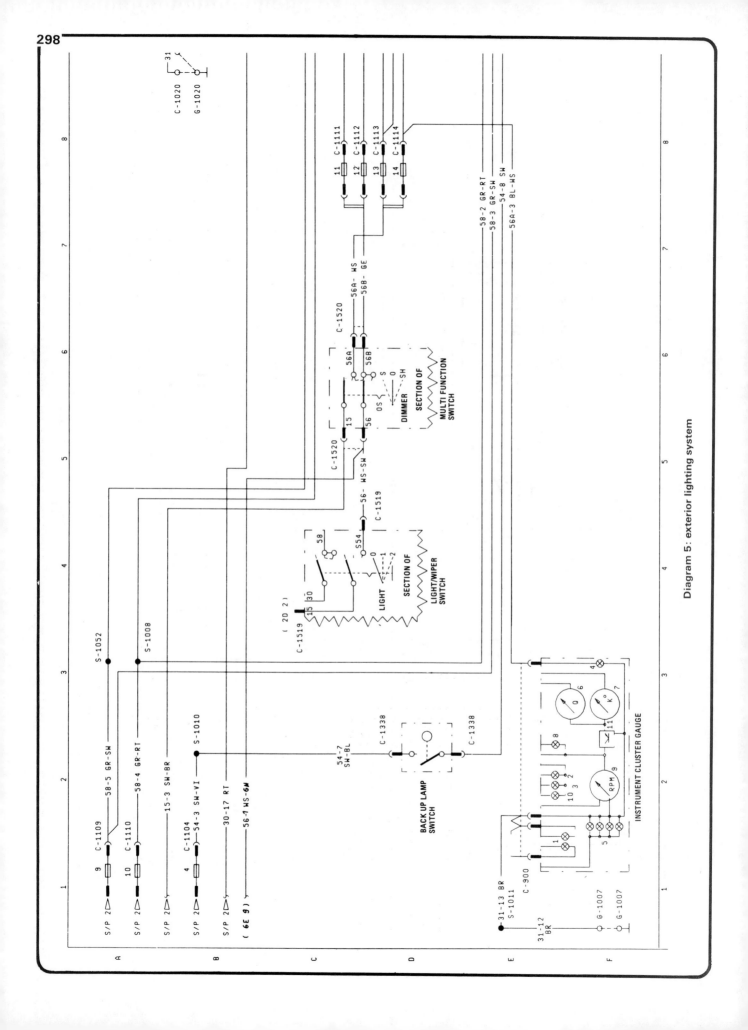

Diagram 5: exterior lighting system

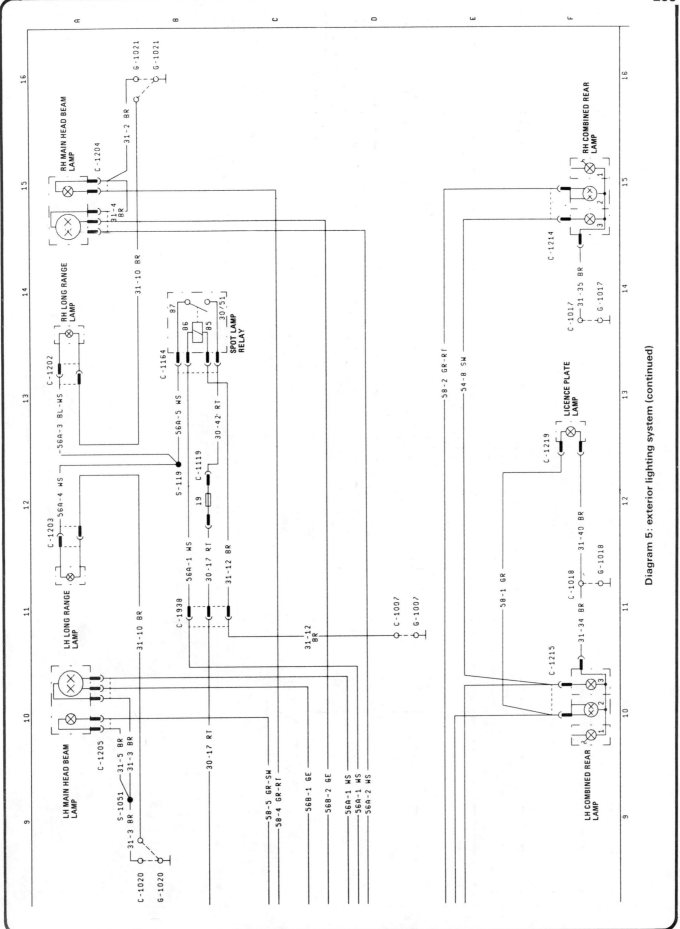

Diagram 5: exterior lighting system (continued)

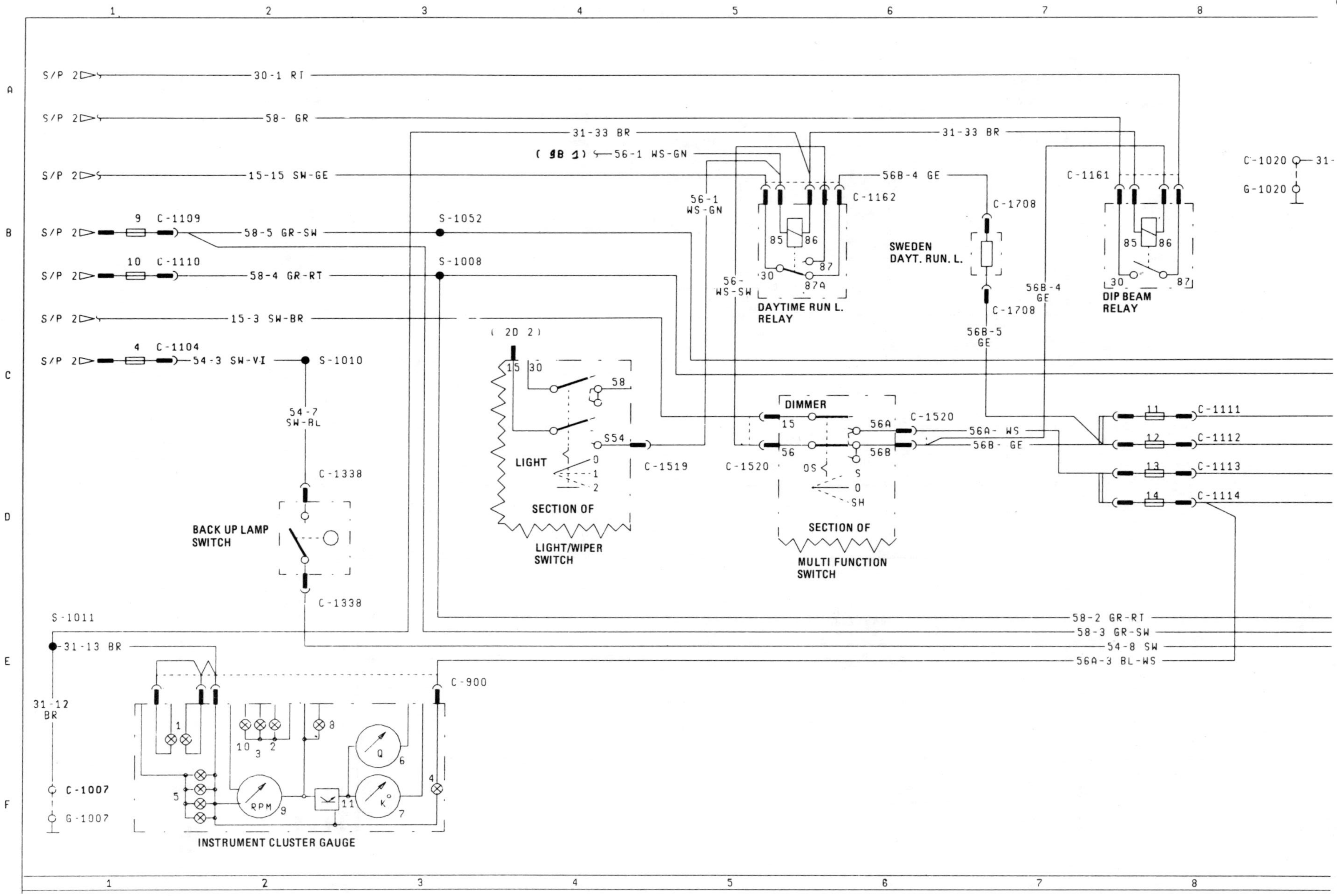

Diagram 5: exterior lighting system (continued)

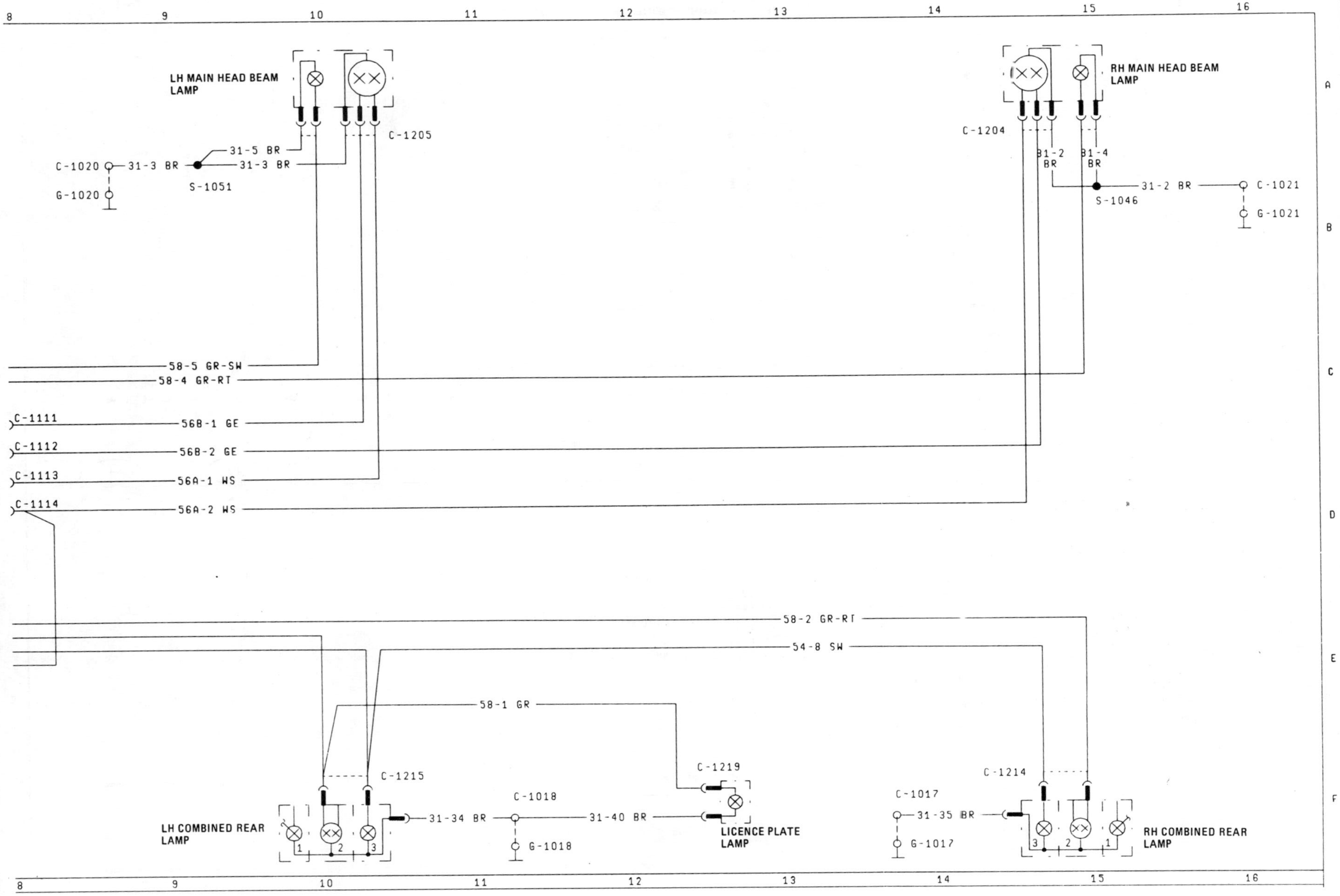

RH MAIN HEAD BEAM LAMP

C-1021
G-1021
31-2 BR
S-1046
B1-4 BR
B1-2 BR
C-1204

LH MAIN HEAD BEAM LAMP

C-1205
C-1020
G-1020
31-5 BR
31-3 BR
S-1051
31-3 BR

58-5 GR-SW
58-4 GR-RT
56B-1 GE
56B-2 GE
56A-1 WS
56A-2 WS

C-1111
C-1112
C-1113
C-1114

RH COMBINED REAR LAMP

C-1214
C-1017
G-1017
31-35 BR

58-2 GR-RT
54-8 SW

LICENCE PLATE LAMP

C-1219
C-1018
G-1018
31-40 BR
58-1 GR
31-34 BR
C-1215

LH COMBINED REAR LAMP

Diagram 5: exterior lighting system (continued)

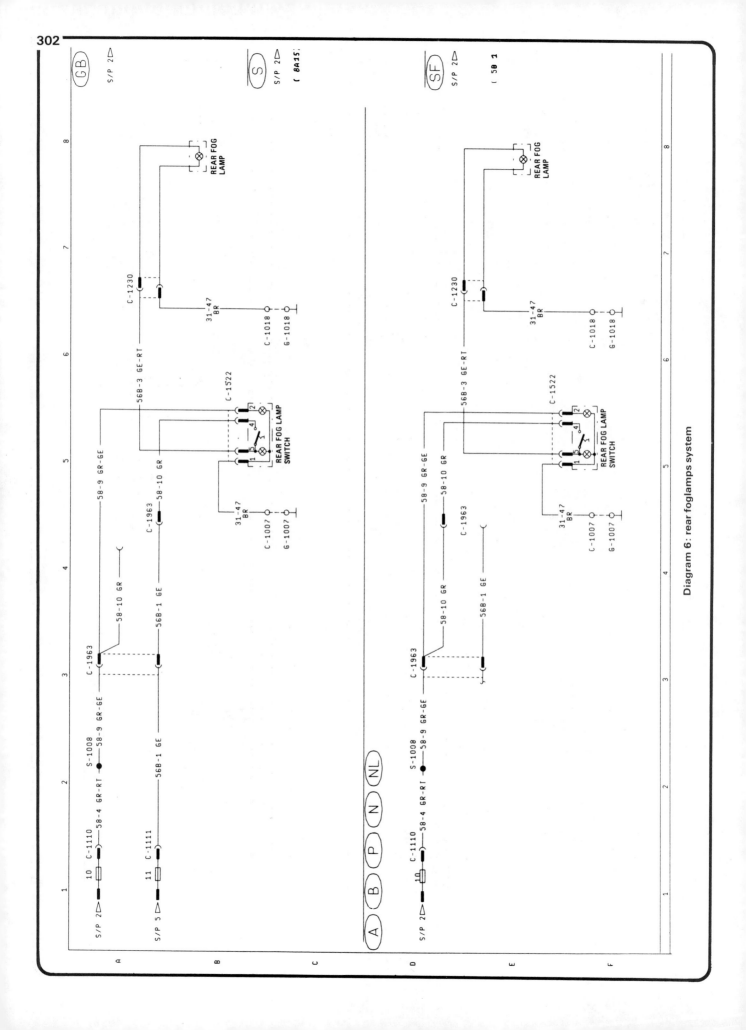

Diagram 6: rear foglamps system

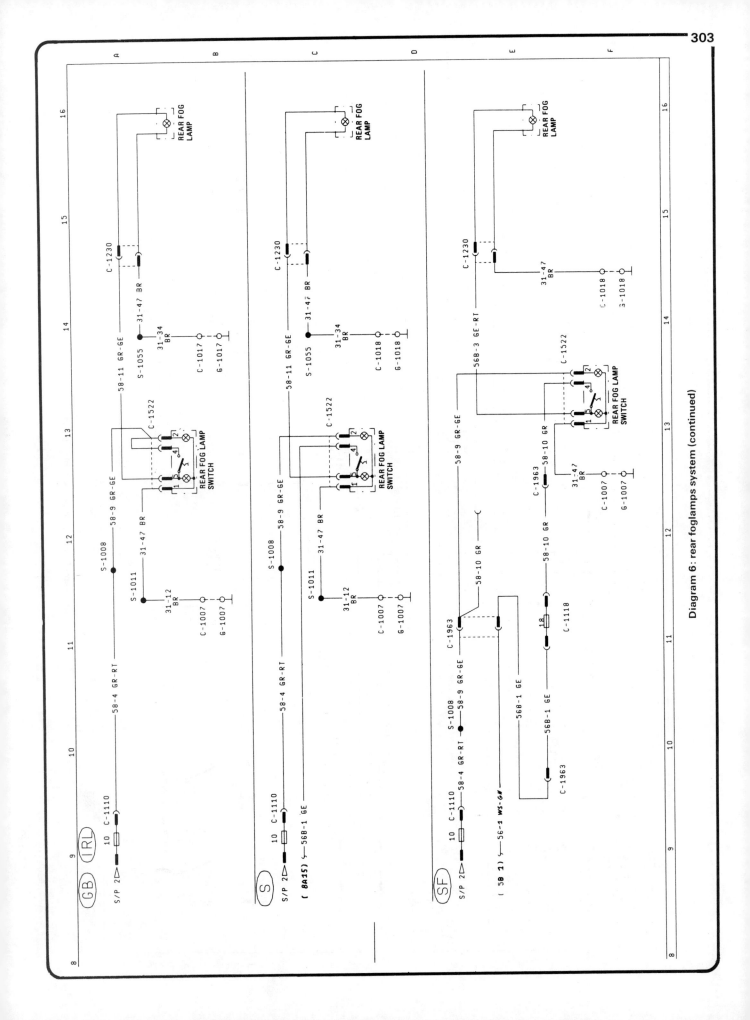

Diagram 6: rear foglamps system (continued)

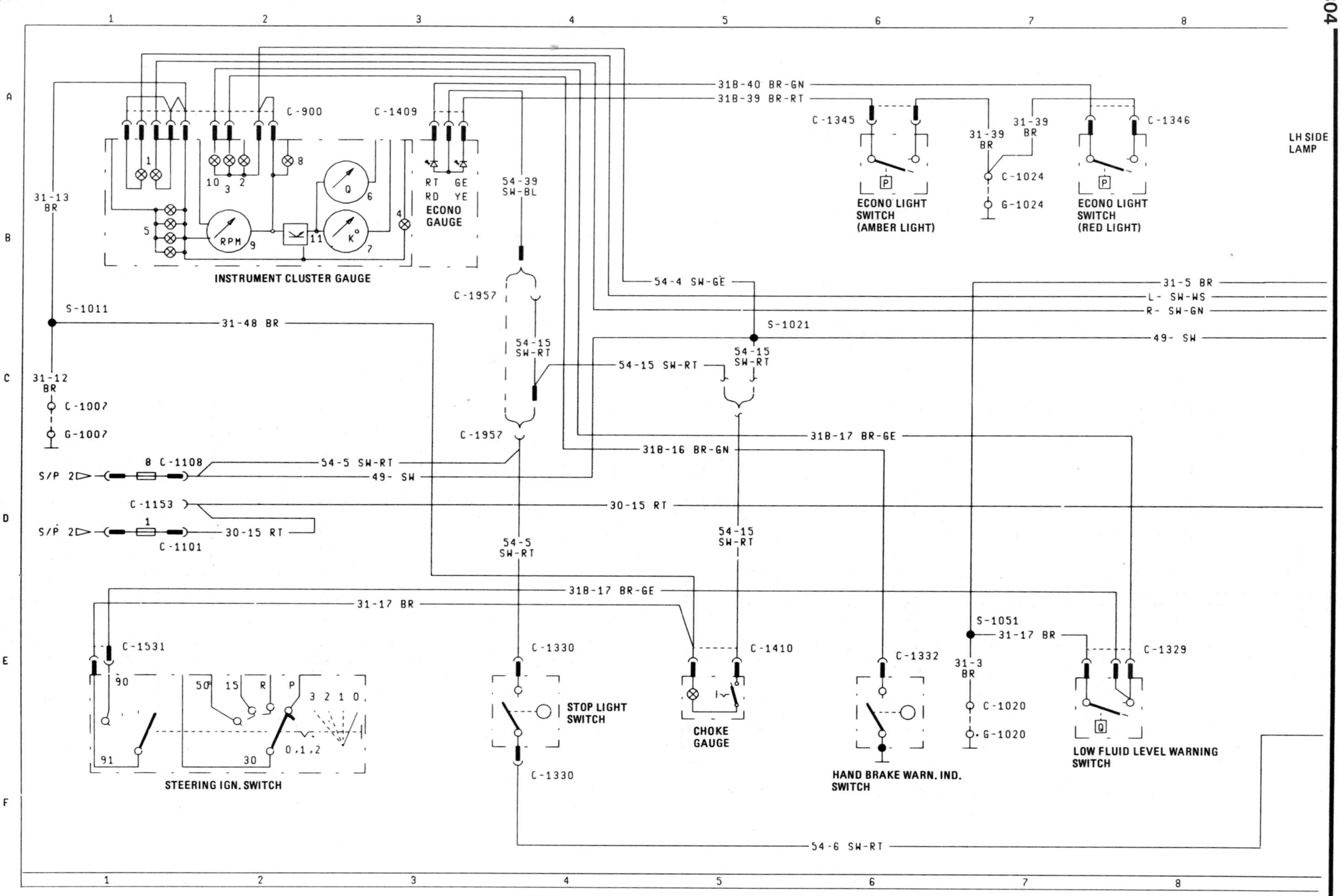

Diagram 7 : indicator and warning systems